The
Brainwashing/Deprogramming Controversy: Sociological, Psychological, Legal and Historical Perspectives

The Brainwashing/Deprogramming Controversy: Sociological, Psychological, Legal and Historical Perspectives

edited by:

DAVID G. BROMLEY
JAMES T. RICHARDSON

Studies in Religion and Society
Volume 5

The Edwin Mellen Press
New York and Toronto

Library of Congress Cataloging in Publication Data
Main entry under title:

The Brainwashing/deprogramming controversy.

   (Studies in religion and society ; v. 5)
   Bibliography: p.
   1. Brainwashing. I. Bromley, David G.
II. Richardson, James T., 1941-   . III. Series:
Studies in religion and society (New York, N.Y.) ; v. 5.
BF633.B73 1983   306'.6   83-4346
ISBN 0-88946-868-0

"Limits to Proselytizing" by R. Delgado;
"Legitimating Repression" by D. Anthony, T. Robbins,
and J. McCarthy; and
"Evil Eyes and Religious Choices" by B. Hargrove
(here retitled "Social Sources and Consequences of
the Brainwashing Controversy") are here
   Published by permission of Transaction Inc.
   from SOCIETY Vol. 17 #3 Copyright ⓒ 1980
   by Transaction Inc.

        The Edwin Mellen Press
        Box 450
        Lewiston, New York 14092

Printed in the United States of America

CONTENTS

III

PSYCHOLOGICAL PERSPECTIVES 161

IV

LEGAL PERSPECTIVES 213

V

CONCLUSIONS AND IMPLICATIONS 295

THE BRAINWASHING/DEPROGRAMMING CONTROVERSY:
AN INTRODUCTION

James T. Richardson
University of Nevada, Reno

In recent years considerable controversy has raged
about the new religions. This controversy represents yet
another chapter in the history of conflict over religion in
America (Bromley and Shupe, 1981; Cox, 1978; Hargrove, this
volume; and Miller, this volume). The current controversy
over new religions has centered on two major issues, both of
which have engendered considerable debate. One center of
controversy is economic: how the new religions raise and
spend money, and whether or not they should be granted tax-
exempt status (Bromley and Shupe, 1980; Richardson, 1982).
The other major focus of conflict -- the one addressed herein -- has been recruitment and socialization practices of
the new religions. These have brought accusations of
brainwashing which, in turn, have played a role in the development of the new quasi-occupation of deprogramming
(i.e., furnishing services to parents who want their children removed from new religious groups). The level of societal concern and the degree of involvement of different
groups in this controversy make a close examination of conversion and related issues an important undertaking in contemporary social analysis.

TRADITIONAL VIEWS OF RELIGIOUS CONVERSION

Conversion studies have, until recently, been dominated by an interpretation based on the conversion of Paul
on the road to Damascus. Paul's conversion has usually
been viewed as sudden, dramatic, emotional, irrational, and
was "explained" by reference to an agent not under the control of Paul. Traditional views of Paul's conversion attribute agency or cause to an omnipotent God. More recent
views attribute agency to unconscious psychological forces,
or to social-situational factors such as peer pressure, affective ties, social networks, or personal influence.
Whatever the characterization of the agent, it was assumed
that Paul did not act under his own volition, but was temporarily incapacitated by the actions of some outside force.

Paul's experience appeared to be a single event that thoroughly changed his life. The conversion has been viewed as a total negation of the old self and an affirmation of a new self. Such a conversion was expected to "last a lifetime;" only some serious problem could require another. Paul's conversion has usually been interpreted in cognitive terms. His experience caused him to change his beliefs, and then his behavior changed accordingly. Behavior follows belief in the traditional conversion paradigm. Thus, in this traditional view, Paul's experience was individualistic, deterministic, and passive, and has been viewed as predestinational (to use a theological term), or predispositional (to use a psychological term), or situationally determined (to use a sociological term).

Early conversion research, most of which used this approach, has led to a psychologizing of conversion phenomena. Also, many psychiatrists in particular have assumed that something was wrong with anyone who espoused religious beliefs, and that religious conversion is often a symptom, if not a cause, of psychological problems (Stark, 1971). Although sound research on new religions is being done by some psychologists and psychotherapists, most of those disciplines seem to accept unabashedly the traditional view of conversion just described. Some involved in the study of new religions has updated the jargon, but the same basic assumptions remain. This view has been called the "invasion of the body snatchers" or "Little Red Riding Hood" theory of conversion to new religions. Instead of an omnipotent God striking down and blinding Paul on the road to Damascus, we have omnipotent techniques and processes of brainwashing, hypnotism, mind control, and coercive persuasion that are used to strike down passive and innocent youngsters, who "snap" into a new belief system (Shupe and Bromley, 1980). That members of the most educated and privileged generation in American history would succumb to the entreaties of strange gurus is accepted ipso facto as proof that the gurus' techniques are omnipotent, and that drastic measures must be taken to rescue those who fall prey to proseltyizing by new religions.

A CONTEMPORARY VIEW OF CONVERSION

Recent work by sociologists and social psychologists, along with that of a few psychologists and psychiatrists, however, has produced a dramatically different view of conversion to the new religions. A representative sample of this work is included in this volume. The major findings of this research can be summarized as follows:

1. Contemporary conversion is usually not a once-in-a-life-
time event. It is better characterized as a series of affiliations and disaffiliations that make-up a conversion
career (Richardson, 1978 and 1980). Many people, particularly younger people, are taking advantage of the many opportunities in our pluralistic society and are trying out
serial alternatives in life-style, some of which are religious. Many people are experiencing ideological and behavioral variety and mobility in their individual conversion
careers. However, only a small proportion of people contacted by new groups actually join, and of those who do,
only a relatively small proportion remain members very long.
A pattern of sampling and then "moving on" seems the predominant style of relating to the new religious groups (Barker,
1982; Galanter, this volume). Just as institutions of the
larger society have a problem obtaining long-term commitment, voluntary attrition is also a major problem for the
new religions. Perhaps the major difficulty of young converts is not becoming overcommitted to any one group, but a
general lack of commitment to any stable social mooring.
What Robert J. Lifton (1963) has referred to as the Protean
style of life has become a dominant theme of the age.

2. Decisions to join or participate in new religious movements can be made suddenly, dramatically, or emotionally --
as Paul's is usually viewed -- but another fruitful way to
view conversion to new religions is as a series of experiments entered into somewhat gingerly (Pilarzyk, this volume). Many join with what Hans Toch (1965) calls "latent
reservations," and, for many, affiliations are temporary
and the groups themselves are often "on trial." Leaving
religious groups and movements is as important as joining,
and about as frequent (Wright, this volume; Skonovd, this
volume; and Richardson, et. al., 1981). Leaving can also
be as sudden and emotional in appearance as was the act of
joining, because the same process is operating -- people
decide to stop occupying one role (member) and opt for another role (nonmember or member of a new group). Such role
changes require public explanation, and it is the individuals who have switched sides in the midst of this intense
controversy (often after having been deprogrammed) who have
been the authors of the "horror stories" alleging brainwashing and personal exploitation (Bromley, Shupe and
Ventimiglia, this volume).

3. Beliefs do not necessarily change prior to joining.
Instead, a person decides to behave as a group member for a
while, as he or she tries out a new role or life-style
(Bromley and Shupe, 1979; Balch, 1980). This deciding to
behave as a proper group member has been mistaken for "in-

stant conversion" or "snapping" by some outsiders, who assume that some sinister force or technique must be at work.
However, cognitive changes are usually much more gradual and
much less complete in most converts than is commonly assumed. Participation in group activities does not necessarily indicate total commitment to the group's ideology. Even
for those who do make a total commitment to a group, normal
processes of maturation and changes of status (such as marriage and childbirth) usually work to undermine that initial
commitment. Research on nearly all new religious groups
(from the Moonies to the Divine Light Mission to radical
Jesus Movement groups) has demonstrated that marriage, having children, and economic problems often overwhelm ideological factors (Richardson, et. al., 1979; Davis and
Richardson, 1976; Bromley and Shupe, 1979; Lofland, 1977;
Nordquist, 1979). These findings support sociological tru-
isms that individuals usually act in ways dictated by their
social situation, and that beliefs are modified to be consistent with behaviors.

4. Contemporary conversion is usually a social phenomenon.
People affiliate with groups because they want affection
from friends and loved ones who, of course, care for them.
This might be thought of as countering a much discussed
trend toward the "privatism" of religious experience
(Luckmann, 1967), as many contemporary youth "communalize"
their religious experiences in the newer religions
(Kilbourne and Richardson, 1982). Affiliation with social
groups is a normal and essential process in which virtually
all people are involved. But especially when ties are
weakened with groups and institutional structures in which
people usually participate, other structures of sociability
will be sought. When ties with the large society are especially problematic, as was the case for many youth in the
late nineteen-sixties and early nineteen-seventies, many
seek out communal groups as substitute communities. Some
new groups have recruited predominantly among those who
have minimal ties with society. But most groups now recruit along friendship network lines, again indicating the
importance of social considerations (Snow, et. al., 1980).

5. Thus, recruits to new religions are active individuals
involved in seeking appropriate life-styles (Straus, 1976,
1979: Richardson, 1980; and Lofland, 1978). The notion of
a passive person absorbing anything he or she is told,
driven by independent psychological and sociological forces,
does not apply to most conversions to new religious groups.
Rational decisions are being made by most educated converts, who are, after all, members of our most educated
generation ever. Converts are usually seeking to affirm
themselves rather than to negate themselves and run away.

Certainly some of these decisions are difficult to understand from the perspective of the outsider, but this does
not change the basic character of the decision from the
point of view of the person making the decision. Most members of new religious groups talk of autonomy and volition
when they describe what they are doing, and they stress
change, not stasis. Some even admit that they are exploiting the groups (instead of the other way around), or that
they are at least engaged in negotiations with the groups
concerning what they have to do and believe in order to remain a member in good standing. Sometimes members will even
reveal plans to leave the group at some future time.

This summary constitutes an ideal-type description of
contemporary conversion; not every individual case fits.
But the new perspective is closely approximated by most of
the people who are associating with the new religious groups
based on a decade of social science research on groups in
the United States and abroad (Shupe and Bromley, forthcoming).

One's perceptions will always be influenced by direct
contact with those whom one studies, and usually for the
better. Many therapists who are opposed to the new religions have not had direct contact with members of the groups
in their everyday life setting. One key opponent of the new
religions, psychiatrist John Clark, makes it a point not to
go near the groups for "scientific, legal, and ethical reasons." He has demonstrated his position by stating in a
professional paper, in all seriousness, that the urgent
question motivating his work is "What kind of nutty people
get into these crazy groups?" (see Clark, 1979b:2). Such
bias suggests that there may be significant limitations in
his research.

BRAINWASHING

The current explanations of conversion to new religious
movements in terms of coercive mind control techniques constitute a continuation of the reliance on psychological paradigms to account for conversion. Brainwashing is a popu-
larized term that has been applied to a supposedly mysterious process whereby Chinese and Russian Communists extract-
ed confessions from prisoners and seemed to change, at least
temporarily, their beliefs and even values. A number of
classic studies and interpretations of this phenomenon have
been offered by scholars, including especially Robert J.
Lifton, (1963), Edgar Schein, (1961), and William Sargent
(1957). Nearly all such studies, with the partial exception of Edgar Schein's work, treat brainwashing as an ex-

treme example of traditional conversion similar to Paul's
experience.

        Most interpretations of brainwashing assume a relative-
ly passive subject under the control of all-powerful (and,
in the case of new religions, evil) external agents who use
coercive and manipulative techniques. The change associated
with brainwashing involves a total negation of the old self
and the substitution of a new one in its place. The change
is viewed as relatively sudden, dramatic, and emotional.
Physical and mental coercion are assumed to be crucial in
bringing about significant cognitive changes.

        Some twenty years ago A.D. Biderman (1962), offered an
analysis of why the term brainwashing came to prominence in
the nineteen-fifties and nineteen-sixties in the West. He
noted that most of the researchers were caught up in the
anti-Communist rhetoric of the cold war, which permeated
their analysis. Biderman stated (1962:560) that there
seemed to be an assumption that Communist beliefs were "fun-
damentally alien to human nature and social reality" and
that "the acceptance of Communist beliefs is consequently
regarded as ipso facto evidence of insanity or a warped,
evil personality, or both." This anti-Communist sentiment
was also antitotalitarian and anticollectivistic in orientation (with even an element of racism) and contributed to a
misunderstanding of brainwashing phenomena in the nineteen-
fifties that still persists.

        As the era of new religious movements arrived, brain-
washing provided a ready-made, simplistic term to apply to
these new phenomena by those who disapproved or who sought
a scapegoat. The use of the "brainwashing defense" in the
trial of Patty Hearst brought the idea even more into common use, although the term had been used to refer to recruitment to new religious groups even before her trial.
The accusation of brainwashing thus became what Robbins
et. al., (this volume) call a "social weapon" to be used
against groups and beliefs that were not acceptable to
those who had vested interests in the society, including
some families of recruits, representatives of certain religious groups and some therapists who found themselves in
open competition with the new groups for members and clients. The charge of brainwashing is now also being used to
discredit new religions in several other countries by representatives of the same groups and others.

        As Richardson and Kilbourne have pointed out (this
volume), the brainwashing view of why and how people join
new religious groups does not mesh well with the data.

Several psychiatrists such as Marc Galanter and Thomas
Ungerleider (whose work is represented in this volume) have
been involved in well-conceived research on the effects of
joining the new religions and on the process whereby affiliation is effected. Some of the major conclusions of such
work are noteworthy: those members of new religions studied
are normal people in nearly every way, and their ability to
care for themselves is not impaired; further, some of those
who join actually benefit from their participation by improved psychological health (a conclusion consonant with
much of the sociological work already mentioned). Of special note is a paper (this volume) by Galanter which presents data on a cohort of people going through a three-week
training session for the Unification Church. Galanter administered personality assessment instruments to over one-
hundred in the cohort, and compared those who joined with
those who did not. He found that only about eight percent
of those who started the training actually joined, and that
they were basically normal. Those who were members for some
time tended to improve their psychological health.
Galanter's paper demonstrates the low retention and high
drop-out rates of this group, a finding confirmed by Barker,
an English sociologist who has studied the Moonies in
England extensively (see Barker, 1982). A study of young
people in the San Francisco Bay Area reveals that only a
minute fraction of those contacted by members of new religions actually follow up on the contact (Zimbardo and
Hartley, 1981). Such low success rates, coupled with low
retention rates and high attrition, support the conversion
career notion that converts are active seekers trying out
many different groups and lifestyles over time. Galanter
reported that ninety percent of the cohort he studied had
been in other religious groups prior to attending the Unification Church training session.

Some researchers have found certain similarities between the tactics used by some new religious groups and
those employed in brainwashing (Taylor, this volume and
Richardson, et. al., 1972). But the key elements of guilt-
inducement and physical coercion are muted or totally absent
in the new religions. Even some outspoken critics of the
Unification Church admit that coercion is not used, and they
have agreed that "nearly all" the participants are present
voluntarily (Rasmussen, 1976). Some of the new groups have
developed amazingly sophisticated tactics to persuade potential recruits to join and remain members, but it is deceptive to refer to these tactics as brainwashing (Lofland,
1978). "Love bombing," a term sometimes used to refer to
recruitment tactics of some new groups, is simply not equivalent to physical torture, although apparently some would
have us believe that love bombing is totally sinister and

actually worse (more effective) than the physically coercive
tactics of the Chinese and Russian Communists. This logic
is spurious as direct experience with these groups on a day-
to-day basis has demonstrated to numerous social scientists.
To call these elements methods in some sinister plot is cyn-
ical reductionism.

Thus it appears that brainwashing is a much-too-simple
answer to complex questions. Brainwashing explanations of
what happened in Russia and China blinded many Westerners
and led to a less-than-complete understanding of the Communist revolution. Reliance on similar explanations to interpret the rise of the new religions also obscures more than
it reveals, and most social scientists have concluded
that such explanations should be abandoned (Solomon, this
volume).

DEPROGRAMMING

What has been termed deprogramming constitutes the reciprocal of brainwashing and makes sense only in terms of a
brainwashing explanation for conversion to new religious
movements. Deprogramming involves the extraction, often by
force, of a member from a new religious group, and incarceration of the member by quasi-professional people, usually
hired by a blood relative, to change the beliefs and behaviors of the member. Efforts to change the person's beliefs
include intimidation and the commission of acts held to be
sacrilegious in the belief system of the deprogrammee.
Sometimes an effort is made to get the subject to affirm a
general version of traditional Christian beliefs (Shupe and
Bromley, 1980; LeMoult, this volume; Patrick, 1976). Deprogramming can be rapid, or it can last for days. In many
cases, the setting is a motel room, and the persons involved
are usually marginal representatives of the ministerial or
psychological professions, or cult ex-members who were themselves deprogrammed.

Solomon (1982, and this volume) has observed that deprogrammees are more prone to espouse a brainwashing interpretation of what they experienced while in the group following deprogramming, a finding also apparently supported
inadvertently by the work of Singer, Clark, and Conway
and Siegelman (1982). Therefore, deprogramming cannot be
viewed as a uniformly successful tactic, unless one believes
that convincing someone he or she has been brainwashed is a
worthy goal. Deprogrammings have had some obvious negative
effects on the groups, though, since they have lost members,
and since a sizeable proportion of deprogrammers have themselves been deprogrammed (Shupe and Bromley, 1980).

Shupe and Bromley (1980) write about a "noncoercive" type of deprogramming that does not include kidnapping and forced incarceration. Instead, the emphasis is on getting the member away for lengthy conversations about his or her beliefs and practices. This has probably become the more often used tactic by those opposed to the new religions, if only because of the expense and legal problems associated with the more coercive deprogramming (Richardson et. al., 1981). Ironically perhaps, given anti-cult contentions, the fact that voluntary separations from new religions may be effective in producing disaffiliations from new religious movements undermines the brainwashing thesis.

It is possible to characterize deprogramming within traditional paradigms of conversion and even so-called brainwashing because of its assumptions of passivity of the subject and the idea of a sudden total change brought about by an external agent. These key assumptions of the traditional view pervade the approach taken by the deprogrammers toward the initial conversion of the member, and they also pervade assumptions about how to change the person's beliefs back to those held before conversion.

In the case of the more coercive deprogramming, the deprogrammers assume that brainwashing has taken place and therefore drastic measures are required and justified to undo the alleged damage. Noncoercive deprogramming relies slightly more on a view of the person as an active agent because it requires that he or she voluntarily cooperate to a degree. But both see the act of affiliation as brainwashing, and every effort is made by the deprogrammers to take control of the situation and effect something akin to a dramatic reconversion in the traditional mode. There are, of course, important differences in classical brainwashing and deprogramming, but there seems no question that coercive deprogramming is more like brainwashing than are the recruitment and resocialization techniques used in the new religions.

TRADITIONAL VS CONTEMPORARY
VIEWS OF CONVERSION

The traditional psychological and contemporary sociological models described in the preceding pages offer very different interpretations of the process by which individuals affiliate with new religious movements. It would be an over-simplification to assert that sociologists and psychologists divide neatly into two camps, with the former defending new religions and the latter attacking them. There have been a number of sociologists whose writing has

been highly critical of new religions (e.g., Enroth, 1979,
1977; Horowitz, 1978; Levine, 1980, 1979; Mitchell,
Mitchell and Ofshe, 1980), and a number of psychologists/
psychiatrists (e.g., Coleman, 1982; Deutsch, 1975;
Galanter, 1980; Levine and Salter, 1976; Ungerleider and
Wellisch, 1979) who have found little cause for alarm.
Nevertheless, on balance, the more vigorous critics of new
religions have been psychologists, psychiatrists and therapists while sociologists, anthropologists and religious
studies scholars have assumed a less hostile posture.

This division has emerged for at least two major reasons. First, sociological studies of social movements have
shifted away from a deprivation/disorganization perspective
which emphasizes individual anomie, inadequacy, or instability as the motivational basis for participation in social
movements. Family systems theory constitutes a similar development in psychology. Proponents of contemporary paradigms in both disciplines have described and assessed new
religious movements in more neutral, value free terms.
Second, the methodologies and data bases of the two camps
differ significantly. Much of the sociological research on
new religious movements has involved participant observation
of one or more groups (e.g., Balch, 1980; Barker, 1981;
Bromley and Shupe, 1979; Daner, 1976; Downton, 1979; Lofland
1977; Richardson et. al., 1979; Taylor, 1978). These recruitment and socialization processes in this type of research are viewed from the perspective of new and ongoing
members, and affiliation typically is depicted as an inter-
active, negotiated process in which both the neophyte member
and the recruiting organization assert their respective interests and make strategic concessions. A number of psy-
chologists/psychiatrists have relied upon a clinical/case
study approach (e.g., Clark, 1979, 1978; Clark, Langane and
Schecter, 1981; Galper, 1976; Shapiro, 1977; Singer, 1979,
1978) and have been the most outspoken critics of new religions. Since the vast majority of their informants are
former members (and many were deprogrammed), their depictions
of the recruitment and socialization processes reflect the
perspective of individuals who have chosen or were forced
to leave a new religious movement. For example, Singer
(1979) reported that seventy-five percent of those she
counseled left new religions through legal conservatorships.

It is quite interesting to note that when psychologists
/psychiatrists have examined current members of new religions (e.g., Galanter, this volume; Galanter and Buckley,
this volume, Ungerleider and Wellisch, this volume) or so-
ciologists/anthropologists have studied former members of
new religions (Beckford, this volume; Skonovd, this volume;

Wright, this volume), the empirical findings converge. The psychologists/psychiatrists find mixed personal/emotional consequences of membership in new religious movements, no consistent pattern of pathology or incapacity, and even salutary effects of various kinds. The sociologists/anthropologists have found that rather standard sets of social variables and well established bodies of theory explain both the affiliation and disaffiliation processes. At the same time there are persistent reports of manipulative recruitment practices, intense socialization techniques, and a variety of negative personal/emotional experiences that have left former members with intense feelings of disillusionment, guilt and depression. So, on the one hand, there is no clear pattern of findings: these movements have salubrious consequences for some members but not for others, and some former members regard their time in these groups to have been well spent while others feel cheated. On the other hand, extreme explanations do not seem necessary. None of these findings clash with what social scientists would expect to observe in high-demand social movements with millenial hopes.

A review of the contents of this volume will confirm that we have emphasized research produced neither by apologists nor antagonists of the new religions. Naturally, any explanation of the affiliation and disaffiliation processes which relies upon established social science explanations will have a demystifying effect. For that reason, the present volume probably will receive a less than enthusiastic welcome from antagonists of the new religions. However, in our estimation, proponents of the brainwashing thesis have not made their case. While they have written numerous articles (see Shupe and Bromley, forthcoming) in popular and professional journals, they have not produced data-based articles which offer hard evidence to support their position. From our perspective, the burden of proof is on those who proffer the brainwashing hypothesis. Until such evidence is forthcoming, we shall place confidence in the rapidly accumulating body of data which yields a more complex, if mundane explanation for the affiliation and disaffiliation processes.

I
HISTORICAL PERSPECTIVES

Even a cursory review of American religious history reveals that the reception given to new religious groups has
been chilly at best. Viewed in historical perspective, the
contemporary new religions controversy is hardly unprecedented; indeed, it has been precisely the warning of imminent
and unprecedented dangers that has been typical of the reactions to new religious movements throughout American history. In the first paper in this section Miller reviews allegations made against the Shakers (e.g., sexual impropriety,
political subversion, self-serving leaders, and deceptive/
manipulative recruitment practices) which are reminiscent of
the current conflict. Bromley and Shupe (this volume) catalogue the almost carbon copy charges made against the Unification Church in recent years, and elsewhere (1980) have emphasized the similarities of the anti-cult and anti-Catholic
campaigns.

Other observers have reached similar conclusions.
Robbins and Anthony (1979) identified five themes common to
such conflict: (1) subversion myths, (2) violence, (3) en-
slavement, (4) over-generalized stereotypes and (5) apostates. Davis (1960:207) noted that anti-cult crusades have
produced strange bedfellows: "As the image of an un-American
conspiracy took form in the nativist press, in sensational
exposes, in the countless fantasies of treason and mysterious criminality, the lines separating Mason, Catholic and
Mormon became almost indistinguishable." Despite the fact
that fears concerning groups such as Catholics, Mormons and
Masons seem, with the benefit of hindsight, to have been
overblown, simply establishing parallels between past and
present allegations does not refute the latter. However,
these historical continuities should cause us to consider
more carefully the sources and merits of such fears and accusations. As Miller stated, these allegations are most
likely to emerge when dominant lifestyles are threatened.
From this perspective, fears about unconventional groups
reflect key interests and major vulnerabilities of the dominant social order and are more instructive in analyzing
the defensive reactions of that order than as accurate depictions of normative violations by emerging religious
movements.

13

The second paper in this section deals with perhaps the most persistent charge against new religions; that they gain and hold members by duplicity or coercion. The more distant others' beliefs and actions are from our own, the more difficult it is to accept or comprehend them. If others' beliefs and actions are literally incomprehensible to us, it is a short step to interpreting them as bizarre, irrational and dangerous. The brainwashing metaphor constitutes precisely this kind of explanation. Richardson and Kilbourne dissect the concept of brainwashing from a sociology of knowledge perspective. They note the commonalities between the brainwashing models of the 1950's, which sought to account for the alleged success of Chinese communist thought reform camps, and contemporary brainwashing models, which offer explanations for the influx of youth into new religious movements. The authors note that anti-collectivist organizations contravene our individualistic, egoistic conception of human nature. Richardson and Kilbourne conclude that the brainwashing metaphor serves to preserve the status quo in the face of challenges from groups which present alternative conceptions of reality and premises for the construction of social order.

DEPROGRAMMING IN HISTORICAL PERSPECTIVE

Donald E. Miller
University of Southern California

American religious history provides an important backdrop for understanding the deprogramming phenomenon of recent times. Although the history of suppression of religious practice in the United States is uniquely modest (if compared to the treatment by Romans of Christians during the first few centuries, or of heretics of the Church during the Middle Ages), an examination of the treatment of marginal religious movements in America is instructive in understanding contemporary attitudes toward new religious movements and their practice.

In spite of Constitutional guarantees by the First Amendment of freedom of religious expression, the history of the United States is strewn with examples of religious intolerance. Anti-Catholic sentiment in the nineteenth century is perhaps the most blatant expression of religious persecution in this country, but that was not an isolated event. One must also look at the murder in 1844 of Joseph Smith in Carthage, Illinois as the mere symbol of continual harassment of the Mormons. The practice of "plural marriage" by the Mormons was tolerated no better by outsiders than was the practice of "complex marriage" by the Oneida Community. Indeed, the utopian groups of the nineteenth century almost all experienced continual legal and personal harassment for their "deviant" beliefs and practices. Anti-Semitism erupted in the late nineteenth century with the emigration of Jews to this country. Quakers faced oppression because of their pacifist outlook, to the point of some of their young men receiving death sentences (which later were commuted) for refusing to bear arms. And hysteria over the Jehovah's Witnesses resulted in persecutions including castration, burning of property, and other hostile acts.

Perhaps the central contribution of an historical perspective to deprogramming and other forms of religious persecution is that religious persecution of marginal religious movements is not unique to the contemporary period. In general, any new religious movement which is "deviant" by virtue of propounding a unique life style and system of

15

beliefs and practices will be subjected to persecution in
direct ratio to their success in attracting adherents and
to the degree to which they represent a clear and attractive option to the pattern of beliefs and practices of the
dominant culture.

A second value of the historical perspective is to
articulate the contribution which "deviant" groups have made
in the past to the processes of social change and cultural
evolution. Marginal religious groups play an important social function in the dynamic of creative societal change by
posing new formulations of the meaning of human existence
in the present age. It is predictable, however, that to
the extent that any group challenges the status quo through
new patterns of thought and practice, they will face opposition. Hence, standing on the ideological perimeter of a
society has both its promise in the possibility of crea-
tively posing new alternatives for seeing the world, but it
also carries the corresponding liabilities of marginality:
namely, persecution.

A third contribution of the perspective of history is
the realization that many groups which undergo religious
persecution often gain official legitimacy within a very
short span of time. The movement toward social acceptance
is often related to two factors: on one hand, historical
observation would indicate that the religious practice and
belief systems of "deviant" religious groups often become
routinized and rationalized over time and consequently become much more acceptable to the mainstream of cultural
life. Second, to the extent that marginal groups are often
visionary of things to come, the general culture may move
closer to some of the ideas and practices which are represented by formerly marginal groups.

In this paper two historical examples of religious
persecution -- anti-Catholic sentiment in the 1800's and
the bias against the Shakers will be examined. First, the
Catholic situation will be examined briefly, followed by a
more thorough look at the Shaker history.

ANTI-CATHOLIC SENTIMENT

Anti-Catholic sentiment in the United States was related primarily to the nativist movement in America. This
movement perceived the tremendous influx of immigrant
peoples into the nation -- many of them Catholic -- as a
threat to the supremacy of Anglo-Saxon Protestant rule.
During the "open-gate" policy of the nineteenth century,
the hoards of immigrants brought to these shores not only

their talents and in many instances their poverty, but also
their potential for casting a vote. The political potential
of the flow of immigrants is realized in noting that whereas
in the 1820's the immigrant total for the period was
128,452, by the decade of the 1830's it had jumped to
538,381, and by the 1850's there were 2,811,554 immigrants
who arrived during a ten year span. Although these immigrants provided a cheap source of labor for an expanding
economy, they also kept the wage level artificially low because of the competition for employment, and many Americans,
even recently arrived immigrants, perceived the new flow of
immigrants as posing a threat to their own job security;
hence, the newcomers were resented at a variety of levels.

In response to the rapid influx in Catholic population
a number of Protestant organizations and journals sprang up
whose primary goal was the articulation of an anti-Catholic
bias. The Protestant Vindicator, founded by the Reverend
William Craig Brownlee in 1834, was just one such example,
and when matched with the American Society to Promote the
Principles of the Protestant Reformation, together they presented a powerful anti-Catholic lobby. A supporting strain
of horror literature appeared concurrent with these many
publications and organizations and sold to an expectant
audience seeking justification for their anti-Catholic feeling. The reported confessions of Rebecca Theresa Reed, published under the title, Six Months in a Convent (1835),
served to fulfill this purpose. This book was mild, however, compared with the much more sensational expose by
Maria Monk, Awful Disclosures of the Hotel Dieu Nunnery of
Montreal (1836). Although these works were later exposed
as fraudulent and contrived, that fact seemed to have little
effect on their sales.

Anti-Catholic sentiment took physical dimensions with
the burning in 1834 of the Ursuline convent in Charlestown.
Although there was considerable public outrage at this act,
events such as these were fueled by the underlying feeling
that the growing number of Catholics posed a threat to democracy. The explicit hint was made in more than one publication that there was a plot by the Pope and the Jesuits to
subvert democracy by promoting Catholic immigration to
America. In May, 1844 violence erupted again, this time in
Kensington, a suburb of Philadelphia. Sydney Ahlstrom
(1972:563) comments:

This disturbance led to the wildest and blood-
iest rioting of the entire crusade. Two Roman
Catholic churches and dozens of Irish homes
were burned, militia fired point-blank upon

advancing crowds, a cannon was turned against
the soldiers guarding Saint Philip Neri Church,
and for three days mob rule prevailed in the
city and its environs. The final toll was
thirteen dead and over fifty wounded.

The ideological backdrop for this violence was supported and
extended in the 1850's when the American Party, promoting a
nativist platform, sent seventy-five men to Congress.

The lingering sentiment of the anti-Catholic bias was
still with us in 1960 when John Kennedy, running for president, was subjected to questions concerning whether his
first loyalty would be to Rome (the Pope), or to the people
of the United States. This question emerged, as we have
seen, from a deeply rooted attitude toward marginal religious groups as representing subversive political interests.
A contemporary illustration of this point is the frequent
charge made against Reverend Sun Myung Moon that he is
funded by the Korean CIA.

THE SHAKERS

The United Society of Believers, or the "shakers" as
they later preferred being called -- a name given because
of their distinctive form of religious dance -- arose during
a time of racial upheaval only somewhat more climatic than
our own. The Great Awakening was at its peak during the
Shakers most successful years and many of their members had
been affected by the sometimes transient spiritual experience incited by itinerate preachers only to seek a more
permanent relationship to a religious way of life which demanded long term commitment, devotion, and sacrifice. The
Shakers were only one of a number of groups who won considerable followings during this period; other successful
groups included the Oneida Community, various Transcenden-
talist communities, the Mormons, Millerites and Spiritualists. It was a time of religious upheaval not dissimilar
to our own in terms of the number of new religious groups
which were spawned and which found ready numbers of adherents.

At its peak a decade before the Civil War, the Shaker
movement counted some 6,000 members, divided into eighteen
branches containing fifty-eight "family" units. Numerically
it was of approximately the same size as the present membership of the Unification Church within the United States.
Likewise, the movement was foreign in origin, having been
born in England under the catalytic focus of one Ann Lee who
fulfilled the expectations of James and Jane Wardley, and

who like the Cumisards in France had been teaching that
Christ's second coming was imminent and the Kingdom of God
was at hand. Ann Lee was born of common stock, the daughter of a blacksmith and one who later married a blacksmith.
She possessed, however, a finely tuned sense of her own
sinfulness as well as the ability to dream and receive visions. Probably as a result of the death of all four of
her children in either infancy or early childhood, she developed a considerable repugnance toward sexuality and
things of the flesh.

Like Reverend Moon, Ann Lee believed herself to be the
fulfillment of the promise of the second coming of Christ.
This divine appointment was granted to her in a dream which
occurred while imprisoned on charges of disturbing the
peace. Her message was one of spiritual perfection, celibacy, community of goods, confession of sins and withdrawal
from the world. These goals, however, were not to be actu-
alized until several years after the emigration of this
emergent religious group to America in 1774. The path to
success, however, was not easy. Even before leaving
England Ann Lee was roughly arrested and imprisoned, placed
in a cell where she could not even lie down, and kept
there for fourteen days. She was miraculously fed during
this period with a straw through the keyhole in the door of
her cell by James Whittaker, later one of the stalwart
leaders of Shakerism. Later she was stoned, threatened
with having her tongue bored through with a hot iron, and
in general persecuted for her theological pronouncements
and the religious practices she was inspiring. Finally she
was directed by special revelation that the kingdom was to
be established in America.

The movement of location to America did not lessen her
travail. For the first year while her band of followers
were forced to disperse in search of work, and when her
husband got sick, she nearly starved. Once the immigrants
were more settled, the teachings of Ann Lee met with success, but not without considerable hostile reaction. She
was driven from one town to another in her missionizing
journeys and must have felt some kinship with the Apostle
Paul. Scandal followed her path. She was accused of seduction, homebreaking, and prison was her not infrequent
bedding place. In 1776 Mother Ann and her followers took
up residence on land purchased in Niskayuna, New York, and
for three and one-half years they lived and worked in relative peace.

After Mother Ann's death in 1784, leadership was
passed to Father James Whittaker who became the spiritual

head of the Shakers. Under his leadership a number of different communities were organized; first at New Lebanon in 1787 and then by 1794 in eleven other locations. Their communalization, however, spawned a new wave of attacks. These difficulties stemmed from seceders who upon joining the Shakers had legally given all of their possessions for the use of the community; later, however, in those instances where individuals elected to leave, they often attempted to recover these possessions, and in some instances even asked to be compensated for their years of labor. These requests often took the form of law suits against the Shakers.

The Shakers were favorably honored by the judicial system in a number of cases of suits brought by seceders -- this action illustrating the important role which marginal religious groups have played in defining for the nation issues of religious choice and freedom of religious practice. Nevertheless, the travail associated with such public attention did much to blacken the name of the Shakers. Two cases in particular provided wide notoriety for the community, both issuing from charges that the Shakers contributed to dispersing families and breaking up marriages. (Again, note the charge of family disruption as being not dissimilar to the frequent criticism leveled against the Unification Church and other new groups.) In the parallel cases of Mary Dyer and Eunice Chapman, both had joined as family units with their husbands and children, but had seceded, leaving their husbands behind as devotees to the principles of Shakerism.

In the case of Mary Dyer, she and her husband joined the community in 1811. She then left the society some four years later, leaving her children under the custody of the Shaker community. The conflict was over who should have legal possession of the children. For years Mary Dyer petitioned the courts for her children and in the process wrote slanderous books and pamphlets against the Shakers alleging misconduct, debacheries, obscenities, deception and cruelties of various sorts. Andrews (1963:208) summarizes the situation:

> If the depostions she assembled in her Portrai-
> ture of Shakerism (1822) were to be accepted as
> true, the movement would go down as one of the
> greatest hoaxes in American history. Ann is
> represented as a hypocrite, a fortune teller, a
> wine bibber and 'rummer,' a sadist, a prosti-
> tute. She was charged with ordering that chil-
> dren be stripped naked and whipped, strung up
> by their wrists, left alone all night in the

woods, and even beaten to death.

In spite of refutation of the charges by her husband,
Joseph Dyer, in A Compendious Narrative, there was a waiting audience to read the revelations of his wife. The
Shakers even produced sworn testimony by the Dyer children
in an attempt to silence the criticism. For example, the
statement of the daughter, Betsy Dyer, was contained in a
countervailing pamphlet (McNamar, 1819:111-112) appropriately entitled The Other Side of the Question.

> And further, as it is reported that we are kept
> in bondage among the Shakers; that we dare not
> speak as we feel, and that we dare not say any-
> thing only what we are told to say, this is false;
> for I have always spoken to my kindred freely,
> without any embarrassment on account of the
> Shakers.

Eventually Mary Dyer lost her case.

The parallel case of Eunice Chapman was not as fortu-
itous for the Shakers. She also alleged that the Shakers
were stealing her children, because in parallel fashion,
her husband had elected to stay with the community and
consequently her children were kept in the custody of the
Society. The Chapman case evoked such public sympathy
that a specific bill was drawn up in the New York State
Legislature for the release of her children from the
Shakers. The bill indicated that in cases such as that of
Mary Dyer and Eunice Chapman that the marriage contract
would automatically be dissolved, any personal property
held by the spouse united with the Shakers would be given
for maintenance of the family, and the children would be
granted to the parent who was not a believer.

Thomas Jefferson was so outraged by this bill that on
June 16, 1817, he wrote a letter to Albert Gallatin in
which he stated (Andrews, 1963:169):

> Three of our papers have presented us the copy
> of an act of the legislature of New York, which,
> if it has really passed, will carry us back to
> the times of the darkest bigotry and barbarism,
> to find a parallel. Its purport is, that all
> those who shall hereafter join in communion
> with the religious sect of Shaking Quakers,
> shall be deemed civilly dead, their marriages
> dissolved, and all their children and property
> taken out of their hands. This act being pub-

lished nakedly in the papers, without the usual
signatures, or any history of the circumstances
of its passage, I am not without hope it may
have been a mere abortive attempt....

The issue of "child thief" indeed has its parallels
to contemporary charges by parents against marginal religious movements. And likewise, the following statements
from McNamar (1819:131-169) by those young people within
the Shaker community have a strikingly contemporary ring
when compared with the statements of those individuals who
have been unsuccessfully deprogrammed:

We whose names are annexed, having perused the
foregoing information from the church, and dis-
covering a deficiency of testimony relating to
our sex, and particularly concerning our being
held in bondage, contrary to our faith and desire -- humbly present to the public the following statement of facts: That the common report
concerning young people, that they are held in
bondage, is false and groundless; or that they
are compelled to work and slave themselves, to
support older ones in idleness, or prevented
from reading the scriptures, or anything else
to which their faith and conscience may lead
them...

We, the undersigned, do certify, that we have
lived among the people called Shakers, for a
number of years, both in a state of minority
and manhood, that we never were compelled to
do anything contrary to our own faith; nor do
we know of any bondage or compulsion to force
the conscience, in any manner whatever; that
when we became of lawful age, we each of us
received our just portion of our parents'
estate, which we used according to our own
minds, and were left free to do with ourselves
and our interest as we saw proper.

Perhaps even more contemporary in tone is the charge made
against the Shakers by those who stood outside:

Their first step toward securing the children
among them, seems to be by teaching them "dis-
obedience to parents," and an attempt to eradi-
cate from their bosoms all filial affection.
Secondly, under deceptious statements to the
uninformed parents, to obtain indentures. And
lastly, should the parents themselves escape

from under their tyrannical control, their
offspring are concealed, sent to foreign
branches of the society, their names changed,
so that it is next to impossible to find them,
and if found, not unfrequently rescued by
force and strong hand -- and dragged from the
embraces of their doting parents, again to become the unconscious partakers of a spirit at
least of folly and madness, if not of infernal
origin.

The only difference between the above statement and many
being made currently against groups such as the Unification
Church is that in the case of the Shakers one of the parents was engaged in the movements. The following statement about the motives underlying the interest of the
leadership in seeking new members again resembles inflama-
tory charges against contemporary cults and sects (McNamar,
1819:118-119):

We are convinced, from the testimony now in
possession, that wealth and power is the object at which the heads of this society aim
-- that they are swallowing up the substance
of the unfortunate, who fall into their net,
as fast as the serpent of Moses swallowed the
serpents of the Magicians -- that they are
holding numbers of our young, innocent, free
born citizens in bondage -- and instilling
the most abominable principles into every
mind that can be duped or deluded by their
vile sophistry.

The Shakers were not without their defenders, as was
noted in the Jefferson quotation cited above. In the case
of the bill entertained by the New York State Legislature
there was an eloquent reply written by a blue ribbon panel
of notables who made the following point (Andrews, 1963:
211):

If the Legislature can constitutionally deprive
a man of his parental rights, merely because he
is a Shaker, they have an equal right, for the
same cause, to disfranchise him of every other
privilege, or to banish him, or even put him
to death.

The Shakers did not rest with the defense provided by good
willed outsiders, they also printed and distributed a number of books and pamphlets which argued their case.

Witness, for example, the following brief testimonial
(Society of Believers, 1828):

> I first became acquainted with the Shakers, at
> Pleasant Hill, Mercer County, KY in the spring
> of the year 1818. On becoming acquainted with
> them, I found them very different from what they
> were generally represented. Instead of that
> superstitious gloom and religious melancholy
> which I expected to see -- cheerfulness, satis-
> faction, peace and tranquility appeared to
> reign throughout their delightful dominions.

In addition, in order to protect themselves, particularly against the suits of seceders, the Shakers constructed a careful legal "covenant" which each incoming member
signed and which entitled the signee to "Just and equal
rights and privileges, according to their needs, in the use
of all things in the Church." What this document was careful to specify, however, was that their right was a religious and not a property right. This Covenant protected
the society against those individuals who after seceding
were not only making their claims for property which they
brought into the community, but also for labor which had
been given for the years that they had been associated with
the community. There usually was some negotiation by
Shaker leadership with the departing member, but only to
the extent of providing the seceder with token discharge
money to ease his/her transition into a new way of life.
As noted earlier, the courts fairly regularly looked with
favor upon the Shakers in these suits. The following
statement, by the court (Andrews, 1963:205-206) indicates
that the Shakers were not universally held in reproach.

> No one can see the improvements made in husbandry
> and manufacture by this sect, and at the same
> time believe the existence of the sect to be
> against the policy of the law. Whatever we may
> think of their faith, their works are good, and
> charity bids us think well of the tree when the
> fruits are salutary. We cannot try the question
> which religion, theirs or ours, is the better
> one....Theirs is equally under the protection
> of the law, as ours...There certainly are some
> reasons for saying that the religion of this
> sect of Christians bears a greater resemblance
> to that of the primitive church than ours does....

In spite of the affirmative attitude by many intellectuals towards the Shakers, the popular mind enjoyed specu-

lating on what went on within communitarian life. Perhaps
because of the rigidly strict discipline of separating the
sexes there were popular novels of the period with titles
such as Shaker Lovers (Thompson, 1846). The basic plot of
this "racy" work focuses on the courtship of two young
people who are forced to secretly meet in order to share
their affection. The obvious bias of this work, and
others, is reflected in the following interlude within the
book.

> But so well known is their meaningless mode of
> worship -- their long drawn, nasal chant of
> Hottentot gibberish, set to the "inspired" tune
> of perhaps Nancy Dawson, or the Roving Sailor;
> (for their tunes as well as the words they
> contend are inspired) their formal, unvarying,
> Kangaroo-like dance, performed with uplifted
> hands and various contortions of features, or
> the occasional exhibition, by some freshly in-
> spired Elder or Eldress, of a new gift for
> clapping the hands, for shaking, jerking,
> jumping, stamping and groaning -- so well
> known are all these, that we will pass over
> them for matters more immediately connected
> with our story....

Somehow the charge of sexually promiscuous behavior was a
favorite issue.

The fear of the public that the Shakers were becoming
financially too powerful also fueled the criticism which
poured forth. The claim was made, for example, that the
Shakers owned too much land, were encroaching upon other
denominations, and threatened to embrace whole towns, and
perhaps even counties. Unfortunately for the Shakers,
some of those who had left as seceders did nothing to dissuade these fears and, in fact, often published accounts
which seemed to confirm the worst possible conditions within the communities (New Hampshire, 1049:6):

> I am eighteen years of age; I have lived with the
> Shakers at Canterbury eleven years....While
> there I was always taught to disown and hate all
> natural affection; was told not to have any re-
> gard for my relations, and never allowed to be
> with them unless some of the leaders were with
> me; I was instructed to look no further than
> the Elders for God; they (the Elders) could see
> and discern what was right, and what was wrong,
> in all cases. The Shakers were accustomed to

have revelations and see visions; used to have
intercourse with Indians, Negroes, and Angels.
I have known children who were obliged to kneel,
and stand for hours together for trivial offenses;
I have been obliged to do it myself....

Another testimonial stated (New Hampshire, 1849:7):

We arise at half past four o'clock in the morning, during the summer, and later in winter;
eat breakfast and work till twelve o'clock; eat
dinner and commence work again, and work till
six o'clock; then eat supper. After eating supper, there is an exercise which is called "retiring." We are required to sit up straight in
our chairs, without touching the chair backs,
perfectly still. If we laugh, fall asleep, or
whisper, or do anything out of order, we must
stand up and make three bows to the Elders,
and confess. Persons frequently fall asleep
from fatigue, after laboring during the day.
Immediately after "retiring" we go into meeting
and after meeting all retire to bed; none sit
up.

A major issue arose around the following incident which
may have had some reference to an actual event (New
Hampshire, 1849:7):

I knew George A. Emery, and was there when he
died. His Caretaker was Ephraim Dennett. I
once saw Dennett seize this boy and beat his
head upon the floor as many as fifteen times.
I was in the meeting the night that the boy
died. We were told, by Elder Johnson, that a
sad accident had happened; that George had gone
down in the field to walk with Ephraim, and
while there had fallen upon a rock, struck his
head and killed him.

No movement is devoid of those with pathological strains,
and surely the citation of one or two isolated events does
not discount the authenticity of the religious convictions
of an entire community.

The case of religious persecution against the Shakers
could be documented more fully, but the quotations and incidences cited above give some indication of the parallels
in criticism between one nineteenth century religious community and marginal religious groups of the present. The

same case I have made with the Shakers could just as easily
be made with the Oneida community, or other nineteenth
century groups. In retrospect we look back on the Shakers
with a great sense of admiration for their industriousness,
simplicity of design, and technological innovations within
their manufacturing industries. We also realize the wisdom
of the courts in honoring their integrity as a marginal
religious movement. Certainly the nation was enriched by
the creativity of their offering at a particular moment in
history. Also, the Shakers met a spiritual need for a number of individuals who were seeking perfection in a world
fraught with rapid social change and disruption. What les-
sons are to be learned from the example of the Shakers in
terms of our relation to marginal religious movements of
the present?

CONCLUSIONS

Each of the situations discussed above were for a time
provocative of negative sanction by the dominant culture.
History shows the pattern of response to be quite uniform.
Often the character of the leaders of a new religious
movement is attacked; First, charges of sexual, legal, and
financial misconduct are routinely made; the attempt by
outsiders being to cast into question the motives of the
leadership of the movement. Second, it is commonly alleged
that the members themselves engage in sexually licentious
behavior or other activity which is cruel, inhumane, or
indecent. Third, a new religious movement frequently is
portrayed as a political threat, either because of the
leader's connection to a foreign country or because of his/
her ideological leanings. Within the United States, the
socialist and communal tendency of many marginal groups
especially opens them to charges of political subversion.
Fourth, it is common to label the education of children,
as well as the process of inducting new members, as "brainwashing," hence evoking the sympathy of the "objective"
outsider to the plight of the helpless.

What lies behind these attempts at discreditation is
undoubtedly the perception that the way of life of the
dominant culture is being threatened. From the perspective
of the values of those within the dominant culture, it is
incomprehensible why anyone would want to forego sex, meat
and sleep, engage in limited consumerism and consumption,
and endure other "privations." Obviously, individuals engaging in such practices are either devoted to some political end which allows them such personal sacrifice, or
they are mentally ill. What often goes unrecognized by

those within the dominant culture because of their social
and economic position, however, is the profound sense of
dissatisfaction felt by members of marginal religious
groups toward the values underpinning the way of life of
those within the dominant culture.

Another point seldom appreciated by those of the dominant culture is the important social role played by individuals holding to "deviant" belief systems and practices.
To address the historical role which has been played by
such groups, it is important to recall that the source of
marginal religious movements is that they are a product of
those who feel acutely the cultural dislocation or dis-
orientation of their period. Hence, the uniqueness of the
belief system, practices and life style of members of marginal religious groups resides in the fact that they offer
alternative ways of achieving meaning and purpose within a
culture which to them does not make sense as defined by the
majority. In this sense, such individuals are cultural in-
novators, responding to the world in a unique way which reflects their "skewed" interpretation of reality. These individuals are willing to break with customary modes of interpretation. It is this commitment which provides their
basis for a new vision of human meaning and purpose -- a
new vision that may be very valuable for a pluralistic
society.

CLASSICAL AND CONTEMPORARY APPLICATIONS OF
BRAINWASHING MODELS: A COMPARISON AND CRITIQUE

James T. Richardson
Brock Kilbourne
University of Nevada Reno

In 1972, Richardson, Simmonds and Harder published the first systematic research applying the models derived from studies of Chinese "thought reform" to the Jesus Movement. These authors, following Zablocki's (1971) application of Lifton's (1961) ideas of the thought reform process to the religious community of the Bruderhoff, identified a number of problems in assuming the equivalence of Chinese thought reform techniques with the resocialization practices of Jesus Movement groups. For instance, the failure of equivalence was indicated by the obvious lack of direct physical coercion in the Jesus Movement and the de-emphasis in the Jesus Movement upon the "stripping process" (the first stage of Lifton's thought reform model whereby an individual's identity is assaulted, a sense of self-betrayal and guilt is fostered, and a socio-emotional breakdown is instigated). The stripping process appeared to be unnecessary for establishing guilt in the majority of members, since many of the individuals came to the movement with a generalized sense of guilt. Additionally, it was found that the "cult of confession" was not as strong an element in the Jesus Movement as in the thought reform camps or revolutionary colleges. Thus, while concluding many of Lifton's elements of totalism were present in their study of the Jesus Movement, Richardson, et. al. observed a significant difference in the intensity and pervasiveness of these totalistic elements.

What appeared as a straightforward scientific analysis soon drew, however, some attention among groups interested in new religions, and appeared, in retrospect, to anticipate the emergence of a substantial body of popular and scholarly writing applying thought reform or "brainwashing" ideas to new religions. Some who were opposed ideologically to the emergence of the new religious groups applied brainwashing or thought reform concepts uncritically to the new religions (see Singer, 1979a, 1979b; Clark, 1978, 1979a, 1979b, for examples) Moreover, an increasing number of social science researchers began to initiate their own research attempts to

ascertain the relationship between new religious groups and
purported thought reform techniques.

        Robbins and Anthony (1979, and reprinted herein) argued,
for example, that current applications of thought reform
concepts to "cults" generally entail a number of gross distortions. These distortions are based upon the pejorative
use of brainwashing models as conceptual weapons to justify
and legitimate the use of coercive measures to abduct allegedly brainwashed victims. The key problems associated
with the use of brainwashing models to explicate membership
in new religious groups are: (1) the use of overgeneralized
cult stereotypes -- all cults are generically equated in
terms of totalistic regimentation, forced dependency, deception, and psychopathology; (2) the implicit equation of religious movements with government operated institutions employing forcible constraint -- the tendency to overlook the
fact that the thought reform process described by Lifton
used peer pressures within a broader context of explicit
physical constraint and forcible confinement, as opposed to
a much higher prevalence of voluntary commitment in the new
religious groups; (3) assumptions that persons subjected to
certain persuasion techniques lack "free will"-- this position ignores that free will is more of a philosophical premise than a measureable concept, and the obvious reality
that there are numerous individuals in today's society who
are not fully autonomous; and (4) methodological issues --
several studies which apply the thought reform literature to
new religious groups over-rely upon the accounts of former
converts. The inherent sampling bias and over-reliance upon
biographical accounts greatly limits the generalizability of
such findings. Robbins and Anthony conclude that "mind control" formulations are better understood as conceptual weapons to indicate deviant groups than as scientific concepts
to advance our understanding of particular social phenomenon.

        From another perspective, Ungerleider and Wellisch
(printed herein) have reported evidence that former and active cult members are fully capable of making sound judgements and legal decisions related to their persons and
property. They reported no evidence of insanity or mental
illness (i.e., in the legal sense) in their study and, interestingly, individuals remaining in the cults tended not to
feel dominated and, in fact, to feel dominant. This clear
trend of sound intellectual functioning coupled with generally reported feelings of dominance by cult members is exceedingly difficult to reconcile with the thought reform
conceptions of helplessness and impaired intellectual functioning. Trudy Solomon (printed herein) has similarly observed the lack of force and captivity in the new religious

groups. In the case of the Moonies, Solomon believes movement leaders and members may use emotional and psychological
pressure; however, they do not force anyone to join or believe. Furthermore, the high turnover rate in recruits of
the Unification Church in their first year (only 10% of new
recruits remain beyond the first weekend and a turnover rate
of 55% in the first year of those who remain) seriously
limits the applicability of thought reform concepts to the
behavior of new religious group members. As quoted in
Ungerleider and Wellisch, Dr. Albert Lubin, chairman of the
Committee of Psychiatry and Religion for the Group of the
Advancement of Psychiatry (GAP) has stated in this regard:

> When the conversion is to a religion that fur-
> thers the status quo, society tends to approve
> of the converts and regard them as normal. When
> it threatens prevailing beliefs or lifestyles,
> society often desires to eliminate them either
> by exile or imprisonment or milder forms of re-
> pression and regard them as mentally ill.

Yet, in spite of the growing reluctance by many social scientists and helping professionals to espouse the use of
brainwashing concepts and allegations, a vocal minority of
professionals and lay persons continue to use this scienti-
fically defunct term in relation to the new religious
groups.

Perhaps more interesting than the comparison of thought
reform techniques and new religious groups is the observation that the stubborn persistence of the brainwashing models of the 1950s and the 1970s appears to be a phenomenon
worthy of study in and of its own right. It may, in fact,
constitute the most important issue in the current controversy about new religions, since the comparability of new
religious groups and thought reform techniques is obviously
contingent upon a certain kind of rhetoric. In other words,
the rhetoric being used defines the person's or group's universe of discourse, and takes for granted or presupposes
certain types of conceptual solutions to rhetorically bounded
problems. The world is thus defined a certain way, and to
the extent we "buy into" certain definitions, so must we
also deduce certain necessary conclusions. Mead (1934) has
observed how the universe of discourse typically provides an
interpretive framework by which individuals live and organize their experiences. Brown (1977) takes the argument a
step further by contending the universe of discourse or rhetoric may, at times, be heavily infused with metaphor. Metaphors are viewed as providing different perspectives from
which individuals may view and describe society. Metaphors

may even acquire the power to influence, if not literally
determine, our understandings of social reality.

It is the metaphor of brainwashing then that concerns
us here. Szasz has previously addressed this issue, and
claims "A person can no more wash another's brain with coercion or conversion than he can make him bleed with a cutting remark" (quoted in Robbins and Anthony, 1978, p. 77).
But, more importantly, it is the selective application of
the "brainwashing" metaphor in particular social situations
to particular people that concerns us most. Namely, the
reservation of the brainwashing metaphor to those disapproved of social influences which are considered by some
to be illegitimate (e.g., new religious groups). Consequently, there is a need to characterize the distinguishing
aspects of the rhetoric used to attack both communist
thought reform camps in the 1950s and new religious groups
in the 1970s; this should allow us to assess how the "mind
control" or "brainwashing" rhetoric has been selectively
applied to certain groups.

One way to analyze the brainwashing rhetoric is from
the standpoint of the "critical theory" of the Frankfurt
school (Horkheimer, 1972, 1974; Adorno, 1973; Marcuse, 1964;
Habermas, 1971, 1973). The Frankfurt school is best known
for its efforts to critique the ideological underpinnings of
commonly accepted knowledge. The questions posed by such
analyses focus on whose interests are served by particular
ideas and ideologies. More recently, critical theory has
manifested itself in social psychology (Gergen and Morawski,
1980) by focusing on social context effects in social psychological knowledge. A critical perspective has been used
to identify the economic, political, ideological, and metatheoretical underpinnings of so-called neutral and objective
knowledge. Thus, from a critical perspective, it is the
main contention of the present paper that the brainwashing
rhetoric of the 1950s and the 1970s can fruitfully be viewed
in terms of the following shared characteristics: (1) a common ideological perspective; (2) a common metatheoretical
structure; (3) a common "stage theory" explanation of attitudinal and behavioral change; and (4) common methodological
approaches.

THE CLASSICAL MODELS OF BRAINWASHING

More than two decades have passed since the first of a
series of brainwashing models (Hunter, 1951; Meerloo, 1956;
Sargant, 1957; Lifton, 1961; Schein, Schneier and Barker,
1961; Somit, 1968) was proposed to explicate the process of
radical behavioral and attitudinal change. These models,

which attempted to explain radical changes in prisoners in Communist thought reform camps, might not have been attended to in recent times had it not been for the rise of the new religious and self growth groups. Unfortunately, the actual value of coercive techniques to extract information and false confessions, to demoralize, to confuse, to break up a group, and to function as an effective propaganda strategy has been largely lost from view as some researchers of the new religions attempt to compare early thought reform techniques with recruitment and resocialization practices in new religious groups.

The problem with this approach to new religious groups is that an uncritical acceptance of the classical models of brainwashing has led some investigators to incorporate various elements of these models into their contemporary explanations of resocialization into the new religions, as if these elements were firmly established and agreed upon. This tendency has resulted in a near hysterical state of affairs. A close examination of both classical and contemporary models of brainwashing suggests, however, that the continuity in explanations is more a function of a common ideological, conceptual, metatheoretical, and methodological base than of similar conditions in thought reform camps and new religions.

The four classic models of brainwashing assume different perspectives in their respective explanations of the same phenomenon; Lifton is neo-Freudian, Sargant is physiological, Meerloo is Freudian and Pavlovian, and Schein, et. al. are cognitive-social psychological in approach. Nonetheless they all share a common ideological bias and cognitive orientation in that "belief change" is presumed to precede "behavior change." Each theorist implicitly and explicitly values individualism and democratic capitalism, and likewise condemns totalism, and even collectivism. Each idealizes America and its institutions. Totalism is generally equated with brainwashing, and becomes the manner in which the individual can be dehumanized by taking advantage of his or her natural limitations. Totalism, accordingly, immerses the individual in the group, and destroys all that is unique and creative in human nature.

Lifton (1961), the most quoted early brainwashing researcher, identifies eight separate criteria that are part of ideological totalism and construed to be inseparable from brainwashing: "milieu control," "mystical manipulation," "demand for purity," "cult of confession," "sacred science," "loading the language," "doctrine over person," and the "dispensing of existence." Sargant (1957) approaches brainwash-

ing from an entirely intra-individualistic perspective, and
concludes that the real spector of brainwashing is the danger of lost individuality and immersion within an amorphous
and unruly mob. His work was initiated after he noted similarities between conversions to early Methodism and the
Pavlovian experiments with dogs. For Sargant, the mob sym-
bolizes the first step toward the total submission of the
individual to a malignant collectivity. But, Meerloo (1956)
offers the most vehement ideological condemnation of the
four models. For Meerloo, brainwashing is "an elaborate
ritual and systematic indoctrination, conversion, and self-
accusation used to change non-Communists into submissive
followers of the party." Totalists use their understanding
of unconscious conflicts and the conditionable natures of
human beings to reduce them to zombies. Lastly, Schein, et.
al. (1961) express their ideological opposition to totalism
when they conceptualize brainwashing in relation to a totalistic social movement.

Biderman (1962), in his critique of Schein, et al. and
of Lifton's work, also suggests an element of racism in both
approaches. His comment seems applicable to all four models,
although in most cases the racism is subtle. On the one
hand, there is the "ethnocentrism" of researchers of Chinese
thought reform techniques who have tended to equate all individuals, social groups and cultures with the stereotypic
response of American POWs in captivity. On the other hand,
there is a played upon element of "fear of the Orient" or of
the "yellow plague" which pervades much of the early writing
on this subject.

Second, all four models generally rely upon the same
metatheoretical assumptions of homeostasis, determinism/pas-
sivity, transformation, and individualism (only Schein, et.
al. provide a less individualistic and more sociological approach). The basic idea of the biological metaphor of homeostasis is that there is a psychological equilibrium point in
humans which automatically corrects psychic imbalances when
they occur. Each model assumes such a state of equilibrium
in humans, and consequently assumes an overly deterministic
and passive view of human nature. This ignores, of course,
the voluntary nature of much of the participation in the
thought reform colleges in China, as described especially by
Lifton (1961), and noted by Biderman (1962). The individual's personality is viewed by those espousing a thought reform or brainwashing perspective as determined by powerful
instinctual, biological, cultural, or social forces. Individuals are simply passive recipients of their personalities
(i.e., it is something that happens to them or is given to
them) from early childhood into adulthood.

The metatheoretical assumption of self transformation is also evident in each of the four models of brainwashing. That is, the person's self can be transformed into new forms of self, similar to the transformation of silkworms into butterflies. This assumption is at the core of all models of brainwashing, and is in fact the traditional view of conversion processes (Richardson, 1982). Finally, an individualistic bias pervades the discussion of all models except that of Schein, et al. Totalism and brainwashing constitute a systematically destructive assault upon the uniqueness, adaptiveness, integrity, and problem-solving capacities of the individual. The healthy individual is supposedly the individual who stands apart from the social group, and who does not depend upon the group for self definitions. Collectivism is, thus, eschewed by all four, even to some extent by Schein, et. al.

Third, all four models of brainwashing proffer similar three stage models to explicate the resocialization process. In general, these three stages consist of the individual's initial socio-emotional breakdown, his or her developing commitment to and identification with captors (i.e., a kind of training phase), and his or her resulting immersion into a new group and the development of a new social self. In the initial breakdown phase of stimulus control the individual is ostensibly overwhelmed with various incapacitating physical and social conditions that produce an abrupt break in the individual's sense of reality. In the second phase of increased commitment, training and response control, the individual's responses are closely monitored and he or she tends to identify with the captors; the individual first manifests signs of succumbing to the various pressures of the first phase of stimulus control, and then begins an attempt to reestablish a semblance of order and predictability. The individual perceives the captors as the ultimate and only source of reality, and attempts to match or align his or her actions and beliefs with those of the captors. In the third stage of group immersion and normative control, in which the person's thoughts and beliefs are largely influenced by the legitimated normative structure, the individual is fully committed to a new system of roles, responsibilities, and relationships. His or her life becomes normalized or ritualized in a new social community and taken for granted. Moreover, the person acquires the social definitions and self-identity(s) associated with the new social role and social community. As a consequence, the person is very likely to be perceived intra-individualistically, analogous to the general tendency for observers to attribute the cause of an actor's behavior to internal causes (Harvey and Weary, 1981), and thus construed as literally changed, over and above their new social commitments and role obligations.

Fourth, all four researchers generally employed quite problematic methods to arrive at their conclusions (see Biderman, 1962). The majority of the so-called brainwashing data was drawn from basically biased small samples that cannot be said to be representative of the populations to which they hoped to generalize. And in most cases the reports furnished from the research were primarily limited to anecdotal accounts, bound by the theorist's subjective interpretations within a particular theoretical framework. These scientific reports are also grossly limited by the biographical nature of the data collected. For example, as Biderman (1962) points out, Lifton only studied 40 people in all, and presents eleven detailed case studies, and Schein's original research was limited to a study of fifteen American civilians who returned after imprisonment in China.

CONTEMPORARY MODELS AND QUASI-MODELS OF BRAINWASHING

The more recent models and quasi-models of brainwashing share similar underlying commonalities with the classical models. Like their predecessors, these models are anti-totalistic in ideology, rely upon the same metatheoretical assumptions (i.e., homeostasis, passivism, transformation and individualism), proffer a three-stage model of resocialization, and employ a narrow data base for their justification (Singer, 1979a; Lifton, 1979; Scales, 1980; Conway and Siegleman, 1978, 1982; Clark, 1978, 1979a, 1979b, 1981; Verdier, 1980; Levine, 1980a, 1980b; Delgado, 1980; Enroth, 1977; Patrick and Dulak, 1976; Stoner and Parke, 1977). However, while the early brainwashing models were used to discredit the "rising tide of communism," the new models have been used to explain and to discredit the so-called "cult phenomenon." They are all anti-cult in their orientation.

The four commonalities of both the new applications of brainwashing models and the earlier models are exemplified particularly well in the Clark, et al. (1981) conception of conversion to new religious groups. The anti-totalistic ideology of their model is apparent in their belief that:

the characteristically totalitarian corporate
structure of the destructive groups which concerns us, as well as the unconscionable degree
to which they use manipulative techniques of
conversion and maintenance, clearly distinguish

them from helpful or relatively benign solutions to private and public problems...

Destructive cult leaders have, as a result
of their evangelism, usually become wealthy
men or women whom their followers have invested with unique, even God-like powers.
They espouse and enforce beliefs and practices which converts hold to be absolutely
true and vital to salvation while at the same
time encouraging a rabid intolerance of other
belief systems and of outsiders who do not
share the same vision. The typical result
among converts is a paranoid view of the non-
cult world and an intrigue-laden, guarded,
and manipulative interaction with it (1981:
8-9).

Conversion to such groups is also conceptualized essentially in terms of a three-stage model of resocialization. The first phase consists of what we have referred
to as stimulus control and the typical stripping process.
Supposedly, individuals are enticed into the group, given
intense personalized attention, subjected to extreme social pressures, bombarded with rituals and activities, deprived of sleep and nourishment, and systematically seduced
into altered states of consciousness. The first stage is
designed to "soften them up" and make the new recruit more
receptive to the "cult's"unique and oftentimes strange
ideas and ideology. In the second phase of response control (i.e., training and identification), the new recruit
is subjected to "marathon classes and intense devotional or
confessional activities calculated to maintain and strength-
en the convert's receptivity" (Clark, et al. 1981:14).
The convert is repeatedly induced to espouse and rehearse
the cult's beliefs, practices, and sanctioned behavior. In
the third phase of normative control and the rebirth of a
new self, "a factitious second personality -- the cult personality -- begins episodically to achieve a certain autonomy as it struggles with the old one for position in the
forefront of consciousness" (Clark, et al. 1981:17).
The individual thus acquires a new self which is supported
by a new world view, special language, roles, activities,
norms and social relationships. At this point the convert
has successfully internalized the new social or normative
order. The convert now polices him or herself.

This description of the Clark, et. al. conversion process serves as a useful example for many of the new quasi-
brainwashing models of new religious conversion. They view
the convert as a passive recipient of life changes who gains

a new personality, resulting from the imbalancing of normal
social relations and biological processes. Consequently,
the new models see this change occurring at the individual
level as the person disposes of their old self and acquires
a new "cult" personality. Interestingly, Clark's data is
primarily derived from clinical observations made in his
private practice (1981) and, similar to other psychiatric
reports of this sort, has been generated from a relatively
small, but apparently growing, number of case histories at
various stages of involvement in the newer religions.

In fact, the new brainwashing models have usually relied upon clinical case histories (see the work of Singer,
of Clark and of Verdier) and snowball sampling techniques
(see the work of Conway and Siegleman, of Enroth, and of
Stoner and Parke) to collect their data. And in both cases
the data base for such brainwashing claims have been collected primarily from former cult members, most of whom
were deprogrammed. Many problems arise, of course, when
collecting data in this fashion; most notable such data
gathering techniques preclude the possibility of drawing
valid generalizations. While snowball sampling allows the
researcher to interview whomever they can contact, it nonetheless cannot be said to be representative of a total population; and is only useful when members of the target population maintain formal or informal communication with one
another (Lin, 1976), an assumption that cannot be made in
these studies. Furthermore, as already suggested, it is
problematic whether the therapeutic setting permits the
therapist simultaneously to provide treatment and to collect
unbiased data.

There are even more severe problems of the reported
data which such brainwashing claims are made. A good example of this is evident in a recent statistical analysis
(Kilbourne, 1982) of a sampling of findings reported by
Conway and Siegleman (1982), the authors of Snapping (1978),
the best known of the popular anti-cult literature. In an
article entitled "Information Disease: Have Cults Created a
New Mental Illness?", Conway and Siegleman report findings
for the five biggest cults in their study (i.e., the
Moonies, Hare Krishna, Church of Scientology, Divine Light,
and The Way International), which consisted of 262 former
members (65.5% of their total volunteer and snowball sample,
N=400). In relation to their study (1982:90) Conway and
Siegleman claimed:

    But our research showed what appeared to be a
    direct relationship between the number of hours
    spent per week in cult ritual and indoctrination
    and the number of long-term effects. In addition,

we found a similar correlation between hours per
week spent in ritual and indoctrination and the
reported length of rehabilitation time. Put
simply: our findings appear to confirm that the
psychological trauma cults inflict upon their
members is directly related to the amount of
time spent in indoctrination and mind-control
rituals (emphasis theirs).

However, Kilbourne's analysis of these reported data
(i.e., group averages and group percentages) indicated that,
except for one instance, total hours per week in ritual and
indoctrination was not significantly correlated (using rho)
with any of the purported long term mental and emotional effects or with average rehabilitation time (all p's > .2).
Only the variable hallucinations and delusions was found to
be significantly correlated with total hours per week in
ritual/indoctrination, but this relationship was negative
(rho=-.90, p > .038). Additionally, the average length of
time in the cult did not significantly correlate with any of
the long term mental/emotional effects or with average rehabilitation time (all p's > .3), and the same general pattern
emerged in relation to the average hours spent per day in
ritual processes by the sampled cult members. Thus, for the
reported data for five major groups in their study, Conway
and Siegleman offer no statistical evidence for their conclusions.

An apparent strength of the newer brainwashing and
quasi-brainwashing models that explains their persistence
in the face of counter evidence is their consistency in application, their greater comprehensiveness and their pseu-
doscientific nature. As already discussed, the classical
models were sharply divided in their theoretical explanation of the mechanism(s) underlying the brainwashing process. Recent models pull elements from all models, but
have particularly used concepts from Lifton and from
Sargant. Some overtly claim to build on but go far beyond
previous work. Especially Conway and Siegleman's (1978)
effort to promote "catastrophe theory" as the logical extension of and improvement on early brainwashing studies
illustrates this tendency. Also, see Verdier's (1980)
claim to have developed a simple test to determine if brainwashing has occurred. While sometimes emphasizing certain
elements over others (for example see Verdier's emphasis on
the biological and Lifton's attention to the social; see
Scales, (1980), contemporary users of brainwashing models

have all combined elements from each of the earlier models
of brainwashing to develop a generally quite consistent application to new religious phenomenon. The new quasi-brainwashing models have developed a remarkably standard and even
stereotypic interpretation of new religious conversion.

    This stereotypic interpretation we refer to as the cult
syndrome. The cult syndrome consists of three components
which are used in combination to explain how brainwashing is
accomplished. These are: (1) personal vulnerabilities --
individuals who join the new religions suffer from some a
priori ailment. They are thought to suffer from identity
crises and meaninglessness (Singer, 1979a), to be discon-
nected from tradition and alienated from materialism (Scales,
1980), alienated by the 1960's (Conway and Siegleman, 1978),
to be unsuspecting and naive (Verdier, 1980), to have strong
personality-dependency needs (Levine, 1980a), to want to escape from freedom (Delgado, 1980), an inherent need to conform (Stoner and Parke, 1977), to suffer from life crises,
confusion and excessive idealism (Enroth, 1977; Patrick with
Dulak, 1976), and to be disillusioned and susceptible to
trance states and having a low tolerance for ambiguity
(Clark, et. al. 1981), etc.; (2) cults use powerful and sophisticated recruitment techniques -- radical changes in new
recruits are generally attributed to the cult's systematic
manipulation of isolation and deprivation, intense emotion
and guilt, information and milieu control, conditioning,
repetition, group pressures, altered states of consciousness,
ideological totalism, confession rituals, charasmatic leadership, lack of privacy, constant activity and induced dependency (see previous citations on Singer, Lifton, Clark,
Conway and Siegleman, Verdier, Levine, Delgado, Enroth,
Patrick, Stoner and Parke); and (3) cult membership results
in negative effects -- cult conversion is purported to in-
capacitate individuals in various ways. For instance,
Singer (1979a) claims the consequences of cult life are depression, loneliness, indecisiveness, slipping into altered
states, blurring of mental acuity, uncritical passivity and
fear of the cult itself. According to Clark, et al. (1981),
former cult members look "depressed much of the time" (1981:
18); "there is often a fixed, intense focus in the eyes"
(1981:18); and there is an uncritical passivity to life, an
"abiding sense of guilt" (1981:20), deep distrust, haunting
fear, outrage toward the cult, obsessional thinking, impairment of intellectual functioning, memory loss, hallucinations, depersonalization, derealization, indecisiveness and
flashbacks to dissociative states. Others allege cult membership results in robot-like personalities (Scales, 1980;
Patrick with Dulak, 1976); breaks down the mind's ability to
process information (Conway and Siegleman, 1978); produces
loss of freedom of choice (Levine, 1980a), narrowed atten-

tion and heightened suggestibility (Delgado, 1980), and destruction of the will to be self-determining (Enroth, 1977);
leads to a loss of career, family and middle-class lifestyle
(Stoner and Parke, 1977); and enslaves minds and directly
assaults a person's sanity (Verdier, 1980).

In sum, the new quasi-models of brainwashing applied by
some to new religions have evolved out of the earlier models
of brainwashing. Similar to the earlier models, they are
anti-totalistic and ethnocentric, overdeterministic, individualistic, view brainwashing as a kind of three-stage model
of stripping, identification, and the establishment of the
new self-new norms, and rely upon a narrow methodological
base and cross-citations. However, while over-relying on
clinical histories and snowball techniques for their data,
some of these new models are more comprehensive and sophisticated than the earlier models. They incorporate elements
of each and appreciate more the interaction of personality
factors (i.e., vulnerabilities) with powerful social factors
(i.e., milieu control).

The new models have been used to discredit and patholo-
gize membership in the new religions, just as earlier work
explained radical attitudinal and behavioral change in Communist thought reform camps. Yet, we can best appreciate
these models in relation to their stereotypic application.
Here we speak of a "cult syndrome" consisting of vulnerable
personalities, powerful recruitment/resocialization techniques and general negative effects. Interestingly, the cult
syndrome is very similar to other syndromes (i.e., the Communist or political radical syndrome, the "hippie syndrome,"
etc.) which have been used historically as social weapons in
American society to discredit new ideas, social forms and
lifestyles of threat to mainstream society. Robbins and
Anthony have stated this aptly:

> The present revival of brainwashing mystiques
> is taking place in the context of a general back-
> lash against forms of dissent and nonconformity
> which flourished in the late sixties and early
> seventies. Feminists, gay militants, and new
> religions are all experiencing retaliation for
> their stridency in the past decade (ironically,
> some guru groups and Jesus sects are antifem-
> inist and socially conservative). Brainwash-
> ing, which failed as a rational for exculpating
> a deviant (i.e., Patricia Hearst), has been
> having some success as a weapon against devi-
> ants. A backlashing "law and order" oriented
> public will not accept mind control as a means
> of absolving dissidents from responsibility

for criminal acts, but it may accept such a
notion as a persecutory rationale (1978, p.
80).

In this sense, there appears to be a need in American society to implement periodically such syndromes, and their accompanying witchhunts, in order to maintain the boundaries
of acceptable and unacceptable behavior (Durkheim, 1938;
Erikson, 1966) and to resolve the conflict between competing
interest groups in society (Darendorf, 1959; Coser, 1956;
Richardson and Kilbourne, 1982; Kilbourne and Richardson,
1981).

A SOCIOLOGY OF KNOWLEDGE PERSPECTIVE

While a critical perspective permits us to appreciate
whose interests are being served by particular ideas and
ideologies and how they are being served, it does not lead
necessarily to a full understanding of the historical, cultural and structural factors contributing to the construction of particular kinds of knowledge and shared understandings. A sociology of knowledge approach (Mannheim, 1936;
Berger and Luckman, 1977) will aid our analysis and furnish
answers to the question, "What was there about the 1970s
that produced the preponderance of the same metaphor, the
metaphor of brainwashing?"

First, an historical analysis of the treatment of new
religious movements indicates that the United States is characteristically intolerant of radically new religious ideas
(Davis, 1962; Miller, this volume). New religious groups
which promulgate unique life styles are generally subjected
to persecution in direct relation to their success in attracting new adherents. In many instances, a uniform pattern of response has been indicated. Members and leaders
are typically attacked in various ways (including even physical attacks) and the movement is often labeled a political
threat or a threat to society's morals. Thus, historically,
any religious group threatening the dominant culture tends
to be subjected to discrediting, discrimination, and isolation.

Bromley and Shupe (1979) have previously elaborated this
point, contending that the societal reaction to a new religious group depends in large measure on the degree of legitimacy accorded the new group. American history reveals that
nearly every major religious group was met initially with
resistance, ostracism, or persecution. The stereotypic
charges alleged against the new religions are in a very real
sense traditional to American society, and do not differ

substantively from their earlier manifestations: political subversion, brainwashing (or an equivalent term), submissive members to an authoritarian leader, and atrocity tales by apostates (see Cox, 1978; Bromley, Shupe and Ventimiglia, 1979; and Hargrove, reprinted herein). In sum, any group which attempts to implement social change in American society tends to become the object of attack by social control agents with the express purpose of maintaining the status quo.

Second, against this historical backdrop, lies an important recent cultural development. Although historically hostile to new lifestyles and new religious beliefs, American society has recently produced an organized oppositional group of anti-cultists (see Shupe and Bromley, 1979). Emerging in the early 70s and hungry for an organization impetus, the leaders of the largest anti-cult groups organized into a united front against marginal religious groups. This merger succeeded, if only temporarily, to increase the financial viability of the anti-cultists, to create ideological cohesiveness, and to expedite administrative effectiveness. The resulting organization announced publicly its goals to disseminate information on the growth and operation of cults, to lobby actively against such groups, and to function as an effective referral service for parents, professionals, etc. More importantly, though, with the help of a few mental health professionals, the anti-cult movement was largely responsible for the re-emergence of the brainwashing metaphor in conjunction with the "deprogramming rationale." Deprogramming is the practice whereby cult members are forcibly abducted, if need be, from the influence of the cult and subjected to intense "resocialization" to force rejection of their cultist ties. Deprogramming has been justified legally and morally in terms of the brainwashing rhetoric of the 1950s. That is, it has been alleged that normal individuals have had their critical faculties impaired by one or more coercive techniques and have been manipulated by the ulterior and deceptive purposes of the new religious groups. A change in religious orientation does not automatically constitute therefore a true religious conversion. The emergence in the public forefront of the anti-cult movement has resulted in not only reinforcing the oppositional stance of mainstream society to new religious groups, new ideas, and lifestyles, but it has also succeeded in "reviving" the brainwashing rhetoric of the 1950s to such an extent that the rhetoric has become almost commonplace as a means to explain any form of undesired social influence.

Third, a full appreciation of the "revival" of the brainwashing rhetoric requires an examination of certain structural relationships and vested interests in contemporary

American society. Certain concepts (e.g., brainwashing or
mental illness) like certain activities (e.g., incarceration
in prison or in a mental hospital) function to allow powerful groups in society (i.e., mental health professionals,
political, military or business interests, etc.) to label
negatively and thus influence or control activities of those
individuals and groups they perceive to be threatening their
particular interests or the status quo. The brainwashing
label functions effectively in a boundary maintenance fashion to define acceptable and unacceptable behaviors, and to
cut the deviant individual off from his/her social group(s).
Moreover, it becomes an effective means to delegitimate legitimate demands and to misattribute the origin of new values and ideas to a pathological state or condition. The
brainwashing rhetoric also provides the victim with a ready-
made excusatory account (i.e., "I know what I did was wrong
but its not my fault") to make intelligible and sensible
their former anti-social behavior of joining an outcase
group. For example, insofar as former cult members acknowledge a brainwashed condition (in much the same way that mental patients must first acknowledge their "sickness" before
they can hope to recover), existing relationships between
the former cult member and their society can be maintained
and the "lost sheep" can be brought back into the fold.

CONCLUSIONS

In conclusion, a critical theory approach to the brainwashing rhetoric of the 1950s and 1970s led to the discovery
that the purported knowledge and technology of that rhetoric
was anti-collectivistic and anti-totalistic. Also, it was
found that the menacing aspects of totalism relate to certain
assumptions made about human nature (e.g., the ease with
which we disrupt human's homeostatic cycle, frustrate the innate desire for uniqueness, mold responses, and transform an
autonomous self into a self indistinguishable from that of
the group). Hence, each of the classical and contemporary
models of brainwashing rely on virtually the same ideological
and metatheoretical assumptions to explain a three stage de-
basing process by which individuals are stripped of their
individuality and transformed into socially unrecognizable
and undesirable non-humans.

The present paper has also examined the common roots of
the brainwashing rhetoric from a sociology of knowledge perspective. In particular it was argued that the historical
rejection of radically new religious beliefs in conjunction
with the emergence of an organized and powerful anti-cult
movement, and the explicit imperatives of certain powerful

groups in society to maintain their social and economic ascendance (e.g., the mental health profession), has led to the current "revival" of the brainwashing rhetoric. This revived rhetoric appears to be of greater consequence for students of American society than continued attempts by certain researchers and laypersons to draw parallels between the new religious groups and early thought reform practices, even though these latter efforts can sometimes be quite insightful.

II
SOCIOLOGICAL PERSPECTIVES

Throughout American history new religious groups have been charged with duping or coercing their members. This "seduction premise" easily leads to the conclusion that neither affiliation nor disaffiliation is a voluntaristic act. Brainwashing simply constitutes the most recent metaphor by which affiliation with disvalued groups is depicted. In this section we present several empirical studies of affiliation with and disaffiliation from contemporary new religious groups. Other papers consider the reactions of outsiders and former members to the affiliation and disaffiliation processes since social positioning is a key determinant of interpretations of the meaning of membership in new religious groups. All of the research has been undertaken in response to the contemporary new religions controversy. As a result, the sophistication of social science understanding of both affiliation and disaffiliation has substantially increased.

In the first of two papers on the affiliation process Pilarzyk distinguishes between what he terms sectarian conversion and cultic alternation processes. The former process is characteristic of groups such as the Hare Krishna while Divine Light Mission typifies the latter process. Conversion involves a radical change in lifestyle, a break with the past and a reorganization of personal identity, all in the context of an all encompassing social organization. By contrast, alternation involves a less radical change in lifestyle, worldview and identity, and fewer organizational demands are made on members. This empirically based dichotomy holds significant implications for the current controversy. At the very least this analysis documents sufficient diversity among new religions that uniform categorization of them as "cults" would be inaccurate and misleading. It follows, of course, that recruitment and socialization techniques also differ, which calls into question assumptions about a uniform "brainwashing" process.

Taylor describes the recruitment and preliminary socialization techniques employed by the west coast branch of the Unification Church, a group Pilarzyk would certainly include in the sectarian category. Taylor analyzed recruitment to the "Moonies" in terms of Lifton's thought reform model. On the basis of his own participant observation experience Taylor reports practices which he concludes were

contrived, manipulative and psychologically coercive. Yet
while he found some correspondence between these practices
and thought reform as described by Lifton, he concluded that
the affiliation process was more transactional than unilat-
eral since individuals actively participated in producing
their own conversions.

Two papers examine the disaffiliation process which
only recently has begun to receive attention from social
scientists. Based on intensive interviews with sixty former
members of various new religious groups, Skonovd argues that
deterioration of group bonds is the most important factor
causing defection. Individuals who lose group support lack
the means to deal with prevalent intellectual and emotional
problems and personal disillusionment. The speed with which
disengagement occurs depends upon whether an individual is
propelled by a critical event or gradually reflects upon the
past, present and future in the context of group membership.
Wright's paper builds upon Skonovd's findings as he identifies four specific sources of conflict/disillusionment which
typically precipitate defection. These factors include a
breakdown in members insulation from the outside world, the
development of dyadic relationships within the group, perceived failure to achieve movement goals and inconsistencies
between leaders' actions and ideals. All of the groups
Wright studied (Unification Church, Hare Krishna, Children
of God) would fall in Pilarzyk's sectarian category; up to
the present there has not been any attempt to compare disaffiliation processes for different types of social movements. Nevertheless, both of these papers confirm that disaffiliation, like affiliation, is a process which can be interpreted in terms of existing social science concepts. It
is also clear that considerable personal pain and emotional
turmoil accompanies the process of disengagement from a sectarian group and re-entry into conventional society. The
personal/emotional problems leavetakers encounter confirm
the contentions of anti-cultists that personal disruption
is sometimes associated with membership in such groups, but
the findings from this research belie claims that individuals lack the will and autonomy to make and carry out the
decision to defect.

The final two papers deal with the reactions of outsiders to new religious movements. Beckford discusses family reactions to family members participation in the Unification Church in England and the United States. He argues
that the use of the brainwashing metaphor by relatives of
members is not whimsical and irrational. Such explanations
emanate from lack of knowledge about the Unification Church,
the perception that information is being withheld from them,

difficulty in seeing and communicating with converts, and
the apparent suddenness of changes in personality and lifestyle. Bromley, Shupe and Ventimiglia approach the issue
of outsiders interpretations of the Unification Church from
a different but complementary perspective. They concur
with Beckford that family distress readily leads to allegations of brainwashing. They also observe, however, that
disillusioned former members contribute significantly to
this ideology. Both parents and defectors have an interest
in portraying individual involvement in non-stigmatizing
terms and defining the groups and their leaders as unscrupulous and conspiratorial. The result is a series of widely
disseminated atrocity stories which substantially shape
the public image of new religious groups. This analysis
suggests a more critical analysis of the interests of various groups and individuals seeking to shape the symbolic
definitions of these groups is imperative if myth reifica-
tion is to be avoided.

*CONVERSION AND ALTERNATION PROCESSES IN THE YOUTH CULTURE: A COMPARATIVE ANALYSIS OF RELIGIOUS TRANSFORMATIONS

Thomas Pilarzyk
Marymount College of Kansas

A proliferation of new religious movements took place with the emergence of the youth culture as an alternative within the life-worlds of modern Western societies in the 1960s. Such distinctive sects as the Jesus People, the Moonies, the Children of God, and the International Society for Krsna Consciousness -- as well as numerous meditation and esoteric cultic groups -- were embodied in this religious revival. While some movements catered specifically to spiritual needs in the youth culture milieu, others offered therapeutic orientations for the general societal population as a whole. The scholarly literature on the religiosity of the American youth culture emphasized three distinctive elements: (1) its "consciousness" as a whole (e.g., Roszak, 1969, 1973; Reich, 1970; Baum, 1970), (2) its different religious manifestations as expressed in ideology and ritual (e.g., Greeley, 1970; Tiryakian, 1972; Shepherd, 1972; Gutmann, 1972), and (3) the specific sectarian and cultic groups which emerged within the larger movement (e.g., Adams and Fox, 1972; Robbins, 1960; Robbins and Anthony, 1972; Truzzi, 1972; Peterson and Mauss, 1973; Richardson, 1973; Robbins et al., 1975). Unfortunately, most analyses failed to adequately analyze the different processes by which some individuals in the youth culture altered their subjective world views through participation in a religious movement.

This article addresses this important omission by exploring the nature of resocialization processes in two religious movements within the youth culture from a contemporary phenomenological perspective. The author distinguishes the processes undergone by members of different religious movements by focusing on the transformation of converts' subuniverses of meaning or subjective apprehensions of social reality. In so doing, the background and situational factors affecting such shifts in Weltanschauung are taken into account. These transformation in world view, meaning, and

identity include (1) attempts to reinterpret a period prior
to contact as one of partial or total discontentment, crisis, alienation, or suffering (a constituent of what struc-
tural-functionalists refer to as the "antecedents" of conversion),(2) different resocialization processes, and (3)
expressions of commitment as members of a religious organization. These elements, often interrelated in everyday
life, are examined through the use of ethnographic data.

Largely qualitative research was conducted among mem-
bers of the cultic Divine Light Mission Movement (DLM) of
Guru Maharaj Ji and the sectarian International Society for
Krsna Consciousness (ISKCON) of Swami Prabhupada at "ashrams" or temples in the Midwest. Field sites included the
Midwest headquarters of the International Society for Krsna
Consciousness (more commonly known as the Hare Krsna movement) in Evanston, Illinois and communities of the Divine
Light Mission in Milwaukee, Wisconsin and Chicago, Illinois.
Participant-observation techniques, intensive taped interviews, and content analyses of movement literature were
utilized. Numerous visitations were made to each field
site for over two years (1972-1974); correspondence and interviews with national leaders of both movements were also
utilized as sources of data. The interview data, presented
below in the form of percentages, were collected among 104
Divine Light Mission members and 63 individuals affiliated
with the Hare Krsna movement. Let us now turn to the theoretical perspective that will aid our understanding of the
processes of religious transformation.

BERGER'S PHENOMENOLOGICAL APPROACH
TO CONVERSION

Sociological approaches to the study of religious conversion have commonly outlined the various social and
social-psychological factors involved in the shift of an
individual's world view.[1] These include background characteristics of the group making it "conducive" for conversion,
thus stressing the importance of social identification or
group reinforcement for changes in subjective outlook (e.g.,
see Lofland and Stark, 1965; Richardson, 1973). Few studies
argue for the equal importance of emotionally charged
"shock experiences" which have intrinsic spiritual or existential significance for the convert apart from group constraints.[2]

A conceptual paradigm which may adequately take both
objective and subjective aspects of personal transformation
into account is commonly referred to as phenomenological or

existential sociology (e.g., see Tiryakian, 1965; Psathas
and Waksler, 1973; Bogard, 1977; Douglas and Johnson,
1977). One important trend within this intellectual movement which is especially promising for my purposes is the
theoretical perspective of Berger (1963, 1966, 1967). While
not restricting himself specifically to instances of religious conversion, he stresses the potential convert's need
for a cognitive redefinition of social reality in order to
justify any new Weltanschauung. Berger (1963:51-52) notes
that each of the multiple world views of modernity carries
its own interpretation of social reality. Transformations
between alternate systems of meaning commonly take place.
Alternation, for Berger, is that process of alternating
back and forth between logically contradictory yet fully
elaborated meaning systems which are radical attempts at re-
organizing everyday life. Alternation, or the "instance of
transformation that appears total if compared with lesser
modifications," requires a process of resocialization involving both social and conceptual conditions. It commonly
includes the availability of an effective social group
which serves as the "Laboratory for transformation through
(which) significant others...act as guides in its ability
to provide such an indispensible plausibility structure for
this new reality."

The importance of the religious group is reflected in
its ability to provide such a plausibility structure. The
convert is reinforced so that he continues to take his new
world view seriously. With Luckmann (Berger with Luckmann,
1966:97-98), Berger has argued that the religious group as
a symbolic universe

> provides for the subjective apprehension of bio-
> graphical experience. Experiences belonging to
> different spheres of reality are integrated by
> incorporation in the same, overarching universe
> of meaning. ...The integration of the realities
> of marginal situations within the paramount
> reality of everyday life is of great importance,
> because these situations constitute the most
> acute threats to taken-for-granted, routinized
> existence in society.... Thoughts of madness
> and terror are contained by ordering all con-
> ceivable realities within the same symbolic
> universe that encompasses the reality of every-
> day life -- to wit, ordering them in such a
> way that the latter reality retains its para-
> mount, definitive...quality.

They emphasize the overriding importance of participation
in the religious group in reinforcing personal transforma-

tions, as well as the role of its system of beliefs and
practices in the reinterpretation of past biographical
events. A religious collectivity then constitutes the
social base of symbolic meaning for the convert.

Travasino (1975) has modified Berger's statements on
alternations, noting that they involve a wide range of
transformations which vary in degree with changes in perspective, identity, and situation. Following Travasino,
the term conversion in this paper will denote a "radical
alternation" or a complete and thorough transformation of
the individual's world view, suggesting the phenomenological import of viewing it as a dynamic process of resocialization. In conversion, the individual's past life is radically reorganized and reinterpreted as one's identity is
reintegrated into a new set of meanings. This transformation of subjective reality usually involves an all-encompassing, absolutist organizing principle. In the case of
religious groups, this principle is typically furnished by
a sectarian ideology and organization. "Sectarian conversion" then implies complete disruption and change in life
within the confines of an all-inclusive system of religious
meanings and a rather authoritarian social structure. On
the other hand, Travasino views alternation as a milder
cognitive transformation. It is a relatively easy change
in life, meaning, and identity. In this paper, the term
"cultic alternation" will be used to denote this rather
transitional change in the individual's identity and lifestyle which is not all-inclusive but which allows for the
simultaneous holding of multiple organizing principles in
the reinterpretation of subjective reality.

Table 1 presents each type of religious transformation
within the youth culture. The scheme remains faithful to
Berger's phenomenological perspective and to Travasino's
necessary modification. Alternations and conversions then
differ in the degree and type of change in identity, subjective meanings, and ties to social organizations. Both
conversions and alternations do include emotional episodes
of illumination, sometimes giving rise to an insight upon
which a cognitive change is based or merely reinforcing the
newly formed world view of the social group. Let us first
explore these types of transformations in relation to sect
and cult followers' prior lives in the youth culture.

TABLE 1

Types of Religious Transformation in the Youth Culture

Sectarian Conversion	Cultic Alternation
1. demands drastic changes in life, meaning and identity	1. involves a transitional change in life, meaning and identity
2. demands negation of former "mundane" identity	2. involves an extension of or minor break with former identity
3. radically reorganizes past life and identity within new meaning system	3. permits reorganization within existing meaning system or subcultural orientation of past life and identity
4. includes a prior period of unrest or confusion over life, meaning or identity	4. includes a prior period of partial, mild unrest or confusion over life, meaning or identity
5. involves an all-encompassing absolutist organizing principle for the radical reinterpretation of subjective reality	5. allows for segmented, simultaneous or multiple principles for the reinterpretation of subjective reality

RELIGIOUS MEANING SYSTEMS AS ALTERNATIVES WITHIN THE YOUTH CULTURE

The relationship between the youth culture and the members of the two movements under study becomes more explicit once we analyze the process by which an individual shifts his subjective conceptions of reality from that of "hippie" or "freak" to that of ISKCON 'devotee' or DLM "premie." Therefore, some of the factors which disenchant members of the youth culture and influence them in "shopping around" on the youth culture's religious marketplace (Berger, 1967) must be considered. Conversion to contemporary religious movements cannot be understood without referring to the quality of their members' prior experiences.

Life within the youth culture of the early 1970s provided a symbolic universe of meaning in the biographical pasts of both the Divine Light Mission and Hare Krsna members. Among other things, the set of symbolic meanings of the American youth culture reflected interests in a diver-

sity of cultural themes including Eastern and Western mysticism and the scriptures of the world religions, political-
revolutionary writings, hedonism, pop psychology, and the
traditional American values of individualism and independence (Partridge, 1973).   This pluralism of cultural themes
had at least two effects. First, it increased the dis-
orientation of those alienated middle-class youth searching
for a single, broad, overarching conceptual framework of
meaning by which to interpret, understand, and simplify
their lives. Second, it provided for the growth, development, and elaboration of numerous groups utilizing one or
more of these symbolic constellations, typifying and rein-
terpreting them as their own.

Recent research suggests that there were a number of
difficulties associated with the personal fulfillment of
needs within the youth culture, including problems with
drug use, competing values, and unstable organizations.   In
the late 1960s, hallucinogenic drugs were viewed as the
vehicle carrying the message of love, sharing, and spontan-
eity. But as Robbins and Anthony (1972) have suggested,
promiscuous drug use over the years became drug-dependence
as an end in itself. This necessitated the manipulation of
peers to obtain drugs through unethical means, contradicting the original "love ethic" of the hip community. Another problem was evident in the conflict between human
needs for "community," or "groupism," and for autonomy and
individualism. Greeley (1970) and Slater (1970) identify
the need for community with the sociohistorical conditions
giving rise to modern society and the intensity of such
needs for 1960s youth. However, the satisfaction of needs
for community were jeopardized by the greater interpretative meaning many youth gave to individual freedom and
autonomy, or "doing one's own thing." Miller (1971) argues
that this dilemma generated a paradox which further frustrated and alienated the young. Other writers, however,
viewed the failure of the youth culture in its array of
organizational problems reflected in the short-lived nature
of many youth communes. Kanter (1972) and Zablocki (1973)
argue convincingly that hippie communes were based largely
on themes of antinomianism and communitarian anarchism,
neither of which provided a sufficient ethos for building
viable communities.

One personal resolution to these interrelated problems
was for the individual to submit to the teachings and authority of a charismatic leader. The cognitive and experiential acceptance of his framework offered the prospective
convert a common set of symbolic meanings by which to interpret one's existence. This was the alternative taken by
members of both the Divine Light Mission and the Inter-

national Society for Krsna Consciousness in the mid-1970s.
Interviews with communal members of both groups indicate
the prevalence of stereotyped behavior patterns associated
with youth culture lifestyles. The backgrounds of many
Hare Krsna people, for example, reflected a specific preoccupation with drug use. Sixty-six percent of those interviewed felt that prior drug use became highly problematic. A Brahmin of ISKCON reflected on his past preoccupation with hallucinogenic drugs and the alleviation of related problems through conversion.

> Man, I was so into acid that I could hardly talk
> without stammering and stuttering. Then one day
> I heard some devotees rapping on the street cor-
> ner and I went over to listen (to them)....They
> made a lot of sense and I kind of needed a place
> to call home, to feel like I was wanted....I
> guess Krsna was just looking after me....After
> staying at the ashram for a month, I began to
> realize that I could "get high" by chanting,...
> that I didn't need drugs,...and my stuttering
> slowly went away.

Not all devotees reflect such dramatic changes. Another Brahmin saw his entry into the group as basically an
"untraumatic process." However, the majority of those interviewed indicated some type of stereotyped youth culture
behavior. Eighty-five percent had used hallucinogens, almost half had cohabitated, and another 30% had lived communally. Informal conversations suggested that unrest, tension, or conflict associated with such activities in their
previous lives was typical of many members. Intensive interviews and conversations with premies at the DLM ashrams
affirmed a similar and yet less seriously perceived disenchantment with such behavior as hallocinogenic drug use
(89%), cohabitation (49%), and communal living (49%).

Many DLM members specifically interpreted only certain
aspects of prior lifestyles as "sick," "obsessive," or "ex-
istentially meaningless," manifested by indiscriminate,
multiple drug use and open value conflicts with societal
systems of meaning. Such feelings reflected the youth culture's failure to establish a viable meaning system as well
as the DLM's ability to fulfill certain needs not met in
conventional everyday life. The Hare Krsna communalists,
on the other hand, expressed little ethical confusion or
value-conflict in their personal biographies, but the ubiq-
uitous problems of identity-construction related to indiscriminate drug use, unsuccessful love relationships, and
unsatisfactory family ties. In many instances, especially
in the interviews, ISKCON devotees stressed the all-

pervasive anomic, alienating aspects of everyday life within
the youth culture, rather than a specific conflict in meaning with the wider society.

    In sum, past experiences associated with the youth cul-
ture and selectively interpreted by movement members as
conditions of crisis, value-conflict, or existential inse-
curity, reflected in dependency upon drugs were more related
to conversion to the Divine Light Mission than to ISKCON.
The DLM's cultic belief system was more universalistic,
syncretic; its religious experience was said to fulfill existential needs for love and understanding while providing
ethical and moral guidelines for its members. On the other
hand, prior situations characterized by all-pervasive feelings of anomie, drug dependency, unsuccessful love relationships, and family trouble were more frequently associated
with complete engulfment of the individual in the conversion
process to the ISKCON ashram. Therefore, crisis-alleviation
held different implications for each movement. Though contact with the DLM and ISKCON ashrams did not reflect significant differences in the performance of a crisis-alleviat-
ing function in their followers, the Divine Light Mission
and Hare Krsna members did exhibit different interpretations
of that function.

ALTERNATION BETWEEN MEANING SYSTEMS

    Background factors alone do not determine whether or
not conversion or alternation will occur, or the form it
will eventually take. As Robbins (1973) suggests, each
social actor must choose which movement to join, interpret
why s/he joined, and determine who or what helped influence
the decision. In other words, it is not the level of felt-
alienation of disenchantment reflected in prior contact
with problematic aspects of the youth culture alone which
influence association with these movements. Such factors
are intimately interrelated with the individual's ability
to choose between various symbolically meaningful alternatives assisting in overcoming feelings of estrangement, unrest, or crisis (see Wieder and Zimmerman, 1976). These
various alternatives have traditionally included religious
and political resocialization. These two alternative systems of meaning existed within the youth culture.

    Timothy Leary, John Lennon, Phillip Slater, and other
youth culture exponents expressed concern in the late 1960s
over the differences among the youth culture's membership.
A general split was believed to have existed between the
politically leftist activist and the "hippie" or "freak"

oriented toward psychedelia, mind-expansion, and spiritual-
ism. While the former was allegedly more determined to
change the wider society's institutional structure through
violent or nonviolent political revolution, the latter saw
the only viable revolution as based on an internal, even
spiritual road to self-realization.

Members of the Hare Krsna and Divine Light Mission have
been associated previously with both types of problem-
solving perspectives. Over 25% of both the DLM and ISKCON
members expressed past participation in such political
youth groups as SDS, Yippies, Zippies, local campus organizations of liberal persuasion, and draft-information and
draft-resistance centers. Sixty-six percent of DLM members
and 68% of Hare Krsna followers had at least some contact
with political organizations in general. In addition, Hare
Krsna members reported contact with other, similarly authoritarian religions with absolutist meaning systems. Sixty-
eight percent of all those interviewed at the Hare Krsna
ashram reported past affiliation with such religious groups;
over one-third were associated in varying degrees with
groups in the current Jesus movement.

> My girlfriend became heavily involved in the
> Jesus Movement and therefore pressured me into
> some kind of spiritual uplifting....But she
> was too much. Our interests, views and needs
> for each other's friendship outgrew.

> I originally came to the ashram to interview
> the president of the Society for Krsna Con-
> sciousness and to share with him the gospel
> of Jesus Christ....But after talking to him
> I wasn't certain if the Bible was the complete
> message. I later returned to speak to devotees
> and joined the ashram about three months later.

> I was a real believer in the "heart-way" in
> Jesus Christ. I felt I was saved at twenty-
> five and freed from sin and its guilt. But
> I didn't realize at the time that I had a
> lot more karma to burn off.

Such comments reflected alternations between or "shopping
around" among structurally similar religious groups and
radical transformations in meaning and identity from one
absolutist system to another. They may also point to the
existence of larger recruitment patterns within the youth
movement which encompass a considerable number of those who
previously used a religious problem-solving perspective.

DLM members expressed a slightly lower incidence (45%) of
such "shopping around." When occurring, it commonly took
place among groups which were also highly syncretic and
cultic, such as the International Meditation Society, mind
expansion institutes, various hatha and raja yoga groups,
and even astrological cults. Many DLM members even held
simultaneous memberships in more than one of these cultic
groups, suggesting the cultic nature of its alternation
process.

The differences between those associated only with
religious or only with political groups were not significant
in either movement. In addition, many members of both movements reported prior participation in both religious and
political groups -- 45% of DLM members and 57% of those affiliated with ISKCON. Therefore, recruitment patterns were
not selective along spiritual or political lines as hypothesized above. On the contrary, recruitment patterns were
more selectively based on structural aspects of youth culture movements. A strict dichotomy between spiritual and
political types of "hippies" may not exist, or there is a
greater association between the two types than had previously been thought. Such findings, if reliable, may also
point to certain developments or historical convergences
within the youth culture itself.

Analyses of alternation, Berger argues, beg a multitude
of related questions for sociological research. For example
what actually constitutes an "insider" and "outsider?" What
guarantees membership? What constitutes alternation? Let
us turn to such questions in attempting to understand the
different processes involved in the subjective transformations of reality among members of both the International
Society for Krsna Consciousness and the Divine Light Mission.

SECTARIAN CONVERSION AND THE
HARE KRSNA MOVEMENT

Like other youth culture sects, the Hare Krsna movement is decidedly "oppositional." It facilitates the exodus of alienated individuals from the wider society or re-
inforces existing alienation and makes it manageable. Such
sects as the Hare Krsna movement and certain radical groups
of the more diffuse Jesus movement totally reject the com-
monsensical Weltanschauung of the wider society and are
therefore largely countercultural, marginal, and structurally insulated groups. Sectarian conversion involves then
the immersion into an all-pervasive, absolutist world view
and social structure. Highly insulated lifestyles also

guarantee severance of ties to the outside world and redefinition of prior lives in that world as sinful, evil, mundane, and/or illusory. As Howard (1974:207) claims:

> Krishna Consciousness offers a relatively safe
> vehicle for the expression of deep estrangement
> from mainstream culture. It also provides a
> way for youth, facing a personal crisis con-
> cerning the values and life-style of the counter
> culture to back off without dropping back into
> mainstream society (emphasis added).

Therefore, such sectarian groups provide alternative forms
of community within which the convert can attain intragroup goals and status positions while alleviating feelings
of crisis, disenchantment, and alienation, and devaluating
outside interpretations of everyday reality.

Actual entry into the ISKCON ashram was quite simple.
An individual who showed serious interest in attaining
"Krsna Consciousness" through continuous visitations   to
the temple was commonly invited by the ashram president, or
head of the community, to remain for a probationary period.
There were no official standards of admission other than a
simple promise by the prospective convert to keep the basic
rules of conduct of temple life, including prohibition from
eating meat, fish, or eggs, illicit sex, intoxicants, and
from gambling. Other formal regulations included prohibitions against blaspheming Krsna, speaking against the movement leader Prabhupada, and contradicting the traditional
Vedic scriptures (Daner, 1973).

Prabhupada's philosophical position grounded in the
Hindu religious tradition of the Bengali Vaisnavas held important implications as an interpretative framework for
daily life at the ISKCON temple. Great stress was placed
upon the attainment of personal perfection through devotional and individual chanting which ideally leads to experiencing the "transcendental vibration." More importantly, the caste system organized and simplified existence for
the devotees while it minimized and managed sexual, economic, and family needs. The emphasis placed upon loving
service and devotion through the ideal of bhaktiyoga also
formed a basis for communal life and provided a rationale
for "getting the work done," for proselytizing in the outside world, and for insuring social insulation through
various intragroup mechanisms.

The first few weeks of residence at the Evanston ashram were crucial in the individual's decision to ultimately
join or leave. Attrition was highest among those affiliated

for the shortest period of time. The temple president
estimated that 50% of all those entering the ashram for the
first time left within a month. In comparison, he felt that
only 10% left after taking up residency there for over a
month. Most crucial for the novice was the initial adoption
of a new lifestyle, not necessarily acceptance of the movement's conceptual worldview. The devotee community recognized that the radical break in lifestyle from one characterized by casualness, informality, and leisure to an
austere, rigid, and structured one was the single most important factor in the individual's initial decision to remain or leave. This was one indicator of the sectarian
nature of the ISKCON conversion process (Daner, 1973;
Stillson, 1974).

Most interested individuals became affiliated with the
movement through friends, family members, or devotees proseltyizing on the street. Approximately 41% visited the
ashram largely out of curiosity, and 26% had previously
established effective ties to certain devotees. Establishment of such ties was an important determining factor in
attending a Hare Krsna vegetarian feast, a devotional chanting service, or in visiting the ashram. A sizeable number
(31%) also initially visited for reasons specifically associated with religious participation and consciousness-
expansion. Regardless of these more mundane reasons, devotees typically gave a spiritual explanation for their
initial entry into the temple. The more committed the individual devotee was to attaining Krsna Consciousness and
to the group, the more likely s/he was to give a spiritual
interpretation for initially joining or visiting the ashram.
These spiritual explanations were themselves indicative of
internalization of the rather complex, absolutist meaning
system of the sect.[3]

The "uninitiated devotee" who decided to stay at the
ashram was normally assigned to one or two "student devotees" who assisted in the adjustment to various routines
of everyday life in the community, including the internalization of both group behavioral expectations and the elaborate Vedic scriptures. Preliminary resocialization to the
demands of Ashram life was successfully undertaken when it
was felt that the new devotee began to give devotional service to Krsna out of love, not by recitation of Sanskrit
phrases or by habitual action. Individual devotees were
aware of this change in perception and reconceptualization
as indicated by increasing importance of the community in
the devotee's evaluation of the alternation process. For
example, one member exhorted, "Realizing that it's not this
material world, that I'm going the right way, and that I've

found so many beautiful people who also know this and are
going the right way too." At this point, the community's
distinctive symbolic worldview was accepted without question as the "nature of things." In phenomenological terms,
the devotee's worldview began to constitute "the world-
taken-for-granted."

The temple president usually determined when this internal transformation had taken place. A recommendation
was then sent to Prabhupada requesting permission to formally initiate the devotee into the movement. If granted,
a "holy name" ceremony marked this step in the conversion
process. The novitiate was given a Sanskrit name, was
formally made a "student devotee," and his dedication to
the movement was made clearly visible to the rest of the
community. He might also receive a set of new social
duties. This initiation commonly took place after a period
of about six months from the time of initial entry into the
movement. New Spiritual demands attached to the position
of student included greater ego detachment, total celibacy,
and "greater loving service to Krsna."

After a period of further commitment, some devotees
were eligible for a second initiation, a "fire ceremony,"
which marked passage into the brahminic or priestly order of
the movement. They received a secret mantra which aided
them in attaining a higher level of spiritual consciousness. This new position also enabled devotees to perform
certain ritual ceremonies, to lead certain communal proj-
ects, and to gain further prestige among the communal membership. Although conversion as social insulation had effectively taken place by this point, the process was not
considered complete by ISKCON standards. There were two
"higher" forms of spiritual existence further along the
road to enlightenment and consequently more detached from
the mundane nature of everyday life in the ashram. These
included the vanaprastha, or retired order of individuals,
and the sannyasas, or ISKCON's order of mendicants.[4]

The degree of social insulation implicit in the conversion process to the Hare Krsna movement guaranteed that
almost all affective ties are kept inside the community.
Even with an emphasis upon active proseltyization, the distinctive dress, jargon, beliefs, and practices help insulate members from the outside world. The extent to which
insulating mechanisms worked with regard to outside affective ties was expressed by various devotees. A common response of many parents to their children's participation in
the movement was reflected by a woman devotee's experiences
with her family.

My parents could not understand why I would be
interested in this lifestyle. They thought it
was too far out. We began having "run ins"
about my going (to the temple), and we began
to grow apart. I began to dislike their morals
(edited field note excerpt).

Another devotee believed that his parents actually disapproved of his current status within the ashram. However,
because of his previous dependency upon drugs, he felt that
they had to accept, albeit reluctantly, this decision to
live as a devotee to Krsna. Most interpretations of family
relationships were believed to be subject to the karmic laws
operating in the illusory world (maya), a central component
of ISKCON's belief system. Many devotees felt a general
parental disapproval of their decision to join the movement. However, such strain was redefined in terms of the
illusory nature of their family's lifestyle and the devotee's past association with them. Similar reinterpretations
were made of previous peer ties in the youth culture, so as
to remain consistent with the teachings of the sect.
Greatest emphasis was placed upon friendship within the communal structure of the ashram and the alleviation of prior
feelings of social alienation.

In sum, communal life at the Evanston ashram provided
the setting for the radical transformation of the individual's identity and worldview through total immersion in
its all-encompassing, alien ideology and social structure.
Precipitating factors included disenchantment with the
wider society previously manifested in youth culture-
associated patterns of behavior. Comments by devotees suggested that the youth culture was unable to provide a meaningful symbolic framework to explain and/or fulfill their
basic spiritual needs. Prior experiences of devotees also
included both a felt-alienation -- expressed literally as a
state of confusion and ambiguity -- as well as a high incidence of selective "shopping" among similarly absolutist
and highly structured religious movements. Therefore, the
Hare Krsna movement represents a viable sectarian "plausibility structure" in Berger's terms by providing a social
structure for cognitively restructuring the individual's
total worldview, minimizing the managing human needs, and
providing a status sytem for the attainment of spiritually
pragamatic goals. The all-encompassing, absolutist system
of meaning and the comprehensiveness of communal life also
reinforce felt-alienation from competing ideologies and
primary and secondary ties to the outside world.

CULTIC ALTERNATION AND
THE DIVINE LIGHT MISSION

The Divine Light Mission is an exemplar of the many
youth culture cults -- these include astrological, mind
control, the yoga groups, Sabud, Zen, and other Hindu
Vedanta movements such as that of the late Meher Baba and
the Church Universal (see Robbins, 1969; Damrell, 1977).
These rather syncretic groups stress the internal, individualistic transformation of subjective worldviews through
contact with a "hidden reality' beyond the world of appearances. The significance of individual experiences is typically reinforced only by a loosely structured set of religious symbols and boundary-maintenance mechanisms which do
not insulate its members from competing commonsense assumptions of reality or to promote intragroup solidarity.
Therefore, there is minimal "bridge-burning" of past relationships and even an enhancement of existing affective ties
to the outside world.

Most cults provide a meaningful rationale for individual action through seances, meditation, and/or emphasis
upon "service" -- specifically in everyday life -- helping
to resocialize or reintegrate members into either the institutionalized occupational structures of society, or the
more fluid organizational hierarchy of the movements (see
Robbins et al., 1975). While they may make "everyday realities" more understandable and manageable from a spiritually "higher" perspective, such cultic movements commonly
attract individuals with varied types of backgrounds which
create problems of membership commitment, solidarity, and
stability (see Wallis, 1974; Pilarzyk, 1978). In any case,
their integrative nature is indicative of the acceptance of
multiple frameworks of meaning and reinterpretations of biography and identity.

The alternation process by which an individual becomes
a DLM "premie" (literally, "lover of God") is very different from the conversion process within the ISKCON ashram.
For instance, there is no real "process of entry" into the
movement since there are few identifiable group boundaries.
There are also few formal standards of admission. Individuals interested or curious about the group usually attend
a nightly "satsang" meeting, where spiritual discourse concerns the mystical experience and Guru Maharaj Ji. Satsang
was the focal point of communal life at DLM ashrams and the
single most important function served for the movement's
large cultic community of 40,000 Americans in 1974.

Members initially visited the DLM centers in Chicago
and Milwaukee for a variety of reasons. Both curiosity and
the prior establishment of relationships with premies were
common situational factors affecting initial entry. Ashram
premies (13%) were less likely to interpret their first
contacts as merely curiosity-seeking or friendly visitations than were nonashram members (65%). Ashram members
felt their initial contacts with the Divine Light Mission
to be motivated largely by a need for spiritual meaning in
life (85%). They commonly interpreted past situations
through their present condition as active cultic community
members. However, the search for religious meaning also
reflected the typical premie's prior contact with frustra-
ting youth culture lifestyles. An ashram premie in Chicago
expressed this search for meaning and its fulfillment
through membership in the movement.

> Since I was . . . in high school I had realized that
> the normal state of awareness that I and the
> people I knew had lacked something and that "some-
> thing," if known, would allow people to open up
> both inside themselves and outside in relation-
> ships to others. At that time I consciously
> started seeking a way of finding that goal. This
> took me through a couple of years of hatha, raja
> and karma yoga and I even taught for a short
> period of time. My intellectual understanding
> greatly increased, but I knew that the key of
> actually experiencing that which I talked about
> was missing....I ended up going to the Divine
> Light Mission ashram in Minneapolis in late
> September of 1972 and heard satsang there and
> felt that the people were actually experiencing
> that which I longed for. I received knowledge
> . . .and later moved into the ashram here
>   Chicago (field note excerpt).

As with the Hare Krsna communalists, the more committed an
individual premie was to meditation and to the movement (as
reflected by ashram residency), the more likely he was to
give a spiritual interpretation for initially contacting
the ashram.

As noted above, the ashram community stressed the importance of hearing satsang (spiritual discourse). The individual frequently used nightly satsang to raise questions
or to resolve doubts concerning the importance of the guru
and his mystical knowledge. DLM communities were highly
aware of the cognitive worldview restructuring taking place
through satsang and ultimately through the mystical exper-

ience in meditation. They typically regarded satsang as
the best means to achieve communal solidarity. Therefore,
the potential premie was asked to return to a nightly satsang service in order to "cleanse" himself of any doubts
and to "open oneself up to the knowledge." The continual,
gradual change in worldview through satsang was believed to
affect the individual's cognitive and cathectic existence,
preparatory to the receipt of mystical knowledge. The individual recognizing the spiritual significance of the
mystical experience after continual attendance at satsang
was considered adequately prepared to "receive knowledge."
The group's rather diffuse and precarious belief structure
stressed the symbolic universality of its religious experience as exhibited in all scriptures of the major world
religions. In addition, the establishment of personal ties
within the cultic community provided added reinforcement
for becoming a serious follower by receiving the meditative
techniques.

Contrary to ISKCON, the path to alternation cannot be
understood through a timetable of integration into the
group. The highly tentative nature of the "knowledge session" and the variability in time needed for spiritual preparation reflected the cult's highly individualistic orientation. Both factors were determined largely by the "mahatma" or disciple of guru Maharaj Ji.[5] Mahatmas commonly
traveled from city to city, staying at DLM ashrams, giving
spiritual discourse, and revealing secret techniques of the
mystical knowledge. They were considered to be further
along the path to God-realization as apostles of the guru
and therefore commanded much respect from the premie communities. They alone determined if the individual was adequately prepared to receive the knowledge or if a knowledge
session would be granted at all.

The mahatma personally selected those individuals whom
he felt to be spiritually prepared through a personal meeting. He questioned them on the diffuse, precarious belief
system of the movement and on the importance of the religious experience. For those selected, the knowledge session
lasted from five to fifteen hours. It usually included more
satsang as well as the revelation of techniques by which one
mediated upon the "fruits of the knowledge." Premies commonly stressed the intensity of their initial spiritual
"shock experiences" (Schutz, 1970; Schutz and Luckmann,
1973) in the knowledge session and the feelings of love and
peace that accompanied them. As one premie declared, "receive Guru Maharaj Ji's knowledge! It was the most thrill-
ing experience I have gotten out of anything I did." Participation in a knowledge session and receiving the mystical

knowledge formally marked entry and membership into the cultic community at large, temporarily suspending prior commonsense notions of what constituted "reality." This finding
is consistent with ethnographic data gathered among other
Vedantic cults (see Damrell, 1977).

While the experience was considered to be a very intense and illuminating event in the lives of most premies,
it was regarded as the beginning of a life-long path toward
self-perfection through daily meditation. The premie who
sincerely accepted this long-range view of the alternation
process normally asked the general secretary or community
leader for permission to join the ashram. The individual
was accepted into the ashram if he could gain the general
secretary's approval. The latter usually considered the advice and counsel of other ashram members who knew the novitiate personally. If admitted, the new ashram member and
the general secretary then talked over his background skills
and the existing needs of the premie community in order to
determine his new position and set of obligations. The member usually was asked to secure an outside job to raise
money for the movement.

Adjustment to the communal lifestyle, regardless of
prior experiences with alternative living arrangements, was
considered an important aspect of the alternation process
in DLM communities. The daily schedule within the community
provided structure for only those aspects of premie life
considered most essential: meditation, satsang, and proselytization. Satsang commonly took on a different subjective
meaning for a new premie after the alternation experience
and admittance into the movement ashram. It became something to be "given" to fellow premies or to interested outsiders, rather than merely a religious meeting or something
the individual "hears" or "receives." The new premie also
became aware of the public dimension to satsang, namely,
that of proseltyization. Closely related to the idea of
satsang was the notion of "selfless service." Service referred to the acceptance and accomplishment of actions in
everyday life offered in devotion to Guru Majaraj Ji, the
cultic leader and exemplary role model for all behavior.
Thus, service justified the acceptance of the more profane
activities outside the community.

The DLM community's fluid organizational structure contributed to the higher rate of attrition among DLM members.
The lack of mechanisms which insulate communal life was evident in the large number of noncommunal members and the lack
of "bridge-burning." Seventy-two percent of interviewed
ashram premies felt relationships with their families had

improved. Only 90% of these attributed such changes to
their personal transformations through meditation. Many
members reported similar changes in peer relationships due
to Maharaj Ji and the Divine Light movement, though some
ashram members felt a general disapproval from past friends
over their allegiances to the guru. These later relationships were frequently redefined as artificial vis-a-vis the
"real" understanding of love and friendship available
through meditation and the cultic community.

In sum, the alternation process into the Divine Light
Mission movement was highly individualistic in orientation.
It involved only a partial transformation of identity and
subjective reality by cultivating a religious experience
through meditation without a rigorous internalization of
numerous group norms and values. Demands for inculcating
the group ideology were minimal. Background factors among
members included disenchantment with the wider society reflected by patterns of behavior associated with the youth
culture. Many premies also expressed displeasure over aspects of prior youth culture lifestyles which were unable to
supply satisfying interpretive frameworks of meaning or to
fulfill their needs for love, belongingness, and security.
"Shopping around," sometimes simultaneously among other
syncretic cultic groups, was another manifestation of feelings of disaffection and of the cultic nature of the alternation process. Its ashrams provided a setting for alternation, facilitation of spiritual growth, management of
economic needs for ashram members, and for cultic meetings
and organizational activities. The movement further provided its large number of noncommunal members, located within the traditional occupational structures of the wider
society, with a practical means for dealing with personal
stress through meditation. The symbolic and universalistic
nature of DLM ideology and the diffuseness of the movement's
social structure allowed its members freedom to maintain
and cultivate ties with the outside world. No attempts
were made to keep all affective relationships within the
commune. Therefore the alternation process involved a
rather easy break with a former identity and a transition
to a new set of meanings.

CONCLUSION

There are at least two distinctive processes of personal transformation among members of youth culture religions. They are sectarian conversion, as exemplified by
socialization into the Hare Krsna movement, and cultic alternation, as represented by affiliation with the Divine

Light Mission movement. They differ in the degree of subjective change in worldview, lifestyle, and biography
undergone by group members as well as in the objective conditions of each movement's ideology and social structure.
The theoretical orientation of Berger has provided the
author with the possibility of examining the interface between each movement's set of subjective meanings and their
objective conditions.

In this paper then, the author has sought to clarify
and extend Berger's phenomenological perspective on alternations between meaning systems. This article can be considered part of the monumental task, recently begun by
Damrell (1977), Hall (1978), and others, of filling the empirical void in the largely theoretical writings of phenomenological sociology. In addition, this article has hope-
fully provided some direction for future research in the
sociology of religion. For example, a comprehensive,
systematic analysis of the relationship between the processes discussed above and the functions performed by the
great variety of youth culture religions would help to further test the generalizability of this author's contentions.

NOTES

1. For example, see the structural functionalist perspective presented by Lofland and Stark (1965) which an-
   alyzes predisposing or background factors (external
   social conditions which facilitate contact with specific religious groups) and situational factors (internal
   conditions which lead to recruitment of predisposed individuals and to the functioning and social cohesion of
   the group). By contrast, Hine (1970) has characterized
   conversion to a specific fringe religious movement
   (Pentacostalism) in terms of two commitment-generating
   events: (1) a subjective experience which restructures
   the individual's cognitive worldview and self-image,
   and (2) a "bridge-burning act" which cuts the individual off from his social ties to the outside world while
   identifying him with the group in which such an act is
   highly valued. She does suggest that commitment-generating acts and experiences differ for different types of
   movements, an issue which is directly relevant to the
   argument presented in this article.

2. Sociological perspectives on conversion grounded in
   structural-functionalism have stressed the sole importance of the social processes in alternation of a
   worldview. However, our analysis suggests the impor-

tance of the shock experience in cultic alternations.
Schutz (1970) noted the finite provinces of meanings
which constitute "shock experiences" and which disrupt
the routine aspects of everyday life. These include
religious experiences, hallucinations, fantasies, day-
dreams, incidences of existential humor and sex, and
the like. In this article, the mystical experience of
the DLM is regarded as a prototype of such a "shock."
Such religious peak experiences are subjectively associated with feelings of love, joy, and blessedness and
are so profound and intense that they may frequently
outshine the individual's previous existence. Their
deliberate cultivation promotes a subjective redefinition of past experiences and self-conceptions. The
specific study of such peak experiences is commonly associated with the late humanistic psychologist Maslow
(1964). The mystical experience was frequently extolled
by Maslow as the paradigmatic peak experience. Greeley
(1974) has argued that the sociological community has
ignored the importance of mysticism for human existence
and has thereby misunderstood or misinterpreted it.

3. These "rationalizations," "justifications," or "explan-
    ations" are common to most transitions in personal bio-
    graphy, including the transition from "lay person" to
    "sociologist." As suggested by an earlier reviewer of
    this paper, sociologists are also prone to giving
    rational accounts of their transitions into the pro-
    fession, although they were initially affected by
    rather mundane events and happenings.

4. Sannyasas of the Hare Krsna movement are East Indian
    followers appointed by Prabhupada who have "renounced
    the world," traveling from city to city while studying
    and preaching the Vedic scriptures as translated by
    him. They are not subject to ashram rules and regula-
    tions although they adhere to a special set of respon-
    sibilities assigned by Prabhupada. The ashram com-
    munity views this renounced stage of Vedic life as the
    ultimate aim in attaining Krsna Consciousness, re-
    flected in the individual's status as a bhakie or a
    "pure, loving, selfless devotee of Krsna" (see Daner,
    1973). The vanaprastha consist of individuals who have
    become more isolated from the outside world for spirit-
    ual reasons.

5. There were over one thousand mahatmas within the Divine
    Light Mission movement around the world in 1974.
    Almost all were middle-class East Indian males. Little

information exists on them, especially regarding the
decision-making processes by which an individual becomes a mahatma or is "de-mahatmatized."

NOTES

* Originally published in Pacific Sociological Review
  21 (October 1978a):379-405.

THOUGHT REFORM AND THE UNIFICATION CHURCH

David Taylor
The Queens University, Belfast

INTRODUCTION

The Unification Church (UC), led by the Reverend Sun
Myung Moon, self-styled evangelist, has been the subject of
increasing controversy during recent years. Accusations of
political affiliation with South Korea, illegal sources of
income, and a questionable tax-exempt status have led to
Congressional inquiries and court cases. The most prominent
charge is that the Church uses brainwashing to recruit members. A legion of traditional church leaders, parents and
portions of the media have described how the Church attracts
young people to isolated indoctrination centers and applies
"mind control" techniques. Critics claim that prospective
recruits experience overwhelming physical and psychological
pressures. Over a period of days and weeks their world
views supposedly change radically, and those individuals who
are successfully "brainwashed" leave the centers as zealous
Church devotees.

What are the necessary conditions of brainwashing or
mind control? To date, research has been limited to retrospective accounts of those who have undergone such processes
and later left the Church. Yet to emerge is an empirical account that describes the Church's indoctrination process in
detail. (See Lofland, 1978, and Bromley and Shupe, 1979 for
the best treatments.) In the mid-1970's, I completed an
ethnographic study of conversion in the UC that provided
some insight into this issue. The research focused on the
Church's conversion methods at one of its larger (and most
notorious) indoctrination centers. On six occasions I assumed the role of a complete participant and observed
Church's members' methods of convincing people to join the
"Family" as they call themselves. The length of my stays at
the center ranged from two to nine days.

After completing the study, I discovered a number of
similarities between my findings and the research on thought
reform, or "brainwashing" in China and Korea in the 1950s
(Lifton, 1963; Schein, 1957). Perhaps the most well known
among numerous inquiries in this area is Lifton's work on

thought reform. Following the Korean Conflict, he conducted extensive interviews with Westerners who were prisoners in China, as well as with Chinese intellectuals who attended "Revolutionary Universities."

The Unification Church is not the first religious movement whose recruitment techniques have been compared to those of thought reform. Lifton (1963:454-456) pointed out the relationship between thought reform and techniques used by revivalistic cults and other religious groups. Zablocki (1971) and Richardson, Harder and Simmonds (1972) applied Lifton's ideas to their findings. Lifton's model of re-socialization of Western prisoners is compared by Zablocki to the socialization of new members of the Bruderhof commune. Richardson, et al's study found similarities between thought reform and the conversion process of the Jesus movement, but noted an absence of physical coercion in the Jesus groups. Later studies by Richardson (1982) led to broader conclusions: that individuals undergoing recruitment into the Jesus movement and similar groups take an active part in the process that leads to their conversion.

Before comparing the Church's recruitment process to Lifton's conception of thought reform, I will describe features that account for recruitment in the UC. My focus is on the socially structured process by which members lead prospective members through successive stages of commitment.

FINDING PROSPECTIVE MEMBERS

Recruitment into most social or religious movements is achieved through pre-existing personal relationships. UC members must attract people without the benefit of these prior ties. Most potential recruits are first contacted in public places. Church members are assigned to specific locations to proselytize (e.g., city streets, public transportation, shopping centers and college campuses). Since these encounters are between strangers, Church members must develop immediate rapport with their contacts if they hope to develop further commitment.

The member's typical style of witnessing is friendly and direct. Usually he or she guides the conversation by extending flattery to, and personal interest in his prospect. To characterize this enthusiastic attentiveness, a former recruit explains, "...They make you feel like the most important person in the world." After a lengthy discussion, the prospect is invited to dinner at a Unification Church.[1] The member emphasizes that the prospect will meet

others with similar interests. While intentionally vague
about specific beliefs, he describes general aims in thought-
provoking terms: "We are trying to build a community where
we can live together in joy, peace and brotherhood."

At the dinner gathering, the prospective recruit is assigned a host and introduced to other Church members and
newcomers. The evening follows a structured routine, and as
members guide their guests through pre-arranged activities,
they display continual exuberance.

> We have a really full evening planned. After
> dinner the world's greatest entertainment, and
> it's the world's greatest because it's us [mem-
> bers cheer]. Then we have a short lecture to
> tell you what we are all about: the principles
> we live by that give us all this joy, love,
> harmony and unity.

Each member cultivates a close personal relationship
with his guest. He probes his background, ambitions and interests and points out commonalities between guest's goals
and ideals and those of the Church. In this regard Neil
Solonen, former President of the Unification Church in
America, (1974) instructed members to

> Find at least one thing to which they will re-
> spond and get a hook in them. Shift to the
> positive. Be firm and respond to things with
> which they disagree, but shift to something
> which excites them. "What do you feel most
> excited about?" and "What do you find most en-
> lightening?" are good questions to think in
> terms of. Write down their hooks so that the
> whole center knows in follow up.

The lecture presentation is non-controversial and
idealistic. To a young, naive audience its over-generalized
insights can have a ring of truth. Cliches like "actualizing the truth," "following conscientious common sense" and
"finding purpose and direction" seem provocative, especially
within the context of highly emotional imagery. The lecture
concludes with an invitation to a weekend training session
at Booneville.

> We are going to explode up to Booneville to
> actualize our fullest human potential. We
> have come to realize that people can experi-
> ence joy, stimulation and full value in a
> harmonious environment.

Throughout the evening the guest is encouraged to go to
Booneville. A slide show depicts people working and playing
together in a pastoral setting. A final appeal to attend
the training session typically is

> If you liked what was said here tonight, your
> question is, "How does it apply to me?" What-
> ever your perspective on the world -- economic,
> political or religious -- we can work out the
> problems together! You wonder how come every-
> one is filled with joy? Well, we are facing
> these problems in the world. Here is your op-
> portunity to be pioneer and help us build an
> ideal world.

Members attempt to make life in the Family as rewarding
as possible. By manipulating all interaction, members seek
to move their guests from a "wait and see" attitude to one
of trust and receptiveness. The evening's events are organized to promote the guest's complete participation. Members
realize that if their guests are involved and enjoying themselves, they are more likely to come to Booneville. A young
woman who attended a Unification Church dinner and eventually a weekend at Booneville had this impression of the evening.

> Amy urged me to come back and to attend a week-
> end. I came away quite unsure what I thought
> of it all. I really liked some of the people.
> Everyone certainly looked healthy and happy.
> I wondered what they had that produced such
> energy and exuberance.

During the course of my study, those who went to Booneville seemed to be most attracted to the intense personal
attention they received, as well as to the opportunity to
spend a weekend with a group of people who promised "...the
greatest weekend of your life."

Nearly all who decide to go on the training session are
in their early twenties. Most are white, middle class, and
have attended college. Many were recent arrivals to the Bay
Area and were either looking for work, a connection to a
communal group, or "just something to happen." A number of
others lived in the Bay Area and expressed dissatisfaction
with their jobs or with whatever they were involved. The
most consistent commonality was an openness to personal
change.

THE WEEKEND TRAINING SESSION; A SOCIALLY
ORGANIZED ACCOMPLISHMENT

The training session has a pre-established pattern of
action deliberately structured to enhance recruitment. Members know beforehand the character and tempo of all formal
activity and play their roles precisely. Neil Solonen's
instructions (1974) to Church members were:

> You must regard all other training sessions as
> past...they didn't make us perfect and didn't
> bring everyone in. We must really pray to learn
> better ways, to be effective and inspiring...
> We should prepare earlier in the week, arrive at
> the site ahead of time and welcome the guests as
> we would to our homes. Everything should have
> the feeling that you have prepared it for them.

The weekend officially begins on Saturday morning.
Guests are roused from bed early with music ("Wake up, wake
up, you sleepy head..."), and are hustled through a series
of pre-planned activities. Singing, group discussions, lectures and recreation alternate in rapid sequence. As soon
as one activity concludes, participants are hurried to the
next. Recalling his first trip to Booneville, a former member (Ross, 1975) said:

> The weekend with its many lectures and group
> activities seemed to rush forward. I felt as
> though I were being pushed forward against my
> will. But the activity was so intense and in-
> cessant I had no time to think about it. The
> only time I had for myself was during sleep.
> Every minute was accounted for.

The atmosphere at Booneville reminded the observer of a
Hollywood musical. One former member said he felt like he
was on stage in "West Side Story" (Stoner and Parke, 1977).
The scenes and events are choreographed to convey specific
meanings and impressions, as well as create an aura of excitement. The dramatic production is efficient and effective because members are cooperative, disciplined and always
in total consensus. Cheers and applause follow every song,
announcement, lecture and group activity. Songs serve as a
dynamic connective mechanism. They proceed and follow all
group gatherings and the lyrics often suggest the virtues
and rewards of being part of the Family.

The guest's attention is absorbed by the incessant
round of activity. Often he or she is mystified by the entire production. Their inhibition and awe toward the in-

tense nature of the workshop allow the routine character of
the performance to be obscured. Moreover, idealized impressions can be created. Because there is such "joy" and
"stimulation" in being part of Booneville's festive scene,
it is taken for granted that everyone will merge easily into
the collective. In this setting it is impossible to remain
on the fringe of action as a passive observer. The question
facing the guest is how to respond, how to act. With rare
exceptions, prospective members are anxious to conform.
Newcomers are given ample social cues to cope with the incessant round of events and members' passion for unanimity.
They are told one must "participate one hundred per cent" to
get the most out of the training session.

     Small groups are the focal point of training-session
activity. They are formed early in the training session to
facilitate prospective members' total involvement. Each
group has about ten people; an equal number of members and
guests. A group leader extends an enthusiastic welcome and
asks everyone to introduce himself. "It's like we are going
to be married for the next thirty-six hours," participants
are told. They are asked to share how they happened to come
to the training session. Church members volunteer informal
testimonies of how their lives have been transformed positively since they met the Family. Nearly all guests eventually share their innermost thoughts and feelings, for
which they receive support and praise from the group. Neil
Salonen (1974) notes the crucial importance of groups in
promoting participation:

          People should want to do everything with their
          group, because it makes possible a deeper and
          richer experience. Commitment and communication
          are so deep that people must reveal themselves....
          When the group is intensely involved and com-
          mitted, the group pressure of the best kind
          inspires students to be involved. We have to
          build a big pressure for a heavy decision by
          the end of the weekend.

     Within the group each guest is paired with a member who
is a constant companion through the duration of the workshop.
The member's task is to ensure his or her "buddy's" total
involvement in all activity. The buddy system assures that
Booneville's collective processional continues on cue. A
member holds his or her buddy's hand during group discussions and while moving from place to place, even to the
bathroom.

     As the weekend progresses members gauge newcomers'
reactions to this stream of events, scrutinizing continu-

ously their responses to each situation and measuring the
extent of their participation. They appraise carefully
prospective members' receptiveness to lectures. If prospects do not seem to be giving full effort during songs, a
member gives them a slight nudge and a broad smile while
continuing to sing and clap loudly to demonstrate the happiness of taking part.

Members' continual attentiveness towards their prospects may appear to be spontaneous and arise out of natural
circumstances. To the contrary, this attitude is prepared
and employed conscientiously. One workshop participant
(World Christian Liberation Front, 1974) had this insight
into the intentionality of members' interactions with prospective members.

On Sunday morning, when I woke really early, I
walked by the building where some of the Family
members had slept. They were up and apparently
having a meeting, I heard a cheer: "Gonna meet
all their needs...Gonna meet all their needs...
Gonna meet all their needs." And that did seem
to be what they tried to do. Whatever I wanted
-- except privacy or any deviation from the
schedule -- would be gotten for me immediately
and with great concern. I was continually smiled
at, hugged, patted. And made to feel very special
and very much wanted.

Taking part in the conversion occasion is exhilarating;
yet this excitement serves as a catalyst for what members
refer to as "the final push for commitment," their effort
to entice their prospects to remain for a week-long training
session. While immersed in an isolated environment intentionally structured to narrow their perspective and perception, prospects make the "heavy decision" segregated from
the outside world. Lifton noted that participants in such
settings are "...deprived of external information and inner
reflection which anyone requires to test the realities of
the environment" (1963:421). Since their attention is dominated totally and they are isolated, prospects have little
opportunity to develop critical evaluations either on their
own or with others. The world can begin to close in on
those prospects who accept the version of life that members
convey consistently.

New people face a dilemma: they can return home, as most
have planned originally, or acquiesce to the urgings of
their respective buddies and stay for at least a week. During the final moments of the weekend many prospects choose
to remain. The overwhelming kindness and attention members

have extended to them frequently is the strongest factor influencing their decision. As one weekend training session
came to a close, a member briefed a colleague on her efforts
to entice her buddy to remain: "He has heard enough of the
truth. What should I do now?" the woman asked. "Well, if
he has heard enough of the truth, then love him some more,"
said the other. "Love bomb" is a term members use to refer
to the attentiveness and affection they offer potential recruits. The love bomb is also applied during the week-long
training session, since members must sustain a close relationship with their prospects to secure further commitment.

FURTHER COMMITMENT

When a prospect remains for the week-long training session, his or her buddy also stays to facilitate integration
into the Family. Once again, the training session contingent is divided into groups composed of a leader, Church
members and prospects. Participants spend the entire day
with their respective groups, engaged in a routine similar
to the weekend indoctrination. Members continue to display
a joyous *esprit* de *corps*, and group leaders work to sustain
cohesiveness. Rather than being optional, it is assumed
that all participants will share their ideas and inspirations. Leaders and other members coax prospects to "reveal
themselves" and reward them subsequently with gestures of
affection for sharing with the group what they "learned from
the lecture" or how they are "actualizing" their goals.
Fellow participants quickly become a new reference group for
prospects, and trust among their new "brothers and sisters"
is emphasized throughout the week.

The training session's intense emotional quality is
most evident during dramatic scenarios, a rigorous hike
taken by everyone up to the peak of a low mountain. The
walk is symbolic; participants are told to think of the
daily climb Moses made to the top of the mountain to show
God his faith. Everyone is to overcome the mountain "together," with the strong helping the weak accomplish the
exhausting journey. When the summit is reached, everyone is
ecstatic. Many are weeping and congratulating one another.
The group gathers in a circle to cheer and sing "Exodus" and
"Shining Fatherland." A leader offers an arousing prayer,
then participants are told to scatter about the slope of the
mountain and pray individually. This and similar scenes are
choreographed carefully to make an emotional impression on
potential members.

Rather than present prospective members with a join-or-
else ultimatum, at the close of the week-long training

session members "invite" guests to remain for one more week.
During my observations, slightly more than half of the prospects chose to stay beyond the first week. Many of those
who remain experience a gradual conversion and become members of the Family after three more weeks of indoctrination.
The second week is identical in procedure to the first.
Lectures and other events are repeated with renewed intensity. The prospective member continues to be confronted
with a sense of urgency and moral obligation to become a
"pioneer" building the "Ideal World."

If the prospect adopts the Church's world view he often
begins to promote actively his new perspective among new recruits, especially during group discussions. Becoming an
agent for Church ideology (The Principles) is a sure indication the prospect is moving towards total commitment. Members introduce other elements to help the prospect forge his
new identity. Experienced leaders are designated as role
models to be followed as patterns for proper behavior.
Group leaders tell participants:

It's so great to have older members around for us
to emulate....Just watch everything they do; how
they move. Learn those gestures of kindness so
that working toward perfection is really easy.
All you have to do is imitate them.

"Older members" share emotional testimonies that include the details of their conversion. When giving their
testimonies, they display a sense of assurance and depth of
faith that newcomers can find admirable. Members and
guests are enraptured and often brought to tears by these
personal narratives. All testimonies are arranged to appeal to the deepest sentiments of prospective members. For
the prospect, emulation of these testimonies has the effect
of confirming his commitment when he declares a personal
transformation before the entire training session.

ORGANIZATIONAL QUALITIES OF RELIGIOUS TOTALISM

Lifton (1963:420) suggests that any particular religious environment must be judged according to its own characteristics:

For in identifying, on the basis of this study
of thought reform, features common to all expressions of ideological totalism, I wish to
suggest a set of criteria against which any

environment may be judged -- a basis for answering the ever-recurring question: "Isn't
this just like 'brainwashing'?

He lists eight themes, each having a totalistic quality
that is predominant in a thought reform milieu (1963:420).
This section describes these themes and how each is related
to UC recruitment process. The themes are milieu control,
mystical manipulation, the demand for purity, the cult of
confession, the sacred science, loading the language, doctrine over person and dispensing of existence.

Milieu Control

The most basic feature of the thought reform environment is the control of human communication. In the UC, conversion is contingent on members' ability to control communication at the training session. They attempt intentionally
to determine what potential members hear, see, and experience. The regulation of all personal interaction among non-
members hinges on the achievement of their total participation. Consequently, this environment can be maintained to
members' satisfaction if their prospects are actively engaged in prescribed events (i.e., lectures, songs and discussions).

When hustled through these activities from daybreak to
midnight, newcomers have little opportunity to share ideas
and opinions with one another. Members consistently keep
prospects separated; thus, in those brief moments when it is
possible to exchange reflections and opinions, conversation
is discouraged, except in group settings.

Lifton concludes that "totalist administrators" look
on milieu control as a just and necessary policy, one that
need not be kept a secret. Prospects at the training session are told:

We have a few rules here. They are really good
rules. First, new people are not to talk with
each other. It is best to talk with someone who
has been around longer and had the same experiences you are having. That way, all the talk is
elevated. Likewise for people who have only been
here for a week; talk only with people older than
you.

A newcomer asked the training session director why this
rule of silence was enforced. The director replied:

When they get together, if there is the slightest
bit of negativity, then they will only magnify
the negativity, and see the bad side...Negativity
expressed to new people holds them back while
they are here.

Leaders deliberately guide their group discussions toward absolute accordance with the themes and rhetoric presented at the training session. Exclusion of viewpoints
they term "negative" and "skeptical" is essential to pre-
serving their definition of the workshop's meaning. Emergence of an alternative interpretation of this projected
reality is limited severely.

Mystical Manipulation

Extensive personal manipulation inevitably follows
milieu control. This manipulation "...seeks to provoke certain patterns of behavior and emotion in such a way that
these will appear to have risen spontaneously and directed
to ...assume, for the manipulated, a near mystical quality"
(Lifton, 1963:422).

The evangelical drama of the Unification Church training sessions appears to have a spontaneous quality. Songs,
lectures and testimonies, along with supportive chants, applause and cheers, are arranged in a way that provokes intense emotional states in the participants. Pre-arranged
scenarios like the march up the mountain, intense group
prayer, constant singing and other displays of exuberance
engross prospects. They are likely to evaluate their experiences on an emotional basis and not realize they are subject
to a system of controls.

Lifton asserts that ideological totalists do not pursue
this approach solely for the purpose of maintaining a sense
of power over others.

Rather they are impelled by a special kind of
mystique which not only justifies such manipulations, but make them mandatory. Included in
this mystique is a sense of "higher purpose",
of having "directly perceived some imminent
law of social development", and of being themselves of this development.

At training sessions members often refer to their
"higher purpose" and view themselves as a vanguard.

Prospective members continually are reminded of the opportunity to be "pioneers." A leader told her group"

> This is a time in history when the minority
> really is right....This is the culmination of
> history, the apex. We have been chosen to do
> this great work. What we do affects the rest
> of eternity. When I remember that, I put all
> I've got into every moment. If we work really
> hard now we can spend ten thousand years in
> the Heavenly Kingdom.

Projection of rewarding imagery through lectures, testimonies, singing and discussions is "mandatory" because
Church members are agents "chosen" by God to carry out a
"mystical imperative," an idealistic certitude that mankind's salvation depends on them. During every lecture the
training session director calls on prospects to accept
their "portion of responsibility." Using a humorous anal-
ogy he prevails upon his audience: "Greetings, Heavenly
Father wants you. Your draft notice is truth. Are you
glad He asked you?" "Yes!" is shouted unanimously.

> If God asks you, does He have a better person
> in mind? God never asks you anything He doesn't
> think you can do. When everyone is in the
> Heavenly Kingdom, someone will ask you, "Hey
> did you help build the Heavenly Kingdom?" You
> can say, "Why, yes I did!" God is longing for
> you. God has been waiting for six thousand
> years. Do you think He likes to see babies abused
> by their parents? The Kingdom of Heaven may not
> return for one thousand years. If we fail, do
> you want to be responsible for that?

"No." everyone blurts out. The director adds, "This is the
final morning. We can't disappoint God now. Are you ready
to establish the Heavenly Kingdom?" "Yes!" is usually the
reply.

Demand for Purity

In the thought reform milieu, the world of experience
is divided into the pure and impure, a total polarization
of good and evil. Lifton adds that goodness and purity are
"...those ideas, feelings and actions which are consistent
with the totalist ideology and policy" (1963:423).

At the UC indoctrination center, the path to perfection
is through emulation of Church leaders and the myriad of
provocative themes that are integrated into lectures and
discussions (e.g., "making oneness," "knowing God's will"
and "self-actualizing truth and righteousness"). Group
leaders set guidelines for purity with statements such as,
"When you follow truth, your conscience just naturally follows...When you learn more about the truth and live it naturally it becomes easier to do what is right."

To actualize these notions of perfection, prospects
are urged to surrender their self-centered concepts of
truth. During a mid-week lecture, the training director
says:

> Those without concepts, the pure of heart, can
> recognize the messiah right away. If we seek
> the way with humble hearts we will know the
> truth. The worst thing is to be arrogant and
> not search to know the truth.

Prospective members usually respond to the demand for
purity with humility and follow the milieu's rules. To not
accept or imitate members' dynamic unity is to stand alone
as a maverick; to be on the evil side of a dichotomized
world is to be subjected to embarrassment or ostracism.
In a group discussion, a member directed this comment towards prospects:

> People point out that we have too many rules.
> But those rules are there because we don't
> have a conscience! We don't know the differ-
> ence between good and evil. I'm glad those
> rules are there, to keep us spiritually cen-
> tered.

Role models, ideological guidelines and idealistic
imagery help prospects harmonize their actions with Church
members. Those participants who do not conform consistently
or obviously show no interest in "perfection" or being a
"pioneer" are told quickly to leave. For example, one
participant was slightly uncooperative within his group,
yet not overtly outspoken or "negative." He asked the
training session director: "Aren't you using mind control
here?" After conferring with the director, his group
leader told him he had to leave. He was escorted immediately from the training session to a bus stop. His group
leader told him she regretted his going but that obviously
he was not ready to hear the truth with a pure heart and
open mind, and that skepticism could influence adversely the
spiritual growth of other new people.

Cult of Confession

At UC training sessions, formal confessions are not a routine part of indoctrination, but occasionally members purge themselves of guilt feelings before their peers. More often they incorporate into their inspirations and testimonies expressions of symbolic self-surrender. They seek to impress upon prospects their devotion to the Family, referred to as "a greater-than-self tradition."

In Lifton's study, individuals who experienced thought reform were required to purge themselves of their past "impurities" (1963:425). Such is not the case with the Unification Church. Rather than pressure their prospects to confess a sinful past, members encourage their prospects to express a sense of hope and renewal. Prospects are required to share repeatedly their "inspirations" over a period of weeks. Eventually, they can believe their own assertions and become committed to the Families' vision of an ideal world.

Sacred Science

Lifton says a "...totalist milieu maintains an aura of sacredness around its basic dogma, holding it out as an ultimate moral vision for the ordering of human existence" (1963:427). The Unification Church's sacred science is the Divine Principle. The members regard the Principles as "...unfathomable, always yielding new truths." They are quite intense in their efforts to convince prospects of the validity and ultimate value of their ideology. One group leader emphasized:

> Listen to the lecture like it was for the last
> time to really know the truth. As if we had to
> take the truth to the front lines which is to-
> morrow. This Principle is the greatest thing
> mankind has ever heard. Think of it as God
> speaking to you through the speaker.

The lectures are designed to move the prospect to feel a tremendous moral responsibility to join the Family. The Church is placed in a moving time perspective, using past history to account for its crucial role in the world. The lecturer presents historical evidence that we are living in the "Last Days." The world soon will experience an Armageddon between the forces of Satan and the Lord of the Second Advent, along with his followers (Church members). The world can be "restored" and the Kingdom of Heaven on Earth established under the rule of this new messiah, but success depends on the collective effort of those chosen to respond to the will of God.

Prospects are lured by the opportunity to be in the vanguard of this Utopian vision. It becomes believable on the basis of careful step-by-step syllogisms, sweeping non-rational insights and members' assertions that the Principles are "logical" as well as relevant to their lives. In Lifton's words, the totalist sacred science offers its adherents "...an extremely intense feeling of truth." As one person who recently had become a Church member said:

> When I first came here, I thought I would listen
> and incorporate what kernels of truth were here
> into my own personal philosophy. As the week
> went by, I realized how unnecessary that is.
> The Truth is already here! All I have to do is
> recognize it.

Loading the Language

Loaded language expresses the claimed certitudes of the sacred science. It is characterized by what Lifton calls the "thought-terminating cliche" (1963:429). At the training session, this style of language is centered repetitiously into all communication: lectures, songs and conversation.

The lecturer's language is selected to fit the majority of his audiences' intellectual maturity. He or she makes extensive use of thought-provoking imagery, cliches, analogies and anecdotes to arouse the inner enthusiasm of non-members and prospective members. Countless phrases such as "maximum creative potential" and "setting a high standard" are integrated constantly into lectures and group discussions, becoming an established part of training session jargon. Such brief, highly reductive, definitive-sounding phrases are memorized and expressed easily.

The conversion milieu expects participants, members and prospects to produce these cliches in public performances, inspirations, testimonies and group skits. Eventually, this language becomes very constricting, since it is all the prospect hears and repeats. After a week or two his capacity to think critically or evaluate can be narrowed.

Doctrine Over Person

This sterile language reflects another characteristic feature of ideological totalism, "...the subordination of

human experience to the claims of the doctrine" (Lifton,
1963:430). Church members tell prospects that their lives
only can have "purpose and direction" if they "embrace the
truth" and work to build the Heavenly Kingdom. The force
of this myth is fused into the Church's totalist doctrine,
the Principles. The resulting "logic" can be so compelling
that it simply replaces the realities of individual experience.

The Principles provide doctrinal legitimacy for the
subordination of individuals to authority. Training session
participants are told to "follow center." The "center" is
vested in the person who happens to be closest to the
source of truth and the order of authority extends down a
hierarchical network of administrators and local directors
to group leaders and finally other members. A group leader
explained to prospects the meaning of following center:

> One thing I work on is sacrificing my own con-
> cepts and follow someone who is more on center.
> It's like God works from a center through a
> person that completely understands his purpose.
> Here [the training session] the person most on
> center is...the director.   ...Everything you
> do goes right if it is centered. Someone tells
> you what to do and the source of that is per-
> fection because the person that told him what
> to do had been told by someone else who was
> just that much closer to the center.

The underlying assumption is that the Principles are
more valid than the personal concepts and judgments of members and prospects. Those who accept this doctrinal pri-
macy can have their character and identity reshaped if they
only are willing to put abstract ideas above their individual needs and sensibilities.

The Dispensing of Existence

The totalist environment divides the world into those
whose right to exist is recognized and those who possess no
such right, (Lifton, 1963:433). The UC does not make such
an extreme distinction, but its world is dichotomized into
believers and non-believers. Furthermore, family, friends
and all others outside the Church realm are regarded as
"spiritually dead." Only people who are "actualizing the
truth" when the Heavenly Kingdom is finally established are
assured salvation. The future of all others is not so
secure, especially those who have heard the Truth and rejected it.

Church members feel an enormous responsibility for all mankind. If they do not work hard to pioneer the Heavenly Kingdom, the world will be lost to Satan. Hence, they pressure prospects to accept their cause.

You know, God gave man free will. He doesn't
have to walk down that road as a world saver ,
but he really has no choice. Once he has heard
the truth, there's no turning back....We're in
the business of saving souls.

Prospects are told the "Last Days" are imminent and "The Whole Universe is groaning in travail." Those ambivalent towards the validity of the Principles and its millennial prediction can experience overwhelming feelings of guilt and confusion. Refusing to "respond" to the truth not only jeopardizes one's own existence, but such a mistake contributes to the down fall of humanity.

SUMMARY

This paper has delineated significant similarities and differences between thought reform in totalist environments and the conversion process in the Unification Church. On the one hand, participants in the Church's recruitment milieu are involved totally in a highly controlled and emotional atmosphere. Their participation entails a contrived socialization process that includes affectionate personal ties, extreme pressure to conform to group life, isolation from the external realities, little opportunity for reflective thinking and a sophisticated ideological indoctrination that confronts them with an opportunity to fulfill historical and personal destiny. Members literally choreograph scenarios that continually subject their prospects to various forms of persuasion while avoiding physical coercion. This organizational momentum provides prospects with feelings of exhilaration and intense comradeship that augment their prior susceptibilities. Whether or not they are victims of "brainwashing" is contingent on how the Church's recruitment practices are perceived; whether the observer, in private or official judgment, regards the Church's form of recruitment equivalent to thought reform.

On the other hand, the recruitment process in the Unification Church resembles evangelistic exhortation more than coercion. Coercion can be separated into psychological and physical levels. Perhaps those who attend Unification Church indoctrination sessions do experience psychological coercion. There is much debate on this issue among psychiatrists, social scientists and legal scholars, as well

as a more emotional polemic between advocates and opponents
of deprogramming. The problems underlying this controversy
begin with a lack of consensus over what is precisely brain-
washing/thought reform. Yet to emerge is a useful framework for understanding the relationship between forms of
coercive persuasion and life in religious groups. Such an
approach would necessitate inquiry into both the psychological and social processes involved. To know both how and
why individuals are attracted to controversial marginal
religions requires careful investigation into how commitment
is generated and sustained.

In regard to the Unification Church, one can only assume some correspondence between its recruitment practices
and Lifton's conception of thought reform. But recruitment
of people into the Unification Church is more a transaction
between their susceptibilities and the Church's organized
appeals (Toch, 1965). Suceptibilities include the prior
motives (Zygmunt, 1972) and other predispositions (Lofland
and Stark, 1965) that characterize conversion into other
religious groups.

Rather than being passive actors in the recruitment environment, individuals bring to it prior motives, needs and
desires (Straus, 1976; Balch and Taylor, 1977). They take
an active part in their own conversion. In this respect it
is argued commonly that individuals enter the Unification
Church (as well as other religious sects) voluntarily and
are not forced to remain; thus, they are not subject to
thought reform. Conversion into religious sects is voluntary in a restricted, legalistic sense, but the emphasis on
voluntariness tends to divert attention from various mechanisms of control of a coercive nature that can be applied
once individuals have volunteered themselves. Conversion
into a sect should be examined and assessed on the characteristics of its recruitment process within that particular
environment.

NOTES

1. During the initial stages of recruitment, affiliation
    with the Unification Church or Reverend Moon may be de-
    nied. Most of my recruitment observations were made in
    the Bay Area in the mid-1970's, where the Church identi-
    fied itself as Creative Community Project. People who
    joined this front organization were often not aware they
    had become members of the Unification Church until a few
    weeks after the fact.

LEAVING THE "CULTIC" RELIGIOUS MILIEU

Norman Skonovd
California Youth Authority

The conversion of thousands to religious movements new to Western society since the late 1960's has been a phenomenon difficult to ignore. Not only was it unexpected that the children of an affluent, relatively secularized society should harken to the gurus and messiahs of esoteric religions, but the type of devotion exacted was often startling. Some of these groups (popularly referred to as "cults") proved to be totalistic, requiring the complete devotion of the individual's mind and body. Charges of brainwashing and mind control soon arose and some parents legally and illegally attempted to force their children to renounce their "strange" religious commitments by hiring individuals to "deprogram" them. Both the popular media and the social scientific community have paid considerable attention to many aspects of this phenomenon, particularly conversion. However, little notice has been taken of the fact that thousands of converts have dropped out of these "new age groups", seeking to return to mainstream life. This paper looks at how "cult" members make the decision to defect and at the strategies involved in the actual leavetaking.

METHODOLOGY

The data for this paper were obtained as part of a larger study of the process of defection from totalistic religious groups (see Skonovd, 1981) and were derived from 60 qualitative interviews (lasting from one-had-a-half to five hours). Thirty interviews were conducted with defectors from the Unification Church, five were from Scientology, thirteen were from various religious groups of Eastern origin, two were from People's Temple, and ten were from extreme fundamentalist Christian groups. Most were taped and later transcribed. Defectors were located through media attention given to their defection and/or anti-cult activities through self-identification at various public meetings and lectures concerning "cults," through referrals from current "cult" members and anti-cultists, and by means of the "snowball" method (i.e., respondents referring others for interviews). The sample obtained exhibits a good mix between those sympathetic and non-sympathetic with the anti-cult

movement. Twelve of those interviewed were deprogrammed in
one way or another, however, this paper is primarily concerned with those who left on their own initiative.

DISAFFECTION

Before addressing the issue of how "cult" members decide to leave, it is necessary to consider briefly how the
believer arrives at a state in which continued allegiance is
problematic.

When we think about apostasy of religious defection, we
typically think of individuals who have "lost their faith"
-- individuals who cease to believe in God and/or become
disaffected by theological and/or ethical contradictions and
are thereafter known as agnostics, atheists, or unbelievers.
However, from my interviews with "cult" defectors as well as
from historical information on the well-known agnostics and
atheists of the 19th century, it is apparent that unbelief
and/or disaffection usually occur after physical and/or
emotional separation from the "fellowship" of the believing
community. Therefore, though it is true that religious defection requires dissonance (see Festinger, et al., 1964) --
a disturbing sense of contradiction between beliefs, between
one's belief (or unbelief) and one's actions, between a
group's ethical stance and its leader's actions, etc. -- a
believer typically does not become an apostate simply because of an encounter with dissonance-creating problems.
Problems are relatively common occurrences, and as long as
the believer remains within the bond of fellowship, they
will be overcome by various means (e.g. repression or avoid-
ance of awareness, justification or rationalization, reformation or "righting" the wrong, withdrawal to an enclave of
the religion where the problem does not exist). In fact, if
the religious group bonds remain strong and are not neu-
tralized by competing allegiances, there is less chance that
the believer will be in a position to encounter problems (or
experience dissonance if they are encountered). With sufficient social support, any reality may be successfully maintained (see Berger and Luckmann, 1967; Holzner, 1968).

When social support breaks down due to physical and/or
emotional estrangement, however, reality maintenance becomes
problematic since the individual no longer receives positive
daily reinforcement for working at "maintaining" (i.e.,
avoiding disconfirming information and negative thoughts,
interpreting events only in light of the belief system, associating only with believers, etc.). When this occurs, the
individual is often relatively defenseless when confronted
with "negative" information concerning the group and is

easily upset when contradictions between belief and actions, for example, become apparent. If unable to rely on the group to help dispel doubts and reassure his or her faith, he or she must struggle to overcome them alone. The struggling believer usually attempts to come to terms with his or her problems by putting them into the larger context of his or her overall knowledge of the group, hoping to find an answer somewhere. However, this often leads to additional problems being uncovered and dissonance therefore increases. An ex-Scientologist described well this process of increasing dissonance:

> As we started looking at Scientology's doctrine and organizational structure we discovered we disagreed with more and more things. I mean we found ourselves remembering what we didn't like about it. We ceased ignoring things we couldn't agree with. Before, we had paid attention only to the things we wanted to deal with and the rest we kind of said, "Oh, God, I'll handle that someday," or "its a minor screw-up on the part of the local people." You see, we began interpreting points differently.

I call this process "review and reflection." Though not involved in attempts to forget or repress dissonance, the believer who faces up to a problem will initially reflect back on past experiences within his or her group and review its dogma and organizational structure with the intention of finding convincing evidence of the validity of the religious belief structure and/or the appropriateness of its institutional framework in spite of the problem. This process is a form of rationalization since attempts are made to justify continued involvement in light of whatever contradictions are perceived. The individual thus typically continues to "review and reflect" until the problem no longer represents dissonance (e.g., appearing insignificant in light of the "overall picture"), or it becomes clear that the dissonance creating problems cannot be resolved within the context of present religious allegiances. In fact, even when the latter occurs, the individual will usually continue this process in regard to the additional problems uncovered in order to further justify his or her disaffection.

DECIDING TO LEAVE

Once it has been realized that the problem or problems cannot be resolved within the individual's present religious allegiance, it is only a matter of time before a decision to

leave is reached (unless, of course, his or her estrangement
with the group is overcome). The decision may come about
quickly due to some critical, precipitating event, or it may
slowly take form as the individual weighs alternatives and
ponders theological and emotional considerations. When the
decision to leave is made quickly, the defector typically
finds that he or she has reached the threshold of tolerance
and simply "cannot take it anymore," as a five-year veteran
of the Unification Church claimed:

> I had reached my threshold -- I couldn't take
> another change. The whole time I was in the
> family it was constant change -- constant mov-
> ing -- constant changing jobs and responsibil-
> ities. They were just constantly reshuffling
> my life -- telling me where I was going to live
> and how I was going to live. The straw that
> broke the camel's back was when Moon came and
> demanded that everybody go out on fundraising
> teams. I couldn't do it. I couldn't muster up
> any more energy to make another change and live
> in a Volkswagon bus for another year -- no way.
> Then it just dawned on me: "Now look man, if
> this guy's the messiah, you know, he would
> definitely have more concern about an indivi-
> dual's life, a person's needs." You know, I
> thought the messiah had at least some compas-
> sion in his nature -- not just a gooddamn dollar
> bill. These kinds of thoughts started enter-
> ing my mind. He's making people pay with
> their health for a financial stronghold. I
> thought human life came before money. I thought,
> you know, the human spirit, the quality of your
> character was more important than building a
> business monopoly or something. I decided
> right then that I was not going to be a puppet
> and do that anymore -- I wasn't going to be one
> of his pawns and be used like that.

An example of an even more instantaneous decision to
defect was related to me by a defector from the People's
Temple. His decision to leave was sparked by a blatant incident of racial discrimination after a considerable period
of disillusionment and unhappiness. Because the progressive
and racially egalitarian appearance of the People's Temple
was a major reason for his joining, this incident was beyond
his capacity to "stomach any further:"

> Jones, you know, had this big beating thing and
> at one meeting a Black girl was given 60 to 70
> wacks. She had only stolen a dime-store item

-- an Afro comb or something like that that she
really needed -- and these wacks were brutal.
At the same meeting a white kid who had stolen
a lady's purse out of her car and who had been
disciplined several weeks before for having
stolen a car only got 10 wacks. Now you weren't
allowed to criticize Jones, but I had access to
the podium and so I wrote him a note, explaining
what he was doing and I said: "This is prejudice."
And he called me up to the white podium and said: "You
don't understand." And I thought, "Well, I sure
as hell don't understand." I didn't say anything
and I pretended like nothing was wrong and I
casually put my camera back in the bag and since
I had free access to move around I went and sat
in the car until my wife came out and I told her
I was never going back again.

This abrupt manner of leavetaking -- after becoming upset over the prejudiced or openly hypocritical attitudes of
a congregation and/or member of the clergy -- appears to be
typical of leavetaking from denominational religions. However, in the case of totalistic religions, leaving is a
serious decision and is rarely decided on quickly. For example, the individual quoted above also mentioned that when
an individual decided to leave the People's Temple "you decided that you'd rather die than go back."

Immediate decisions to defect may also occur without
explicit critical events. Long periods of disenchantment --
during which problems and dissatisfactions are generally un-
vocalized -- may culminate in an instantaneous realization
that "it's all wrong and I want out." The following account
related by a four-year veteran of the Unification Church is
illustrative of this:

Because I was an older member and because they
knew I was having spiritual problems they had me
do all these little tasks -- one of which was
typing up Reverend Moon's speeches. I always
hated reading his speeches because they always
got me upset -- I always started having spiritual problems when I would read them. They're
really incoherent -- just disjointed sentences
and ideas. I was typing this speech out and it
went "Your parents and your family...are like
an anchor and they're tied around your leg.
You're on a rope between God and Satan and your
parents are the anchor and they want to pull
you to Satan. You've got to cut that rope,
you've got to cut that rope. Your parents and

the deprogrammers and all the fallen people are
on this side trying to pull you away from me.
But run to me, run to me. And if you don't have
enough strength everyday to go out to battle and
overcome for me, go and pick a fight with somebody and beat them up and let the adrenaline just
flow through you so you can go out and..." I was
sitting there typing this stuff, you know, and I
said: "Oh, God! This is crazy." It was the first
moment I actually voiced all the things I had
actually felt bad about. I said "This is crazy,
and this is not right. I don't believe this,
etc." This was the first time I actually disagreed with what he said consciously. I really
put myself in a different place than him. I just
stopped typing and I said to myself: "I've got to
get out of here!"

Most individuals, however, do not make decisions which
are of such strong existential importance this quickly. The
individuals quoted above had, of course, been disaffected
for some time even though the actual decision was not made
over an extended period of time. They came to realize that
they wanted to leave because some specific, critical event
or instantaneous realization made it clear that they could
not continue for one reason or another. Although critical
events occur in most defections, they more typically create
dissonance and contribute to disillusionment rather than
prompt instantaneous apostasy. The following account, related by a defector who had been a Unification Church member
for five years, is typical:

For a whole year I didn't leave because you don't
think you can leave -- or you'll die -- or you're
going against everything you believe. You try
your darnedest, but I finally just gave in: "I
can't do this anymore! Its not worth it to me!"
Its not a sudden thing -- you've thought about
it for awhile, weighed alternatives, and then you
decide rationally and calmly that it's wrong --
that your worst fears are true and you have to
leave for the sake of your own integrity.

Sometimes the reasoning involved in the decision-making
is explicitly instrumental. Since many contemporary totalistic religious groups are youth-oriented, tension arises
when individuals reach the age when career and/or marriage
decisions cannot be realistically postponed. The following
account by a three-year veteran of the Unification Church
illustrates this well. She had joined partly because of the
"attractiveness" of the young men in the organization:

It came full circle -- the reason I joined was
the reason I left. I looked at these guys --
now I was 21 instead of 18 -- and I thought in
so many words: "Moon has them by the balls."
He controls their total sex life -- you even
have to do it in a certain position after you're
married. You can't live your own life. Somehow
its acceptable for women to submit to that, but
in our society its hard to respect a man who would
submit to that. I had a dream of being married
to this guy in the group -- a real loser -- after
I thought: "Well, I won't have the life I want but
maybe the kids will." Then I thought: "How terrible to have to live through your kids." Further,
I knew that college wouldn't be the end of my
career and I thought about law school, but I realized that the group would never tolerate that.
My interests started diverging from what they
demanded and I couldn't deliver. I couldn't
marry the way they wanted me to marry and all of
a sudden it wasn't this game anymore in college.
It was real life and adulthood and I just wasn't
willing to make all those compromises. I knew
that if I didn't leave than I would probably
suffocate.

Another Unification Church defector described his decision to leave as being basically instrumental. Not experiencing problems of faith, he felt the movement (after being
a member for seven months) was ruining his mental health:

It was all pretty conscious. When I left, even
though I expected to somehow be harmed by evil
forces, I believed that someday I would be all
right. You see, even if I were to be completely
overtaken by that evil force, according to Moon's
theology, someday good would reign supreme so
that my period of time in that hell would be
limited -- especially relative to infinity. So
that was the thing that tipped my decision to
leave the Moonies, besides the fact that I just
felt my survival depended upon it. I sort of
felt the whole process of conversion and socialization into the group had been one of destruction. If you use the image of my mind being a
series of threads, those threads were all but
destroyed and it was like one last remaining,
hardcore life thread was ready to snap if I
stayed there any longer.

For those who continue to "review and reflect" upon
their experiences with the group and its doctrine, the decision making process is often long and involved. The following account by a nine month Unification Church veteran is an
excellent example of this:

> During my time of doubt and crisis one thing that
> really impressed me and led me to leave was some-
> thing Moon said himself at Barrytown. He told us
> about this little old lady who kept coming up to
> him and wanting to talk to him and -- you know --
> I can't remember exactly what it was she wanted
> from him but it was on the order of wanting to be
> around him and needing some food or something.
> He said: "Well, she kept coming up to me and this
> kind of thing and I said 'yes' to her and I was
> nice to her but finally she just started bother-
> ing me so I told her to get out of my way."
> That's not necessarily an exact quote but it's
> the general idea. And so then I reflected on
> things like that and I said: "Wow, how could a
> real messiah treat an old lady like that?" I
> mean even if she had problems and was trying to
> cling to him more than would be appropriate,
> how could he excuse himself by saying she was
> bothering him rather than saying something like:
> "she was overly affectionate toward me, therefore
> I told her I had other things to do and that it
> would help her to serve me better by doing such
> and such away from me rather than hanging around
> me." So, I mean just more and more things like
> that came up and I can name you a whole bunch of
> contraditions like that. Basically the thing
> that most effectively got me out was looking at
> the contradictions like that. Basically the
> thing that most effectively got me out was look-
> ing at the contradictions over and over -- both
> in the Divine Principle itself, and In Moon him-
> self -- you know, by his behavior and in his
> speeches whether in person or in The Master Speaks.
> Then I reflected upon the whole hierarchical
> nature of the church and how it was just totally
> fascist from top to bottom. I also began think-
> ing about how it was totally against my inner
> feelings of what was right. It was more like
> God saying: "Be a puppet," rather than "Come to
> me of your free will." It just kind of got to
> the point where after awhile I felt I no longer
> belonged in the Unification Church and I no longer
> wanted to have anything to do with it. So, I left.

ALTERNATIVES

Many individuals, particularly long-term members, require an alternative to the "cultic" interpretation of reality before they can make the decision to defect. They need
a map by which they can chart where they are, where they can
go, and an assurance that life outside the confines of the
movement is possible or even desirable. If the alternative
contains a sophisticated world view or theology which can
take the individual's beliefs and experiences into account,
the decision process may be relatively easy. Thus movement
from one religion to another may be a relatively smooth
transition. In fact, confrontation with an alternative
religious system that is perceived as superior may create
the original crisis, provide an explicitly integrated framework by which to critique other doctrine and organizational
structure, and provide a rationale for defecting as well as
an alternative paradigm with which to restructure one's
life. More typically, however, an individual will encounter
dissonance-creating inconsistencies or contradictions within
the movement's doctrine and/or organizational structure, become generally disaffected after a process of "review and
reflection," and then encounter an alternative framework
which provides both the impetus to defect and the necessary
rationale. Typical is the experience of a two-year veteran
of the Hare Krishna movement who claims to have been unable
to make the decision to leave until she adopted a fundamentalist Christian framework:

I had become absolutely alienated from a lot of
what was occurring at the ashram -- the arranged,
loveless marriages, the deceptive fundraising.
The real lack of concern for other people had begun to really upset me. For over a year I really
longed to leave, but I was afraid that if I left
I would end up back in maya -- you know, the illusion and have to go through another cycle of
deaths and rebirths. Finally, I met this group
of Christians -- they were really beautiful loving people -- very different than the people I
live with at the ashram. Through them I began
to see that I had been spiritually deceived by
Satan and that the whole Hare Krishna movement
was under Satan's control. I just really began
to understand all the things that had happened
to me -- the things that had gone on in the
group which were really evil. More importantly,
I found Jesus -- I had a way out. I don't
think that I could ever have done it otherwise.
I was just too caught up in their world, even

though I had begun to hate it.

An encounter with such an alternate conception of reality is important because it destroys the movement's power to
define reality and rationalize its inconsistencies. However, even here a decision to leave is not necessarily easy.
The individual must come to assure him or herself that the
alternative is true -- not an easy accomplishment in light
of the fear many individuals must overcome before they can
relinquish their old faith. For example, a four-and-a-half
year veteran of the Unification Church overcame his fear of
defecting only after being introduced to fundamentalist
Christian ideas (through another member who secretly shared
with him Christian books and pamphlets brought back from a
visit to her family).

> There was a problem, you know, if Unification
> Church theology was right, you couldn't leave
> it whether it was bad or not. But Christianity
> became an alternative there and when she came
> back she started sharing with me.... I didn't
> turn her in and the whole Christian alternative
> kind of opened up to us. We had time to our-
> selves to discuss things that were going on be-
> cause we were taking care of the children of
> the center director and we were taken out of
> some of the main activities at that time so we
> could observe what was going on more than other
> people normally could. And, we could talk
> about it with each other without having to fear
> that the other one would run to the leader and
> say: "Hey, so and so's got negative feelings
> and you had better do something." It just
> reached the point finally that we made a deci-
> sion that we were going to become Christians
> instead of Divine Principle people and that we
> would just follow that up and on that basis
> we would leave and begin whatever life we would
> begin. We weren't really sure what we would do
> but we'd come to the conclusion that what we
> were doing was wrong and that, in fact, when it
> claimed to be a higher expression of Christian-
> ity, it in fact misused the quotes and, you know,
> was really quite different theology. And so, we
> experienced a release from that bond of fear or
> that tie to the Unification Church and just left
> it.

Deprogramming, a controversial method of inducing apostasy, relies heavily on this need for alternatives to "cultic" interpretations of reality. After inducing dissonance

(or even as a method for inducing it), deprogrammers typically present a "brainwashing model" of conversion and membership in religious "cults." This is a type of "medical
model" which absolves individuals of responsibility for
their conversions, for remaining with the group, and for be-
having in "abnormal" ways while in, based upon the argument
that they were brainwashed into converting and then manipulated by mind control. The "brainwashing model" also holds
out the promise of "health" -- the promise of a viable existence apart from the movement in which the individual can
experience independence and intellectual freedom once again.
This facilitates apostasy in a way similar to that of adopt-
a competing religious world view. Such a model or paradigm
provides a cognitive structure with which individuals can
reinterpret the cultic world view and their respective experiences in it, as well as anticipate a life outside it.

STRATEGIES OF LEAVETAKING

Once a decision to leave has been made, the problem of
how to effect the actual leavetaking remains -- a problem of
method, timing, and emotions. In totalistic groups, leaving
is not simply a matter of packing up and walking out the
door. The individual, though estranged, remains physically
and emotionally involved with what is essentially a total
institution. Therefore, a public leavetaking is extremely
difficult, if not impossible, for most. Because dissension
is forbidden for the sake of maintaining religious solidarity, public announcement of defection would be shocking to
the group and would result in tremendous social pressure being placed on the individual to repent and remain within the
group. Therefore, the individual is faced with either telling one or two individuals who might be empathetic, or leaving stealthily. Only one person interviewed attempted to
leave publicly -- a four-year veteran of the Unification
Church. However, after attempting to obtain the tacit "approval" of the individual in charge of the group, she was
eventually forced into leaving furtively:

> I called _____ and I tried to say: "listen
> I don't want to be here." And I was really up-
> set -- I mean I was even crying. I was more up-
> set than I'd been in years. He said: "Well, just
> don't do anything rash." I said: "I just can't
> do this and I want to leave openly. I want to
> tell the people here. I don't want to have to
> sneak away." So he said, well, you have to talk
> with Reverend _____ first. So I called him
> and he said: "You've got to give me three weeks."
> I said: "Sorry, I can't. I'm leaving." Mean-

while I'm getting very upset again and so he
finally agreed to talk to me that night. Meanwhile I packed up my car and was ready to go.
Finally at eleven o'clock that night he called
to say he was coming over to talk to me. However, when he came he wouldn't listen. He just
wouldn't listen to anything and I mean I got
really upset. Basically all he did was sit
there and judge me and finally I said: "I'm
sorry Reverend _____, but this is just going
in one ear and out the other. It doesn't mean
a thing to me. You can't accuse me into staying." And he just gave me this disgusted look
like "forget her" to his translator -- he was
talking to me through a translator -- and walked
out with me sitting there. So, I turned to some
girls and said: "Well, goodbye." And they said:
"What? You're leaving?" Only one other girl
really knew that I was going to leave. They
couldn't believe it and they followed me out to
the car and one girl climbed through the window
and wouldn't get out. I couldn't believe this
was really happening. They said: "Well, what
about the messiah? He's the messiah, you know!"
I said: "It doesn't mean anything to me -- it
just doesn't mean a thing to me." But they
wouldn't let me go so I said: "Okay, I'll go
back in." But I refused to take anything out of
my car. I laid down on the floor in the room
where I was supposed to go to sleep. At four in
the morning I got up and the girl who was supposed
to be on watch was asleep and so I went out, got
in my car and drove straight up the coast to my
parents' home.

Individuals appear to have a need to say goodbye formally to at least one person -- to confide in someone concerning their disaffection and their intention to leave.
However, the individual takes a risk in doing so because the
person in whom he or she confides may tell others and make
the exiting more difficult -- or even impossible. Therefore, individuals are wary of who they tell -- if they tell
anyone -- since each member generally knows the probable social consequences should his or her decision to leave become
widely known. The following comment from a three-year veteran of the Unification Church is illustrative of this:

I didn't tell the leaders that I was leaving because I knew if I did I would never get out.
They'd only care about keeping me in. I did tell
one guy I was really close to. However, when I

told him he tried to talk me out of it for 10
straight hours. He was a friend, but I couldn't
have lasted if I had told anyone else. He was
threatened because I was a pillar in the group.
Finally he said: "Can I tell the group you're
just going home for a rest?" And I said sure --
I didn't care what they said.

Announcing that one is going home to rest is, in fact,
sometimes a successful way to avoid confrontations over
leaving totalistic groups. However, only members of long-
standing are usually allowed to go home unaccompanied.

Because the groups are so tightly knit, it is difficult
to make preparations to leave -- particularly when one is
obviously unhappy and/or experiencing "spiritual problems."
One cannot simply start packing because others will become
suspicious and alert the leaders. Therefore intricate planning is often involved as two ex-Unification Church members
indicate:

> It took me two or three days to sneak my stuff
> out. What I did was put on two sets of clothes,
> snuck over to the Greyhound Bus Station, got a
> coin locker, took off one set of clothes and put
> them in. I was able to get quite a bit of my
> stuff over there by the time I walked out the
> door for the last time.

> The camp was kind of isolated and it was an in-
> between day -- between seminars and people were
> cleaning up and going here and there. There was
> a busload of people going back to the city --
> people who had to go to the dentist and stuff
> like that. Of course, I wasn't supposed to be
> let out (she was known to be having "spiritual
> problems"), but then the girl that was driving
> the bus didn't know that because I was older and
> could use, you know, my spiritual authority: "I've
> got to go down to the Bay Area, I've got an im-
> portant appointment." So I get down to the city
> about eleven o'clock that night and I was staying
> at the Ashby Street house in Berkeley.... Be-
> cause I was an older member they didn't always
> question what I was doing... so I got all my
> stuff and went over to an old friend's house
> which was nearby and called up my dad and he
> came over and picked me up.

Situations of group transition or disruption -- in addition to weakening the group's sway over individual members

-- also provide individuals with the social conditions in which to effect an easy and unobserved exit. The situation described above is typical. However, if a group-wide transition does not present itself, even relatively small events can be exploited for purposes of exiting. The following account of a short-term member of the Unification Church illustrates one such strategy.

> After I packed everything up there was a lecture on anti-communism. So, after it began I excused myself to those sitting around me and told them I had to go to the bathroom. Usually, you can't just up and go to the bathroom, but no one said anything. I went upstairs, grabbed my stuff and ran out the back door going through the kitchen. Well, a couple of people accosted me, asking if I'd gotten permission from several different people to go and I lied to them and said: "Yes, I've already checked it out."

Even though an individual has made a decision to leave and has devised an exit plan, the process of actually walking out is complicated often by emotional matters. For example, one ex-member of the Unification Church told me that he had attempted to leave three times before he was able to make it out on a fourth try. Because he still had possession of his car, this was relatively easy. Nevertheless, he twice turned back and returned to the group after traveling many miles away from his local center. A third time he was talked out of leaving by several leaders when they observed him making preparations to leave. Though disaffected, the prospective apostate is often so attached to the group that leaving is a very highly charged emotional experience. The following account, by a woman who had been a member of the Unification Church for five years, is typical of the level of emotional trauma leaving brings on:

> It wasn't easy to leave. I even had my bags packed one day and I couldn't do it. I sat there and just cried and cried. I cried my soul out that day, but I just could not leave. But I knew I couldn't stay. I had to get out of there. So finally what I did was -- I had everything packed. I had it all packed so people could send me my stuff in the mail. What I did was I just took what I had on -- I had some money -- that was how I could do it. I did have enough money. I took my knitting bag, put a few things in it... and just walked out of there -- took a taxi to Kennedy Airport and flew home. I didn't tell anybody -- I couldn't do it. It would have been too painful,

however, I did leave a note for this guy I was
working with along with twenty dollars to send
me my stuff, and that was it.

Only for individuals who are openly troublesome and in
direct conflict with the group is leave-taking relatively
uncomplicated. An individual may get into a heated alterca-
tion with group leaders and be told to "shut up or leave."
Some individuals who are disliked also have relatively easy
exits. In these instances -- not common among those I interviewed -- the individual does, in a sense, simply walk
away.

CONCLUSION

This paper has explored the conditions under which continued "cultic" religious involvement is problematic, the
manner in which decisions to leave are made, and the strategies involved in physically leaving. It has been argued
that the critical factor underlying religious disaffection
is the deterioration of the individual's group bonds. Without the social support and nurturance of fellow believers,
the individual is left on his or her own and is thus much
more susceptible to dissonance creating problems. When
problems cannot be resolved, and others appear, the believer
becomes disaffected and is faced with making a decision regarding continued involvement. The decision is sometimes
made quickly due to a critical event which makes continued
involvement appear impossible. In other cases, it is made
slowly by reviewing and reflecting on the group's beliefs
and organizational practices, by a consideration of the individual's personal future with the group, or by seeking out
viable alternatives to the "cultic" life. Leavetaking has
been shown to center mainly on strategizing to physically
depart without creating attention that would impede leaving,
and in overcoming emotional attachments.

We end this discussion with the disaffected individual
walking away from his or her "cultic" environment. However,
it must be noted that we cannot consider such an individual
an apostate at this stage. In fact, the most difficult aspect of the process of religious defection is still ahead --
that is, the creation of an identity, life style, and world
view apart from that of the rejected religion.

DEFECTION FROM NEW RELIGIOUS MOVEMENTS:
A TEST OF SOME THEORETICAL PROPOSITIONS

Stuart A. Wright
Center for Urban Church Studies

The controversy surrounding "cult brainwashing" and "deprogramming" in the last decade has centered largely around the issue of voluntary participation and commitment of members. Much has been said and written about deprogrammed ex-members who later claim to have been victims of "mind control" and brainwashing techniques (Conway and Seigelman, 1978; Delgado, 1977, 1979; Edwards, 1979; Enroth, 1977; Patrick and Dulack, 1976; Singer, 1979; Underwood and Underwood, 1979; Verdier, 1977). The rationale of deprogramming itself rests on the assumption that members of the new religions have been unwittingly "programmed" (see Shupe and Bromley, 1980:70-78). Yet most persons who join these movements leave on their own, without the aid of deprogramming. Research suggests that the attrition rate among these groups is high and that probably only a small percentage of defections are directly a result of deprogramming (Shupe and Bromley, 1980:108; Solomon, 1980). In a random sample survey of 200 members of the Unification Church living in centers, Judah (1978:206) found that "fifty-five percent of those surveyed had been in the Church for one year or less." Robbins and Anthony (1980:77) note that "movements such as the Hare Krishna or the Unification Church...exhibit a rapid turnover and high dropout rate." Similarly, Bromley and Shupe (1979:93) attribute the difficulty of obtaining accurate membership figures from the new religions to the "rapid turnover" of members. Consequently, the question arises: If deprogramming is not imperative to bring people to a personal choice to leave, then how and why do members leave on their own? This study is undertaken to address the question of voluntary defection from new religious movements. More specifically, it examines defection from those new religious and communal movements that have been most commonly accused of brainwashing their members -- the Unification Church, the Hare Krishna, and the Children of God.

Only a few studies have examined voluntary defection from the new religious movements. Beckford (1978) has analyzed withdrawal of members from the Unification Church in Great Britain. He found that "accounts of withdrawal are

usually hesitant, fragmented and rarely conclusive.... The
result is that most informants show considerable confusion
about the overall meaning to them of the events making up
their withdrawal from the Unification Church and remain
strongly ambivalent in their attitudes toward the cult"
(Beckford, 1978:111). Beckford concluded that the confusion
derived from the attempts of ex-members to reconstruct accounts of withdrawal that make sense to them ex-post facto.
More recently, Skonovd (1981) has examined defection from
"totalistic" religious groups. Unlike Beckford, however,
Skonovd uncovered and identified shared social and psychological categories of withdrawal that are common to ex-members.
Members shared similar experiences and perceptions that undermined belief maintenance and followed identifiable patterns of withdrawal. Skonovd's study laid important groundwork for testing some theoretical propositions regarding defection from new religious movements.

THE NATURE OF VOLUNTARY COMMITMENT

Bromley and Shupe refer to groups such as the Unification Church, the Hare Krishna and the Children of God as
"world-transforming movements." World-transforming movements
are essentially aimed at bringing "total, permanent, structural change of societies across all institutions" through
peaceful means (Bromley and Shupe, 1979:22). Though world-
transforming movements seek rapid and total change, they initially have only a small number of members. This has at
least two implications for mobilization and growth if these
groups are to achieve their goals. First, commitment must
be total because the movement organizations require maximum
effort and energy from the few members they claim in order
to realize the new social order. Second, recruitment must
be aggressive and vigorous in order to win new converts and
warn society of the impending transformation. Thus, these
groups must rely on rapid and effective tactics of recruitment, resocialization, and commitment-building. Because of
the expediency with which they envision their mission and the
limited control of resources they possess, they exhibit "a
low capacity to exercise selectivity in recruitment (and)
new members are subjected to intensive socialization in order to achieve the desired behavioral orientation" (Shupe
and Bromley, 1980:235).

Intensive socialization is accomplished in part through
certain organizational requisites that act as commitment-
building mechanisms. Daily schedules are structured so that
members will spend several hours a day in collective activities, rituals, teaching sessions, religious ceremonies, etc.

Communal living arrangements encourage unity with the group while discouraging individualistic actions and pursuits. Members are expected to minimize outside ties with families and friends in order to devote full time and energies to the movement. Members are often encouraged to donate their worldly possessions to the movement and to change behavior, dress and even their names. Unconventional marriage and family life-styles are practiced in order to secure primary emotional attachments. These organizational requisites are absolutely crucial to the success of world-transforming movements from both an organizational and social psychological standpoint. Kanter (1972) has shown that these requisites serve as commitment-building mechanisms that strengthen collective identity, cohesion, and social control. She has argued that intensive socialization procedures increase the survival ability of communal groups. Other research supports this contention. Zald and Ash (1966:332) have argued that movement organizations with easy conditions of membership are likely to fade away faster than ones with rigorous conditions. Similarly, Richardson, et al. (1979:332) stated that "groups which early develop rigorous resocialization procedures have shown more survival ability."

Commitment is a perpetual process that must be continually renewed, strengthened, and sustained. Individually, members must continue to make social and psychological investments in the group so that commitment will be perceived as meaningful and worthwhile. Collectively, world-transforming movements must continually implement processes that reduce the value of external ties and increase the value of attachment to the group. Commitment is sustained to the extend that these processes of giving up and getting augment attachment to, and dependence upon, the group. Commitment, therefore, is more than an initial decision, or conversion to a group or perspective, it is an ongoing process which is developed and strengthened through interaction, identification, and cooperation with other committed followers. The primary task of building commitment among members lies in leading them to a point at which personal identity and subjective reality comes to be seen as coextensive with the group. "Commitment," states Kanter (1972:499), "refers to the willingness of social actors to give their energy and loyalty to social systems, the attachment of personality systems to social relations which are seen as self-expressive." However, this process is always subject to interruption whereby prior socialization can be impaired and leaving becomes an alternative. Organizational requisites employed by world-transforming movements simply try to reduce the likelihood of interruptions occurring.

World-transforming movements must employ strong socialization mechanisms in order to prevent members from being
lost to the larger social world. These mechanisms are designed to produce a total commitment of members' time, energy, and loyalty. The preservation of high level commitment in this type of movement is both difficult and precarious. Members face the inherent paradox of attempting to
change the world at the same time they seek to protect themselves from its corrupting influence. The maintenance of
socialization mechanisms help to create more durable "plausibility structures" (Berger and Luckmann, 1966) that are less
likely to be penetrated and disrupted. But there are conditions under which the process of commitment-building and socialization can be impeded, interrupted, and weakened increasing the likelihood of defection. In this paper we shall
examine four factors which increase the probability of voluntary defection from world-transforming movements: (1) a
breakdown in members' insulation from the outside world, (2)
unregulated development of dyadic relationships within the
communal context, (3) perceived lack of success in achieving
world transformation and (4) inconsistencies between the actions of leaders and the ideals they symbolically represent.

Data for this study have been gathered from ninety
structured in-depth interviews. These are divided equally
among defectors (N=45) and a control sample of current members (N=45). The sample is further subdivided among the
three movements (Unification Church, Hare Kirshna, and Children of God) so that defectors and members from each are
equally represented. Interviews with defectors have been obtained by the use of a snowball sampling technique which involved the use of posters and newspaper ads in several major
university settings in the Northeast. Interviews with current members have been obtained with the permission of local
organizational authorities of each group.

Social Insulation

The less a world transforming movement insulates members
from the larger society, the greater the likelihood of defection. Insulation is important for all members of a movement
operating in a hostile environment which constantly challenges the movement's right to exist and the integrity of
each member. The changes that members will be confronted by
a constant flow of negative information or be placed in a
defenseless situation that might produce dissonance are reduced through social insulation (Skonovd, 1981:33). When insulating boundaries are disrupted, weakened or dissolved,
commitment is much more likely to be undermined by disconfirming evidence, and the likelihood of defection is thereby
increased.

The most important means through which insulation in a
world-transforming movement is disrupted is by prolonged
separation of a member from the group. When extended periods of separation are permitted, the effects of insulation
are more likely to be weakened and undermined. Data from
this study show that persons who were separated from a world
transforming movement for a prolonged period of time were
less likely to return to the group. Of the twelve persons
who reported separation and isolation from other members for
a period of three weeks or more, only four (33%) continued
as committed members; the remaining eight (67%) pointed to
the time spent apart from the movement as critical to their
decision to leave. Segregated from the ordinarily stable,
reality-supporting measures of the religious group, these
individuals found that increased time spent away from fellow
believers and the social milieu of the movement perpetuated
doubts and uncertainties about their future involvement.

The following case represents an example of how insulating boundaries can facilitate defection. Lisa, a former
member of the Children of God, attributed her decision to
leave the movement to an extended separation after she returned home from Europe for a visit with her family and her
husband Roger from whom she had separated the year before.
While on leave she stayed at her parent's home and purportedly had full intentions of returning to the movement. But
after two weeks, her parents took the liberty of confronting
her about her future plans and goals, and about her marriage
to Roger, and attempted to persuade her to stay by offering
her furniture. Lisa responded by accepting the furniture
and calling Roger in an attempt to reconcile their differences (Roger had defected and was opposed to the movement,
though not vehement) and try living together outside the
movement on a trial basis. During this period, Lisa reported struggling with her strong ties to the "family" and her
divided loyalties, but as time spent apart from the movement increased, the effects of socialization were eroded
and alternative plausibility structure adopted.

> I guess it was actually just the amount of time
> I spent away from them (Children of God), and
> seeing that I actually wanted to stay away and
> live my life with Roger doing our best on our
> own....It was nine months to a year before my
> definite decision to leave. It was so difficult.

There were many times I wanted to go back to
Europe, or find another colony here in the
States that would take me. Once I made the
decision, there was no more question about it
and I was happy with my decision.

When I first came home to visit after Roger
had already left, my parents asked me if I
wanted some furniture and confronted me with
what I was going to do. Out of the blue, I
just decided to go ahead and take it and I
called Peter and asked him to find a place for
us to live in Boston.

Interviewer: "So when did you make the firm decision to
leave?"

I made the decision to get a place with Roger
a few weeks after arriving back in the States
for a visit. But it wasn't until the following December that I made up my mind that things
were wrong with the Children and that I didn't
want to be part of them. There was nothing
specific that brought me to that conclusion, I
just began to see, and let myself see, things
clearer and from a different perspective. One
thing interesting is, the decision really had
to come from me, whenever Roger tried to push
his feelings on me it had a bad effect and made
me hold tighter to the past (Interview #7).

It could be argued that Lisa's defection was influenced
more by her loyalty to her husband than the absence of insulating boundaries. There can be no doubt that Lisa's
marital life to Roger was one factor in the decision-making
process. Yet Lisa suggested that her husband's efforts to
influence her decision had an adverse effect ("...when Roger
tried to push his feelings on me it had a bad effect and
made me hold tighter to the past.") Further, consideration
must be given to the fact that the Children of God discourage "...private marriage ties (that) interfere with Our Family and God ties..." and that "...they can be readily abandoned for the glory of God and the good of the Family!"
(Moses Berg, 1976:1367). Such teaching obviates against
private two-person intimacy and loyalty. Since Roger and
Lisa met and were married after they joined the Children of
God, it is certain that these teachings and principles
shaped their marital expectations. Emotional energies were
supposed to be directed toward the "larger Family," and
those married couples who demonstrated stronger loyalties
toward each other than toward the group ran the risk of be-

ing separated. As the teachings of Moses David made clear,
"...even if God has to break us these little private two-
somes in order to make up conscious of the greater unit of
the Family, He will do it!" (Moses David, 1976:1367).

        Lisa was a full time member of the Children of God for
four and a half years. Thus, it is not surprising that she
struggled with her decision to defect for almost a year after separation from the movement. The effects of Lisa's
socialization or commitment were forcefully demonstrated by
her choice to remain with the Children of God when her husband left. Her decision not to return came only after the
insulating boundaries were removed and a prolonged separation eroded the bonds of commitment.

Interpersonal Intimacy

        The less a world-transforming movement is effective in
regulating two-person intimacy, the greater the likelihood
of defection. One major source of defection arises when one
partner of a dyad wishes to leave the movement and attempts
to persuade the other to defect. Kanter (1972:86) has argued that "two-person intimacy poses a threat to group cohesiveness unless it is somehow controlled or regulated...
(Thus) an intense private two-person relationship, where
neither person is tied into the community in other strong
ways, is the sort of unit that can potentially withdraw from
involvement with the group." Exclusive two-person bonds
create rival interests and divert emotional energies from
the movement. When world transforming movements do not effectively control such dyadic attachments and redirect commitment to the larger group, they face an increased possibility of defection by couples. Marital and romantic relationships are the best illustration of this requisite. In
all of the groups examined here marriage is permitted, but
each group exercises strict controls over mate selection,
marital lifestyles, child rearing and family structure.

        The data showed that in every case where one spouse or
mate defected the other also left the movement. By contrast
none of the continuing members interviewed reported that
their spouse or mate had defected. However, the low incidence of this type of defection, only seven of forty-five
cases (16%), suggests that these movements have been reason-
ably successful in regulating potentially disruptive sexual
relations. This regulation is accomplished primarily by requiring endogamous marriage and deferring marriage until
members have demonstrated a sufficient period of loyalty to
the movement. For example, the Unification Church demands a
three year oath of celibacy before unmarried followers are
eligible to be "matched" by Reverend Moon.

The success of these movements in controlling dyadic
attachments is partly attributable to the fact that most individuals are single when they join. The movements thus
have an opportunity to prevent the development of disruptive
relationships and to control and legitimate the relationships which do develop. When married couples do join world
transforming movements, curtailing dyadic ties to increase
group commitment is a more difficult task. Of the six
couples who entered these movements already married, four
left. In the case of couples already married, a movement
must challenge established ties in order to gain comparable
self-sacrifice and group commitment. For example, interviews with Unification Church leaders revealed that persons
already married when they join are expected to separate and
adopt a celibate lifestyle for a minimum of seven months in
order to prove their faithfulness to the church. The low
retention rate of married couples reflects the strength of
pre-existing marital bonds.

Unmarried members who become emotionally attached and
form dyadic commitments do so without the knowledge or consent of the group and its leaders. Under conditions where
there exist insufficient constraints, ordinary interaction
may lead to exclusive attachments that simply go unnoticed
by other members. Though movement ideologies strictly for-
bid "private ties" that "interfere" with the goals and purposes of the movement, long hours of mixed gender association through fund-raising or recruitment activities may give
rise to unintended emotional involvement. Members who find
themselves in this situation face an agonizing dilemma.
Since dyadic arrangements are exclusively selected and regulated by the movement, the couple will most likely be asked
to separate. Thus, the persons involved must choose between
the group or the dyadic partner.

One such account of an emotional attachment leading to
a dyadic defection was given by a former member of the Unification Church. Sandy and her husband Paul met while fund-
raising in Texas. They were both members of a large musical
group sponsored by the movement. The band was required to
fund-raise when it was not performing and Sandy and Paul
were assigned to the same mobile fund-raising team. Paul
became the team leader, and Sandy was selected as his assistant. A short time later, they reportedly fell in love.
Sandy explained in detail the course of events leading up to
their exit from the movement.

> The biggest thing was the fact that I met a guy
> while I was fund-raising in Texas and he and I
> were fund-raising on the same team. He was the
> team captain and I was the assistant and we were

both members of the band...Anyway, we were sent
out to fund-raise for the band and we got to
know each other, and after a certain amount of
time we fell in love.

Interviewer: How much time?

Well, you know how it is. You become interested
in someone and it just develops over a period of
time. But I would say within a couple of months
we were pretty far gone, pretty deeply in love.
And that was very much frowned upon by the church,
it was actually forbidden. In the Unification
Church, you are not allowed to choose your own
mate. Now if you happen to be married before
· you go into the church, then you are separated
from your spouse for, well it depends on how
long, lots of times it is three or four years,
and, you know, you only see them occasionally.
Thats to prove your loyalty is to the church,
to Reverend Moon, and not to your spouse. Eventually, you know, they will allow you to get
back together through a special ceremony and so
on. If you are not married when you go into the
church, your mate will be chosen for you by Reverend Moon, if you are ever to get married. You
are not allowed to choose the person you want to
marry because, according to their beliefs, you
are not competent to make that decision; only
Reverend Moon is able to choose the perfect mate
for you. And once you are married, according to
their ceremonies and so on, you become a perfect
couple and produce perfect children. So, any-
time you started to become involved with a person, that was usually cut off as soon as anybody
found out about it.

We were in a unique situation in that we were out
fund-raising and he was the team leader and I was
the assistant. So, we had an opportunity to develop the relationship, whereas if it had taken
place in another situation it probably would have
been squelched before it had a chance to even
start. But by the time they really found out
about it and everything, we were already pretty
deeply in love, pretty emotionally involved. But
what happened was that, first, they started telling us, well, you have to go for a certain period
of time, like twenty one days without talking to
each other. But we never did that. Then, even-

tually, after about four or five months, someone else saw us walking down the street holding hands and reported us to the person that was my particular superior at the time. So they gave us a choice. They gave me a choice of either leaving the movement immediately there in New York without any money or any means to get anywhere, or to be sent to California to be with a group out there that was fund-raising and witnessing. So I chose to go out to California. They gave Paul the same choice, only they were going to send him to Ohio. So he fund-raised for the money for his bus ticket, and that was during the time when you could get a bus ticket anywhere in the U.S. for a certain amount of money; I believe it was like $52 or something at the time. So he went ahead and bought his bus ticket and he didn't stop in Ohio but he went ahead and went out to California and got me out of the movement too and we both left.

I believe that it would have been difficult for me to leave if it hadn't been for him because they tell you that if you leave the movement you are spiritually dead. And, you know, you might as well be dead. You can get so involved in it that its hard to imagine a life outside of the movement. So if it hadn't been for Paul and myself falling in love, I probably wouldn't have left.

...Another thing was that we had asked people in higher up positions if there was any possibility at all that we could ever get married. We were willing to be separated for two or three years, or whatever it took if we could get married, and they told us absolutely not, that there was no chance of it at all (Interview #17).

Sandy had joined the Unification Church in January of 1976 and was a full-time member for a year and four months prior to her departure. Paul had been a full-time member for two years. Before becoming emotionally involved, both persons fully intended to abide by the church's practice of an arranged marriage. However, their assignments as leaders to the same mobile fund-raising team forced them into a situation of having to work more closely together than ordinarily would be expected. It is quite common in the movement that team captains meet with their assistants in the evenings, after a day's fund-raising activities have been completed, in order to tabulate and record incoming funds and

discuss strategies for the following day. This routine mode
of interaction not only provided a vehicle for the development of a dyadic attachment, but it also served to camou-
flage the relationship in the eyes of other members. After
the dyadic attachment developed, over a period of several
months, commitment to the exclusive relationship began to
rival commitment to the movement, though neither person perceived it in this way. When told by the leadership to terminate their involvement, Paul and Sandy quietly and pri-
vately refused. When the issue was forced upon them, to
choose between the two commitments, the eventual outcome was
a dyadic defection.

The Imminence of Transformation

The less members of a world-transforming movement perceive
the regulation of their time, lifestyle, labor and sexual
conduct, the greater the likelihood of defection. Because
the new age or new world order is believed to be imminent,
urgency plays a crucial role in providing justification for
extreme sacrifices made by members. World transforming movements claim to be privileged agents of imminent and total
change. The special status of the movement as the agent of
the new order is an important and attractive feature to new
recruits. If over time these initially high expectations of
immediate and sweeping success are unfulfilled or if the
urgency of the groups mission is not effectively maintained
and redefined, members' willingness to make extreme personal
sacrifices may diminish.

      Among those individuals we interviewed eight left for
this reason. Defectors tended to voice complaints about the
lack of change they were effecting in society and about the
failure to see any promising signs that things were going to
change in the near future. Conversely, members rarely expressed complaints or frustrations about the "success" of
the movement.[1] Members tended to exaggerate their growth and
impact within society while offering countless interpretations of current events as "proof" of the forthcoming transformation. Indeed, none of the present members could be
singled out as voicing complaints about the progress or suc-
ess of the movement. Even occasional remarks by present
members that could be construed as expressions of disappoint-
ment were vigorously restated and defended as positive
statements by those who voiced them. "We have had more than
our share of problems in this country," one Hare Krishna devotee stated, "but even through bad publicity people are
still chanting the name of Krishna....When people just mention the name of Krishna there is spiritual advancement"
(Interview #63).

One such example involved a former devotee of the Hare
Krishna movement. Bernie was a full-time devotee for about
one year before leaving in 1977. His frustration grew out
of a daily routine of austerity in the absence of any visible signs of movement growth or progress. According to
Bernie, more persons actually left the movement than joined
indicating a dismal contradiction of prior claims to usher-
ing in the "Golden Age." Against the perceived backdrop of
stalled growth or stagnancy, Bernie described the dissipa-
tion of fervor and commitment preceding his departure from
the Hare Krishna movement.

> It was very tough to lead that type of life; I
> mean it was very austere being celibate, being
> a Brahmacari. I didn't like being celibate and
> I didn't feel that if you wanted to attain God-
> consciousness it was necessary to do all the
> things they asked; you know, to go to those ex-
> tremes.

Interviewer: Why not?

> Well, you know, I lived in the temple for a year
> and I followed the four regulative principles and
> I chanted sixteen rounds and I did sankraton and
> I did all those things. But you don't have to
> live in the temple to practice Krishna conscious-
> ness, you can do it on your own, at home. Krishna
> consciousness just means God-realized, being a
> servant of the Lord. Besides, there were some
> things I just didn't like about living in the
> temple. I felt that we should be preaching about
> Krishna more and spreading the philosophy. But
> there was so much emphasis on book distribution
> and getting donations from people anyway we could.
> We even had quotas...And I don't think most people
> ever read the literature anyway; they would give
> a donation just to get us off their backs....Also,
> not that many people ever came around or joined
> while I was there. Devotees would come in from
> other temples, but I only saw a few people join
> the whole time I lived there. I think more
> people left than joined.

Interviewer: How many left?

> Oh, I don't know, maybe six or seven. And that's
> not exactly the kind of thing you expect when you
> first become a devotee. Don't misunderstand me,
> I'm not putting it down. It takes a lot of dedica-

tion and self-discipline to be a devotee. But
I just couldn't see giving my whole life to
that. I guess I was just frustrated with the
way things were in the temple (Interview #47).

The comments made by this ex-devotee point to demorali-
zing conditions at the temple that reflect unrealized ideals
and goals. Bernie's discouragement was directly related to
such conditions and gave rise to the perception that extensive personal sacrifices were not warranted by commitment to
a stalled cause. The perceived stagnancy of the movement
described by Bernie parallels what Zald and Ash (1966:335)
have referred to as a "becalmed movement." A becalmed movement is one which has created or found a niche in society,
but its growth has slowed down or ceased. Goal attainment
is not expected in the near future, or as in the case of
world-transforming movements, the time-frame for completing
the agenda is vaguely defined and ambiguous enough so that
the prospective transformation appears within reach but is
never actually achieved. A becalmed movement is vulnerable
to a loss of emotional fervor among members and, therefore,
the leadership is faced with the problem of generating commitment incentives to curb apathy and discouragement.

Leadership

The less members perceive the leadership of a world-
transforming movement as "exemplary," the greater the likelihood of defection. Weber (1963:55) described the role of an
"exemplary" leader or prophet as one who directs others down
the same path of salvation he himself has traversed. Wilson
(1973:309) has argued that commitment "has meaning for the
individual only so long as his leader and those around him
seem to warrant that loyalty..." Commitment to a movement
characterized by charismatic leadership thus emerges out of
an investment of "trust" made by members. Most of the literature on charismatic leadership has focused on the individual personality or prowess of leaders. However, "the other
side of the charismatic relationship," Wilson (1973:204) has
stated, "is that the followers have complete personal trust
in the individual." Charismatic leadership must be recognized and validated by others who are willing to give up
previous commitments and realign loyalties to the leader or
leaders of the movement. Consequently, one problem all
world-transforming movements face is that followers need to
be convinced that movement leaders are legitimate embodiments
or representatives of moral truths and, therefore, worthy of
their sacrifice and dedication. If, however, invested loyalty or trust is betrayed through actions that are perceived
as morally inconsistent with espoused ideals or goals, the
likelihood of defection is increased.

Data from this study provide rather strong support for the importance of exemplary leadership. Thirteen defectors from the sample pointed to unexemplary leadership as their primary reason for leaving. These ex-members reported disillusioning experiences with leaders which they clearly interpreted as ethically inconsistent, hypocritical, or immoral. On the other hand, current members registered no such complaints of invalidating experiences with leaders. All of the present members interviewed affirmed the belief that their leaders were placed there by divine will, such arrangements being defined as legitimate and sacred.

Ethan, a former devotee of the Hare Krishna movement, recounted a dissonance-creating experience when the prophet-leader, A.C. Bhaktivedanta, responded to an organizational problem in an unanticipated way.

> Well, the movement changed in a lot of ways. The Hare Krishna movement today in 1981 and the Hare Krishna movement in 1971 are completely different. When I joined in 1971 it was very low-key, very loving, you know, the late sixties and the whole hippie-thing, it was very much a family type atmosphere. But that changed very drastically. About 1975, we started getting these letters from India saying there is going to be a change. Now the guru tells us that we have got to stress book distribution because if the person on the street gets a book, he is getting Krishna. He said, "Don't bother wasting time preaching on the street. My books are so potent that if they read one page their lives will be changed," because he is a pure devotee. We are such mudhas (asses), if we preach for half an hour it is useless. But if he speaks one sentence, it will go right to their hearts and change their lives. So we were told to get out and sell those books.

> Well, it wasn't too long after that that things started getting out of hand. Devotees were trying so hard to sell books they began using deception, transcendental trickery I mean, we got this absolute order from the guru, which is as good as having an order from God, to go out and sell books. But the only problem is people don't want them, and they certainly aren't going to pay for something they don't want. So what do you do? You get them to take a book anyway you can. Just get a book in their hands. They will help eradicate their ignorance and stop suffering. That will stop their sinful life and save them from

material illusion....But it got so deceptive that
anything went because the mission was so important.

Then finally, in 1976, we wrote a letter to
Prabhupada saying, "At the airport girls are
cheating. While in line they are stealing service-
men's wallets. All these things are being written
up in the newspapers." We sent one of the newspaper clippings to India thinking that the guru
was going to read this and straighten everything
out. He was going to see all this and put a stop
to it. Things had really gotten out of hand and
we just knew he was going to blow the whistle on
the whole thing.

Well, a letter came back from India and he says,
"This is very good, This man has said Krishna many
times in his article. Therefore, when people read
this article, they will have the name of Krishna
in their minds, and they will be purified. It does
not matter good or bad; all we are interested in is
having the name of Krishna implanted in people's
consciousness. As far as these techniques are concerned, its not important." And then he said, "The
end justifies the means."

I couldn't believe it. I mean, I almost fell over.
I remember thinking, this can't be. He can't say
this. How can he say this? He is supposed to be
a pure devotee; perfect, holy, and sinless, and he
is saying that lying and stealing is not wrong? I
just couldn't believe it. That just really burst
my balloon (Interview #41).

For Ethan, this experience proved to be critically un-
settling. His perception of Bhaktivedanta's integrity and
legitimacy as an exemplary leader was severely damaged creating unresolvable dissonance. The actions of his leader violated the nature of the charismatic relationship built on
trust. Trust includes a set of expectations that demand con-
sonance with such attributes as "holy," "perfect" and "sinless." When the authenticity of these imputed qualities was
seriously questioned, the bond of trust became strained and
weakened and the likelihood of defection was increased.

Research suggests that American converts to new religious movements have often been motivated by the moral ambiguity they witnessed among dominant cultural institutions
and values (Bellah, 1976; Doress and Porter, 1981; Judah,
1978; Robbins and Anthony, 1980). Therefore, it should not

be surprising that observed inconsistencies between espoused
ideals and actual practices by leaders of world-transforming
movements would produce among some members the same disillusionment that motivated them to initially reject mainstream
culture. Pavlos (1982:43) observes that "charismatic leaders have what psychologists label credibility, the perception by others that they possess expertise and trustworthi-
ness." But as in the case of Ethan, morally ambivalent behavior by movement leadership destroys the credibility of
the mission and robs the movement of its special moral status precisely because it demonstrates the same flaws one
finds in the corrupted social order outside the movement.
In religious language, one's spiritual calling as a member
of an elect group is demythologized and desacralized as the
all-too-worldly limitations of highly esteemed leaders are
revealed.

CONCLUSION

Implications of these findings address the issue of voluntary defection from the more highly controversial new religions: those that have been accused of brainwashing their
members, thus making deprogramming imperative. This study
specifies the conditions under which voluntary defection occurs. There is no intention here of either defending or attacking these groups or assessing the desirability of these
movements. But much of the popular literature is highly
sensationalistic and does not lend itself to sober and systematic treatment (see Conway and Siegalman, 1978; Edwards,
1979; Patrick and Dulack, 1976; Wood, 1979). Social science
has been slow to direct any research toward the subject of
defection from new religions and, therefore, has contributed
little to the understanding of how and why people leave.
This study is intended to help fill that vacuum and it is
hoped that future research will benefit from the groundwork
laid here.

NOTE

1. Of course, the objection may be raised that members are
   not being entirely honest with the interviewer. But I
   suggest another explanation. Members are provided with
   alternate interpretations of unfulfilled claims which are
   at least plausible enough to sustain their commitment.
   This amounts to the successful dissonance-management tactic of negotiating social reality. According to Prus
   (1976:127), dissonance is a "socially negotiable" phenomenon in social movements. Defectors reflect instances
   where the negotiation process is absent or inadequate.

'BRAINWASHING' AND 'DEPROGRAMMING' IN BRITAIN:
THE SOCIAL SOURCES OF ANTI-CULT SENTIMENT

James A. Beckford
University of Durham

It is clear from previous descriptions of the anti-cult movement (Patrick and Dulack, 1976; Robbins and Anthony, 1978; Shupe and Bromley, 1980) that this movement has been able to generate and mobilize large amounts of human energy and material resources in the attempt to stem what is considered by its activities to be a dangerous flood of young people into new religious cults. The perceived danger seems to have three principal aspects: cults allegedly brainwash their adherents; encourage young people to engage in nonproductive, and possibly immoral, forms of unpaid employment; and cults disrupt normal family life. It is not my intention here to suggest that these allegations have any reasonable foundation in fact. My aim is merely to catalogue them as a necessary preliminary to a sociological understanding of the vehemence of anti-cult feeling among some people directly affected by a cult's operations in Britain.

This article arises from research[1] which I have conducted into the response of close relatives of members and ex-members of the Unity Cult (UC)[2] in Britain to its activities (see Beckford, 1978, 1979). My general concern has been to understand what happens in nuclear families when a member either joins, or withdraws from the UC. It was hypothesized that difficulties in personal relations would be experienced by all family members and that the difficulties would result in part from the patterns of thinking, feeling and acting instilled in UC members. A further hypothesis was that difficulties would also arise in part from the way in which relatives are commonly disposed to account for recruitment, participation and withdrawal. What follows is largely an analysis of the patterns and consequences of relatives' accounting procedures. A brief description of the UC in Britain and of its organized opponents will precede the analysis.

In the face of the UC's active obstruction to my research project it was not possible to construct a reliable sampling frame of members and former members. Tape-recorded

interviews lasting several hours have, however, been conducted with 30 ex-members who had been contacted by means of
the "snowball" procedure (Polsky, 1967). The sample may
therefore contain a disproportionately large number of cases
of extreme reaction to the UC.

THE ANTI-CULT MOVEMENT IN BRITAIN

The UC, which originated in the Far East in the mid-
1950s, was brought to Britain in the late 1960s by an
American missionary. It has grown more slowly in numbers
and financial strength than in many Western democracies and
at present has about 600 members resident in about 15 communal centres. They spend most of their time either selling
the cult's literature and other goods to raise funds, or
witnessing to the public in the hope of recruiting new members. Their main beliefs are that a second Messiah is already on earth preparing to complete the task which Jesus
Christ failed to accomplish and that the benefits of millennial perfection are available to those who abide by the
spiritual principles enshrined in their founder/leader's
published works.

Britain has had two groups of organized critics of the
UC.[3] The People's Organized Workshop on Ersatz Religion
(POWER) was founded and administered apparently single-hand-
ed by a young man whose aims were once described as follows
(Heys, 1976:2):

> The cults must be totally destroyed; the govern-
> ment will not act, so people must take the law
> into their own hands. We must have hundreds, if
> not thousands of deprogrammers up and down the
> countryside.... Cult members should not be al-
> lowed to own property, drive cars, or vote.
> Cult members should be placed in a higher tax
> bracket for their non-productivity... Police
> should harass (sic) the cults into leaving the
> soils (sic) of Britain. Contingency plans should
> be drawn up by the armed forces to move into
> centres controlled by cults in cases where pub-
> lic disturbance is likely... The Vatican should
> lend a hand by training Jesuits as deprogrammers.

But this group's operations were shrouded by such secrecy
and mystery that it was impossible to know what its real objectives were, where its resources were drawn from, and who
its supporters were. It certainly attracted publicity, not
least for its notorious brochure "Deprogramming: The Con-

structive Destruction of Belief. A Manual of Technique"
(Power, n.d.). But POWER went into decline, if not inacti-
vity, after 1977. Very few opponents or critics of the UC
ever gave any support to its objectives, and it was publicly
criticised for its intemperance by leading members of the
other anti-UC group in Britain -- Family Action, Information
and Rescue (FAIR). POWER's brief and stormy contribution to
the anti-cult movement amounts to no more than an exotic pre-
lude.

By contrast, FAIR has attracted the sympathy and support
of many relatives of UC members and defectors. It was formally established by Mr. Paul Rose, M.P. in March 1976 at a
meeting in the Houses of Parliament. By this time there was
already an informal network of communication among a wide
variety of people concerned about the UC, and the elected
officers of FAIR were mainly drawn from this network. A
core-group of members has remained active in fund-raising,
publicity work and case-work in consultation with some of
the families affected by the cult. Mr. Rose delivered two
speeches (one on October 22, 1975 and the other on February
23, 1977) against the UC in the House of Commons where his
words were protected by parliamentary privilege from writs
for libel. He resigned from the chairmanship of FAIR in
1978 and subsequently declined to stand as a candidate in
the General Election to Parliament in 1979. At the time of
writing there is a joint chairmanship held by an Anglican
clergyman and a twin brother of a UC member.

It is difficult to assess the impact of FAIR on the UC's
fortunes in Britain. There have been a few cases in which
FAIR members have succeeded in either removing someone from
the cult or dissuading someone from joining. And it has allegedly been of assistance to many of my informants in providing guidance, reassurance and practical advice about methods of coping with the problems arising in families when a
member joins or leaves the UC. There have also been sugges-
tions that the cult has modified some of its more controversial policies and practices as a result of FAIR's campaigning. However, many people have been offended by the strident tone of its criticism and by its apparently implacable
opposition to every facet of the UC. And the cult loses no
opportunity to warn its members' relatives against involvement in what it sees as a Satanic, communist-inspired plot
to subvert the second Messiah's plans.

The response of governmental agencies to FAIR's campaign has been largely negative. The Under-Secretary of
State for the Home Office, in reply to Mr. Rose's impassion-
ed denunciation of the UC in a House of Commons debate on

23rd February 1977, affirmed the government's refusal to interfere with the activities of the UC's two registered charities unless it could be shown that a criminal offence had
been committed by them. Her reasoning was that:

> If these organizations keep within the law, it is
> a very serious matter indeed to suggest that the
> Government should take action against them none
> the less. My right Hon. Friend and I may as indi-
> viduals take the view that the doctrines advanced
> by the UC's founder-leader are lunatic. We may
> be particularly suspicious of the motives of peo-
> ple who, while claiming to benefit humanity, have
> substantially enriched themselves. But these are
> matters of opinion, and surely it is one of the
> principles of a free society that people may pro-
> pagate ideas which the majority of us do not share
> and do not like.

This argument follows very closely the line taken sixteen
months earlier by a different government spokesman in reply
to Mr. Rose's first speech against the UC. And it is tempt-
ing to speculate that the British government's reluctance
to act on the promptings of Mr. Rose might have been part of
a legacy from the late 1960s when a previous Labour government had acted in a heavy-handed fashion against the Scientology movement. For after the Minister of Health had undertaken to curb Scientology's growth by denying entry to
Britain to foreign nationals who wanted to follow courses at
its College in East Grinstead, an official enquiry concluded
in 1971 that "...most of the Government measures of July
1968 were not justified" (Foster, 1971:v).

There is an apparent paradox in the fact that FAIR, in
contrast to its American counterparts, has failed to secure
any official investigation of the UC. The main problem facing the American anti-cult movements, according to Shupe and
Bromley (1980) has been to achieve national integration and
organization. Yet, this was something that FAIR achieved
with relatively little difficulty in Britain. By contrast,
the American groups' continual agitation at state and federal levels has resulted in the conduct of several official
and judicial investigations of various cults. This is something that FAIR has been unable to achieve. The paradox
dissolves, however, when it is recognized that centraliza-
tion and national integration are no guarantee of success
for anti-cult groups. For it is relatively easy to establish nationwide organizations in a country which is much
smaller and more homogeneous in culture than the United
States, but this has no necessary implications for the suc-

cess of such organizations' campaigns.

A further point of contrast between Britain and the
United States lies in the different fields chosen for the
conflict between the cults and their opponents. Firstly,
since there is no provision in English law for the appointment of conservators over adults, it is simply not possible
for the conservatorship issue to arise in English courts.
Secondly, there have been no judicial or quasi-judicial en-
quiries into the activities of religious cults in Britain
since the Foster Report (1971) was written on Scientology
between 1969 and 1971. FAIR has certainly tried to have the
UC's tax exempt status revoked, but the Charity Commissioners
could only take such a step if the cult's activities could
be shown to be no longer charitable in law. Thirdly, the UC
has taken advantage of the relatively generous provisions in
English law for plaintiffs to seek redress in law for the
publications of allegedly libelous statements about themselves. American law does not offer equally generous faci-
lities for cults to suppress or to penalize adverse comment.

These differences between the position of anti-cultists
in Britain and the United States must be taken into account
when considering the place of deprogramming in the former.
The legal, political and social institutions are quite different from their American counterparts, and the differences
help to explain the differential trajectories of the anti-
cult movements in the two countries. This will be illus-
trated by means of two case-studies of attempted deprogramming in Britain.

It must be emphasized that the number of deprogrammings
in Britain has been very small and that the issue of deprogramming, as it has occurred in the United States, has really not entered the arena of public debate. Consequently,
anti-cult sentiment and agitation have been relatively mild
and, by comparison with the United States, less polarized in
terms of attitudes towards the highly divisive issues of
brainwashing and deprogramming. The comparatively lower salience of extreme opinions in Britain permits a clearer view
of the subtle, yet intensive, processes whereby people
standing in various relations to cults have tried to come to
terms with them. In some respects this represents a considerable advantage over the position in which most American
commentators find themselves, for they have become so preoc-
cupied with trying to understand the more violent and spec-
tacular aspects of cultism and anti-cultism that the very
real, painful experiences of individuals involved in the
matter have often been overlooked. The narrower focus of
this paper on two cases in detail has been selected in order

to permit a view of anti-cult sentiment in the manner in
which it was actually experienced. From my point of view,
many of the diatribes against anti-cultism in the United
States are simply red herrings which attract attention away
from more immediate and real difficulties arising from the
conflict and tension generated between cult and society in
Britain.

Two things should be made absolutely plain: (1) not all
members of the UC feel the need to withdraw, and (2) most
defectors are able to leave of their own accord. But both
cases analysed below help to highlight in clear terms some
aspects of what is undoubtedly a common pattern of reaction
among those parents and other relatives of UC members who
are worried about the cult's activities and its effects on
its members. It should not be overlooked, however, that
there are relatives who support the cult and encourage participation in it.

Case 1

The first case concerns Martin, a twenty-five year old
British university graduate who was recruited in 1975 to the
UC while in California. He remained with the cult in California for ten months against the wishes and advice of his
family, eventually returning to visit his dying father. He
was detained at home for a week while two deprogrammers im-
ported from the United States tried to talk him out of the
UC, but he found his way back to its headquarters in London
and is still a member.

The first remarkable feature of this case is that it
concerns someone recruited abroad into a movement which was
totally unknown to his relatives. The extreme difficulty of
communicating with him and what was seen for a long time as
his apparent disregard for his father's ill health were both
considered by his family to have been out of keeping with
his character. In short, his relatives tried to reason out
what had happened to Martin against a background of ignorance and puzzlement. In the United States, by contrast,
there was far greater public awareness of the UC's presence
even in 1975 and a consequently lower level of ignorance
about its activities. This is not to deny, however, that the
American public necessarily had a correct understanding of
this movement.

Nevertheless, his relatives were able to construct a
coherent and plausible account of Martin's recruitment and
resistance to deprogramming when interviewed by me. Their
account showed that they had picked up sufficient clues from

his letters, telephone conversations and eventual conduct in
England to be able to "explain" what had happened. The
structure of their account is typical of relatives' reactions
to the growing awareness that a member of their family has
joined a deviant religious movement, and it is therefore
worthy of close analysis.

Firstly, their ex post facto account is inclusive of all
Martin's actions from the time of his initial contact with
the UC to the time of the interview. It omits nothing in its
drive towards a completely plausible reconstruction of events
and states of mind apparently recollected nearly eighteen
months later. Thus, they said that he was only rarely available in California to speak on the telephone and that when he
did speak:

> ...it wasn't Martin. There was somebody with him
> and you knew there was somebody with him... We
> did notice his letters were getting a bit obscure,
> you know... He sounded sort of delirious way-out
> (Brother and sister-in-law).

So Martin's father thought he had nothing else
to do but write a letter to him saying "Come
home." Of course, when it didn't have any effect,
his father got worried... Nobody knew how to
handle the situation... Do you know, he couldn't
tell us which flight he was coming on, what aero-
plane he was on, he didn't know anything (Sister-
in-law).

A second typical feature of the account is that it turns
around the conviction that "something must have happened" to
Martin and that there was a strong contrast between the before-and-after states of his person:

> We took him to a pub deliberately, you know...
> He said it was a den of iniquity. He didn't
> like it... But you couldn't get him away from
> drink once. I said, "Oh, come on, you used to
> love it." But he thought it was dreadful
> (Sister-in-law).

Actually, his mother has got all the letters from
Martin when he left home right until the present...
You can see the change in letters... He was a
different boy completely (Brother and sister-in-
law).

Martin gets the salt, the holy salt, and puts
salt round his meal and all these kinds of things.
I mean, Martin -- the old Martin -- he'd have
laughed at all this, wouldn't he?... He would
have said, "You're crazy"... Yes, "Crackers." He
would have had a great laugh (Brother and sister-
in-law).

A third typical feature of this account is that the discrepancies with Martin's previous character and the perceived
incongruity of his actions after joining the UC are presented
as cumulative reasons for adopting strong measures to deprogram him. Thus:

We could see him filling the visa application form
in, and he couldn't think; he could hardly write...
He filled quite a few things in wrong. I said "God,
look at that"...he absolutely couldn't think for
himself (Brother).

Although we realized he was brainwashed we didn't
realize the full implications of this. At least
we thought he was brainwashed. We didn't realize
how much he was brainwashed, and actually the more
we went through the deprogramming , the more we
realized that it should be done (Brother).

In at least three ways, then, this account is typical
of the way in which many relatives talk about people who
have joined the UC. A vague notion of "brainwashing" is
usually central to the "vocabulary of motives" (Mills, 1940)
employed, but, as I shall show later, such accounts can be
understood to serve more purposes than vaguely explaining
inexplicable phenomena. Nor should talk of "brainwashing"
be understood as a purely irrational or hysterical reaction;
for it is clearly woven into a complicated but rational account of events. The notion may be vague, but it certainly
helped the speakers to make sense of puzzling phenomena and
it was used with considerable consistency. Some features of
the second case for analysis will make this point clearer.

Case 2

Marilyn, a nineteen year old trainee nurse, was contacted in the street by a UC member on the first day of her
hospital training in a city about 80 miles from her parents'
home. She attended a meeting that evening and was soon a
regular participant in the local group's activities. Eventually she moved into the residential centre and gave notice
of her resignation from her training course. She was, to

all intents and purposes, a member of the UC for two months
in the Spring of 1974 and was removed from it against her
wishes by her parents.

My general comments on Case 1 are equally applicable to
this case, but there are some additional features which deserve special attention. First of all, the affiliation process took place in Britain and her parents met several other
UC members when they visited the group shortly after Marilyn
had joined it. In her father's words:

> They were very hospitable and most friendly...
> It was all a sort of evangelical atmosphere
> which struck me as very non-real, unreal, highly
> idealistic; but they all seemed very happy...
> Well, they seemed awfully nice and so back we
> went and I was a bit -- well, it seemed eerie
> to me -- and, you know, uncanny the whole thing.
> I didn't like the atmosphere, but our daughter
> was terribly happy, deliriously happy with them,
> so that was that.

In other words, Marilyn's father had initially picked up no
clues which would have helped to classify the UC as an object of suspicion.

But when Marilyn telephoned home two days later with
the news that she had agreed to spend a large inheritance on
buying a house for the UC, her parents were sufficiently
disturbed to try to dissuade the trustees of the inheritance
from releasing the money. Their disquiet increased sharply
when the group's leader, in a telephone conversation with
Marilyn's father, revealed that arrangements for the house
purchase had already been well advanced when the parents had
visited the group, although no mention had been made of it.
The leader's response to his accusation of deceitfulness was,
according to Marilyn's father, that:

> ...they were completely unrepentant; there was no
> word of apology or embarrassment, nothing of the
> sort. They insisted that Marilyn was of age, she
> was nineteen. Marilyn can do with her money what
> she likes and that we must not be in her way; it's
> got nothing to do with us; if Marilyn wants to
> give them money, she can give them the money.

> They were extremely impudent over the phone, and
> from that time onwards Marilyn completely broke
> with us, didn't know us any more. We rushed up
> to Angleton several times. She looked through us

like a piece of glass, rigid. Nothing; she wanted
to have nothing to do with us... She was obviously
not herself.

The dispute over the inheritance made Marilyn's parents
suspicious of the UC, and the apparently sudden and unexpected change in her attitude towards them was taken as further
evidence that she must have been involved in something un-
pleasant. The contrast between before-and-after in this
case relates both to Marilyn's own character and to her parents' opinions of the UC. Again, as in the case of Martin,
the account is constructed in a cumulative manner with indications of ever increasing disquiet at the growing sense of
before-and-after contrasts.

This case differs from the case of Martin however, as a
result of Marilyn's father's dogged pursuit of information
about the UC and about his legal rights. Through a series
of contacts initiated by his Member of Parliament he finally
got in touch with a young man who had lived for a short time
with the UC and who could pass on some information about it.
What Marilyn's father heard about the cult merely confirmed
all his worst suspicions, and he tried to convey his views
to his daughter. By this time he had deliberately sought
information from the police, a lawyer, a Member of Parliament, a University chaplain, and a former associate of the
UC.

But what finally galvanized him into action to remove
Marilyn from the UC was the advice given by her nursing Tutor. She had telephoned to say that Marilyn had resigned
from her training course in order to join the cult full-
time. Her father's raction was that:

> It was obvious to me there was something very
> wrong, and the Tutor said "Well, I tell you in
> confidence she's out of her mind; she is dis-
> turbed, mentally disturbed, and if I were you
> I would take her away. She's on duty tonight
> till 9 o'clock."

The parents immediately dashed to the hospital and invited
Marilyn to join them for supper. Once she was in the car,
her father drove home non-stop despite Marilyn's protests.
She was kept at home under constant watch for several days
and forbidden to use the telephone. Her father's description of her physical condition supplies further insight into
his process of reasoning about what must have happened to
her:

...she cried for three hours and she was most distressed. She looked like a ghost, an absolute
ghost. She had a rash all over her face; she had
a running ear. She was unrecognizable, physically
and mentally unrecognizable.

After three days of isolation from contacts outside the
parental home Marilyn eventually broke down under the pressure of arguments about the UC's allegedly unwholesome poli-
tical-cum-commercial activities. In her mother's words she
blurted out, "All you say is right, it all fits. How did
you find out? How did you discover? It's true what you
say." She took about three weeks to recover emotional stability and to feel confident enough to face the world and
begin re-making her nursing career. It should be added that
in her own account of her involuntary departure from the UC
Marilyn explicitly denied that she would have withdrawn from
it if her parents and her nursing Tutor had not put strong
pressure on her. In fact, she claimed that she would probably still be a member if she had not been forcibly removed
from the UC.

Marilyn's parents both professed an utter horror of
American-style deprogramming, but they were also adamant
that they had been entirely justified in removing their
daughter against her wishes from the UC. As in Case 1 the
justification for extreme action was dependent on the charge
that Marilyn had been brainwashed. Their accounts of her
recruitment and withdrawal were therefore coherent and plausible if it could be accepted that control of her mind had
been misappropriated. Their accounts stress that at every
turn in their deliberate investigation of the UC they sought
evidence to confirm their charges.

THE RHETORIC OF BRAINWASHING

One of the interesting features of both these cases is
that the relatives' accounts of what happened display a logic of congruence between, on the one hand, their allegations
of brainwashing, and on the other hand, their implicit justifications for attempting to remove Martin and Marilyn from
the UC. The brainwashing rhetoric provides for the deprogramming rhetoric. How does this logic work?

First, it should be noticed that talk about brainwashing was used to present an image of the UC member as the
kind of person who might either fall voluntarily for this
type of religious cult or fall victim to its sophisticated
techniques of recruitment. For example, Martin's brother

was insistent that Martin "was searching for something" in
his late teenage and that "he got worse when he went to University." In fact there was even a sense of guilt in his
sister-in-law's suggestion that they had not taken Martin's
questioning seriously enough and had "let him down." This
kind of account turns the UC recruit into a victim of various
circumstances: personal, familial and religious. Similarly,
Marilyn's parents' accounts of her recruitment provide for
her convertibility in terms of a traumatic experience in
childhood, the difficulty in reconciling herself to being
Jewish, her quest for religious understanding and her search
for warm companionship. According to her father:

> She was a little -- not a misfit -- no certainly
> not. I shouldn't say a misfit, but she didn't
> know herself. She hadn't found herself. She
> didn't know what she was all about. She was
> searching... She was very isolated... She was
> not one of those popular girls because again
> she was a very tense youngster, always tense...
> She would have been a complete pushover, let me
> put it that way, for the UC.

The brainwashing image calls for a distinctive vocabulary of motives -- or, more accurately in these two cases,
non-motives. For the charge of brainwashing serves to de-
pict the recruit as a victim of prior circumstances, a person more acted upon that acting. This explains the apparently inexplicable in terms of the conditions which made it
possible for it to happen in the way that it allegedly did.

Secondly, the relatives' accounts present a strong contrast in both cases between the UC converts' personality before and after recruitment, and they make it clear that adverse circumstances had conspired to dispose the recruits
towards joining a group like the UC. Brainwashing is allegedly the device which explains why they joined this particular cult, and it is used as an excuse for actions which
the relatives initially found it difficult to excuse (e.g.,
indifference or hostility towards their close relatives).
The evidence of radical personality changes, incongruous affect or defective cognition may be scattered throughout relatives' accounts, but the cumulative effect is to support
the argument that the recruits could no longer be held responsible for their actions. "Guilty but insane" is their
implicit verdict. Thus, in the words of Martin's sister-in-
law:

> You know, he is brainwashed, no matter what you
> think and how he is at the moment. Sometimes I
> think I could hit him right in the face. Then

> I think "No, he's brainwashed and it's not
> Martin."

And Marilyn's father was equally insistent:

> I realized very quickly that she was brain-
> washed... She had this sort of glazed look...
> I realized that she was not with us... She
> was no more my Marilyn, she was quite a dif-
> ferent person.

Thirdly, there seemed to be no doubt in my informants'
minds in both cases that a fundamental change had been "engineered" in the UC members' personality and identity. Since
the members were no longer considered to be "themselves,"
their close relatives felt justified in taking extreme measures to override their express wishes. Not unexpectedly,
relatives' accounts were replete with self-justifying phrases and arguments which could be heard to absolve them from
the guilt of having committed what many people would consider a major infraction of the UC recruit's personal rights.
No doubt the unavoidably inquisitorial setting of a tape-
recorded interview elicits such defensive ploys, but for
present purposes the interesting thing is that the self-
justificatory themes are so skillfully woven into the relatives' accounts. Self-justification is not a separate item
in their speech: it is part of the very materials with which
their accounts are constructed. And it is made to connect
logically and smoothly with the brainwashing image.

Finally, my informants' accounts contain implicit reasoning about the UC's objectives and practices. They imply
that the UC must be the kind of organization which would try,
or need, to brainwash its recruits and turn them against
their families. The logic of their accounts is that the
"immorality" of the cult must be matched by morally questionable counter-measures: in their eyes it is a question of
adopting the lesser of two evils even if this entails overriding the rights of their close relatives and denying their
dignity as human beings. This explains why Martin's brother
and sister-in-law actually experienced a sense of relief
when arrangements for the deprogramming had been finalized:
"We thought at least we're doing something; we felt so terrible all the months we never did anything; we thought
'great'." And it explains why Marilyn's father was adamant
that he had acted correctly in the circumstances and that he
would act no differently if the situation ever recurred.
Again, the image of brainwashing is crucial to the accounts'
coherence, but in this instance it can be heard as a means
of accusing the UC or morally indefensible tactics. It is

charged with emotion and moral indignation. This usage follows logically from the common practice among relatives of
presenting the UC as the kind of organization which would
engage in brainwashing.

I am not suggesting that relatives learn to produce
these features on purpose, nor is there evidence that the
accounts have been rehearsed to achieve a certain effect.
Rather, my hypothesis is that relatives may have a vague
conception of what "brainwashing" involves and that their
speech is clearly conditioned by a distinct "vocabulary of
motives" (Mills, 1940) associated with it. They may not be
able to articulate this conception at all clearly, but this
does not prevent them from using it in a practical sense to
produce a coherent account of what in their opinion seems to
have happened in the recruitment process.

The brainwashing image or metaphor can be used as an
effective social weapon, as Robbins et al., have shown elsewhere in this volume, and it has figured prominently in the
hysterical mass-media presentations of the hostile public
reaction to some new religious movements (Robbins and
Anthony, 1978). What this chapter has tried to show is that,
in a far less dramatic way, if the brainwashing image is
used as the crux of accounts of recruitment to the UC, it
enables speakers to achieve a number of important objectives.
They can plausibly be heard to explain, excuse, justify and
accuse. And, in so doing, they can go some way towards re-
pairing what form them is an unacceptable breakdown in normal social order.

The logical congruence that I have detected in the procedures whereby relatives typically account for a UC member's
affiliation to the cult and of their attempts to remove him
or her from it must be situated in their social context. In
other words I would now like briefly to investigate the social conditions which can dispose relatives towards constructing the kind of account which links accusations of
brainwashing to justifications for deprogramming.

First and foremost, in all the accounts that I have
collected is the fact that relatives typically had no real
idea of the kind of movement with which they were dealing.
They had no personal experience of, or knowledge about, the
UC -- or indeed about any comparable cult -- and all their
attempts to improve their knowledge were to no avail. The
point should not be overlooked that many parents searched
frantically for any scrap of information that might have
told them something about the cult in question. Their hostile response to it arose more from fear of the unknown than

from prejudice against a deviant minority movement.

A second factor was that the UC member was usually felt to be concealing from relatives the real nature of the cult by refusing to answer questions about it. Inquiries about its teachings, practices, history, personnel, etc. were met with either silence or incomprehensible statements of faith and conviction. In fact, those members who did write letters to their relatives were often so enthusiastic in their attempts to convey their sense of total submission to an alien system of beliefs that relatives' anxieties were only heightened. This placed both the member and the relatives in a double-bind. The more the member enthused about the UC, the more hostile was the response; the less that was revealed about the cult, the more intense was the relatives' anxiety. And on the other side, the deeper the relatives probed into the member's actions, the more evasive and defensive was the response; the less the relatives showed interest in the cult, the more worried they became that the member would interpret this as tacit approval. I want to emphasize that these double-binds were experienced as very real dilemmas to which the actors could see no easy and mutually acceptable solution.

A third factor which weighed heavily with many relatives was the difficulty encountered in trying to arrange a meeting with new recruits outside the confines of UC premises, and in some cases even inside such premises. To perplexed and anxious relatives the apparent refusal to discuss affiliation to the cult represented a clear-cut sign either that the recruit was being held against his or her will or that the recruit had something to hide. Naturally, the UC viewed this situation very differently, and it is a measure of the very real dilemmas and deadlocks generated by the clash of interests between the cult and some of its members' relatives that acceptable solutions were rarely produced. Recourse to charges of brainwashing must be located in the context of the rage and frustration experienced on all sides as a result of the many impasses into which relationships commonly slid.

A fourth condition of widespread anxiety among relatives was the suddenness and apparently irrevocable nature of the recruits' commitment to the UC. Even in cases where the decision to affiliate was taken after gradual intensification of interest over a long period of time, relatives were often disturbed by the apparent lack of any provision for a probationary period of a chance to reconsider the decision in circumstances free from the cult's influence. Many relatives reported that they had found it impossible to

accept that a member had committed himself or herself so totally, so suddenly and so irrevocably to a religious movement which remained so mysterious and impenetrable to outsiders. It was almost as if they found the idea of total,
irreversible commitment to a religious ideal obscene.

Let me make it clear that I am not suggesting these
four conditions or factors amount to a justification for the
charges of brainwashing commonly levelled against the UC.
But what I do want to emphasize is that, given these typical
conditions within which relatives of UC recruits had to reason about the recruitment, it is not difficult to understand
their recourse to such a powerful, catch-all, but empirically elusive metaphor as "brainwashing." And let me also
add that the policy of the UC towards the frightened and aggressive relatives of its members is also understandable in
part in view of its single-minded orientation towards the
realization of what it considers to be absolute values. No
concessions to human weakness and mundane attachments are
permissible, and no chinks must be left in the armour protecting the cult against satanic attacks.

CONCLUSIONS

What I have tried to show is that recourse to the
brainwashing metaphor and its associated rhetorical appara-
tus is far from being an irrational response on the part of
people who are confronted with the problem of coming to
terms with the fact that a close relative has joined the UC.
On the contrary, the metaphor can be used to good effect in
a number of different ways and is thus instrumentally rational to some degree. Moreover, it must be added that my
informants did not use the metaphor lightly or without what
they considered to be good cause. Its use should also be
firmly situated in a context of extreme bewilderment, fear
for the "victim" and concern for the restoration of "normal-
ity" in family relationships. And, since both cases pre-
ceded the formation of any concerted anti-cultism in Britain, it would be wrong to attribute the use of "brainwashing" to the influence of a social movement for the suppression of deviant religions. Indeed, what the cases reported
above bring to light is the very real, painful and, in many
respects, desperate, plight of people facing the apparently
sudden and total transformation of their formerly easy-going
and warm relationship with a close relative into a relationship marked by secrecy, fear, mutual incomprehension and indifference. No amount of rationalization of events in terms
of a reactionary, prejudiced, law-and-order backlash against
religious deviations should be allowed to obscure the very

real pain and anxiety experienced by those directly affected
by the recruitment of young adults in some cults.

NOTES

1. The research was funded by the Social Science Research
    Council, and I am grateful for its generous financial
    assistance.

2. In order to preserve anonymity, all proper names have
    been altered.

3. In addition, a number of evangelical Christian groups
    have also published anti-cult literature and sponsored
    conferences on the general theme of the dangers of
    cultism.

THE ROLE OF ANECDOTAL ATROCITIES IN
THE SOCIAL CONSTRUCTION OF EVIL

David G. Bromley
Anson D. Shupe, Jr.
J.C. Ventimiglia
The University of Texas at Arlington

There are times in the histories of societies when the
entire society or a subgroup of it feels threatened by an
impending evil which usually is perceived as the product of
the actions of some individual or group. These feelings may
be generated by a variety of conditions such as a series of
rapacious crimes, bellicose relations with traditional enemies, signs of unrest among oppressed minorities, or sub-
cultural lifestyle patterns which clash with those of the
dominant social strata. In some cases there may be a perception of threat to a basic cultural value which is widely
shared and deeply felt, as when there have been a series of
brutal rapes or murders. When the violation is of a commonly cherished value, merely calling attention to the infraction will suffice to evoke moral indignation and yield support for the imposition of punitive sanctions. If the norm
has legal standing, a formal labeling process is readily
available by which the individual can be discredited and his
status degraded. This process has been aptly described by
Garfinkel (1956). Legitimation of reactions to deviance in
this situation is seldom at issue.

If, by contrast, the less consensual interests of a
group are threatened, that group is likely to attempt to
vest its interests and activities with the mantle of legitimacy by contending that its rights and privileges flow from
and support some basic cultural value, hence those interests
deserve or require protection. In this situation, legitimation of extreme measures against some deviant group is con-
testable. An argumentative process between the threatened
group and the alleged violators of its interests then ensues. What occurs in this subsequent war of accusations is
a struggle for the construction of social reality. What we
shall refer to as "atrocity stories" constitute a major weapon in such struggles. Each side attempts to construct definitions of its own and its opponents' motives that serve
to legitimate and gain acceptance for its own activities and
discredit those of the other side. In concrete terms this
means that to the extent that new religious movements (and

their civil libertarian sympathizers) are successful in pro-
mulgating its definition of the situation, severe legal
sanctions could be brought against deprogrammers and even
parents. Conversely, if the "deprogramming movement" is
successful, deprogramming will at least be tolerated, conservatorships will be granted, and a variety of other legal
pressures will be brought to bear on the new religions.

An atrocity may be defined as an event which is viewed
as a flagrant violation of a fundamental cultural value.
Accordingly, an atrocity tale is a presentation of that
event (real or imaginary) in such a way as to (1) evoke moral outrage by specifying and detailing the value violations,
(2) authorize, implicitly or explicitly, punitive sanctions,
and (3) mobilize control efforts against the alleged perpetrators. A pure case of an atrocity story should contain
each of these three elements. However, since the "deprogramming movement" has (until recently) been a relatively
uncoordinated effort, and the telling of atrocity tales is
filtered through journalists who may or may not accept or
alter the presentations, individual atrocity tales are presumed only to approximate the pure type.

The intent of such tales is not to present the complex-
ity of events dispassionately but rather, as Garfinkel
(1956) noted, to make the event and individual stand out
from the ordinary. Each contestant in this struggle to define reality will portray events as it sees them or as it
wishes others to see them. Whether such stories represent
some kernal of "truth" is not only difficult to validate in
many cases but is also of minor importance in understanding
their construction. The stories gain their persuasiveness
and motivating power from their larger-than-life quality.

In the case of new religious movements the labeling
problem faced by their critics in applying labels is that
the church membership in new religions is composed largely
of the young adult offspring of parents who are leading and
supporting the "deprogramming movement." To argue that new
religions are evil, therefore, is to cast aspersion upon
those "children" one hopes to save and, indirectly, upon the
parents who raised them. One way of resolving this dilemma
is to label the organizations, rather than its members, as
evil, and to treat individual members as victims. A recent
study (Shupe, Spielmann and Stigall, 1977a:951) outlined
four progressive steps in this labeling process: The implicit reasoning involved in denying cult believers' belief
legitimacy seems to reduce to the following: (1) my (son,
daughter, family member) has embraced a "strange" religion;
(2) only inherently "strange" people would be voluntarily

attracted to such a religion; (3) my (son, daughter, family
member) is obviously not an inherently "strange" person; (4)
hence, he or she must have been hoodwinked or brainwashed
into participating. This is the logic of what Toch (1965:
226) called "the seduction premise." Atrocity tales function as a prerequisite step in such a labeling process by
providing dramatic "evidence" that new religious groups are
indeed "evil." In this way, individual members are absolved
of responsibility for their "bizarre" actions while under
the "control" of a "cult." Upon their "return" to conventional society they may resume their "normal identities,"
and parents are relieved of any feelings of guilt for "kidnapping" children or for inadvertently predisposing the latter to take up "strange" beliefs.

Finally, when deprogramming is undertaken, the process
creates its own justification. If it is successful, the individual leaves the "cult" and usually issues a public
statement of renunciation. This has the effect of confirming that the former member indeed had been brainwashed and
was unable to break the "cult's" hold on him independently.
However, if deprogramming is not successful, the brainwashing premise is also confirmed. The individual is seen as so
strongly possessed by the evil that even the best efforts of
the deprogrammers and confrontation with the "trust" cannot
break its grip. This outcome only serves to further validate the atrocity stories and to authorize more drastic action against the "cults."

METHODS

In this study, a sample of atrocity tales told by opponents of cults about the Unification Church will be analyzed
in order to describe how atrocities are presented so as to
discredit the target group and marshal opposition to it.
There are, of course, atrocity stories told by the opponents
of deprogramming as well (ACLU, 1976). Although these are
not included in the present study, a preliminary analysis
indicates they are quite similar in all important respects
to those examined here. Our sample of contextual units
(newspaper articles) in which the search for atrocity tales
occurred consisted of 188 newspaper articles published
throughout the United States. While the sample was not random, an examination of the newspapers' regional distribution
showed fair representativeness following expected differences among clustered populations.

The content analysis generally followed the guidelines
suggested by Holsti (1969) and particularly resembled
White's (1951) analysis of values. Conceptually, the format

of Lasswell et al. (1952) underlay the procedure: "Who says
what, to whom, how, and with what effect?" In this case
"what" is the atrocity tale as defined earlier, "to whom"
refers to the journalist's readership, "how" was not recorded in our analysis though the format is obvious, "when" is
the year of publication, and the "effect" is explored in our
discussion. The variables were the alleger, subdivided into
six categories; the atrocity tale, also subdivided into six
categories of violated cultural values; and the year of publication (1974-1977). The perpetrator was always assumed to
be Reverend Sun Myung Moon or officials of the Unification
Church. Whether the victim was an individual or a social
system was not relevant for our purposes.

     The six coding categories of violated values were: the
physical (nutritional, rest, comfort, safety, locomotion),
the psychological (independence-autonomy, achievement-recog-
nition, cognitive stimulation, ego security), the economic
(members' property ownership, fair exchange with non-members), the associative (family loyalty, heterosexuality,
other relational freedom, veracity with non-members), the
political-legal (patriotism, fair play, observance of law),
and the general cultural. Each specification served as an
empirical indicator of its respective value.

     Only one occurrence of a specific value-typical atrocity
was coded for each relevant article no matter how many times
the article may have repeated the same atrocity. This
placed an upper-limit of six atrocities on each article.
Acting as coders, the three authors observed 709 coded atrocities (though the actual number, considering repetitions
within articles, far exceeded that number), noting the presence or absence of a specific indicator. In the interest of
simplicity, atrocities were unweighted by frequency or by
intensity. Almost all the articles contained alleged atrocities, and the average article contained at least three.
The coding system satisfied the criteria of exclusivity (no
two categories overlapped), exhaustiveness (no tale fell
outside the category scheme), parallelism (all categories
were abstract nouns), unidimensionality (all referred to
values), independence (no atrocity tale could be twice cate-
gorized), and standardization. Close collaboration at all
points of the content analysis was maintained to ensure
high reliability.

FINDINGS AND DISCUSSION

Value Violations

Examination of the frequency and type of atrocities in the newspaper articles by year (1974-1977) revealed no discernable patterns. "Bad press" for the Unification Church had, by those middle years of the decade, perhaps hit a plateau.

Analysis of the identity of the 239 individual allegers recounting value violations revealed that over forty percent were former Unification Church members. Parents and experts (religious leaders, legal officials, psychiatrists, and political leaders) each accounted for approximately twenty percent, while the remainder of the allegers were journalists.

While our coding scheme discriminated among violations of six distinct values, we nevertheless noted a commonality or core dimension underlying all the atrocities: <u>loss of individual freedom</u>. Specifically, this freedom refers to personal choice, not only choice among belief systems and/or styles of worship, but also choice as to the manner in which an individual integrates his or her religious affairs into the broader mosaic of a lifestyle. Violations, however they imposed extrapersonal constraints on otherwise freely determined choices in these three aspects, thus strike at an extremely basic premise of religion in American culture.

For this reason, the most frequently reported atrocity fell under the category of <u>violation of personal freedom and autonomy</u>. No matter how many atrocities were alleged, psychological violations were cited most frequently. For example, when only one violation was mentioned, it fell into this category in fully half of the cases. Only associative atrocities approached psychological violations in frequency of mention; if two or more violations were mentioned, the set usually included both of these. Within the psychological category it was violations of individual independence and autonomy that were cited most frequently, and within the associative category disruption of family loyalties was most often mentioned.

In fact, all the coded atrocities, either explicitly or implicitly, served as incremental evidence to establish the ultimate religious atrocity of removing the free will necessary to consciously direct one's own religious fulfillment. The fact that not all tales were explicitly linked to this common dimension can in part be attributed to journalists'

lack of experience or motivation to construct a coherent set
of atrocities necessary to foment outrage against a target,
and partly to the sheer shock value (hence readability)
which many atrocities provide independent of any larger context. However, as the following examples illustrate, the
issue of deprivation of free will reads like a red letter in
atrocity tales, if only as a larger implication of each a-
trocity.

Psychological Atrocities

Psychological atrocities strike closest to the underlying value of free will, particularly when stories explicitly
claim deliberate manipulation on the part of Unification
Church leaders. This general type of atrocity story conveys
an imposition of constraints on free choice that initially
concern religion but which gradually extend to all areas of
a person's life. As an ex-member recalled:

> The philosophy teaches that your time, your life,
> is not rightly your own, but belongs to God who
> works through Moon, who works through the hier-
> archy of the cult. You have no free time be-
> cause every moment must be given to God through
> your immediate superior. You must give your
> self completely ("The Moon Store," The Farming-
> dale, NY Observer, 30 October 1975).

This "totalism" a la Lifton (1963:419) leads ex-members
and unsympathetic observers of the Unification Church to refer to "entrapped" members as "zombies," "robots," "mental
three-year-olds," "automaton," and to employ other metaphors to express this loss of autonomy: "As she looks back,
Kathy Knight said she believes her mind has been in a strong
box for the past three years" ("Young Woman Freed of Moon's
Cult Home Again," The Ft. Wayne, IN News Sentinel, 20 November 1976).

Other atrocity tales describe the techniques by which
this extraordinary compliance of "Moonies," working and en-
during their apparent deprivations with relish, is achieved.
Such techniques can be discussed in terms of recruitment and
indoctrination. Atrocity tales of recruitment procedures
emphasize the alleged deception involved in proselytization
(see also Associative atrocities), particularly when young
converts are unacquainted with specific elements of the
"Biblical authority" legitimizing the Church's claims and
when they are involved in a period of personal transition,
such as when separated from family and friends at college or
when taking a first job in a new location. Thus, for example, one anti-Unification Church spokesperson advocated

that "parents teach their children the Bible, because the
book is distorted by the cults for their own purpose and an
unprepared person is easy prey ("Moonie Details Break Away
From Cult," The Mystic, CT Compass Comment, 23 July 1975).
Two typical ex-members commented on the Church's interpersonal tactics with potential recruits. The first said:
"They look for a person's weakness, make him feel bad about
it and then accept him, relate to him, and bring him into
the group...." ("Former Moonie Describes Subtle Method of
Persuasion," The Albany, NY Evangelist, 29 July 1976). A
second elaborated on "traps" for the unwary, noting that
"They seemed very much interested in my ideas, encouraging
me to share more of my knowledge with them and telling me
how intelligent I was. They were just flattering me to encourage me to join the group ("He Was Walking Zombie," The
New York, NY Knickerbocker News, 16 May 1976). Sexual en-
ticement, along with suspicions that drugs are slipped into
food, are also occasionally alleged.

Indoctrination encompasses a number of tactics, including rote learning, creating "childlike dependence," enmesh-
ing the recruit in a network of personal relationships from
which it is emotionally traumatic to wrench oneself, and
even directly "capturing" the will of the person by Svenga-
lian art. For example, one apostate claimed "the movement
uses hypnosis and peer culture techniques to rule your mind.
...You become more and more divorced from your own decision"
("Newton Youth Back Home, Leaves Moon Movement," Newton, OH
Mennonite Weekly Review, 27 November 1975). Another recalled, "We had to answer word for word from the lecture....
There was no freedom of thinking, dialogue, or originality
allowed" ("Moon Glow Dims for 2 Followers," Columbus, OH
Evening Dispatch, 20 August 1976). One tale combined a se-
quence of such techniques:

> I think I was hypnotized at first. Basically by
> the girl that met me because she kept staring
> into my eyes and I kept being attracted to her
> eyes. Then, during the meal, it's very possible
> for some sort of a drug to make me more suscep-
> tible to the lecture. Then after that it was
> brainwashing because I was hooked. I wanted to
> stay there; I wanted to learn what they had to
> say. There was repetition all the time. Very
> appealing ("I Was Slave...Zombie, Returned Son
> Relates," The Cleveland Heights, OH Sun Press,
> 16 October 1975).

Extreme examples of compliance and of the members' surrender of their free will and personal responsibility serve
to reinforce the sense of atrocity. One ex-member lamented,

"Even though I have been deprogrammed, I still don't have my full mind back yet" ("Man Tells How Religious Cult Brainwashed Him," The Cleveland, OH Press, 13 October 1975), while another testimony put the extent of such compliance more bluntly: "I would have killed for him," she said. "I would have done anything Moon said" ("I Was Moon's Programmed Robot," The Dallas, TX Morning News, 19 October 1975).

An additional element that accentuates the gravity of such compliance concerns the successful lives that Unification Church members might otherwise be enjoying had they not become "ensnared." Descriptions abound of these persons as honors students in college, complete with scholarships, active social lives, and promising careers. Compliance with the hectic demands of fund raising and other Unification Church service at the expense of individual development and achievement within conventional society serves to reinforce the apparent irrationality of their religious commitment. Young adulthood, customarily a time of life when preparation is made for participation in secular educational, occupational, and domestic institutions, becomes seen as a tragedy of great waste, of diverting youthful exuberance away from "productive" channels. As one ex-member expressed it, "One of the prerequisites to becoming a member in good standing of the Unification Church is to suppress all personal ambitions" (Former Moonie Describes Subtle Method of Persuasion," The Albany, NY Evangelist, 29 July 1976).

A final type of psychological atrocity concerns violations of ego security and imposed guilt. The implication of these tales is that Church doctrines produce a morbid preoccupation with illusory sins, weakening personality integration by harming the person's otherwise relatively consistent sense of positive self. Many tales report how rigorous standards of doctrinal single-mindedness and asceticism are quickly internalized by new members and how this internalization serves to enforce conformity. As one female ex-member recalled: "It's virtually impossible to leave on your own...because you're afraid of letting the rest of the world down and you're afraid Satan is going to get you" ("Moonie Church Cleverly Set Up, One Thinks God Is Leading You," The New Brunswick, NJ Home News, 21 October 1976). Another apostate confirmed the role of guilt: "They make you feel guilty all the time. They say you are Satonic [sic], and any thoughts contrary to their religious ideology are evil," ("Deprogramming Procedures Harsh But Necessary," The Manketo MN Free Press, 9 June 1976).

One particularly lurid variation of the psychological security atrocity is sexual. Conventional heterosexual be-

havior, expected by larger American society among healthy
young people during their peak mate-selecting and reproduc-
tive years, is tabooed by the Unification Church except a-
long its own narrowly prescribed lines. If a member strays
from the high expectations of pre-marital abstinence, even
at the relatively "innocent" level of unspoken interest in
another person, the member is visited by relentless pangs of
guilt.

> "I even had guilt feelings about thinking about
> it," Richard said. "Guilty about past sexual
> experiences when I thought about them. Anything
> sexual involves Satan until we are saved by the
> Messiah and we are one with God. Then sex was
> OK. That's one of the ways they alienated us
> from our parents...by saying that they had
> created us without true love for God, so the
> sex they had was Satanic ("I Was Slave...Zombie,
> Returned Son Relates," The Cleveland Heights,OH
> Sun Press, 16 October 1975).

Such atrocity tales have an outrage potential cross-
cutting several values. They provide families with evidence
that the Unification Church is stifling the full human development of youth by forbidding culturally accepted heterosexual contact and generating guilt over it. At the same
time, the energies of young members are redirected into
seemingly endless fund-raising campaigns. Furthermore, this
extreme Puritanism appears hypocritical when contrasted with
occasional stories of Reverend Moon's own alleged "esca-
pades":

> Mike said he and other members of the Church
> had questioned one of the girls who was sup-
> posedly "blessed". She explained that Moon,
> his oldest son or one of Moon's top honchos
> will have relations with a girl coming into
> the cult who is not a virgin. She told them
> that this will supposedly purify the girl
> ("Youth Continues Running from the Unifica-
> tion," The New Haven, CT Register, 30 July
> 1976).

Physical Atrocities

Atrocity tales in this category typically focus on violations of a trio of values: proper nutrition, sufficient
rest, and physical safety. Some simply report deprivations
that have prima facie outrage value to a presumably well-fed,
rested, and secure reader. For example:

"There was very little protein in the diet," he
continued, "The food was almost totally carbo-
hydrates (cookies, ice cream, coke, peanut butter
and jelly sandwiches). On Sunday you might get
a drumstick" ("Ex-Moonie Attacks Movement," The
Mount Kisco, NY Patent Trader, 5 August 1976).

Other tales explicitly portray such debilitation or in-
security as part of a systematic conspiracy to undermine
free will and induce suggestibility.

Breakfast was oatmeal, just enough to go around,
served in styrofoam coffee cups. There was sugar
but no milk. Although members of the Church told
him that milk was too expensive, Kevin believes
that Moon's recruits are intentionally kept on a
low protein diet to induce physical weakness and
docility ("Ex-Moonie Tells of Threats on Life,"
The Wenham, MA Chronicle, 2 June 1976).

This category also included lesser atrocities that
under other circumstances (e.g., summer camp or a slumber
party) might be viewed as adventurous inconveniences, such
as sleeping on floors (rather than beds) in sleeping bags in
overcrowded, stuffy rooms, or participating in workshops
staged in remote rural locations.

Economic Atrocities

While psychological and physical atrocities are generally unfamiliar occurrences to non-members, economic violations have a more widely experienced, concrete referent.
Members of marginal religious groups, whether of the Unification Church, Hare Krishna, or others, have become a common sight to Americans as the former solicit funds on
street corners, in parking lots, or in places of public con-
veyance. Ex-members of the Church usually reserve their
bitterest condemnations for this aspect of service in the
Unification Church, perhaps because of its high priority in
members' expenditures of time. Remarked one:

"What it all comes down to," concluded Terry,
"is that it is just one big money-making scheme
and they brainwash you into thinking you're doing God's work. It's the greatest rip-off of
them all" ("He Was Walking Zombie," The New
York, NY Knickerbocker News, 16 May 1976).

Economic atrocity tales focus on two dimensions. The
first includes violations of members' private property

rights, such as the Church "absorbing" their saleable possessions (cars, electronic equipment, clothing) and savings
accounts upon joining, or exploiting them to work long hours,
with only a subsistence return, for the financial gain of a
few leaders. Typical of this type of atrocity tale are two
told of ex-members. "Miss Frank said a car she owned when
she joined the church was declared community property"
("City Woman Asked Deprogramming, Said She Lost Control of
Her Thoughts," The Grand Forks, ND Herald, 28 May 1976).
The other woman reported that "they said they averaged between $60 and $100 a day, and the money was always turned
over to the church which is headed by the Korean Reverend
Sun Myung Moon" ("Ex-Moonies Say They Used Lies," Fosters
Democrat, 30 July 1976).

    A second dimension allegedly violated by Unification
Church followers is the value of fair exchange, meaning that
a person contributing money should be given an honest account of the purposes to which it will be put and/or an implicit norm of reciprocity that the quality of goods ex-
changed for fixed donations will in some way approximate the
donation (while still permitting some profit). The atrocity
tales which we coded were replete with claims of members being encouraged to disguise the destination of contributions,
i.e., constructing stories of bogus charities to play on the
sympathies of non-Church members (a technique referred to by
members as "heavenly deception"), and of selling candy and
other inexpensive goods at exorbitantly marked-up prices.
For example:

> She described the process of "heavenly deceit"
> in which so-called Moonies would buy boxes of
> candy for 79 cents and sell them for $2. "We
> were conditioned to believe that everyone we
> approached was being given the opportunity to
> pay indemnity for his sins by buying our candy,"
> Jill said ("Moonie Experience Not Sunny," The
> Costa Mesa, CA Daily Pilot, 1 August 1976).

Associative Atrocities

    Associative atrocities are concerned with violations of
conventional patterns of relationships, in this case between
members of the Unification Church and non-members. Many of
these violations involve breaking off previously established
relations, both from "physical" families and from friends.

    The most sensational variation of this atrocity deals
with the severing of the parent-child bond. Unification
theology teaches that parents not "saved" (i.e., not accepting the Church's grace-imparting doctrine) conceived their

children in sin; hence the biological children, if "saved,"
have an obligation to accept their "true" spiritual parents
(Rev. and Mrs. Moon) and reject the biological parents if
the latter oppose them.

At the same time, rejection of one's biological parents represent a culturally heinous breach of reciprocity.
Parents' functions include not only procreation, nurturance,
and socialization but also social placement. Particularly
in the case of many middle class young persons attracted to
the Unification Church, parents have subsidized (perhaps at
marked sacrifice) educational and career opportunities.
Rejection of this subsidy and its goals, aside from the
emotional concern during a period of estrangement, causes
the parents initial confusion coupled with despondency and
is followed by a suspicion that the locus of such an abrupt
change can be sought outside their young person.

A complete break in communication as part of Church-
encouraged estrangement is one frequently cited atrocity.

> "She didn't even send her father a birthday
> card," Mrs. Ballerini said. "She said she
> didn't even consider us her real parents,
> only her physical parents. Moon and his
> wife were her real parents" ("Devotee Left
> Family to Follow Course of Moon," The New
> Brunswick, NJ Home News, 12 October 1975).

Ex-members often claim that such a communication gap
was never their own wish even with committed members but
rather was Church policy. Such claims add to the "evidence" of conspiracy:

> I wrote my Dad and he never got one of the
> letters. And when he sent a message to me
> that he was coming to Yankee Stadium I never
> received it ("Youth Continues Running From
> Unification Church," The New Haven, CT
> Register, 30 July 1976).

Familial atrocities also include the ultimate cultural
taboo -- extinction of the biological parents if necessary
-- to drive home the complete loss of free will among members:

> He was taught that if parents stand in the
> way of your duty to God (belonging to the cult),
> killing the parents would be permissible ("Steps
> to Prevent Spread of Moon Cult Requested," The
> Burlington, VT Free Press, 24 February 1976).

We earlier discussed sexual violations in terms of psychological security, basic sexuality, and guilt. One similar but distinct category of associational violations concerns heterosexual marriage. The mass arranged marriages within the Unification Church (for which members must pay $400 apiece), often joining American Caucasians with Asians, violate not only an explicit American value on free mate selection but also an implicit, still widespread norm against miscegination. Such atrocity tales relegate Unification Church marriage to a non-marriage status:

> They want to arrange your marriage with an Oriental and then they totally destroy the family unit by putting the children in day care centers and sending the husband and wife on their separate ways for mission ("I Was Moon's Programmed Robot," The Dallas, TX Morning News, 19 October 1976).

Restrictions placed on members' locomotion and the often hectic pace of service in the Unification Church sharply restrict "Moonies'" opportunities to develop relationships with non-Church persons except within their solicitor witness roles. This is often viewed by concerned families as further evidence of their children's increasing entrapment in the Church. However, a more serious aspect of the member's relation to non-members centers on veracity, i.e., on the integrity of their encounters. The solicitor-witness role stresses several goals, most important of which are at least informal financial quotas for fund-raising terms, and converts (or at least a high turnover of persons exposed to the initial messages).

Our field observations and interviews with Church members at several Texas locations indicate an ethic motivating success in both fund-raising and conversion closely resembling the Weberian Protestant Ethic. Specifically, both activities, if conducted in the proper spirit, are "God-centered," hence success in raising money or gaining new members does not reflect a member's own talents or persuasive powers as much as it indicates God's favor and reward for proper faith. These tangible indicators of success, therefore, become translated into spiritual achievement (in the Calvinistic sense). This spiritual achievement, in the crucial days of "the advent of the Third Adam" preached by Reverend Moon, encourages a pragmatic emphasis on the ends at the expense of the means and thus promotes breaches in veracity with "outsiders."

Violations of the value of fair exchange, previously discussed under economic atrocities, touched upon deception

in fund-raising. Violations of veracity in the wider associational sense involve proselytizing with identifying
one's beliefs and purposes as related to the Unification
Church. The following testimony puts this atrocity into
sharper relief:

> Moonies put an ad in an Austin paper that read,
> "Conscientious, creative people who want to
> help the world, call Janis at (phone number)."
> We received 70 calls a day and were taught how
> to lure the callers into the center by twisting
> the conversation around to their interests and
> then relating to them. They poured into the
> center, one scheduled every 15 minutes. Our
> purpose was to get them to attend a weekend
> workshop ("I Was Moon's Programmed Robot," The
> Dallas, TX Morning News 19 October 1976).

Such a story reaffirms to anti-Church persons that
free will and "normal" inhibitions have been completely
suppressed when their children relate such seemingly unscrupulous deeds.

Political-Legal Atrocities

Atrocity tales of this type describe violations in the
areas of loyalty to America, fair play in American politics,
and law-abiding behavior. The general tenor of these stories
is to portray the Unification Church either as a conspiratorial force directed by a foreigner or as a public nuisance.
Since many of the articles we coded had appeared before the
press had delved far into possible connections between Moon's
hierarchy and the Korean CIA, we encountered few accusations
that Moon is really an agent for the South Korean government.
Rather, the threat conveyed in most patriotic atrocity tales
is reminiscent of older "Yellow Peril-Fu Manchu" genre.
"Jansen said the 'master plan' of the Unification members
were eventual political take-over of the United States and
then the world" ("Lies and Abuses Within Unification Church,"
The Newport, VT Express, 30 July 1976). There were other
similar allegations:

> Doug says he thinks that Moon wants to control
> the government and rule the world....If he
> gets enough people in his cult, according to
> Doug, Moon can elect his own senators, congress-
> men and even the President when and if he ever
> gets big enough ("Woman, Man Tell of Religious
> Cult Experience," The Waseca, MN Journal, 16
> April 1976).

The tactics of this incursion into America's political affairs spill over into the fair play variation of political legal atrocities. The Unification Church, as a legally recognized religious organization, is prohibited from political lobbying. Yet some atrocity stories, tinged with hints of sexuality, describe Moon's ongoing lobbying efforts (often referred to as "love-bombing") on behalf of South Korea.

Meanwhile his inroads into Congress, while not too successful, have already resulted in Representative Carl Albert having "Moonies" on his staff. Moon has said he needs 300 pretty girls, three for each Senator ("The Rabbi Makes Penthouse Magazine, Is That Success?" Indianapolis, IN Jewish Post and Opinion, 21 May 1976).

Friction between the Unification Church and local law enforcement officials constitutes a third variation of this category of violations. The Church members' offending acts are not so much prima facie atrocious as they are merely misdemeanors: ignoring "no soliciting" signs, blocking traffic at intersections as they peddle flowers and candy, peddling without licenses, and so forth. Nevertheless, ex-members' accounts of having casually ignored local ordinances in pursuit of their "higher ends" adds to the stereotype of "blind" obedience and ordinarily law-abiding youth "manipulated" into devious activities.

Cultural Atrocities

There are, in every cultural system, some sacred symbols, some heroic-divine statures, and some reverend roles to which most mortals should not aspire lest they be accused of outrageous arrogance or irreverance. Claimants to such exalted levels cannot, in present American society, be formally punished for sacrilege. However, such pretentions still constitute an atrocity in the eyes of conventional society. For example, while exoteric presentations of Unification theology may allude to, but never directly claim, Christ-like status for Moon himself, there is an unmistakable impression in the minds of most ex-Church members that Moon considers himself the "Third Adam," "the new Messiah," and the fulfillment of Christian soteriology. "Moon has proclaimed that 'the world must be made pure by 1980 because of the coming of a new Messiah who will take the place of Jesus who failed in his mission because the Jews killed him before he could marry a perfect mate" ("Korea Messiah Tricks Youth, Rabbi Charges," New York Jewish Week and American Examiner, 28 September 1974). Another report carried a similar theme:

Protestors, mostly parents and children who have
been "deprogrammed" from Unification Church assert that when his followers use the term "God,"
they mean "Moon" ("Anti-Moonies Demonstrate,"
San Francisco, CA Jewish Bulletin, 11 June 1976).

AUTHORIZATION

Actions may be said to be authorized when they are
deemed appropriate tacitly or explicitly by some group (or
its representative) which is recognized as legitimately
evaluating or controlling those actions. The distinction
between explicit and implicit authorization is significant.
In most circumstances authorities voice direct approval or
disapproval of actions; however, activities may be implicitly sanctions by the authorized agent simply failing to ex-
ercize authority. Under such conditions the authority is
tacitly accepting or rejecting the individually based action.
Implicitly approved activity is likely to occur, for example,
when the authorized agent faces competing principles and re-
solves the dilemma by inaction or when the authorized agent
would prefer an action which cannot be legitimated and condones it by choosing not to apply penalties.

Deprogramming typically involves implicit authorization which emanates from the construction of the offender-
victim relationship. The individual Church member is portrayed as a victim of manipulative and coercive mind control
by the Church. Parents and deprogrammers thereby become
agents of restoration, transferring the locus of control
from the Church back to the individual. The Church, rather
than being a victim of harassment, is seen as the offender,
having violated individual freedom of choice and action.
Once the individual Church member is defined as having diminished competence, tacit authorization is relatively easily obtained.

Atrocity tales recount this tacit authorization from a
number of sources such as religious leaders, parents, law
enforcement agencies, and former Church members. Statements
are provided which clearly discredit the Unification Church
and separate it from other religious bodies which are recognized as representing legitimate religious activity.

The National Council of Churches in New York
refused him admission. The Archdioces of New
York has condemned him as have the Lutherans,
the Presbyterians and the Episcopalians ("More
Moonie Madness," Ardmore, PA Main Line Times,
10 February 1977).

When stories providing tacit authorization are presented, they often detail the agonizing nature of the decision
that had to be made. The decision to proceed with deprogramming is presented as the resolution of a conflict between the values of conformity to the rule of law and family
sanctity and loyalty, with the latter being defended as the
pre-eminent value. Extraordinary times require extraordinary actions which, it is readily acknowledged, would not be
tolerated under normal circumstances. One of the most outspoken critics of the Unification Church was quoted as follows:

> Davis is not a body snatcher, as is the contro-
> versial deprogrammer Ted Patrick, whom he knows,
> and says he has "great respect" for. Snatching
> is not his way, says Davis. "I have a couple of
> hangups about it. I just can't do it. But, God
> forbid, if either of my two sons were to join
> the Moon movement, there's no law I wouldn't break
> to bring them back" ("Foe Equals Moonies Fanati-
> cism," The San Antonio, TX Light, 10 June 1976).

Parental and legal authorization frequently are linked
since deprogramming may require forcible abduction and confinement. Both parental assertion that the actions taken
were in the best interest of their offspring and the willingness of authorities to "bend" the law are necessary to
gain full authorization.

> "We felt if we did not do something to get her
> to think for herself we were never going to en-
> joy having our daughter with us again and she
> would never enjoy living in this world," explain-
> ed Gordon, a Lake county supervisor.
> "I do not agree with or condone the actions
> taken," said D.A. Davis Luce. "However, after
> interviewing the Gordon family last week, he
> decided not to file charges" ("The Deprogram-
> ming of Ann Gordon's Mind," Santa Rosa, CA News-
> Herald, 28 October 1975).

Even when the Church or its members attempt to defend their
legal rights formally and publicly authorization may be
granted.

> Antonio leaped from the car and got a headlock
> on his screaming daughter. Moonies joined the
> scuffle, resulting in severely bruised ribs for
> Antonio. Within minutes, both a laywer for the
> Unification Church and a New York policeman ar-
> rived on the scene. While the Church lawyer

delivered his spiel about kidnapping, the police-
man whispered to Jolin Antonio, "Get the hell out
of here" ("Moonie Experience Not Sunny," Costa
Mesa, CA Daily Pilot, 1 August 1976).

Perhaps the ultimate authorization is provided by
statements from former Church members who themselves have
undergone deprogramming. The apostate role, which has been
largely neglected by sociologists, plays a significant part
in discrediting a deviant group and in authorizing social
control measures. As an individual who has foresaken the
faith to which he formerly adhered, the apostate is a valuable source of information who can perform as the star witness in public proceedings or propaganda campaigns against
the group. He can reveal the group's inner workings and
secrets in such a way as to confirm suspicions and allegations about it, condemn the group with a knowledge and cer-
tainty no outsider could muster, and reaffirm the values of
conventional society by voluntarily and publicly confessing
the "error" or his ways.

Apostates contribute substantially to the larger-than-
life quality of atrocity tales. Having flouted the dominant
value system, the apostate can hardly expect to regain acceptance in conventional society after merely losing interest in the deviant group. It is incumbent upon him to demonstrate convincingly that his reaffirmation of the domi-
nate values is genuine, that he shares with others negative
sentiments toward the group, and that his former commitment
was false witnessing.

Along with formulating an acceptable public confession
the apostate is likely to feel some need to account for his
own conduct. Others may ask, if the group is as transpar-
ently evil as he now contends, why did he espouse its cause
in the first place? In the process of trying to explain
his own seduction and to confirm the worst fears about the
group, the apostate is likely to paint a caricature of the
group which is shaped more by his current role as apostate
than by his actual experiences in the group.

An apostate's story in our sample typically depicted
the member as initially resisting efforts to separate him
from the Church but later conceding that his parents had
been right all along. Such a statement would be accompanied
by expressions of appreciation for parental love and concern
even though the process was painful and admission that the
individual was too completely "hooked" to have secured his
own freedom.

Here I would like to conclude that had it not
been for the strong action of my parents in
actually forcing me to be "deprogrammed" from
this "brainwashed" state, I would still be a
totally dedicated member. There was little
way for me to break the bonds of their control of my own, and I would have continued to
sacrifice myself, ready to lie, cheat, steal
and kill for the cause of the cult. I am
thankful that after ten months of blind submission I am now free of this system and its
manipulation. I am deeply grateful to those
people who worked behind my back and in spite
of my protest to accomplish this ("The Moon
Store," The Farmingdale, NY Observer, 13
November 1975).

The unique role of the family in securing and protecting individual freedom is publicly acknowledged.

After spending six days with one of the leading "deprogrammers" in the nation, Carper
decided not to return to the Unification
Church. "I was lucky my parents cared enough
for me to reach out and grab me," said Carper.
"There are many kids whose parents don't
care at all" ("Former Moonie Says He Lost the
Right to Think," Hillsboro, KS Star Journal,
19 May 1976).

MOBILIZATION

Mobilization involves motivating, organizing and focusing individual actions toward a socially defined goal. It
therefore includes some assertion of normative compliance
and of the appropriate social context for action. The atrocity tales about the Unification Church attempt to motivate
individuals, first by portraying the evil involved as being
very powerful, growing in strength, and not amenable to conventional social mechanisms, and second by providing specific individual and collective actions which can be undertaken
or supported.

In a world filled with problems effective mobilization
requires establishing the immediate salience of the problem
for the individual. Many of the newspaper story headlines
boldly proclaimed the impending threat: "Cult Called U.S.
Greatest Threat" (Ft. Worth, TX Star Telegram, 1 October
1975); "Moon's Church Called Clear and Present Danger"
(Mamaroneck, NY Daily Times, 27 October 1975); "The Dangers

of the Moon Cult to Our Youth" (The Plainfield, NY Courier
News, 1 February 1977); "Escapee Says Cults Want 1984
World" (The Mexico City News, 4 December 1975). The text
accompanying such headlines describes the evil associated
with the Church as so powerful that anyone is susceptible:
"I don't believe myself to be unusually susceptible to political or spiritual causes," he wrote, "but the propaganda
system set up at this center was infallible" ("Harvard Student's Dream Vanished in the Movement," The Dallas, TX Morning News, 19 October 1976).

One means of impressing the reader with the magnitude
of the danger was to compare the Unification Church with the
Hitler Youth Movement and the Manson family, groups which it
is widely agreed committed particularly heinous atrocities.
In testimony before a U.S. Senate committee Rabbi Maurice
Davis stated:

> Rabbi Davis admitted that he is "scared" of the
> similarities he sees between Moon's group and
> Hitler's. Senator Dole, the last time I ever
> witnessed a movement that was totally mono-
> lithic, that was replete with fanatical follow-
> ers prepared to do anything, that hated every-
> one outside and festered suspicion of parents
> -- the last time I saw this was the Nazi youth
> movement, and I tell you, I'm scared ("Cult
> Compared to Nazi Youth Organization, Tarrytown,
> NY News, 19 February 1976).

Indeed, the danger is portrayed as being so great that individuals are warned about even personally seeking further
information about the Church for fear they might not be
able to resist its power despite being forewarned:

> During the question session, 19 year-old Jeff
> Rosenthal of Cherry Hill, asked if it would be
> possible to attend a Moon meeting "to find out
> about it" and then leave at the end of the
> night. The deprogrammer replied it would be
> risky, especially since a few reporters and
> investigators attempted to do so and found
> themselves "slipping under". He said some
> never returned to finish their stories ("Do
> Cults Brainwash Members?" Burlington, NJ
> County Times, 29 August 1976).

Immediate action is mandated because the power of the
evil is growing so swiftly that unless steps are taken to
confront it, it may become too potent to control. "Rabbi

Davis said he is convinced that Moon's motives are political and that "five years from now we won't be able to do anything about it" ("Rotarians Hear Rabbi Slam Moon," Tarrytown, NY News, 11 February 1976). Nor can containment of the Church be left to conventional authority because, it is alleged, the Church has cunningly used its status as a religious organization to thwart prosecution.

There is somewhat less emphasis in the atrocity stories on specific actions than might be expected. Much greater attention is paid to detailing the atrocities, establishing authorization for "rescue" and proclaiming the imminence of the threat. In large part this seems to be due to the fact that the deprogramming movement is a small, highly decentralized movement which acts only when parents request information or assistance. Without a broader agenda, there are relatively few opportunities for formal participation which can be offered. However, since the stories provide authorization to parents who decide to deprogram their offspring, and the names and addresses of key deprogrammers and deprogramming organizations also frequently are contained in the articles, further mobilization may be unnecessary.

> For families, there are defenses, too. First,
> a close relationship of trust. But if your son
> or daughter gets caught up in the movement,
> don't argue over the phone or in a letter. Try
> to re-kindle favorite memories of home life.
> Get in touch with our parent group, Citizens
> Engaged in Re-Uniting Families, Box 112-H,
> Scarsdale, New York 10583, and let your Con-
> gressman and Senator know what is happening
> ("Devotee Left Family to Follow Course of Moon,"
> The New Brunswick, NJ Home News, 12 October
> 1975).

CONCLUSIONS

In a recent essay, Smelser (1971) speculated on the ways in which excessive violence and coercion (i.e., social evil) can be legitimized, authorized and rationalized. He also suggested methods by which persons might be mobilized to support actions that exceed conventionally moral limits. Among the factors important to the support for such excesses were the expectation of impending harm and the perspective of some threatening agent as so powerful that it can resist conventional control agents.

This paper was documented, through a content analysis of anecdotal atrocity tales directed at the controversial Unification Church, the processes with which Smelser was concerned. We have seen how atrocity tales help construct a moral basis for otherwise immoral actions, providing deprogrammers and their supporters with what Smelser (1971: 23) called "simple reassurances that the actor need not bear all the guilt for the deed because special circumstances justify it". By associating deviant groups with reprehensible violations of fundamental values, atrocity tales function at a seminal stage of the labeling process. They are the elements out of which a social context for evil is formed. By their outrageous, larger-than-life quality, they help mobilize reactions against targets. Most importantly, they provide the "evidence" (at both visceral and intellectual levels) for negative labels that later may justify formal degradation ceremonies.

III

PSYCHOLOGICAL PERSPECTIVES

The papers in this section address several important issues that have been raised in scholarly and popular literature regarding the mental health of members of new religious movements. As the introduction to this volume noted, there have been persistent allegations that individuals are recruited through a combination of deceptive, fraudulent and coercive techniques (collectively termed brainwashing). Severe emotional disturbance and protracted problems in readjusting to conventional society have been alleged to follow separation from these groups. These charges have dominated the agenda of psychological/psychiatric research in this area. The four papers in this section provide some of the best data and most interesting insights on these issues.

Solomon, a social psychologist, establishes a link between sociological and psychological approaches to understanding attitude and behavior change. She utilizes concepts and findings from the widely studied phenomenon of interpersonal influence. Distilling from the extensive literature on brainwashing the major elements of that process, she assesses the extent to which programming (by new religions) and deprogramming (by anti-cultists) approach this extreme form of influence exertion. Solomon concludes that while manipulative practices can be found in both processes, neither is mysterious from a social science perspective and each can better be understood in terms of existing social psychological concepts than through the brainwashing model.

Galanter's work on the psychological implications of affiliation with new religious movements has been regarded as objective and balanced by all sides in the new religions controversy. In this paper, he reports on data collected during a twenty-one day recruitment workshop operated by the Unification Church on the West Coast. Over this three week period he administered a variety of psychological tests to workshop participants. Galanter observes that groups like the Unification Church function as therapeutically oriented self-help groups. Indeed, he concludes that many individuals ultimately manifest improved psychological well-being as a result of membership in such groups. This finding and his observation of high turnover in membership clash with contentions that new religious movements inevitably

produce deleterious consequences for members and trap individuals in these unhealthy environments.

A second paper by Galanter, co-authored with Buckley,
reaches similar conclusions. Based on 119 interviews with
members of the Divine Light Mission, Galanter and Buckley
report a significant decline in psychiatric symptoms among
members over a several month period. They also note that
the Divine Light Mission has been able to restructure and
refocus peer groups in such a way as to eliminate rather
than encourage drug use. These findings, like those in the
preceding paper, clash with the brainwashing hypothesis.

In the final paper in this section Ungerleider and
Wellisch report the results of research involving the admin-
istration of several personality assessment instruments and
psychiatric interviews with members and former members of
various new religious groups. The sample included current
members, deprogrammed individuals who left their respective
groups permanently, individuals who were deprogrammed but
later returned to their respective groups, and individuals
who voluntarily disaffiliated from their respective groups.
The authors found no indication that members of these groups
lacked the capacity to make independent personal judgements;
they did observe that these individuals were motivated by
"ideological hunger" and concern for ambivalence in their
own lives. Ungerleider and Wellisch reported salutary effects associated with membership in these groups and a decline in reported psychiatric symptoms and drug use. Since
the best predictors of these declines were "group-related
variables," organizational characteristics of at least some
new religious groups appear to be associated with ameliora-
tion rather than exacerbation of emotional distress.

Taken together, these papers suggest a much more complex pattern of psychological consequences associated with
membership in new religious movements than those predicted
by the brainwashing model. There is little doubt that some
recruitment/socialization techniques have been manipulative,
and it is clear that many individuals experience emotional
turmoil during the transitional periods of affiliation and
disaffiliation. Yet this kind of intense religious commitment has salutary effects for many individuals, and neither
the intense, peak experiences nor the affiliation/disaffil-
iation processes require extraordinary explanations.

PROGRAMMING AND DEPROGRAMMING THE MOONIES:
SOCIAL PSYCHOLOGY APPLIED

Trudy Solomon
National Science Foundation

The rapid proliferation of new religious movements in America during the last two decades has awakened not only a host of social scientists attempting to explain the phenomenon, but also a plethora of legal scholars caught in the concomitant constitutional crisis it has spawned. For by their very existence these movements have brought into focus the meaning and application of one of our nation's most coveted guarantees, the First Amendment. Questions concerning religious freedom, freedom of speech, of association, and of travel, thought to be fundamental to the American culture have been shown to be dependent upon the values and beliefs of those who interpret them. At issue is whether young people, the most frequent adherents to these new religions, are free to participate and believe as they choose, or if opposing parents and governmental agencies will be permitted to intervene and thereby limit individual participation.

Should this kind of intervention be allowed in light of what appears to be flagrant violations of First Amendment rights? The answer, though far from simple, rests on the assumption of the opponents of these new religions that there exists an even more fundamental right than those guaranteed by the First Amendment -- freedom of thought -- which is allegedly taken away by these movements. It is the contention of opponents to new religions that without this most basic human right, freedom of religion, speech, association, and its ancillary liberties are rendered utterly meaningless.

In a desperate search for remedy, both sides of this controversy are embroiled in a protracted battle whose outcome will most probably be determined through the courts. The issues involved are far from black and white. It is hoped that the following discussion will shed light on methods used by these new religions to gain converts (programming) and techniques that have been developed to counteract their influence on an individual (deprogramming). Alternative theoretical perspectives to the popular one of brainwashing will be explored. Before turning to those issues,

however, it is imperative to understand the definitional
framework that will be used throughout this discourse.

TWO PROCESSES IN SEARCH
OF A THEORETICAL FRAMEWORK

Given the seriousness of the rhetorical and legal
charges currently on the minds, if not the tongues, of com-
plainants adhering to either side of the programming/depro-
gramming controversy, it seems imperative that researchers
formulate testable, theoretical perspectives to more realistically and empirically explicate the hows of programming
and deprogramming. A proliferation of explanations have
been offered for these processes, most of which center a-
round the highly debatable concept of brainwashing. Since
this perspective has gained the most notoriety, it will be
discussed first, followed by the potentially more viable
alternative of applied social psychology.

What is meant by brainwashing? Broadly defined it is
said to be a method of indoctrination which has as its primary goal coerced behavior (Santucci and Winokur, 1955).
More specifically, it is seen as a process which has two
major elements: (1) the exposure and renunciation of past
and present "evil" through systematically applied psychological and physical coercion; and (2) the re-education, or
the remaking, of the person to obtain the desired point of
view (Lifton, 1961). Although space limitations will not
permit an in-depth discussion of each of the formulated
theoretical approaches to brainwashing it should be noted
that three of the best delineated have been characterized
as Psycho-physiological Stress Theory (Hinkle and Wolff,
1956; Hunter, 1951, 1956; Sargant, 1951, 1956), Learning
Theory (Meerloo, 1954, 1956; Sargant, 1951, 1957; Hunter,
1951, 1956; Santucci and Winokur, 1955; Farber, Harlow and
West, 1957), and Psychoanalytic Theory (Moloney, 1955;
Meerloo, 1951, 1954, 1956; Lifton, 1956, 1961).

Although crude forerunners of the process of brainwashing were surely used throughout history for the manipulation
of human behavior, the techniques were thought to have been
refined in Russia during the purge trials of the late 30s.
The process was then soon exported to the Communist satel-
lite countries of Europe and then to Communist China
(Hunter, 1956). Even though the vast majority of what has
been written on brainwashing since its popularization in
the 50s has focused on the Chinese techniques as the final
step in an evolutionary process, it should be noted that
the Chinese methods differed from their ancestors in several important ways which can be grouped around what Singer

(1977) has called the six essential questions (see Table 1). It is thus the Chinese and not the Russian techniques which have most recently been indicted as the primary tools of the programming process in indoctrination and the deprogramming process in its attempted reversal.

TABLE 1

A COMPARISON OF RUSSIAN AND CHINESE
BRAINWASHING TECHNIQUES

Question	Russian	Chinese
1. Is the person expendable or usable?	Expendable	Usable
2. Is confession or conversion the desired end product?	Confession	Conversion
3. Is coercion or persuasion the primary tool to achieve this end?	Coercion	Persuasion
4. How is the procedure best characterized?	Scientific	Evangelistic
5. Is the primary change agent an individual or a group?	Individual (Interrogator)	Group (Cellmates)
6. Is understimulation or overstimulation utilized in the process?	Understimulation (Isolation from others)	Overstimulation (Immersion in the group)

Though the Chinese techniques may be more applicable to the processes involved in both programming and deprogramming in new religions, it should be clear that brainwashing has throughout its conceptual history shown itself to be an entity which defies a single definitional framework and all major theorists on the topic now look to an amalgam of ideas to explain its alleged effects (Lifton, 1961; Schein, 1961). One reason for such conceptual discrepancies could stem from the fact that soon after its introduction the concept of brainwashing was applied to a variety of contexts including indoctrination techniques in other countries and to past phenomena such as the Inquisition and a variety of witch trials. Because of the predominantly evil and negative con-

notations that rapidly became associated with the term
brainwashing, a number of more neutral, semantic deriva-
tives were invented, such as mind control, mental coercion,
thought reform, coercive persuasion and menticide. It was
in these later incarnations that the brainwashing concept
has throughout the years been applied to nearly every form
of human influence, including hypnosis, psychotherapy,
mass media, advertising, education, socialization, child-
rearing, behavior modification and a myriad of related
forms of attitude and behavioral change techniques.

     This broad range of applications and terminology pro-
duced a number of contrasting mythologies concerning the
process by which brainwashing was accomplished. On the one
hand, brainwashing was seen as a mysterious and all powerful device, an irresistable, magical method of achieving
total control over the human mind. Hunter (1956:43) stated,
for instance: "The newly devised pressures of the mind --
mind atrocities called brainwashing -- were as modern and
devastating an advance in war as nuclear fusion had been
only a few years before when it made its unannounced debut
with a hellish flash and a gigantic mushroom of pallid
smoke over the luckless city of Hiroshima." Yet it was only
the next year that Bauer (1957:43) proposed that the techniques used in brainwashing are: "...indistinguishable from
the shrewd common sense practices of journalists and sales-
men of all times and places, and are based on psychological,
physiological, and physical principles known to interroga-
tors regardless of national or political allegiance, or any
academic persuasion."

     Almost every field of psychology was explored in an at-
tempt to explain the process called "brainwashing," resulting in an outpouring of contradictory explanations, primarily due to the variety of operational definitions utilized
(Solomon and Pines, 1977). The confusion in the literature
on brainwashing caused Lifton (1961:4), perhaps the most
frequently quoted author on the topic, to conclude: "...the
term has a far from precise and questionable usefulness;
one may even be tempted to forget about the whole subject
and return to more constructive pursuits." Indeed, the intensive use and overuse of the concept, has nearly emptied
it of any value.

     Throughout its historical evolution some critics have
questioned whether brainwashing as an entity existed at all.
Thus, West (1964) dubbed it "the great brainwashing hoax"
stemming, he felt, from a loose original definition and a
number of highly publicized, misleading statements by a few
individuals about the behavior of United States' prisoners
of war in Korea. Even within the last year, brainwashing

has been attacked on a number of fronts. Within sociology, Robbins, Anthony, and McCarthy (1977) proposed that brainwashing could best be understood as a "social weapon" to legitimate repression of deviant minorities. And, finally, within psychiatry, Thomas Szasz (1976:11), famous for his mental illness metaphor, accorded brainwashing the same status by saying:

> Actually, it's all quite simple. Like many dramatic terms, "brainwashing" is a metaphor. A person can no more wash another's brain with coercion or conversation than he can make him bleed with a cutting remark. If there is no such thing as brainwashing, what does this metaphor stand for? It stands for one of the most universal human experiences and events, namely for one person influencing another.

It should be obvious that we do not apply the term brainwashing to <u>all</u> forms of personal and psychological influence, but rather our culture seems to reserve the term for influence processes of which we disapprove while more societally valued influence processes go under one of the more neutral, derivative terms. It should be clear that words can be instruments of power, according to Meerloo (1956:137), and in order to use that power effectively one must: "...coin new labels and new words with emotional appeal while allowing the same old practices and institutions to continue as before -- the trick is to replace a disagreeable image though the substance remains the same." Words also have the ability to mask <u>process</u> similarities by emphasizing rather superficial <u>content</u> differences.

Superficially, much of what transpires during programming and deprogramming does follow some of the classic steps in the brainwashing process. However, it is crucial to realize that brainwashing and its component parts are <u>not</u> dichotomous variables in any sense of the term. If one eliminates this "all or nothing" orientation and explores the more feasible and intellectually appealing alternative of a continuum delineation of the process with, for example, mass media advertising or child-rearing as one endpoint and the Korean or Chinese POW experience at the opposite extreme it is possible to understand a myriad of influence processes including brainwashing as a question not of existence, but of <u>degree</u>.

Surely programmees and deprogramees alike are isolated from their present environments, subjected to a variety of group influence techniques (including repetition, monopolization of input and selective reinforcement), and are forced

to undergo some form of physical and/or mental coercion
within a tightly controlled environment. Yet it is the degree with which these elements are applied and not merely
their presence or absence which should be used as the criterion for whether brainwashing can be equated with either,
both or neither of the processes under discussion.

It is no secret that most religious groups (old and
new) indoctrinate through a variety of subtle and not so
subtle techniques. When this indoctrination process is acceptable to society it is called "religious training" or
"religious instruction," yet when a sect, cult or movement
is new, unpopular or unacceptable, it has in recent years
been called brainwashing or subversion (Eiga, 1977). Some
in our society are attempting to distinguish between kinds
of control that are "good" and those that are "bad." If
such a delineation continues, our culture may begin judging
persuasive techniques by investigating the motives of those
involved rather than by studying their form or substance.
Just such a proposal for distinguishing between programming
and deprogramming was recently set forth by Patrick (1976:
70-71) who said that the evidence would seem to suggest
that:

> I'm fighting fire with fire -- or that, at best,
> I'm no better in my methods than the cults.
> But let's look at motives....Motives are impor-
> tant. The cult's motives are destructive --
> this can be demonstrated. My motives, I hope
> I have demonstrated here, have nothing in com-
> mon with those of the spiritual gangsters.

It would appear that such reasoning is fallacious since
Patrick is counseling us to look at content and not process
factors in making our judgments about a method's validity
or efficacy. This is just as misguided as those who would
counsel us to judge a method only by its outcome, ignoring
its means. However, such a level of analysis is clearly
shortsighted; a better approach to judging a movement, a
technique, or a new religious order is by analyzing its process.

SOCIAL PSYCHOLOGY APPLIED

Removing the processes of programming and deprogramming
from the realm of brainwashing is a crucial step in freeing
them from the bonds of mysticism and facilitating their empirical study. Since brainwashing has previously been characterized as the extreme on a social influence continuum, it
would seem reasonable to conceptualize the processes of pro-

gramming and deprogramming as simply less extreme points on the same hypothetical continuum. It is an applied problem in that these processes are naturally occurring phenomena that must of necessity be studied in their field setting. It is a social psychological problem in that their underlying premises speak to two crucial social psychological issues: (1) how and under what circumstances can social influence processes impact upon individual participants and (2) what is the nature of the relationship and the direction of causality between attitudinal and behavioral changes.

Historically, the posing of the first question signals a return to the very roots of social psychology and to the theoretical formulations of one of the field's most influential thinkers, Kurt Lewin. Lewin (1947) first made the notion of social influence a concrete entity by proposing that all human behavior is a function of the person interacting with his or her environment. That programming and deprogramming are social influence processes which foster active and intensive interaction between individuals and their immediate environments cannot be denied. Yet, just what weight should be assigned to the person or the environment is a prime topic of debate.

To social psychologists, one of the most interesting aspects of these two processes is its relevance to the second question posed in that both programming and deprogramming are striking field examples of what researchers in the laboratory have been attempting to do since our discipline's creation, namely to produce a concrete link between attitudes and behavior. Numerous studies have shown that a change in attitude produced by the social influence of a persuasive message is often unrelated to behavior change (Zimbardo, Ebbeson and Maslach, 1977). An investigation of the programming and deprogramming processes could reveal evidence of this as yet elusive link. The mysterious feature of these processes is that peoples' beliefs can apparently be changed. Clearly coercion can affect behavior, but what can persuade people to radically change their beliefs?

Traditional social psychology studies which discuss attitude or behavior change reveal that, even when a link has been found it is difficult to generalize from the laboratory experiment to the field with any confidence. It readily becomes clear that stimulus materials with certain characteristics (such as relative simplicity, ease of measurement and lack of intrinsic interest) have been employed most frequently and that only rarely have experiments involved the type of activities that are a regular part of our daily lives. In addition these experiments often have been "artificial," making it difficult to draw general conclusions

for use in interpreting reactions in more "real life" situations. The types of influences exerted in a laboratory
rarely approximate the existing pressures felt by prisoners
undergoing thought reform in Korea, new recruits training
to be "Moonies," or deeply committed Moon movement members
experiencing deprogramming. Indeed, laboratory analogues
have often consisted of merely a subject's hearing a report
on the adjustment being made by others to the situation
(Blake and Mouton, 1961). Nonetheless, several theories
advanced from such studies, if taken in their proper perspective, can be useful in explaining these processes.

Thus, the following discussion of applied social psychology is put forth to make the processes of programming
and deprogramming understandable. The discussion will focus
on the seven component techniques touched upon earlier
which have been used as evidence to equate brainwashing with
the methods used during the programming process (isolation,
group pressures, sleep and food deprivation, repetition, reinforcement, monopolization and coercion). These seven
techniques are here collapsed into three general categories:
(1) isolation; (2) group pressures (including repetition,
reinforcement and monopolization; and (3) coercion (including sleep and food deprivation). Let us examine the applicability of each to both programming and deprogramming.

Isolation

One of the most effective ways of producing a break
with a person's present identity is to isolate him from all
contact with present and past environments. Through isolation, it is possible to externally impose a stripping of self
akin to the "mortification process" which Goffman (1961)
states new mental patients experience upon entering an institution. It is also possible through this method to foster an
in-group (present) out-group (past) animosity which helps to
maintain cohesion and loyalty within the new environment
(Cartwright and Zander, 1953). This cohesion is further
strengthened by the censorship of informational input producing a contextual vacuum within which reality rapidly becomes
relativistic.

Programming - the Unification Church isolates its converts
and new recruits and in so doing shields them both from their
old environment and from any negative information that environment could give them about the Moon movement. Members
stress that isolation is necessary to be separate from the
"temptations of evil" and to increase concentration without
undue interference (De Maria, 1978). Critics of the Unification Church charge that through isolation members are being
"turned against their parents" and are even taught not to

visit or communicate with them since they are "agents of the devil."

It is not difficult to see how this kind of isolation could readily foster the notion that all inside the movement is good while all outside is evil. Within this system, converts quite usually experience an intensification of affective bonds to replace any familial and friendship ties lost or damaged when the decision to become a "Moonie" was made. As inside ties become stronger, outside ties usually grow weaker, furthering the insulation and isolation of the movement. This is either accomplished by choice or by the rejection of the recruit's newly found belief and "family" by those outside the movement. Interestingly, persecution of the movement from the outside has most probably made it even more cohesive and resistant than before. Thus critics may be working at cross purposes by strengthening the movement's defenses through their attacks (see Buckner, 1964, and Barker, this volume).

However, several researchers have provided evidence for the thesis that many recruits had weak or non-existent external ties before joining the movement and that in some cases disaffection with geographically distant families, spouses, or friends was one of the original problems they were seeking to solve (Lofland, 1966; Judah, 1977). More often than not, however, an intense belief in the new produces an intolerance of deviation and a total rejection of old beliefs. Sometimes converts even change their names, ridding themselves of that symbol of their old self conception as well (Shibutani, 1961).

The recent proliferation of new religious groups has, not surprisingly, elicited fear and anger from some parents who cannot understand why their children affiliate with movements the parents consider alien and antithetical to their beliefs and values. It is instructive to note that parents who approve of their children's new beliefs, or at least tolerate them, do not espouse the same accusations. Thus, it was proposed by Thomas Szasz (Sage, 1976:45) that: "Parents want to believe in brainwashing so badly because otherwise they have to admit to themselves that the kid they devoted 15 or 20 years to has rejected them and their values." Zaretsky (Sage, 1976) emphasizes that such movements do not necessarily change a pre-existing parent-child relationship but rather that "the cults often become scapegoats for the problems of both parents and their sons and daughters." Indeed, it is common knowledge among deprogrammers that in a majority of cases, deep-seated family problems which have perhaps been festering for years are uncovered during the intense drama of the deprogramming situation. It has been proposed that such problems are among the primary reasons why many of the individuals initially joined.

Deprogramming - In deprogramming, complete isolation from the present environment is the obvious first step. According to the deprogramming viewpoint, unless Moonies are removed from the implicit and explicit mind control thought to be rampant within the Unification Church, these individuals will never be able to think for themselves nor leave the Moon movement of their own free will. Isolation within the deprogramming process is accomplished dramatically, usually during an abduction situation, rather than the relatively more gradual methods used by the Unification Church. Deprogrammers reverse the process originally set in motion during the programming process, namely, they utilize isolation to break down the affective bonds between the deprogramee and other Moon movement members, they force contact with and dependence upon the past environment (family, friends, etc.) by involving these previously significant others in the actual deprogramming process, and finally they too censor informational input to create their own brand of reality.

Group Pressures

At the core of any attitudinal and behavioral changes which occur during the programming and deprogramming processes are group pressures or social influence techniques. Experimental research on small groups has provided an opportunity for detailed investigations into the conditions and determinants of change induced in an individual's behavior through his or her direct or indirect experience of the behavior of other people (Tajfel, 1954). Although of somewhat limited generalizability, a discussion of the most relevant findings within this vast literature is crucial to an understanding of the programming and deprogramming processes. Since repetition, reinforcement, and monopolization are in essence component parts of the broader category, group pressures, these three techniques will be discussed together.

From a cognitive perspective, the individual subjected to social influence techniques within a group setting is viewed as an active organism, continually involved in organizing and evaluating informational input. During this time one is most open to such input from others in the milieu and from oneself. This openness stems from a need to make sense of one's environment, to find a cognitive mechanism which will make further adaptation possible, and to gain social reinforcement. It is in this way that an active, cognitively functioning individual is thought to analyze his or her current situation and the pressures at hand to facilitate adaptation (Schein, 1961).

One of the most significant theories in this area is Festinger's theory of cognitive dissonance (1957) which assumes that when two or more cognitions (thoughts, perceptions, implications of behavior) are inconsistent with each other, this inconsistency creates dissonance which motivates the individual to do something which will reduce this state. Dissonance can be reduced either by changing one's beliefs or changing one's behavior. Since the latter is usually much more difficult to accomplish, the former is the most common response. One of the most frequent situations which creates dissonance is an individual engaging in behavior at odds with his or her beliefs. It should not be difficult to see the relevance of this theory to the two processes under study.

An alternative interpretation of Festinger's cognitive dissonance phenomena was more recently proposed by Daryl Bem (1967). Self-perception theory, states that we come to know our own attitudes in much the same way that we evaluate another's beliefs, by observing our own behavior. Thus, Bem (1967) suggested that self-descriptive attitude statements can be based on the individual's observation of his or her own overt behavior and the external stimulus conditions under which that behavior occurs.

Evidence has been gathered by a number of researchers to confirm that behavioral commitment and active participation are key devices in producing attitude change. For example, role-playing or forced public compliance have been shown to be useful in changing attitudes previously contrary to one's beliefs (Janis and King, 1954; King and Janis, 1956). Subjects came to believe what they had said more than what they had heard or read. Lieberman (1956) found that workers promoted to foreman would change their attitudes in the direction of prevailing foreman attitudes within a matter of months, and, if demoted, would readopt the prevailing attitudes of the worker group. In related research, inducing subjects to comply with a small behavioral request has been shown to increase their tendency to comply with a bigger, more discrepant request -- the "foot-in-the-door technique" (Freedman and Fraser, 1966). All of these studies lend strong support to the conception that active participation and behavioral commitment are key devices for producing attitude change.

The famous studies of group pressure conducted by Asch (1951, 1952, 1956), although they explain only modifications in a single perceptual response rather than an integrated series of beliefs or attitudes, did nonetheless show how

individual judgments can yield to group pressure even when
that majority opinion is obviously wrong. Asch's findings
have obvious relevance to several aspects of the programming
and deprogramming processes, especially that of documenting
the tremendous influencing potential of an unanimous majority. Thus, theoretical interpretations seem to indicate
that both perception and behavior can be made to conform to
group definitions when the other members of the group define
the situation consistently.

From the earliest days of psychology, a great deal of
research has been done on the effects of repetition on persuasion, in part because of its relevance to the popular
topics of learning (McGuire, 1954). Researchers have found
that a certain amount of repetition facilitates attitude
change (Peterson and Thurstone, 1933; Staats and Staats,
1958), and that in conformity situations, the impact increases as the size of the unanimous majority grows from one
to four persons (Asch, 1956; Stukat, 1958; Thorndike, 1938).
However, it should be noted that experiments investigating
the link between repetition and learning have focused on attitudinal change, leaving any consequent behavioral modifications a matter of debate.

A basic principle of learning is that responses which
are rewarded tend to occur more frequently. Most reinforcements at the human level involve the approval or affection
of others (Middlebrook, 1974). It is therefore not difficult to understand the relevance of principles of reinforcement to those modifications of attitude and behavior which
occur within a group setting during the programming and deprogramming processes. In addition, according to Bandura's
social learning theory (1971), reinforcement appears to play
the crucial mediating role between the observational phase
of the learning process and its eventual culmination either
through verbal output or behavioral performance. However,
the permanency of such a change will, of course, depend on
the maintenance of the milieu and its ability to provide
continual reinforcement.

If the complete manipulation of information within an
environment can be achieved, this technique in and of itself
is capable of having a great impact on one's identity, and
by implication has been thought to facilitate a concurrent
change in attitudes and behavior. Combine this kind of limited informational input with a setting in which there is
either no time for individual reflection and thought or such
solitude is simply not allowed, and the effect of that world
view on an individual could be quite profound. Goffman
(1961) has discussed the damaging consequences of a similar

system in a mental institution setting as "negative feed-
back looping." In this setting, mental patients are kept
under the constant surveillance of their fellow patients
and staff with little time or attention given to privacy
needs. In addition, their past behavior is continually reviewed and serves to remind inmates that regardless of their
current level of functioning, past errors or present trans-
gressions can be powerful in the shaping of future behavior.

Programming - Group pressure is an integral part of the entire indoctrination process and is an effective method in
the long-term maintenance of beliefs within the Unification
Church. If after the initial contact with a Unification
Church member an individual accepts the subsequent invitation to a dinner or lecture, that person will seldom if ever
be outside a group situation from that point forward while a
member. The new recruit's contact person is far more than
merely his or her "spiritual parent," but rather the contact
becomes an appendage of sorts, following each bodily movement, anticipating questions, and taking care of the recruit's material and social needs. This kind of intense
contact creates an affective bond quite rapidly, a process
greatly facilitated by the fact that new recruits are usually brought into the movement by a Unification Church member of the opposite sex. Thus, new recruits are made a part
of the "Family" and made to feel loved and needed. The member's sincerity and concern give the newcomer a sense of belonging, perhaps for the first time. Acceptance in a new
group also helps to restore one's level of self esteem. New
recruits become convinced that if other people care about
them then they are surely worthy of care (Shibutani, 1961).
Thus, the development or presence of some positive, interpersonal response seems necessary to bridge the gap between
exposure and conversion. As Balance Theory (Heider, 1946)
would predict, affective bonding also furthers the acceptance by the new recruit of the ideology and beliefs embodied
in the Divine Principle.

All activities, including eating, fund-raising, lectures, and games within the Moon movement take place in
groups, many of which are sex-segregated. Without time for
private reflection new recruits and more advanced members
have little time to dwell on doubts or to think about social
and material characteristics of the outside world. This
technique, then, is useful in breaking up past memories and
external ties as well as keeping the information input to
members sufficiently convoluted to avoid contact with the
environment outside the Unification Church.

At weekend workshops, usually the first major step in
new recruit training, group pressures become even more pro-

nounced. Small groups are formed upon arrival at the retreat. These groups consist of a majority of committed Unification Church members and a sprinkling of recruits in
each. Thus, recruits are always surrounded by a larger proportion of members more advanced in their training. During
the exhausting weekend schedule these groups do everything
together and become a crucial component in the training process.

One of the most effective methods used by the Moonies
to gain conformity and compliance within these groups is a
technique known as "sharing." Through this method, group
members are counseled to open up their hearts and share
their experiences and thoughts with the group. Cohesion in
the groups is greatly emphasized. Focal topics for this
technique include discussions of lecture concepts, personal
backgrounds, reactions to the weekend's experiences, and
anything else a group leader decides is relevant to the
growth of the group and its members. These "sharings" usually begin with testimonials of more advanced members and
are followed by the recruits. Regardless of the topic,
Unification Church members tend to be somewhat uniform in
content and surely set the tone for the group. As in the
test situation designed by Asch, if a person hears five
people say X, chances are that person will also speak to X
rather than Y, even if X is not something in which he or
she truly believes. As one visitor to a weekend workshop
put it (San Francisco Chronicle, 11 December 1975):

> For two days I was swooshed and swished around
> in a maelstrom of conflicting messages and
> emotional appeals. I was told I was free to say
> what I liked and also strongly pressured not to
> rock the boat. I was assured I was experiencing
> the "unconditional love" of the whole "family"
> and yet not permitted to engage in casual con-
> versation with anyone. I heard "creativity"
> touted and saw only conformity.

It would almost seem that the Moon movement has learned one of the most basic rules of social psychology and applied it to nearly every form of human interaction, namely:
social and especially positive social reinforcement is far
more effective in shaping human behavior than are material
or negative reinforcements. With love as a reward and its
withdrawal as a punishment, behavior and beliefs can be
molded and influenced. Movement members, therefore, engage
in a great deal of touching, smiling, direct eye contact
and emotional espousals of fellowship and love, all of which
are allegedly withdrawn if "deviant" behavior is exhibited.
Some comments from recent recruits are instructive:

I realized I had to believe like them to get their
love. That conditional love made me very uncomfortable.

How can you expect me to make a decision when you
are controlling all the social reinforcements?

When you have no time to reflect, to think your
own thoughts, to talk with people with whom you
have something in common, you have to survive
somehow. The easiest way to do that, I found, is
to please.

The message is clear: conformity is praised and deviation
from the group is unacceptable. To those for whom the Moon
movement is particularly attractive, conformity to the norm
becomes that much more important as a step toward acceptance.

Repetitive singing and chanting are also a regular part
of the "Moonie" regime. Although critics suggest that such
repetition produces a kind of "mind-numbing" through a var-
iant on Pavlovian conditioning, this has not as yet been
proven. More realistically, this kind of repetition in
songs and chants creates an artificial feeling of together-
ness while the repetition of lecture concepts serves to reinforce key ideas (e.g., Satan, evil, negativity) and de-
sensitizes recruits to potentially mind boggling restructur-
ings of biblical and historical facts. It should be clear
that even though at this stage recruits may not believe the
words they utter or accept their behavior as parts of their
own repertoire, the groundwork has been laid for future acceptance. Whether one adheres to Festinger's notion of cognitive dissonance or Bem's theory of self-perception, it is
not hard to see how in time and with the aid of more intensive training and contact, change on both the attitudinal
and behavioral levels will be forthcoming.

Deprogramming - Just as group pressure forms the backbone
of indoctrination into the Moon movement, similar techniques
are crucial in what deprogrammers see as restoring an individual's free will and facilitating extraction from the
group. From the moment deprogrammees are abducted they are,
primarily for security reasons, never left alone, not even
to dispense with their own personal hygiene. It soon becomes abundantly clear that the deprogramee is the minority
or deviant figure in a group which can be quite large and
which most often consists of a team of deprogrammers (including ex-members of the Unification Church), the individual's parents, and sometimes a smattering of significant
others from the person's past.

The use of ex-members in the deprogramming process is an important element in the social influence process, since they, like the more advanced members of "Moonie" training groups, can give the "proper" direction and reinforcement necessary if change is to occur. Additionally, the use of family members in the deprogramming process often creates a positive inducement to change. The more attractive the group is to the deprogramee, the more compliance he or she will exhibit throughout the process.

Since most deprogrammings take place either in locked motel rooms or other small, secure locations, monopolization of time and attention is not hard to achieve. The deprogramee is the focal point of all attention, and from the process' commencement, constant repetition of key concepts becomes the major technique utilized. Whether through tape recordings, printed material, personal testimonials, or Moon's own words, the major tenets of the Divine Principle are relentlessly attacked and their alleged inadequacies and flaws are perpetually repeated. In the initial stages of such a barrage of information so highly inconsistent with a "Moonie's" belief system, fear surely interferes with absorption. However, as the deprogramee grows accustomed to his or her plight, perhaps realizes the futility of fighting a so obviously stacked deck, and begins to be positively reinforced by members of the group for any show of "true emotion" or "free thought," change usually becomes merely a matter of time.

Coercion

The use of sheer physical coercion, as in the extreme brainwashing situation, in an effort to change both attitudes and behavior, has been shown to produce little in the way of permanent effects. Although one can relatively easily gain temporary compliance in such a coercive environment, once people are removed from the coercive setting their attitudes and behavior will usually shift back toward their preimprisonment repertoire. Though mere behavioral compliance (a change in behavior to gain reward or avoid punishment) may be an acceptable end-product in the brainwashing situation, it is clearly not the desired result of either programming or deprogramming. For either of these processes to be effective (in the absence of an extremely totalistic environment such as a prisoner of war camp) any overt change in behavior must be accompanied by a higher order of attitudinal change. Such changes include identification, where one conforms to others to establish a satisfying relationship, or internalization, where one changes because of a recognition that the content of the new behavior is intrinsically motivating and it therefore fulfills

some need (Kelman, 1958). This shift from extrinsic sources
to motivation to intrinsic ones is crucial in the maintenance of change over time. Once behavior or beliefs are no
longer being conditioned by external motivators (i.e., compliance, reinforcement) and are instead replaced by internal
or intrinsic motivators, the changes which such a process
produces can be quite dramatic and permanent (Lepper, Greene
and Nisbett, 1971). In addition, Zimbardo (1966) has argued
that attitudes shift into line with behavior when the individual perceives him or herself to have chosen the behavior
and that attitudes fail to do so when the behavior is under
the control of environmental contingencies and constraints.

Programming - Arguments over whether the Unification Church
physically restrains its members or uses physical coercion
to gain and maintain converts has been a central element in
the brainwashing charges that have been levied against them.
Leaders of the Unification Church deny the use of coercion
in the conversion and maintenance of beliefs, but it is
clear that the self-generated pressure members feel toward
Church dictated beliefs and behavior must have derived from
sources external to the individual. However, force and captivity are simply not conditions that apply to Moon's recruits. Movement members and leaders may use emotional and
psychological pressure to be sure, but they do not force
anyone to join or believe. As Rice (1976:47) put it:

> While one might question the independence of a
> convert's mind, no one has proven the Church
> holds its members against their will. It might
> be fairer to use the term conversion instead of
> brainwashing. If conversion requires the sus-
> pension of critical faculties, at least the
> Moonies do so willingly.

Labeling as brainwashing of any indoctrination, teaching, or philosophy that is engaged in voluntarily is surely
an erroneous if not dangerous practice. This potential
danger and the key issue of coercion was recently addressed
by the American Civil Liberties Union (ACLU) in a statement
opposing the use of temporary conservatorships, mental incompetency proceedings, or denial of government protection
as a method of depriving people who have reached the age of
majority of the free exercise of religion. That statement
read in part:

> Modes of religious proselytizing or persuasion
> for a continued adherence that do not employ phy-
> sical coercion or threat of same are protected by
> the free exercise of religion clause of the First
> Amendment against action of state laws or by state

officials. The claim of free exercise may not
be overcome by the contention that "brainwashing" or "mind control" has been used, in the
absence of evidence that the above standards
have been violated.

Yet critics of the Unification Church are quick to
point out that the fallacy of making such analogies between
the methods used by the Moon movement and those utilized by
other secular and religious institutions is that people enter the latter of their own volition and therefore know the
consequences of joining. These critics claim that converts
to the Unification Church do not join voluntarily and furthermore that they are actually lured into conversion by
deception. This accusation derives from a practice known
within the Church as "heavenly deception." Members will
sometimes disguise their true association or identity for
proselytizing or fund-raising purposes. Its use has been
widely criticized within the Bay Area by Moon himself, and
it is reported to be on the wane. Further, "heavenly deception" is not employed as frequently on the East coast or
in Europe as on the West coast (Anthony, 1977). Although
the origins of heavenly deception are not certain, leaders
within the movement have ascribed it to the priority ori-
entals have sometimes given to the accomplishment of duty
rather than to the means of its fulfillment (Judah, 1977).
Critics of the practice of heavenly deception see it this
way (Day of Affirmation and Protest Hearings, 18 February
1976):

> In the Unification cult, two wrongs make a right.
> Because in the Garden of Eden, Satan deceived
> God's children, now God's children -- that is,
> the Unification Church members -- are justified
> to deceive Satan, that is the Satan-controlled
> world.

Further evidence that attests to the lack of physical
coercion and the charge of involuntary detainment of recruits and converts can be found in statistical data collected on the Unification Church. It has been shown that
the movement has a 55 percent turnover rate in recruits during their first year. This means that over half of the new
recruits will not even fulfill one year of their commitment
to the movement. Other studies (Galanter, this volume) have
shown that only 10 percent of the recruits will decide to
stay on in the movement after their first weekend workshop,
while a full 90 percent will leave on their own volition.
This same study (Judah, 1977) surveyed ex-members' reasons
for leaving the Unification Church, which generally fell

into two major categories: (1) dissatisfaction with cultural differences within the movement (i.e., sexism, reliance
on old vs. new traditions, especially pertaining to marriage) and (2) disaffection with the strict discipline which
is enforced within the movement (i.e., rules regarding celibacy, regimented routine, living by strong moralistic doctrines). These kinds of statistics and ancillary evidence
no doubt prompted Zaretsky (Sage, 1976:49) to state: "If
such groups are practicing brainwashing as such, they are
doing a tremendously sloppy job of it."

In addition to more overt kinds of physical coercion
charged by the critics, sleep and food deprivation are also
cited as "physical coercion" and a prime method of producing vulnerability to indoctrination. Moonies are said to
receive five to six hours of sleep a day and three primarily vegetarian meals, hardly the conditions under which
POWs were kept. Nevertheless, in contrast to ordinary
American standards, these seem Spartan indeed. It should
also be noted that while these so-called "deprivations" may
be externally induced in the initial stages of programming,
the new convert soon begins to engage in "conditions" or
self-imposed food, sleep, and other restrictions to pay
"indemnity" to God for "sins or failings." While there
have been some reports that these "conditions" were externally imposed as well, these are as yet unsubstantiated.

Yet simply because physical coercion may not be a part
of the Moonie regime does not exempt them from claims of
psychological or mental coercion, which though far more
subtle, might in some cases be more salient. The kind of
mental coercion that can be readily studied stems from the
Divine Principle itself which states that everyone outside
the Unification Church is influenced by Satan. Implicit in
this ideology is the notion that if a convert leaves the
fold he or she will also "be of Satan." Deprogrammed
Moonies have asserted that leaders use this threat often by
teaching that if a member leaves the Unification Church they
automatically damn not only themselves but also their ancestors and descendents to eternal hell. Leaders also are alleged to counsel that "Satan works through your loved ones
to get you away," as well as its corollary, "Anyone who
tries to get you to leave the movement is Satanic." It is
easy to see how these could be potentially horrifying instruments of fear, guilt, and superstition which some would
argue constitute a form of mental coercion.

Deprogramming - Although many of the methods used in the deprogramming process are quite similar to those used in the
original programming of the Moonies, one of its most central

elements is the forcible abduction and involuntary physical
confinement of movement members. Statistics are also useful in documenting the long-lasting effects of this kind of
physical coercion, for in comparison to those gathered on
the Unification Church members, it has been reported that
90 percent of the members who are deprogrammed remain outside the movement while a mere 10 percent return (Benson,
1977). However, it should be emphasized that many of the
horror stories concerning the physically coercive nature of
the deprogramming process have truly been blown out of proportion by the media (see Testa, 1978). Abuses in food and
sleep deprivation and physical brutality may occur, but
they most assuredly are not the norm.

CONCLUSION

By utilizing this applied social psychology perspective to explain programming and deprogramming, these processes become far less sensational and more comprehensible
to researchers and laypeople alike. Additionally, each
component of these two processes can be explored using a
variety of social science techniques including, participant
observation, survey research methodology, interviews, and/
or quasi-experimental design. In this way, programming and
deprogramming need no longer be viewed within the inappli-
cable and untestable perspective of brainwashing, but rather as phenomena amenable to research and study.

- - - - - - - - -

NOTES

1. This paper is based on research conducted by
   the author at the University of California
   at Berkeley during 1976-1978.

2. Any opinions, findings and conclusions expressed in this publication are those of the
   author(s) and do not necessarily reflect the
   views of the National Science Foundation.

*GROUP INDUCTION TECHNIQUES IN A CHARISMATIC SECT

Marc Galanter
Albert Einstein College of Medicine

In the last decade charismatic religious sects have attracted a considerable number of followers in the United
States. The results of a study on the psychological issues
relevant to decisions made by a sample of young adults about
joining one of these sects, the Unification Church (or as
its members are called, the "Moonies") are reported in this
paper. We have previously studied the psychological traits
of persons who joined charismatic religious sects; these
were studied by means of objective tests (Galanter, 1978;
Galanter and Buckley, 1978; Galanter, Rabkin and Rabkin,
1979). Similar approaches have been used for persons who
left various religious cults (Ungerleider and Wellish, 1979).
For two reasons, however, it seemed useful to consider a
group of individuals making their initial contacts with a
charismatic religious sect. First, the psychology of the
individuals themselves is important. The characteristics
defined thus far in sect members do not necessarily differentiate them from many persons who have never joined a sect.
If those who consider joining a sect were evaluated, it
might eventually be possible for us to differentiate between
persons who finally elect to join and those who do not.
Second, these sects dramatically illustrate certain aspects
of group dynamics. For example, responses evinced by them
bear similarity, in certain respects, to the responses evoked
by many of the therapeutically oriented self-help groups
(Galanter, 1978). Therefore, by studying the induction process of these sects we may obtain valuable information on
the mechanisms by which affiliation is established in large
therapeutic groups. This may then enhance our understanding
of psychologically oriented group treatments.

An initial study (Galanter, Rabkin and Rabkin, 1979)
was made that examined the attitudes of Unification Church
members, including an examination of their experiences a-
round the time of joining the church. When it became desirable to study the church's induction procedures, the sect's
officials subsequently granted further interviews and site
visits to clarify the operation of their "workshops". These
officials expressed the opinion that an objective study of

the induction procedure might serve to demystify the process
of joining, which some critics have referred to as "brainwashing." The process examined in this study was not necessarily typical of the procedures used by the church in all
parts of the country, but it reflects procedures used in
late 1978 as workshops serving a number of areas, including
Boston, New York City, Washington, D.C., and southern California. The actual sample was drawn from the latter location.

METHOD

A full workshop experience runs 21 days. Eight workshop sequences were studied over a 2-month period. There
were 104 persons who attended one of these workshop sequences. A description ensues of the workshop sequence and the
disposition of these persons. Because the interactional
context of the workshop may not be familiar to the reader,
an attempt has been made to convey the nature of the group
context in some detail so that associated psychological responses will be more understandable.

People who attend the initial "2-day workshop" are generally invited by a member of the church whom they may have
met in a public place while that member was "witnessing,"
i.e., recruiting for the church. The motivation of persons
attending the "2-day workshop" may be limited, as may be
their understanding of the church's religious creed. Prospective members usually leave for the Workshop Center from
a large city or academic campus on a Friday evening. The
Workshop Center is usually in a secluded rustic setting, a
few hours from the city of debarkation, as it was in this
study.

The schedule for the next 2 days is filled with planned
activities from 8:00 a.m. to 11:00 p.m., including three
meals a day. The principal activity is a series of six 1½-
hour lectures, which convey the most salient points of the
"Divine Principle," -- the religious doctrine of the Unification Church. Each lecture is followed by a 1/2-hour small
group discussion. The discussions and some other sharing
experiences are more oriented toward intellectual exploration of religious concepts than emotional catharsis; they
do, however, delve into personal attitudes and experiences.
The remainder of the time is filled with group activities,
typically singing, sports, and preparing and giving skits.
Participants, or "guests," spend most of their discussion
time in groups with 2 or 3 other guests, a leader who is a
church member, and the 3 or 4 "hosts" who originally invited

each of the guests to the workshop. Virtually all the guests' time, therefore, is spent either in small or large groups where more than one-half the individuals are active members in the Church. In the evening of day 2, following discussions of their continuing the workshop sequence, guests are encouraged to stay at the Workshop Center for the "7-day workshop" (which actually runs 6 days). Thirty guests (29%) opted to remain; 74 (71%) of the guests, designated as "early dropouts," did not continue beyond the initial weekend. The status of each guest was reviewed by me with the workshop staff after each weekend. Two of the guests leaving before the second workshop had been taken away by family members who came to the Workshop Center, as were two more later on in the 21-day sequence.

During the second segment, the "7-day workshop," breakfast begins at 8:00 and is followed by a 3-hour lecture and discussion; lunch is followed by 2 hours of sports, hiking, or working at the Workshop Center. In late afternoon there is another 2-hour lecture and discussion, which is followed by dinner and further sharing and discussion. The day ends with the guests filling out their "reflection notebooks;" they may choose to discuss their entries in this notebook with the larger group.

Persons participating in the "7-day workshop" engage in considerable discussion and introspection regarding their interest in the Unification Church. Workshop staff, however, also evaluate the guests' suitability for membership in the group primarily, as they describe, to exclude persons who lack the psychological stability and maturity for the arduous and dedicated lifestyle. Thus, by the end of day 8, the majority of the remaining guests elected to stay on beyond the initial week for the next segment. Therefore, 18 individuals (60% of those who completed the "7-day workshop but only 17% of the original cohort) proceeded to the next phase. Of those who left, 3 had been asked to do so after extensive discussion among the staff. During the ensuing segment 3 more were asked to leave.

This next segment, the "21-day workshop," consists of 1 week that is dedicated to fund raising, and a second week to "witnessing." In this study the "21 day workshop" was conducted in Los Angeles and its environs. This phase has a somewhat more rigorous daily schedule. Guests arise at about 6:00 a.m.; most of the day is directed toward intensive public fund raising or recruiting, for which the group is well known. In addition, there are prayers, lectures and some group activities around meal times. The day ends before midnight after a period of "sharing" and filling out

the "reflection notebook." During the day workshop guests
mix with people who are not in the Unification Church, although their compatriots are generally nearby.

At the end of the "21-day workshop" guests may elect to
move into a communal Unification Church residence, as did 9
individuals (50% of those who completed the "21-day workshop but only 9% of the original cohort), who we have designated "joiners." Application forms may be filled out, but
this formality can also take place before or after they move
into the church residence. Church members often move at
this time to remote parts of the country for fund raising,
recruiting, or other church activities, and it can be difficult to track new members. The new members were followed,
however, through contacts with the state membership directors, the original workshop coordinators, and the central
membership office of the Unification Church in New York.

It was possible to ascertain the status 4 months later
of the 9 persons who had joined after the 21-day workshop
sequence. Of these, 6 (67% of those who completed the "21-
day workshop but only 6% of the original cohort) were still
active members. Of the 3 who had left the group after joining, 1 chose to return to his family who lived overseas; 1
was reported to have been abducted while visiting his aunt's
home on the way to another church Center, and 1 was felt to
have been "not serious" in his commitment.

TEST BATTERY

In order to examine the psychological experience of the
workshop guests a test battery was formulated utilizing some
of the approaches previously employed in our studies on
group cohesiveness and religious beliefs (Galanter, 1978;
Galanter and Buckley, 1978; Galanter, Rabkin and Rabkin,
1979). In addition, by means of interviews and subsequent
pilot studies with church members, additional scales were
developed to address issues relevant to the psychological
state of workshop guests. Demographic and background items,
as well as the General Well-Being Schedule, were administered in the first 2 days of the sequence. With the exception
of the general well-being scale, the scales described below
were given as part of a repeating battery on days 1, 2, 5,
7, and 9.

General Well-Being Schedule

A 16-item scale for general psychological adjustment
was developed by the National Center for Health Statistics

(Dupuy, 1973). Its background and the derivation of an age-
and sex-matched comparison group not affiliated with the Unification Church have been discussed previously (Galanter,
Rabkin and Rabkin, 1979). Typical items, each with a choice
of scaled responses, are "How have you been feeling in general?" "Have you been bothered by nervousness or your ner-
ves?" "Have you been feeling emotionally stable and sure of
yourself?"

Cohesion Scales

These employ eight cue sentences, developed for use in
previous studies (Galanter, 1978; Galanter and Buckley,
1978; Galanter, Rabkin and Rabkin, 1979; Schutz, 1966), that
reflect different aspects of social affiliation, such as,
"They care for me," "They are suspicious of me" (scored in
reverse), and "I like being part of their activities." Responses are made along a 5-point scale ("not at all" to
"very much") in relation to two target groups. The first
group is composed of "the ten or so people from the workshop you know best" from which is generated a score for affiliative feelings toward persons inside the workshop group
("affiliations inside"). Responses toward the second target
group, "the ten or so people outside the Church and workshop
you know best," generates a score for "affiliations outside"
the group.

Creed Scale

The Divine Principle is a compilation of the sect's
religious creed. Six items of creed were chosen from the
Divine Principle that were specific to the Unification
Church; they were also presented to the guests during the
workshop sequence. Guests were asked to use the same 5-
point scale noted above to indicate the degree to which they
"agreed with each Unification Church belief." Examples,
which may sound idiosyncratic to one unfamiliar with the
sect, are "Some of the problems I see around me began with
an immature use of love by the first human ancestors," and
"My understanding of Jesus' mission to restore God's Ideal
of Creation will lead to a more meaningful life for me.

Sense of Purpose Scales

Six cue sentences each reflect some aspect of an existential sense of purpose. Samples are "I feel that my life
can have a meaning," "I can experience worthwhile relationships with others," and "My life can really make a difference." Guests were asked to use a 5-point scale to indicate
their own sense of purpose, yielding a score designated "own

purpose." They were then asked to indicate how much the
Divine Principle contributed to their feeling for each item,
generating a "purpose/Divine Principle" score.

Group leaders and workshop coordinators were rehearsed
in the format of administrating the tests, and questions
that might be asked by the guests were reviewed. Weekly exchanges with workshop staff were also arranged to deal with
problems that arose. The tests, or questionnaires, were
prepackaged in envelopes for each small workshop discussion
group; instructions were attached to each envelope and were
read to the group by the group leaders and coordinators.

A record was kept on the face of each envelope of those
who had completed the questionnaires, but the questionnaires
were kept anonymous. The following system was used to allow
for tracking of each subject's questionnaire. Subjects selected a 5-letter word and a number as their personal code,
which they inscribed on all their questionnaires. After
each workshop sequence it was therefore possible to link a
series of each guest's questionnaires that reflected how
long each guest remained in the workshops. Although this
allowed for anonymity and fostered frank responses, it did
not allow for designating questionnaires from those guests
who were either asked to leave or were picked up by their
families. On the other hand, in order to differentiate between those guests who joined after completing the entire
workshop sequence and those who did not, the joiners were
asked at the end of the 21-day sequence to reveal their respective codes. It was explained that the information would
be used solely to segregate them from the latter two groups.
All agreed to do so.

                              RESULTS

Because some test items described above were used previously in our study of long-standing members of the Unification Church (Galanter, Rabkin and Rabkin, 1979), it was
possible to compare the guests from this study with long-
standing members (N=237). On the whole, the groups were
quite similar in demographics and background. The workshop
guests who responded (N=104) were predominantly male (77%),
single (95%), and white (77%). Comparable figures for the
long-standing members in our previous study were 61%, 89%,
and 83%, respectively. The guests' mean age (+SD) was 21.6+
3.4 years; this was .3 years younger than the long-standing
members had been when they joined. Eighty percent of the
workshop guests had both parents living; 79% of the long-
standing active members had both parents living. The work-

shop guests also did not differ significantly from long-standing church members in their assessment of the degree of religious commitment their parents had. The workshop guests and the long-standing members indicated that 74% and 78%, respectively, of their fathers had no more than moderate religious commitment.

Scores for both groups on the general well-being scale are listed in table 1; they reflect the workshop guests' emotional state during the month before testing. As reported previously (Galanter, Rabkin and Rabkin, 1979), long-standing members had significantly lower scores than the matched comparison group (N=305). In the current study, workshop guests who continued with the workshop sequence after day 2 (N=30) scored significantly lower than the long-standing members; the guests who finally joined scored lower than either group.

TABLE 1

Psychological General Well-Being Schedule Scores of Long-Standing Members of the Unification Church, a Nonmember Comparison Group, and Nonmembers Attending Church Workshops

Group	General Well-Being Scores		Comparison with Long-Standing Members	
	Mean	SD	t	Signi.
Long-standing members (N=237)	74.4	17.2		
Nonmember comparison group (N=305)	83.4	16.2	6.24	p>.001
Guests attending workshop				
Dropouts after "2-day workshop" (N=74)	74.7	17.9	.28	
Guests who continued beyond "2-day workshop" (N=30)	67.2	19.2	1.95	p>.05
Guests who joined after 21-day workshop sequence (N=9)	61.9	20.1	1.89	p>.05

Results of the repeated battery were examined next using one-tailed t tests to compare guests who dropped out at the end of each workshop segment to those who did not. The

early dropouts, those who left by the end of day 2 (N=74)
had mean scores (+SD) lower than day on the affiliations inside scale than those who continued attending the workshops
(20.2+5.7 and 24.0+5.3, respectively, t=3.01,p > .005). They
also scored higher on the affiliations outside scale (17.6+
6.0, 13.4+6.9, respectively, t=2.91,p > .005).

In the previous study of long-standing members, the
same scale items had been used to demonstrate affiliations
inside the sect, i.e., "the ten members of the Unification
Church you see the most." Responses of those members can
therefore provide some basis for comparison. The workshop
guests who continued beyond the second day (N=30) scored as
high on the cohesion scales as long-standing members (mean
score, 23.7+3.9), even as early as day 2. The early dropouts, on the other hand, did not (t=5.76,p > .001). Early
dropouts also scored lower on the creed scale than those
who continued (mean score, 22.3+7.2 and 26.0+6.0, respectively, t=2.39,p .01) and the purpose/Divine Principle
scale (mean score, 20.9+8.6 and 25.6+6.1, respectively, t=
2.61,p > .01). There was, however, no significant difference
in scores on the own purpose scale between the early dropouts and those who remained.

The 30 respondents who continued beyond the second day
and completed the test batteries were divided into two
groups: those who ultimately joined at day 22 (N=9), designated as "joiners," and those who dropped out between days
3 and 22, the late dropouts (N=21). The cohesion scale
scores of affiliations outside the church were compared. On
the cohesion scales there were no significant differences at
any of the test points between the two groups on the inside
affiliations scale, but there were significant differences
at all points on the outside affiliations scale; the early
and late dropouts scored significantly higher on the outside affiliations scale than the joiners. For example, mean
scores on day 2 for the joiners and late dropouts on the inside affiliations scale were 25.3+4.7 and 25.0+3.8, respectively; on day 9 they were 25.5+3.1 and 26.3+2.9, respectively. The outside affiliations scores on day 2 were 15.8
+6.6 and 7.4+6.2, respectively, t=2.80,p .01; on day 9 they
were 20.0+4.07 and 9.3+7.2, respectively, t=2.99,p > .01. In
addition, the joiners and the late dropouts were not significantly different at any of the test points for creed, own
purpose, or purpose/Divine Principle scales.

DISCUSSION

In a previous paper (Galanter, 1978) I discussed the therapeutic large-group as a clinically useful model for the study of certain clinical phenomena, such as self-help groups and membership in charismatic sects. The large-group was defined as a cohesive association of a large number of persons who often meet in small groups and espouse a zealous philosophy with attendant rituals. The social roles and behavioral norms of group members were redefined in relation to the group's goals and functions. The model was developed from the examination of one particular sect where social cohesion was studied with questionnaire instruments similar to those employed in the present study. Comparisons were drawn to other sects and quasi-therapeutic self-help groups, such as est and the drug-free therapeutic communities. An ensuing study on the Unification Church (Ungerleider and Wellisch, 1979) dealt with the regulatory role of the belief system as well. The present study now provides an opportunity to examine the process of affiliation to such a group. This is of interest because it reflects a psychological phenomenon of considerable potency in light of the profound influence such a group may exert and the potential adaptability of this model to psychotherapeutic ends.

How were the people who joined the Unification Church different from those who dropped out? The early dropouts were found to differ on the basis of weaker affiliative ties toward the group and less acceptance of the church's religious beliefs in contrast to those who stayed beyond the initial workshop segment. Late dropouts, however, showed a high level of affiliativeness toward fellow workshop members, which was comparable to that of the longstanding members toward their compatriots. They also achieved a commitment to the sect's beliefs comparable to the guests who ultimately joined. The later dropouts, however, were different from those who joined by their greater affiliative ties to people outside the sect. This appears to indicate that an important factor in joining the sect is the presence of relatively weak ties to family and peers. Apparently, at least at this stage in the affiliation process, considerable enthusiasm for the group may be countered by the strength of outside ties.

It is interesting to compare these findings to ones reported by Trice (1959), who studied affiliation motives in members of Alcoholics Anonymous (AA), another quasi-therapeutic large group where consensual belief is important. Persons who maintained a long-term membership in AA, rather than dropping out after an initial affiliation, were found to have greater need to establish social affiliations. For a religious sect such as the Unification Church, however, a greater isolation from previous ties accompanies membership. The relative balance between affiliation to members and to old associates therefore becomes important.

In our previous studies (Galanter, 1978; Galanter and Buckley, 1978; Galanter, Rabkin and Rabkin, 1979), long-standing members gave responses to a neurotic distress scale in relation to multiple time periods. The responses indicated apparently greater neurotic distress before affil-iation compared to neurotic distress after a period of mem-bership. In the absence of prospective data, however, it was not possible to ascertain whether this reflected an ac-tual difference between these two periods or whether it was primarily the product of unintentional distortion due to cognitive dissonance. Although the number of joiners in this study was small, it seemed worthwhile to compare the general well-being scores of those who ultimately joined to those scores of the long-standing members. Significantly lower mean general well-being scores were found among the new joiners than the long-standing members. This supports the interpretation that members actually do experience amel-ioration in psychological well-being long after joining.

Members and workshop guests scored lower than a compar-ison group for psychological general well-being. The com-parison group was drawn from a residentially and socially more stable population than that usually associated with persons entering this sect, although the comparison group was matched for age and sex. The difference in scores might therefore be partly attributed to the considerable amount of social disruption experienced by many persons who elect to come to the workshops. This latter phenomenon merits fur-ther investigation because it may provide a key to the role of social instability in valency to join a quasi-therapeutic large-group.

This explanation, however, may be contrasted with the possibility that considerable psychopathology unrelated to situational issues is common in sect members. Indeed, a global solution may appeal to the psychologically distressed. Deutsch (1975) examined in detail the presence of prominent psychopathology in members of a smaller Eastern sect. In addition, we had found that 6% of the members from the Uni-fication Church and 9% from the Divine Light Mission had been hospitalized for emotional problems (Galanter, Rabkin and Rabkin, 1979; Galanter and Buckley, 1978). In this study the workshop staff, apparently respecting the vulner-ability of some guests, asked 6 of the 30 guests who stayed beyond the "2-day workshop" to leave because of "psychological instability." The staff accepted the fact that not all those interested in joining were suitable for membership. It should be noted, however, that an apparent therapeutic response has been observed for those who join other modern self-help-oriented large-groups, such as est (Simon, 1978; Babbie and Stone, 1976), consciousness-raising groups (Lieberman, Solow and Bond, 1979), Gestalt-oriented growth centers (Lieberman and Gardner, 1976), as well as other religious sects.

In this study there was no significant difference between the joiners and the dropouts regarding an absence of existential meaning in their lives. For the potential member perhaps only a certain degree of absent meaning in life is necessary to elicit interest in the Unification Church. The church must present its belief system in such a way that the potential innate resistance is relieved and the creed can be accepted. To this end, the social context plays an important role to rapidly generate a strong sense of cohesiveness during the workshops, as observed here. This was promoted when the workshop guests continued through the initial workshop segment in close relationships with the hosts who originally invited them.

The milieu of the lectures and discussions is consequently influenced by the fact that Unification Church affiliates constitute half of the membership of the group. This presents an interesting parallel to the sponsorship system in AA. It also has antecedents in other Christian sects, such as the Moravian Protestants (Piette, 1936) and the Anabaptists (Ahlstrom, 1972), which employed group-oriented explorations of belief and feelings. Indeed, technique of mixing "successful" veterans and initiates in conjoint group experience for modeling and identification is regularly seen in contemporary self-help programs. It might also be useful in strengthening the induction process in more traditional mental health settings.

NOTES

* Originally published in <u>American Journal of Psychiatry</u> 137 (December 1980):1574-1579.

*PSYCHOLOGICAL CONSEQUENCES OF CHARISMATIC RELIGIOUS EXPERIENCE AND MEDITATION

Marc Galanter
Peter Buckley
Albert Einstein College of Medicine

William James (1929:247) quoted a convert as follows:

Realization of conversion was very vivid, like
a ton's weight being lifted from my heart; a
strange light which seemed to light up the whole
room (for it was dark); a conscious supreme
bliss which caused me to repeat "Glory to God"
for a long time.

Can the lifting of "a ton's weight" change the psychiatric status of a convert, and if so, are such changes more than transient? What role can "strange lights," the meditative or transcendent experiences, play in this process? A recent growth in evangelical sects has highlighted the value of examining these issues. This is particularly important, since little systematic, quantitative research has been conducted to study the integration between religious experience and psychopathology.

This study was undertaken because of anecdotal reports rewarding one particular evangelical religious sect, the Divine Light Mission. It appeared that for certain members initiation yielded significant psychological benefits as well as relief from alcohol and drug abuse. The study was intended to examine whether this impression could be validated, and in that way improvement might be correlated with particular aspects of membership.

THE DIVINE LIGHT MISSION

The Divine Light Mission (DLM) had its origin in the United States in 1971, when its spiritual leader, a 13 year-old Indian, Guru Maharaj Ji, visited this country, after which chapters soon developed in a number of American cities. Initiation into the movement occurs when agreement is reached with one of the apostolic figures of the Mission that the potential member is ready to receive Knowledge.

After the spiritual ceremony the initiate, designated a premie, may live in a religious residence called an Ashram in
which celibacy, vegetarianism, and full obedience to the DLM
are practiced. Other premies live in communal residence
with less stringent regulations.

Premies are expected to fulfill the tenets of the DLM
which include service and meditation. Service refers to all
activities dedicated to the DLM, ranging from the formal
religious tasks to a variety of good deeds, benefiting either premies or nonpremies. Meditation generally consists
of a period of up to 1 hour in both the morning and evening,
during which the meditator sits in a lotus position with
eyes closed, and experiences various spiritual and sensate
aspects of the Knowledge. Meditation is also observed by
experiencing the holy "Word" throughout the day by rooting
one's consciousness in that experience, no matter what activity the person is engaged in.

METHODS

An arrangement was made the the DLM national organization to conduct a survey on a sample of members attending a
DLM national festival and four premies with counseling experience were trained to assist in administering research
questionnaires. A random sample of 119 premies was selected
among those members registering at different points during
the festival. While supervised in small groups, they filled
out the research instrument, a 170 item multiple choice
questionnaire which was coded for data processing. Items
were presented so as to minimize the potential influence of
respondent bias. In addition to demographic characteristics
questionnaire items fell into the following categories:

Group functions

A number of items on work patterns, residence, and meditation practice were used to clarify the relationship of
the premie to the larger group. Other items designed to tap
interpersonal affiliativeness were based on a related study
by one of the authors (Galanter, 1978; Galanter, Stillman
and Wyatt, 1974). Responses on a five-point scale ("not at
all" to "very much") were elicited for a series of cue sentences, related to feelings of social affiliativeness, such
as, "I like being part of their activities." The cue sentences were applied to each of three stimulus groups "the 10
or so premies whom you see the most," "the 10 or so nonpremies whom you see the most," and "all premies the world
over."

Psychiatric symptoms

Respondents perception of the presence and intensity of specific symptoms was ascertained by ratings on the five-point scale for the following series of statements, each followed here by its corresponding symptom: (a) I felt nervous and tense (anxiety). (b) I felt depressed and glum (depression). (c) I had thoughts of ending my life (suicidal ideation). (d) I had the feeling that I was being watched or talked about by others (referential thinking). (e) I was unclear about how to lead my life (anomie). (f) I got into trouble with my job, at school, or with the law (behavioral problems). (g) I heard voices that other people did not hear (hearing voices). (h) Emotional problems interfere with my adjustment in life (general emotional maladaptation).

Ratings of intensity were given for each symptom during each of the four following 2-month periods: (a) when the symptom was most intense at any time prior to introduction to the DLM; (b) immediately before exposure to the DLM; (c) immediately after initiation (i.e., after receiving Knowledge); and (d) in the last 2 months.

Data were analyzed by computing the incidence in the respondent sample of each symptom during each of the four periods. The statistical significance of differences between the four periods was ascertained by the Cochran Q-test. A change score for each symptom for each of the members was then computed for the difference between symptom ratings from right before exposure to right after initiation. These scores were entered into a stepwise multiple regression analysis as dependent variables, in order to ascertain significant predictors of symptom change. Questionnaire items relating to DLM activities were entered as predictors.

Drug use

Frequency of use for the following categories of drugs was evaluated for the four 2-month periods listed above: marijuana, alcohol, hallucinogens, stimulants, depressants, and heroin. Frequency of use was rated on a five-point scale for the particular 2-month period and data were analyzed by the techniques described above.

Meditation

Meditation practices were also examined, and respondents were asked to rate the occurrence and intensity of specific transcendent experiences they felt during meditation,

chosen on the basis of reports in previous pilot interviews.

RESULTS

Characteristics of the members

Premies were typically unmarried (82%) and white (97%)
and primarily in their 20s (73%). They had received Knowledge about 2 years before. Their social class was reflected in the fact that the large majority had attended
college (76%), as had one or both of their parents (71%).
There was a high incidence before joining of both seeking
professional help for psychiatric disturbance (38%), and of
hospitalization for emotional problems (9%). In addition,
one in four (27%) had been arrested at some time.

The amount of drug use prior to joining was considerable. Nine-tenths had smoked marijuana (92%) at some time;
two-thirds had used hallucinogens (68%) and 14 percent
heroin. With the exception of alcohol, the use level for
all drugs was two to four times that reported by a representative national sample of college students for that same
period. The same number had used alcohol in each of the
two groups (80%) (National Commission on Marihuana and Drug
Abuse, 1973).

Group functions

By the measurements made, there was a strong sense of
cohesiveness and communal sharing. Respondents generally
lived with their compatriots, 20 percent in Ashrams and another 50 percent with other premies in nonritual residences,
and the spouses of all married and common law respondents
were also premies. Most respondents, however, were involved
in some activities outside the movement at least half-time;
half (51%) in work, and another fifth (21%) at school.

Feelings of affiliativeness and trust were felt very
strongly toward the "10 or so premies" each respondent saw
the most. For example, the large majority of respondents
(88%) felt that they enjoyed being part of activities with
this group "a lot." Only a few (10%) felt that these premies were at all suspicious of them. Attitudes were very
similar toward "all premies the world over" (81% and 16%,
respectively). Significant differences did exist between
attitudes toward the two premie groups and a third group,
the "10 or so nonpremies" whom respondents saw most. For
example, only 21 percent liked "a lot" being part of the
nonpremies' activities (Q=64.3, df=3,p > .001); and the ma-

jority felt that this group was suspicious of them (66%,Q= 151.6, df=3,p >.001).

Decline in perceived psychiatric symptoms and drug use

Table 1 illustrates the decline in the reported incidence of moderate and severe symptoms, and moderate to heavy drug use. Compared to the periods before joining, these were reported by significantly less respondents right after joining and at the time of the survey. For example, there was a two-thirds decline after initiation in the number who felt that emotional problems affected their adjustment to life a lot, followed by a similar decline to the time of the study. The only symptom which did not decline in incidence was hearing voices, which was stable over the four time periods. The regular use of both social intoxicants and acknowledged drugs of abuse declined considerably after joining.

Predictors of symptom decline

By means of a multiple regression analysis, questionnaire items related to the following variables were tested as predictors of decline for the psychiatric symptoms and for alcohol and marijuana use: group cohesiveness, group activities (residence in an Ashram, job in DLM), and meditation (time frequency and transcendental experiences). The multiple correlation coefficients for criterion symptoms were all highly significant (df=117,p >.001), for example, .58 for decline in depression, and .38 for decline in marijuana use.

The multiple correlation coefficient for decrease in the sum of scores for all psychiatric symptoms was .69 (p > .001). That is to say, the group-related predictors tested here accounted for 48 percent of the variance in the decline of the total score on psychiatric symptoms. Predictor variables which contributed significantly to the variance of the total symptom score were: the degree to which the respondent was made happy by all premies; cared for the 10 premies he saw most often; felt better than ever before at some time while meditating; meditated during daily activities; and lived in an Ashram.

Meditation experiences

Almost all respondents (97%) set aside a specific time to meditate more than once a week, and 80 percent meditated at least twice a day. In addition, virtually all (99%) indicated that they meditated during daily activities at least

TABLE 1

PSYCHOLOGICAL SYMPTOMS AND REGULAR DRUG USE IN 119 SUBJECTS:
REPORTED INCIDENCE DURING FOUR PERIODS

	Scale Scores[a]	Symptomatic 2 months Before Introduction to DLM	2 Months Right Before Introduction	2 Months Right After Joining	Most Recent 2 Months	Q-Value
Moderate to severe psychological symptoms:						
Anxiety	4-5	45	33	5	6	99.8*
Depression	4-5	43	33	5	2	101.6*
Suicidal ideation	3-5	34	17	1	3	142.6*
Referential thinking	3-5	45	34	6	4	81.0*
Anomie	4-5	65	52	9	3	163.7*
Behavioral problems	3-5	31	22	6	1	71.0*
Heard voices	3-5	7	8	6	8	2.7b
General emotional mal- adaptation	4-5	39	29	9	3	112.5*
Moderate to heavy drug use:						
Marijuana	4-5	65	45	0	7	152.3*
Alcohol	4-5	17	13	1	0	47.7*
Hallucinogens	3-5	28	12	1	0	79.7*
Stimulants	3-5	18	7	0	1	49.4*
Depressants	3-5	15	5	1	1	39.9*
Heroin	2-5	14	7	1	0	37.0*

a Answer choices and scale scores. For psychological symptoms: 1 = not at all; 2 = a little bit; 3 = moderately; 4 = a lot; 3 = very much. For drug use: 1 = none; 2 = one to three times; 3 = about once or twice a week; 4 = about once a day; 5 = more than once on most days.

b Not significant

* p > .001, Cochran Q-test

some of the time, and over half (54%) did it "usually" or
"always." In the regression analyses the time spent in both
modes of meditation were found to be significant predictors
for decline among both psychiatric symptoms and drug use
items.

Having transcendental experiences during meditation was
also a predictor of symptom relief. Those experiences are
listed below. Following each one, in parentheses, is the
answer representing the highest score of four possible
choices, followed by the percentage of respondents who reported experiencing this choice: (a) I saw something special that no one else could see (clearly, with my eyes, 30%).
(b) I had a special and unfamiliar feeling in my body (...
very intense, 49%). (c) Time passed faster or slower than
usual in a very special way (...very intense, 34%). (d) I
felt myself to be different from my usual self in a very
special way (...very intense, 56%). (e) I saw a special new
meaning in my life (...very intense, 61%). (f) I felt better than ever before in a very special way (...very intense,
66%). (g) I had strong sexual feelings without physical
sexual contact (...clearly more intense than orgasm, 14%).

CLINICAL ILLUSTRATIONS

Psychiatric interviews were conducted with premies reported to have psychiatric and drug abuse problems. The
following vignettes illustrate certain aspects of the relationship between these problems and membership in the movement.

A 28 year-old single chemist lived in an Ashram and
worked full time as a technician. During childhood and ad-
olescence in a Protestant family, he had minimal religious
interest. Throughout that period, he had relatively few
friends and limited dating, but attained good grades at
school. Four years prior to interview he began smoking marijuana with some acquaintances and soon began daily smoking
while alone at home and while at work. He also began regularly using psychotomimetics. His goal was to "expand his
awareness of himself," he reported. He became progressively
more isolated and moved alone to a house in the country.
Over the ensuing year he became interested in the occult and
at times felt that his "soul was moving out of him." He recalled seeing an illuminated orb land in the woods in front
of his house on one occasion and assumed it was a flying sau-
cer. He continued to work, but realized that his behavior
with co-workers was often strange. Although in retrospect
he could provide no specific basis for his fears, he became
convinced at times that he was being set up for arrest on

marijuana charges. In time, he began to fear that he was
going out of his mind. Around this time, he met a premie
who introduced him to the DLM. After 2 months of daily attendance at services he received Knowledge and moved into an
Ashram shortly thereafter. The period was characterized by
a marked decline in anxiety and in feelings of alienation;
he began to feel more safe. In the 2 years since that time,
he made some friends in the Ashram, but not close ones. He
has been a principal in developing an active part time prison counseling program in collaboration with a local addic-
tion treatment program. Other premies confirmed that he was
respected and liked by his peers.

For certain disturbed persons, psychiatric symptoms apparently served as a basis for the leap of faith. These
persons appeared to be in need of some restitutive experience at a time of severe anxiety and disorganization or of
major situational stress. In this respect, the pressure of
the symptoms may have strengthened both faith in the religious creed and affiliative feelings for the group. As in
this case, the conversion sometimes appeared to serve as the
alternative to decompensation. The practice of service,
such as the prison counseling work here, appeared useful in
sustaining the restitutive process.

An 18 year-old high school senior who lived with her
Catholic family came for counseling to the medical unit at
the DLM festival. She was distressed over being unable to
meditate, and felt obliged to undertake a great deal of service to make up for this. When approached by a premie counselor, she immediately burst into tears, exclaiming her mis-
ery and feelings of helplessness and guilt. The counselor
was an empathic college teacher with no formal mental health
training. She reviewed at some length the particulars of
the "patient's" difficulty with meditation, in a compassion-
ate manner. She then gave the patient examples of how such
problems are overcome in time with fuller devotion to the
Guru, and reassured her that it was not necessary to perform
an undue amount of service. By now the girl was visibly reassured and composed. One of the authors was granted permission to speak with her at this point. On interview she gave
a history of having a brief sexual affair with an older married man. When he terminated the relationship 2 months before, she became acutely depressed and was unable to attend
to school work. It was at this point that she began having
difficulty meditating and began feeling the need for doing
more service. The girl had not discussed these particulars
with anyone else. After a measure of clarification and reassurance regarding the nature of her conflict, she expressed relief and appreciation.

Clear parallels exist between certain DLM religious approaches and traditional psychotherapy. Both techniques
provide patients with assistance in dispelling distress by
offering them in a supportive manner a series of assumptions
about their distress which are compatible with their underlying attitudes (Frank, 1963). It appeared in this case
that both a response based on DLM dogma and one based on
psychodynamic psychology were comprehensible and palliative.
Many of the exchanges at the medical unit which seemed related to religious practice appeared to have a clear-cut
therapeutic effect. In fact, at times premies spoke of
their reactions to Satsang too as if they were responding to
a large group therapeutic experience.

DISCUSSION

In planning the systematic psychiatric study of religious movement it soon became clear why recent serious work
in this area has typically employed the same methodology
used by James (1929) 75 years ago in The Varieties of Religious Experience: citation of case histories and personal
observations. Unlike general psychiatric patients who may
be observed as an adjunct to treatment, religious sects are
generally reluctant to bare themselves to outside scrutiny.
In addition, most phenomena of interest in the religious experience are highly subjective and poorly suited to experimental validation.

Since retrospective reporting on symptoms was subject
to distortion, questionnaire items were worded so as to minimize respondent bias. Cue questions for psychological
symptoms were worded so as to be both comprehensible to the
respondent and to represent psychological phenomena regularly dealt with by the mental health profession, and transcendent meditation experiences were probed on the basis of descriptions previously given by a sample of premies. Nevertheless, the changes reported here were subject to exaggeration based on subjects' unconsciously mediated need to justify their own decision to join the group.

It was, however, quite striking when respondents indicated such a widespread decline in symptoms of psychological
distress, a decline which persisted from the time of conversion, an average of 21 months before, This was corroborated
by numerous interviews; one striking example has been cited.
Such relief has been reported anecdotally among a selected
sample of converts in relation to more general attitudes
(Wilson, 1972). The diversity of specific psychological
symptoms alleviated here is notable. A decline was reported

in symptoms affected by behavioral norms, such as drug taking and job trouble; it was also found in subjectively experienced symptoms, such as anxiety, not readily regulated.
The one exception to this, the incidence of hearing voices,
may reflect less susceptibility to psychosocial influence
for this symptom associated with psychosis.

With what other aspects of membership are these effects
correlated? Clinical observations had suggested the importance of commitment to the group and participation in meditation. This was borne out by regression analysis, which allowed for statistical testing of the correlation between
these two variables. In the regression equation, items relating to interpersonal cohesiveness were high ranking predictors for decline in psychological symptoms. This no
doubt reflected the central role of a shared world view a-
mong members of the subculture. Frank (1963) dealt with
this in relation to the symptom relief of both religious and
psychotherapeutic origin, and it has been described in relation to faith-healing practices such as those of Protestant fundamentalists (Pattison, Labins and Doerr, 1973) and
Puerto Rican spiritualists (Ruiz and Langrod, 1976).

With regard to shared group functions, a similarity
might be noted to the ongoing relationship of participants
in "growth centers" (e.g., centers employing Gestalt techniques) to the overall self-actualization movement. Lieberman
and Gardner (1976) found this relationship to be an open-
ended one, directed at goals similar to those of traditional
psychotherapy. Nonetheless, this subculture was found to
operate without formal promise of treatment. It serves as
another example of a movement whose announced agenda may not
reflect its therapeutic effects. Maslow (1964) indeed, has
drawn the thesis of a wedding of psychology and religion
around phenomena such as transcendental peak experiences.

For the generation of youths studied here, the group
subculture has been seen to produce patterns of drug use.
For example, Kandel (1973) demonstrated that the adolescent
peer group predominated over all other variables as the apparent determinant of a student's marijuana use. We found
here that the youth subculture, properly reconstructed,
could reverse this pattern of use by its potent social forces. This finding itself raises a number of questions for
future investigation: Can the constellation of antecedent
stresses or psychological traits which predispose individuals, like those studied here, to a conversion experience
be ascertained? Who is likely to drop out from such a sect
early, and what are the psychological consequences of dropping out? With regard to the underpinnings of the intensive group experience, one of us has written a sociologi-

cal hypothesis for the utility of such group behaviors
(Galanter, 1978).

A second group of predictors of symptom decline in the
regression equation related to meditation. Quantitative
studies on the clinical effects of meditation have until
now been restricted to transcendental meditation. Clinical
findings have been reported with regard to general psychiatric symptoms (Glueck and Stroebel, 1975), and for diminu-
tion in alcohol (Shafi, Lavely and Jaffee, 1974) and marijuana use (Shafi, Lavely and Jaffee, 1975). The DLM uses a
meditation based on intensive imagery as well as a modified
form practiced during daily activities. In these respects
it differs from transcendental meditation, in which a primary goal is to set the mind free of thoughts or images for
a defined period of time. Apparently, both approaches can
be beneficial.

The intensity of the transcendental experiences reported during meditation is striking, and each of these experiences served as a predictor for decline of one or more of
the symptoms. Effects of such experiences on general psychiatric status (Deutsch, 1975; Shimano and Douglas, 1975)
and suicidal intent (Horton, 1973) have been reported, and
the relationship between their clinical and neurophysiolo-
gical manifestations has been discussed (Gelhorn and Kiley,
1972).

The future of religious feeling and transcendental experience in relation to clinical psychiatry cannot be lightly predicted. Interestingly, patients' religiosity has been
found to be significantly correlated with success in outpa-
tient psychotherapy (Shapiro et al., 1976). In addition, a
recent increase in religious interest in the young has promoted discussion of issues raised for the clinician by
youthful patients who have undergone conversion (Levin and
Zegans, 1974; Nicholi, 1974). Further investigation into
such common phenomena may yield useful insights for more
effective psychosocial treatments for mental illness.

NOTES

*Originally published in The Journal of Nervous and Mental
Disease 166 (October 1978):685-691.

THE PROGRAMMING (BRAINWASHING)/DEPROGRAMMING
RELIGIOUS CONTROVERSY

J. Thomas Ungerleider
David K. Wellisch
UCLA Medical Center

The purpose of this paper is to discuss some aspects of a recent controversy involving religion, the law and the mind. Parents and their children, usually adults themselves are the main characters in this controversy. Our personal involvement began in the spring of 1977 when we had occasion to visit a communal group, living in the environs of a picturesque California city. Some 200 members lived in several locations within this city and in the surrounding mountains and valleys. There they engaged in a variety of activities including raising crops and livestock which were sold in a food store, running a health food restaurant and rebuilding sailing schooners. This particular group had formed along Christian religious principles. They practiced morning and evening meditation, the latter accompanied by singing and guitar music. A carpenter had started the group, which has an age range from newborn to over 70. No drugs and and no sex were permitted among the residents. Some members had earned higher degrees and some were in school; however, while television, radios, and newspapers/magazines were available, members were not encouraged to spend time in such activities. Parents were welcome to visit their children, and the residents had the option to visit their parents' homes as well.

During one visit we were made aware that two of the residents had disappeared and were victims of "deprogramming." Some other residents had received letters and news clippings from their parents about this procedure and were concerned that they also might possibly be deprogrammed. The leader of the group asked us to evaluate the mental status of some of the residents. His primary concern was whether these individuals were mentally sound from a legal perspective. Our additional concerns were had they been "brainwashed" by the group, were they subtly being held against their will, and had they lost the freedom to think rationally? We had initially planned only to talk to those who had feared deprogramming, but the two persons who had

been abducted subsequently escaped their captors and sought
legal counselling. Their attorney consulted with a judge,
who then asked us to evaluate the mental condition of these
particular individuals. We were also interested in the
vulnerability of the members of this group to drugs and to
their sexual and angry impulses. (There was no visible anger from what we had seen.) Some residents were rugged
outdoorsmen who appeared physically very healthy. Many were
athletic; one was an Olympic gold medalist.

We began to examine these people, doing psychiatric
histories (including mental status examinations) and administering a battery of psychological tests which consisted
of the Weschler Adult Intelligence Scale (WAIS), the
Minnesota Multiphasic Personality Inventory (MMPI), the
Leary Interpersonal Check List and the Draw-A-Person.

Soon word of our study spread and members of other
groups including the Unification Church, the Hare Krishna,
the 3HO, and the Children of God contacted us. A number of
the members of these groups who feared deprogramming came
to us asking for tests to determine if they were mentally
sound. Others who had been "deprogrammed" and subsequently
either left their religious movement or went back to it also came in to volunteer for these tests. Finally, members
of the Church of Scientology and the Divine Light Mission,
a variety of parents, deprogrammers, psychiatrists, Rabbis
and civil libertarians all requested meetings to provide input, ask questions, and express concerns. Our sample eventually expanded to over 50 persons from throughout the
United States. We divided them into four groups: those
"cult" members who feared deprogramming, those who were deprogrammed and subsequently returned to their "cults,"
those who were deprogrammed and had left their "cults," and
as a control group, those who had "out-grown" their "cult"
membership with no deprogramming. Salient characteristics
in and differences between these four groups have been described elsewhere (Ungerleider and Wellisch 1979).

RESULTS

Of the 50 individuals on whom data are reported here 20
had been deprogrammed; 11 of the 20 deprogrammed individuals
subsequently returned to their respective groups. The remaining 30 individuals had not been deprogrammed. The vast
majority of these (22) reported fearing deprogramming; the
other 8 individuals "outgrew" and left their respective
groups.

Length of membership had a number of implications for cult membership. Of the eight individuals who left one of the groups studied, one did so in the first three months, two exited after between four and twelve months membership, and the remaining five left after at least a full year's membership. The twenty deprogrammed individuals reveal an interesting pattern. Of the nine individuals who were deprogrammed "successfully" (i.e., did not return to the cult) all had been members less than one year. By contrast, all but one of the "unsuccessfully" deprogrammed individuals had been a member for more than a year. Among the current members fear of deprogramming seemed to increase with length of membership. Taken together these findings seem to suggest that the defection rate increases with length of membership while "successful" deprogramming is inversely related. No one we examined was in any legal sense at all psychiatrically impaired to the point where a conservatorship law would apply. On the Mental Status Examination all persons tested were oriented in all three spheres, with intact sensorium and good fund of general information. Several 7's and/or 3's were subtracted well and both forward and backward digit repetition were normal. Proverb interpretation in all cases was normal, with no evidence of concreteness, and problem solving ability was not impaired. No one reported delusions, hallucinations, ideas of reference, severe depression or anxiety. No person examined appeared to be actively hallucinating or delusional, nor were any of these individuals severely depressed or anxious. Varying degrees of insight into their methods of coping and /or handling of problems were demonstrated by the subjects but all were within the normal range.

WAIS Data

The four groups did not differ significantly on the verbal, performance or overall IQ scores. The range of group means on the verbal IQ were from 103 to 114, with a total verbal mean of 111. The range of group means on the performance IQ was from 114 to 120, with a total performance mean of 116. The range of group means for the total IQ was from 115 to 119, with a total IQ mean of 117.

All of those in our sample scored very high on the alcoholism vulnerability scale and the over-controlled hostility scales of the MMPI. Most were idealistic and searching; most were not highly sexually stimulated. Some had been heavily into polydrug use to the point of dysfunction.

ICL Data

The group data on the ICL -- dominance/submission variable revealed that individuals who were deprogrammed and
returned to their group and current members who feared deprogramming were closely paired, viewing themselves as becoming highly dominant in the cult. Those who had left of
their own volition viewed themselves as somewhat less dominant in the cult while those deprogrammed individuals who
did not return to their group viewed themselves as becoming
frankly submissive while in the cult.

MMPI Data

The MMPI data were analyzed by collapsing the original
four groups into two main groups, those who were still members at the time of this study and those who had left. In
an overall sense both groups fell within the grossly normal
range, with the "out" group having peaks on Scales 4, then
3 (Psychopathic-Deviancy and Hysteria) while the "in" group
showed peaks on scales 8, then 6 (Schizophrenia and Paranoia). It should be noted that the "in" group had an elevation on the Lie scale such that their group profile must
be regarded as exemplifying: (1) an intentional attempt to
make a good impression and to deny faults ("fake good") and
(2) neurotic characteristics including the prominent use of
the defenses of repression and denial, coupled with a generalized lack of insight. Thus, it is likely that many of
the "in" group's sub-scales would have been elevated had
the conscious response -- skewing not existed.

DISCUSSION

The data on longevity of stay in the groups did reveal
that for some members, the time spent in the group was far
more than what can be justifiably termed "an experimental
interlude." For others, a natural attrition rate is seen.
Most clear from our data was the finding that forcible removal of individuals from the groups which takes place over
twelve months after entering becomes exceedingly difficult.

The ICL data indicated that those who tended to drop
out without outside intervention appeared to have different
motivations for joining the cults than did those who left
the cults via outside intervention (deprogramming). It appeared that for those who left on their own, the needs were
less intense for a safe, structured, predictable environment
which would permit relatively conflict-free emotional affiliation with others. The other three groups appeared to join
these religious cults partly out of intense needs for such

structured opportunities to make emotional connections with
others, which had been viewed by them as highly difficult
prior to joining the groups. The data did show, however,
that the provision of a safe milieu for affiliation with
others is not enough to hold all those who join. For those
who left after deprogramming, the attraction of affiliation
appeared to be counterbalanced by a rejection of the group
due, at least in part, to a negative reaction to a sense of
being dominated and forced into an unendurably submissive
role. The fact that those who remained in the cults did
not feel dominated and actually felt dominant may be par-
tially explained by a cognitive-dissonance model, as proposed by Festinger (1957). Their perceptions appear to differ from the reality that all of the cults function on a
hierarchical model of power. This structure, by definition,
excludes most members from major decisions or from positions
of dominance over the cult.

Data from the MMPI serve to delineate substantial in-
trapsychic and interpersonal differences between cult group
members and those who have left. Those in the cult groups
indicated difficulty with impulses in several areas with attendant super-ego deficits such that the cults appear to
serve as externalized super-ego substitutes. These difficulties are particularly strong in the area of hostility
management, with the net result being the high level of internalized hostility for all groups,but particularly high
for those who remain in the cults. The trend toward concerns over impulsive and dependent use of alcohol and other
chemical substances illustrates what might be viewed as
frustrated oral dependency needs.

These threatening impulses appear, on the testing, to
have been dealt with by over-conventionality, repression,
denial, and lack of insight. All of these can easily be
seen to be incorporated into a lifestyle based within the
cults. The basis or etiology of the difficulties with hostility present an enigma not readily answerable by this
study. Some evidence exists, however, to point to the existence of hostility prior to joining the cults. The finding that those in the cults experienced hostile feelings
toward their families far in excess of those who had left
the cults is noteworthy. It is highly probable that the
threat or actual experience of being deprogrammed increased
the hostility. It would seem unlikely that the hostility
only stems from the deprogramming issue and not at all from
the pre-cult family process. It also seems equally unlikely
that the overcontrolled, internalized hostility would only
be in regard to the family. The data suggest that the cult
members might also feel hostile toward other authority figures, including cult leaders. The conscious realization or

experience of hostility toward cult leaders would very likely be heavily repressed, or denied. Alternatively, this
denied or repressed hostility might be projected onto figures outside the cults.

The MMPI data suggest that those in our study who left
the cults are anything but free of psychological difficulties manifests differently than for the other groups. For
this group social alienation, emotional alienation and lack
of ego mastery are dominant themes. Complicating these
feelings are other feelings of distrust, resentment, brood-
ing and also an indirect form of hostility projected onto
others. This may leave them somewhat suspicious of others
and account for the elevation on the paranoia scale significantly beyond that of those in the cults. Thus, those
who left appeared to reexperience conflicts which were admittedly felt prior to joining the cults, which may potentially have been aggravated and worsened by cult involvement. The data suggest that it is not valid to say that the
cult experience is responsible for the formation of these
emotional difficulties, but that the cult involvement and
separation process may have served as a catalytic agent in
the experiencing of these feelings. Clearly, those in this
study who left the cults could use some form of psychological intervention, especially those who were deprogrammed.
Although those who left appeared to be able to face their
problems and feelings with less repression and denial, the
data indicates that discomfort with self and others is
acute.

Thus, no one theory or model of coercive persuasion
explains our data, but rather an amalgam of those suggested
by Schein. In a lengthy review of the process of group
manipulation, termed "coercive persuasion," he identified
six theoretical models and their main contributions which
he felt were explanatory psychological mechanisms for the
actualization of coercive persuasion (Schein, 1961). These
include: (1) psycho-physiological stress mechanism (Sargent,
1957; Hunter, 1951; Hinkle and Wolff, 1956; Miller, 1957),
(2) traditional learning theory, either Pavlovian or Instrumental (Forbes, Harlow and West, 1951; Winokur, 1955;
Santucci and Winokur, 1955; Meerloo, 1954), (3) psycho-ana-
lytic formations (Meerloo, 1956; Moloney, 1955), (4) identity, or identity-crisis, (Biderman, 1957; Schein, 1956;
Goffman, 1957), (5) cognitive processes, including shifts
of frame of reference and semantic manipulations (Strauss,
1959; Lifton, 1956; Schein, 1960) and (6) psychology of social (group influences (Kelman, 1958; Asch, 1951; 1952).

The psychoanalytic model fits well with the conflicts
over repressed impulses, as does the identity crisis model.

The social (group) influence model fits well with data indicating dependence on the cult for emotional contact. The psycho-physiological model, whereby cult members are theoretically broken down and debilitated to the point of acceptance of a cult ideology, does not fit our data, for their cognitive abilities were intact. The one model not proposed by Schein is that of a Family Systems orientation where the cult is viewed as an extension or replication of the nuclear family, with the degree of adaptation of the member being related to this variable. The nuclear family system parameters for cult members was not extensively focused upon in this study. The nuclear family thus becomes the logical and critical next step for focus in the evolution of research into the area of the core motivational aspects of the youthful religious cult member.

SUMMARY

In this communication some aspects of the controversy over "brainwashing" and "deprogramming" as they relate to religious cults have been presented. Precise definitions of the terms are lacking and strong differences of opinion exist between and among members of the legal, and mental health professions as well as religious leaders, parents, and their children. Observations on some of the individual psychodynamics and family interactions of a studied sample of 50 involved members have been presented and discussed.

A crucial question in regard to the members of these groups concerns their ability to make sound legal decisions as related to their persons and property. No data emerged, either from intellectual, personality, or mental status testing to suggest that any of these subjects are unable or even limited in their ability to make legal judgments. Rather, the groups all emerged as intellectually capable on testing. Clinically they revealed an intellectual and philosophical bent which resembles what Lifton has termed "strong ideological hunger" regardless of status in relation to the cult. These cults appear to provide, at least for a time, nourishment for these ideological hungers as well as relief from the internal turmoil of ambivalence. As Lifton (1956) stated:

> Thus political and religious movements, as they
> confront Protean man, are likely to have much
> less difficulty convincing him to alter previous
> convictions than they do providing him with a
> set of beliefs which can command his allegiance
> for more than a brief experimental interlude.

IV
LEGAL PERSPECTIVE

Legal issues have been pivotal in the new religions controversy. Various of these new religious groups have engaged in public proseltyization or public fundraising, and most have sought tax exempt status. There has been considerable opposition to new religious movements on all these issues. Further, based on the presumption that members of new religions have been subjected to coercive thought reform techniques, strident anti-cultists have forcibly abducted individuals from these groups for purposes of deprogramming and have sought legal sanction for their actions. As we shall see, the legal situation remains ambiguous. In some instances deprogrammers have been vigorously and successfully prosecuted, while in other cases they have been acquitted in jury trials. Civil suits have been initiated successfully by some deprogrammed individuals; other similar suits against deprogrammers have failed. Parents have achieved variable success in gaining conservatorships and guardianships. And, finally, legal scholars continue to debate the legality and merit of various types of restriction and control of new religions. It is to such issues that the papers in this section are addressed.

The most articulate legal spokesman for the anti-cultists has been Richard Delgado. He has put forward an array of arguments supporting state intervention against new religious movements based on the presumption of the use of injurious thought reform techniques by these groups. The nucleus of his argument is that individuals never possess knowledge and capacity for autonomous judgements simultaneously and hence the basis for informed consent is lacking. Delgado therefore supports a variety of intervention options ranging from mandatory self disclosure in recruiting and "cooling off" periods prior to membership to conservatorships and civil suits.

LeMoult takes the opposite point of view, depicting deprogramming as counter-conversion and defending the rights of members of new religions to their respective beliefs and practices. He views formal or informal state support for deprogramming as a direct violation of religious liberty. Deprogrammers, he contends could be prosecuted for unlawful imprisonment or kidnapping, and legal defenses which they

tests. Nor will expanded conservatorship provisions pass
constitutional muster. By contrast, LeMoult argues that deprogramming victims may initiate civil suits against deprogrammers based on civil rights legislation. He concludes
with a warning about the civil liberties implications of
legitimating deprogramming.

Shepherd has written extensively on the new religions
controversy (1982a, 1982b, 1978) and has a strong civil liberties orientation. He notes that failure of deprogrammed
individuals to achieve success in prosecuting parents or deprogrammers on either civil or criminal charges during the
1970's. However, concurring with LeMount, Shepherd anticipates greater success for civil suits under civil rights
statutes. He discerns a trend in recent constitutional adjudication toward affirmative state duties to prevent injury
from discrimination, a trend which could set the stage for
successful suits by members of religious minorities.

Finally, Bromley reviews the various legal arguments
made over the last decade concerning brainwashing and deprogramming. The weight of these arguments suggests that efforts to gain legal custody of members of new religions
through mental health or conservatorship provisions will not
be successful in the long run. The trend in such legislation seems to be in the direction of greater protection of
individual rights and more stringent standards for state intervention. Further, opponents of new religions have not
been able to formulate an intervention strategy that would
avoid direct confrontation with first amendment liberties.
Despite such constitutional protections, however, deprogramming is likely to continue. Bromley points out that law enforcement agencies and courts are reluctant to intervene in
what they regard as "family disputes," deprogrammers and
family members are willing to assume substantial legal risks,
and deprogrammers have discovered numerous legal loopholes
by which to avoid heavy legal sanctions. Thus, at least in
the near future there may be substantial divergence between
constitutional provisions and political/legal realities.

*LIMITS TO PROSELYTIZING

Richard Delgado
University of California, Los Angeles

Claims of coercive persuasion or thought reform ("brain-washing") have been heard with increasing frequency in con-nection with the activities of certain extremist, youth-oriented religious organizations, such as the Unification Church, the Children of God, the Hare Krishna, and the Love Family. These groups have come under fire from parents, church groups, and government officials for recruiting young persons by deceptive means, making them dependent for emotional support on the cult (a word I use without pejora-tive overtones in its strict dictionary sense -- "a system of religious worship or ritual"), and gradually conditioning them to accept a completely controlled, highly restricted lifestyle and a world view greatly at odds with that of the prevailing society. Critics charge that religious cults recruit young persons when they are especially vulnerable and entrap them by a sophisticated process that exploits known human weaknesses and propensities. Cult leaders re-spond that they are bringing religious values to spirit-ually starved youths and that they are doing nothing that is not done by other highly regimented organizations, such as established religious orders or military academies. The recruiting and indoctrinating practices of these groups give rise to a number of legal and social issues. Are their activities completely protected by the Constitution? If not, at what point and in what manner may the state in-tervene?

Under the Constitution, religious freedom is of two kinds -- freedom of belief and freedom of action. The first is absolutely protected by the First Amendment. A person may believe in a system which society labels bizarre or ridiculous; the state has no power whatsoever to interfere. It is when religious belief spills over into action that the degree of protection afforded to an individual or group is no longer absolute. Instead, religious practices are sub-ject to a balancing test, in which courts weigh the state's interest in forbidding or regulating conduct against the in-terest of the religious organization in carrying out its activities. In determining the state's interest in inter-vening in religious activities, the court must ascertain

both the individual and societal harms presented by these
practices. Should the court find that a competent adult
freely and knowingly consented to these religious activities
the case for intervention would be weakened since our legal
traditions oppose intervention justified on paternalistic
grounds alone. In defining the interest of the cult in
carrying out these activities, the court must look to see
if the group's religious beliefs are sincerely held and the
practices involved are central to these beliefs. In close
cases, the court may consider the extent to which the practices in question comport with the values sought to be protected by the First Amendment as well as whether their impact on society is detrimental or beneficial. In its analysis, a court must differentiate between those instances of
thought reform that are so extreme and so harmful that they
should not be tolerated and those milder forms that are acceptable to society. At this time, the court must decide at
what point a cult leaves the arena of permissible uses of
influence (as exercised by established religious orders and
in military training programs and advertising campaigns) and
enters a region of illegitimate activity. This is, of
course, the familiar "drawing the line" problem.

Judicial review of cult proselytizing must address constitutional interest balancing -- with its associated problems of consent, sincerity, and centrality -- as well as
drawing the line. This article outlines the terms in which
such a judicial inquiry will proceed. Discussion of a
third step -- determination of permissible preventive and
post-induction remedies -- will not be discussed for reasons
of length. Suffice to say that any judicial decision to
regulate or interfere with religious cults or their members
will proceed according to these terms, subject to modification in light of future work that might suggest that modification of these premises is in order.

The state's interest in regulating the recruiting and indoctrinating practices of extremist religious groups varies
according to the perceived harmfulness of these practices.
A review of legislative hearings, reports of attorneys general, court opinions, and writings of clinical psychologists
and psychiatrists suggests that the harms are severe enough
to warrant judicial concern.

INDIVIDUAL HARMS

The pressure, anxiety, and intense guilt manipulation
characteristic of the induction process of certain cults
have been found by some to induce mental and emotional dis-

orders in relatively well-adjusted youths. Individuals who
have more severe personality problems at the beginning of
the induction process may become acutely ill or suffer psychotic breakdowns. At an August, 1976 Vermont Senate hearing, a number of psychologists and psychiatrists testified
about the mental health implications of cult membership.
Dr. John G. Clark, Jr., a psychiatrist associated with Harvard Medical School, testified that the dangers, which he
found generally to be "extreme," varied according to whether
the young person's entry into the group was an expression
of "restitutive" or "adaptive" forces. The restitutive
group came to the cult with fragile, borderline personalities. Often they were "seekers," persons uncomfortable with
themselves and with reality, attempting to find psychological wholeness in a different reality. Their efforts could
be compared to those of schizophrenics who create a new,
simplified world in place of the complex world they wish to
leave. A substantial portion of the cult indoctrinees fell
into this group. A second group, the adaptive group, was
relatively free of pathology at the start. The members of
this group tended to be normal, developing young persons,
frequently college students, going through ordinary adolescent crises at the time of induction into the cult.

According to Dr. Clark, members of the first group were
very much at risk, since their tendency to find refuge in an
unreal, fixed thought system was accelerated by living with
a group whose thought, speech, and behavior patterns encouraged these traits. Their diminishing chances of regain-
ing a relationship with outer reality could be compared
with those of schizophrenics of former years whose condition
deteriorated to the point where they could no longer think
or act effectively as a result of confinement to the back
wards of mental hospitals.

Individuals from the adaptive group presented a somewhat different picture. Relatively normal at the start,
these young people joined the cult as a result of a fortu-
itous combination of opportunity (a temporary condition of
discouragement, depression, or anxiety, which can be produced by exams, leaving home, or a disagreement with a boy
or girl friend) and contact with a recruiter. Drawn into
the group by misleading representations and induced to remain through the initial stages by flattery, peer pressure,
and feigned affection, the members of this group were assumed to have undergone a series of changes. These alter-
ations, while not so pathological as those of the restitutive group, were nevertheless substantial, and if not interrupted, potentially irreversible. The unremitting sensory barrage, dietary and sleep deprivation, and lack of

opportunity for reflection and reality testing, combined to produce in these individuals a state of narrowed attention and heightened suggestibility that Dr. Clark compared to a trance. Once in this condition, the subject was encouraged to reorganize his or her past life and relationships into stereotyped patterns of right and wrong, good and evil. Subjects were compelled to sever attachments to friends and family, to drop out of college, and to give up outside employment. This forced rejection of the past, together with the exaggerated focus on the present -- with its intense preoccupation with the supernatural and cosmic struggles between good and evil -- accelerated the young convert's dependence on the group for a framework in which to resolve these frightening problems.

This dependence was also facilitated, according to the psychiatrist, by changes in the language base in which thought and discourse are carried out. Old, emotion-laden words were given new, rigid, simplified meanings. New speech patterns were adopted that demonstrated a lack of humor or ability to appreciate and use metaphor. Critical thinking was discouraged: the converts were taught to feel and obey -- not to think. Complex rational thought, a career, and ordinary love relationships became impossible. The new member appeared simplistic in his or her thought processes, stereotyped in responses to questions, and unable to make even simple decisions unaided. The possibility of human intimacy was impaired, and the victim's judgments about events in the world were damaged because of a constricted ability to perform ordinary reality testing. The final stage for both groups, according to Dr. Clark, often included classic psychotic or neurotic symptoms, such as schizophrenia, suicide, loss of ego boundaries, and an inability to differentiate between reality and fantasy.

This legislative testimony is echoed in conservatorship, habeas corpus, and child custody cases in which the courts have considered the question of psychic harm resulting from cult membership. The description of a young cult member contained in a psychiatric deposition introduced at a conservatorship hearing is illustrative: the individual had "a mood of false euphoria; a...glassy-eyed stare...." He was "fixated -- almost hypnotically -- with a perception of all people and things cast in a fierce conflict between 'good' and 'evil'." The young person's "memory of his past human interaction with the ordinary world has been remolded into a conception of guilt and self-worthlessness."

Reports by some observers and ex-members indicate that some cults utilize intensive exploitation of guilt to in-

duce compliance, enhance their control over converts, and
facilitate a break with the past. Some ex-members also may
experience personal guilt for having lied to their friends
and family or for having assisted in recruiting new members
into the sect. Aftereffects related to guilt may include
terrifying dreams, often of suffering an illness or accident as punishment for having left the cult. While in the
cult, the forced preoccupation with guilt and damnation
drives some members to engage in self-mutilative behavior,
sometimes as demonstrations of faith. One youth committed
suicide by lying down in the path of an oncoming train
after running away from a Unification Church training center. Physicians and residents of Duchess County, New York,
site of one of Reverend Moon's training centers, have noted
the unusual number of trauma cases and suicide attempts involving cult members seen in local hospitals. The Unification Church teaches that the individual must "pay indemnity" for his sins, which include thinking evil thoughts.
An individual who owes indemnity is required to do something
painful or difficult, such as forfeit a night's sleep. One
who wishes to become a core member of the Unification
Church must fast at least seven days. Some psychiatrists
who have dealt clinically with ex-cult members find that
the feelings of guilt and worthlessness induced by the cult
experience can contribute to depression, feelings of impending doom, and apathy toward one's surroundings lasting
months after release.

Limitations placed on language, thought, and experience;
loss of ego functioning; physical stress; and forced ac-
quiescence to the will of the leaders gradually reduce the
decision-making ability of some cult members to such a degree that their behavior comes to resemble that of much
younger persons. As the developmental process ceases, the
cult maintains the individual in a regressed state by "re-
capitulation of themes" from early stages of life. In this
condition the possibilities for individual growth and development are severely impaired. Once-bright university scholars have written letters of childlike simplicity to their
parents or siblings. Parents who have visited their offspring while in the cult have found them unable to make
simple decisions. A psychohistorically oriented physician
has likened the processes involved to those exploited by a
totalitarian society. Other psychiatrists believe some
youths unconsciously use cult membership as a means to escape the responsibilities of adulthood. Unaware of their
own motivation, these youths became ensnared in an unreal
world and their "escape from freedom" is difficult to reverse.

The health threatening effects of a low protein-high carbohydrate diet, insufficient sleep, overwork, and substandard, cramped living conditions are compounded by the belief, common to many cults, that medical science is useless and that illness is a sign of spiritual shortcomings. In addition, a number of cults, including the Unification Church, allegedly encourage self-mortification as a means of purging the self of sin. Members of one cult were found to ingest dangerous substances in order to attain spiritual insights. Children born to some cult members may suffer from neglect and inadequate medical attention. During a hearing conducted by a California legislative subcommittee, the runaway daughter of the leaders of the Alamo cult told of a boy who died of malnutrition, colitis, and dysentery; medical advice had not been sought. Another report described children with fevers of 104 to 105 degrees who were not permitted to be taken to the hospital and babies who were denied medication needed to combat disease. Chronic vitamin deficiency and protein deprivation are reported to be common in some groups.

One of the most striking outcomes of cult indoctrination processes, observed by some psychiatrists, family members, and ex-cult members, is a severe impairment of autonomy and the ability to think independently. A typical observation is that of an Arizona court psychologist that physiological debilitation, guilt, and anxiety "gradually reduce the decision-making process, the ego functioning, till the person almost becomes 'autistic-like.' He doesn't go outside his little self-encapsulated beliefs," but instead accepts automatically the views and commands of the leaders. Other observers have recounted that long-term cult members appear "zombie-like," or "programmed." Others described qualities such as a "glass-eye stare," a "fixed facial smile," and stereotyped, robot-like responses. Psychological submission can serve as an essential step in preparing a recruit for membership, since some cults require members to subordinate their will to that of the leaders in virtually every aspect of life. Members may live in the commune where their mail and telephone calls are monitored. They may not receive visitors or speak with their parents unless an elder is present. Marriages may be arranged by the leaders, who also assign members to daily tasks. Life consists of fundraising on the streets, proseltyizing for new members, and carrying out household chores. New converts are often required to donate all their possessions to the group; they may also be required to make a will in favor of the cult and sign a power of attorney authorizing the cult leaders to act for them in legal matters. Obedience to the elders is often described as God's will; leaving the

cult or being otherwise disobedient will result in punishment. This obedience in the physical sphere is often carried over into the mental life of the new convert. As the
recruit's external world becomes regimented and his actions
become like those of the other members, his inner life
ceases to be his own. Questioning or critical thinking is
seen as evidence of Satanic influences. The member is
taught to permit the leaders to do his thinking. The literature and teaching of some cults contain phrases such as "I
am your brain."

Our legal system is reluctant to impose restraints on
the self-regarding actions of competent adults. Consequently, the state's interest in intervening in religious
activities because of harm to an individual would be
greatly weakened by a finding that a competent adult freely
gave his informed consent to these religious practices.
However, coercion, deception, physical or mental weakness,
and abuse of a fiduciary capacity traditionally have been
held to militate against a finding of voluntary choice in a
variety of contexts, ranging from consent to medical procedures to waiver of constitutional rights.

CONSENTING ADULTS

Coercion sufficient to override the will of an individual is generally recognized as a factor negating his free
choice, although other requirements, such as the duty of
reasonable resistance, vary from one context to another.
Coercion may be based on the actual use of power to subordinate the will of another, or on a reasonable fear that
the individual in the superior position will use that power
to harm the other.

Some cults have reportedly resorted to threats of physical harm in order to discourage members from leaving the
group. More frequently the pressure takes less physical
forms. The candidate may be told that his salvation depends
upon remaining with the group and that leaving will result
in spiritual punishment. He may be warned that leaving the
cult will cause him to be struck down with cancer, become
insane, or suffer a fatal accident within a year. Cult members may be told that their loved ones may fall ill and suffer a lingering death. The isolated setting in which indoctrination takes place makes it more difficult for the convert to evaluate these threats according to his ordinary
frames of reference.

Apart from a few cases involving witchcraft and voodoo,
there are few decisions concerning the legal effect of

threats of spiritual or physical sanctions which are inherently unlikely but believed by the victim. Cases turning on undue influence hold that when a spiritual or religious adviser convinces a believer that failure to make a gift to the adviser will result in spiritual penalties (even though these may be inherently improbable), the victim's act will be set aside. Since the cult may be found to be responsible for the threat as well as the erosion of a victim's mental processes which causes him to acquiesce to the threat, courts may well deny a cult the defense that the victim acted freely. Of course, when physical pressures accompany the spiritual threats, the likelihood that a court would find an invalid consent increases greatly.

Deception also vitiates consent, since an individual cannot be said to have consented to an act when he has been deceived as to the essential nature of that act. The use by some cults of front groups, concealment of the identity and purpose of the organization to newcomers, and various techniques to ensure that trainees do not have an opportunity for reality testing all combine to make it likely that their recruiting and indoctrinating process will be found nonconsensual because of concealment of material elements from the potential convert.

Courts have found in a number of contexts that mental or physical debility, particularly where known and exploited by one who receives the benefit of an action, is an important element militating against voluntariness. Because some cults systematically maintain conditions designed to weaken resistance and induce a state of physiological and psychic depletion in new members, the victim's choice to cooperate with the cult's processes becomes open to scrutiny.

Gifts to doctors, nurses, and religious advisers have been regarded with skepticism by courts when it appeared that the gift was initiated or solicited by the beneficiary, and when that person occupied a position of special trust with respect to the giver. Because some cult leaders, at the time they solicit a commitment to membership, pose as and perhaps may be regarded as spiritual advisers, it seems likely that they will be held to the high standard of integrity and fair dealing developed by courts in these cases. Any finding of insincerity, pecuniary motive, or exploitation would thus cause the "gift" of the new member's resources and energies to be set aside.

Another factor which should increase a court's skepticism is the deliberate manipulation of knowledge and capacity. The process by which an individual becomes a member of certain cults appears arranged in such a way that knowledge and capacity, the classic ingredients of an informed consent, are maintained in an inverse relationship: when capacity is high, the recruit's knowledge of the cult and its practices is low; when knowledge is high, capacity is reduced.

When the newcomer attends his first meeting, his capacity to make rational choices is relatively unimpaired. He may be experiencing a momentary state of depression or suggestibility; nevertheless, his rational faculties are probably relatively intact. Such persons, if given full information about the cult and their future life in it, might well react by leaving. For this reason, the cult may choose to keep secret its identity as a religious organization, the name of its leader or messiah, and the more onerous conditions of membership until it perceives that the victim is "ready" to receive this information. These details may then be parceled out gradually as the newcomer, as a result of physiological debilitation, guilt manipulation, isolation, and peer pressure, loses the capacity to evaluate them in his ordinary frames of reference. The recruit never has full capacity and full knowledge at any given time; one or the other is always impaired to some degree.

Related to this manipulation of capacity and consent is segmentation of the joining process into a series of stages, whereby the convert's assent is obtained before proceeding to the next step, but the final stage or end result is concealed from view. Thus, the individual at the end of the initial meeting may be pressured to join the group at their three-day retreat; at the end of their retreat, he may be urged to commit himself to attend a longer, seven-day training session. At the end of this session, he may be encouraged to attend an even longer training camp, generally of one to two months' duration. At each step, the intensity of the indoctrination and guilt manipulation increases, together with the pressure to make a permanent commitment to the group.

When this segmentation occurs, the potential convert may be given a general idea of the activities and teachings that will be offered at the next stage, but may be given no opportunity to elect to embark on the entire journey. The consequences of the final step are in such cases concealed until the victim reaches the penultimate stage, at which time he has been "softened up" to such a degree that commit-

ting his life and fortune to the cult seems but a small
step. The process could be compared to a hypothetical one
in which a patient visits a physician for treatment of an
abscess. The physician first obtains the patient's permission to disinfect and examine the affected area. Next,
the physician obtains the patient's consent to administer
a local anesthetic, then to make a small incision. By
stages, the phyician proceeds until he has amputated the
patient's limb -- his undisclosed objective since the in-
ception of treatment. This example, outrageous in the context of the ethical standards we require in the physician-
patient relationship, is arguably no less offensive when
the relationship is that of pastoral trust and confidence.
If, under the circumstances described, the law would protect
the patient from the harm of an unconsented invasion of his
body, it seems equally likely that the law would protect
the cult recruit from any nonconsensual tampering with his
mind and psychic autonomy.

SOCIETAL HARMS

     Apart from the dangers that cult membership can pose
for the well-being and autonomy of the individuals involved,
some cult recruitment and indoctrination practices may appear to threaten certain societal institutions. These
dangers claimed by some observers include harm to the family relationship, a potential for violence; and the social
impact of the aftereffects of cult experience.

     Cult membership is regularly followed by abrupt with-
drawal from and limited communication with the family, a-
part from periodic efforts to obtain monetary donations or
to convert siblings still at home. Parents, particularly if
they show concern or attempt to persuade the young person to
leave the sect, may be said to be agents of Satan. If the
cult believes a parent is contemplating legal action to remove the new member, it may hide the convert or send him to
a remote colony. Words such as father, mother, love, and
family are often given new meanings. In Reverend Moon's
organization, for example, father means Reverend Moon and
mother means Moon's wife.

     Although most cults now exercise at least some care to
ensure that only persons who have attained the age of majority are admitted to full-time membership, some still accept
minors; others proselytize actively among high school and
even junior high school age youths. When a seemingly happy,
well-adjusted son or daughter abruptly disappears and re-
fuses to communicate with his parents, the emotional shock

the parents experience is often intense. High-achieving, popular, well-adjusted youths may disappear without notice or explanation; if the parents succeed in locating the child, he may behave like a stranger. As one parent has observed, there is a double trauma: grief at seeing the son or daughter disappear, and shock at realizing that often little can be done about it. Some parents have suffered mental and physical illnesses as a result of the stress of forced separation from and concern over the welfare of a loved child.

Within the cult, the new relationships may display some unusual characteristics. In some groups, elders select and marry, at mass ceremonies, couples who may not have met before the ceremony. Such marriages may be performed without legal sanction, while remarriages sometimes take place without a prior legal dissolution or divorce. In many groups sex is rigidly regulated. Women may be treated as inferiors, taught to be subservient, and relegated to the performance of domestic tasks. Infants may be raised communally and not considered as belonging to their biological mothers. Their training and discipline are often carried out in rigidly regimented fashion, with stern punishment for behavior that impinges on the adult business, prayer, or consciousness. Babies are frequently born without the benefit of medical care; older children may not receive inoculations, dental care, or pediatric examination. In some cults children of school age are not permitted to attend public schools, since this might expose them to improper thoughts and ideas; they attend a school organized by the cult where they are educated according to a highly restricted curriculum. Although not enough time has elapsed for the results of these approaches to childrearing to be fully evaluated, physicians familiar with the processes involved are concerned that the rigidity, lack of emotional support, and inattention to ordinary developmental needs may well portend severe personality distortions, if not overt psychoses, later in life.

Some ex-cult members have reported that while in the group their state of induced obedience was so absolute that they would have willingly killed their parents or others if commanded by their leaders to do so. One member told a prospect who was determined to leave that he would break both the prospect's legs if that would change his mind. Some members have expressed the view that the struggle between the forces of Satan and the forces of God may soon break out into physical warfare; if it comes, they are prepared to fight and die as "heavenly bullets" for their cause. A tract from the leader of the Children of God sect,

described in a recent California hearing, implies that the
cult could demoralize America through acts of sabotage,
poisoning water supplies, posting snipers on rooftops, and
destroying gasoline supplies. Some cults, including Reverend Moon's organization and the Hare Krishna, reportedly
have set aside stockpiles of firearms for "self-defense."
Members of one cult are known to have kept records of the
names of those they would punish when the spiritual tide
turns in their favor.

While it is difficult to assess the seriousness of
these threats, it is clear that some cult leaders have extensive control over their followers, who would willingly
carry out any order, legal or otherwise. It is also evident
that isolated acts of violence have occurred. Some members
who have succeeded in leaving the cult have been threatened
and harassed, some parents attempting to visit their children have reportedly been beaten. Others who have expressed
an interest in removing their children from the cult have
been told that if they persisted, they would never see their
child again or that the child would be hidden or would
commit suicide. Some professionals and others who actively
oppose certain cults have been threatened with death.

A final concern is that the habits of obedience to authority and simplistic black-and-white thinking forged
within some cult groups will have effects on individuals
long after they have left the organizations and returned to
the outside world. Some social observers have expressed the
fear that these persons will prove ready prey for other such
"totalistic" movements. This concern is supported by the
writings of psychoanalytically-oriented historians such as
Erich Fromm, who see mankind as possessing an impulse to
"escape from freedom" -- an impulse which they see as explaining the rise of such regimes as that of Nazi Germany.
Robert Lifton has written of well-educated Western academics,
physicians, and priests who underwent "re-education" in
Chinese thought-reform camps in the early 1950s and returned
as dedicated communists. Other returnees appeared "deeply
confused," and a number of others apologized for the acts of
the regime that had treated them so brutally, explaining
that these were necessary for their own progress. While the
fear that dropouts from religious cults will retain the im-
print of their conditioning to such an extent that they will
again seek closed, totalistic systems of belief is consistent with earlier human experience and the theoretical writings of psychohistorians, it is difficult to evaluate fully
the likelihood of such an effect. Little systematic research appears to have been done concerning the impact of
the cult experience on members who have left these groups;

too little time may have elapsed for patterns to become
visible.

   Although the state has a number of demonstrable interests in restricting the use of psychologically and physically harmful indoctrination techniques, defenders of religious cults have urged that these are insufficient to overcome the constitutional interest of these groups in practicing their religions. Traditionally, protection of freedom
of religion, along with that of other First Amendment rights,
has been deemed absolutely essential to our constitutional
form of government. The individual's freedom to believe
what he wishes is, and always has been, absolute. The definition of religious belief is very broad; a religious faith
need not be based on belief in a supreme being or involve
conventional forms of worship or church attendance. Thus,
religious cults may not be excluded from constitutional
protection merely because they are different or because
their practices and beliefs appear to others to be heretical
and strange. Indeed, if constitutional guarantees of religious freedom mean anything, they must include the protection of newly established and unpopular groups who will ordinarily lack allies in government and in the established
churches, and will thus be in special need of judicial protection. Because religious thought and practice historically have been afforded great deference under our scheme of
government, it could be argued that noninterference is the
only position that is consistent with American constitutional and political traditions. But where conduct rather
than belief is concerned, courts have applied a less stringent standard of review, and lowered this standard even more
where the practice was found to be insincere or only inci-
dentally religious.

RIGHTS AND LIMITS

   Conscientious objection and other religious exemption
cases establish that religious practices are entitled to
constitutional protection only to the extent that the beliefs underlying them are sincerely held. As consent will
limit state intervention into practices harmful to the individual, fraudulent, deceptive, or predominately secular
practices by a cult will lessen the protection normally
given to religious activities by the courts.

   Deception can enter the recruiting process at several
points. Such violations are reported with particular frequency during the early stages of recruitment. Except in
the rare case in which the recruiter perceives that the vic-

tim is extraordinarily receptive to being converted, the recruiter may neither inform the individual that he is being
asked to attend a function of a religious organization, nor
advise him that the purpose of the meeting is to initiate a
process that will change the prospect's mental processes
and his relationship with the rest of the world. Some cults
utilize front groups with innocuous names in order to allay
the possible suspicion of potential converts that the organization might have overtones of religious totalism.
Frequently, potential converts are told that the group is
concerned only with "making the world a better place," or
addressing the problems of disease, poverty, war, drug ad-
diction, immorality, or racism. Another practice that evi-
dences an attempt on the part of some cults to bypass the
rational processes of their victims involves the selection
of potential converts. Recruiting guides used by some
groups include instructions to concentrate on "the hungry"
and on those individuals whose resistance is temporarily
lowered because of loneliness, worry over exams, or other
adolescent crises.

Deception can continue after the youth has been attracted into accepting his first contact with the group. At
the first meeting, he often finds himself surrounded by
smiling, friendly young persons, very much like himself,
who look him sincerely in the eye and appear to demonstrate
great interest in him, his studies, and his ideas. The initial picture the recruit receives may be of a group of
happy young people primarily involved in secular aims and
ideals. The first lectures tend to be little more than de-
nuniciations of the impersonality and immorality of modern
life. There is little reference to religion: topics such as
the spirit world, the apocalypse, and salvation, as well as
the role of the cult's messiah, may be introduced in a
carefully staged sequence, when the recruit is perceived to
be "ready" for them, and in physical circumstances designed
to lessen the probability that he will withdraw. If the
candidate asks questions or expresses doubts, he is usually
encouraged to suspend these, since they will be answered
during later lectures.

These practices are justified by certain groups as
"heavenly deception." Since candidates are, at the start,
under the influence of evil forces and may thus have a negative attitude toward religion in general or the cult in
particular, concealment and deception are excusable. When
the individual learns about the group's nature, he may be
unable to confront this knowledge because of impaired
judgment resulting from lack of sleep, isolation, peer
pressure, and guilt. In these cases, the act of commitment

may be made at a time when the individual is physically and
emotionally exhausted, as well as surrounded by persons who
press him fervently to make a commitment. His decision may
be the culmination of a carefully staged series of experiences, each designed to generate excitement and guilt, and
to reduce his objectivity. Deception may be utilized at
the outset to attract potential converts to participation
in a process that they might not otherwise choose, as well
as during the actual process of conversion. Where such
techniques are utilized, reduced First Amendment protection
may be appropriate.

Draft and tax exemption cases demonstrate that ostensibly religious conduct will be considered insincere if the
underlying motivation is dominantly secular, rather than
religious. Particularly suspect is activity motivated by
political or pecuniary considerations. Although some religious cults are wholly apolitical and show little interest
in national and civic affairs, others are intensely active
in lobbying and other attempts to affect the political process. Moon's organization, with its recently publicized
ties to a foreign government and possible involvement in
covert intelligence operations, is a prime example. Its
political interest stems from a belief that the world, to
be saved, must become a theocracy under the leadership of
the cult's messiah. The Unification Church utilizes, as do
other cults, the services of hard-working young people, particularly females, to gain the ear of congressmen, especially those with positions on prominent committees. In their
recruiting, some cult organizations may seek out individuals they know will be able to perform these roles. They
also recruit actively among the families of persons who
are believed to possess political power, such as business
leaders, elected officials, and high-ranking military officers. Apart from these special cases, some cults concentrate on recruiting young, upperclass youths, both for the
financial gain they represent for the cult and for the hope
of increasing their access to and acceptance by persons in
positions of power. Despite the monastic simplicity in
which rank-and-file members live, cults such as the Love
Family, Hare Krishna, the Children of God, and Reverend
Moon's organization demonstrate considerable interest in
amassing material wealth. Often, new members are required
to donate all material possessions to the organization.
Cult fund-raisers, through sales of flowers, trinkets, or
literature on street corners or solicitations of donations
for sometimes nonexistent social programs, average one
hundred dollars to three hundred dollars per day; figures up
to one thousand dollars are not uncommon. Much of the proceeds from such activities are often funneled to the elders.

At the top levels, some leaders are reported to live in luxury, surrounded by servants, Persian carpets, antique furniture, and limousines. Excessive economic orientation of cult activities, including proseltyizing, would render the group's religious claims vulnerable to charges of insincerity.

Religious practices offensive to social norms, such as the ritual ingestion of peyote or the refusal to send children to school after they attain a certain age, may be tolerated if they are essential to the practice of the religious group involved. But where the nonconforming practice represents only an optional or minor aspect of the belief system, the practice is likely to be denied complete First Amendment protection. Under this test, the use of cults of coercive or deceptive techniques to attract and indoctrinate new members could be found to fall outside the perimeter of First Amendment coverage. Refusing to allow a cult to use these techniques does not prevent it from continuing to adhere to its belief system, engaging in ceremonies and rituals of its own choosing, or maintaining communal living arrangements. Although it would deny the cult an efficient means of expanding its circle of adherents, ordinary methods of persuasion, education, and propagandizing remain available, as they are to other religious denominations that wish to increase their memberships. It seems unlikely that the interest of any religious group in utilizing extraordinary methods of assuring membership growth can be shown to be so central to its belief system that it warrants First Amendment protection as a core value.

In close cases it becomes necessary to ask whether extending constitutional coverage to coercive persuasion utilized by religious groups as a membership-increasing device is consistent with the values sought to be forwarded by the religious liberty clause of the First Amendment. A number of views exist concerning the objectives of this clause. According to one view, a central purpose is the protection of the individual's right of privacy in making fundamental decisions concerning the conduct of his personal life. Using this approach, it seems unlikely that protection would be extended to coercive persuasion techniques, since these may diminish the ability of the victim to make private decisions about his life. In another view, the protection of religious liberty is designed to prevent oppression of small struggling minorities, who might suffer intolerant treatment at the hands of the majority. But this view seems aimed at preventing the extinction of such groups, rather than affording them a right to become more powerful relative to other groups. A final view, espoused by Thomas Jefferson,

perceives religious freedom as an aspect of freedom of the
mind. Since forceful or deceptive persuasion techniques
may diminish the scope of the mental processes, it appears
these practices are unlikely candidates for protection
under the Jeffersonian view of religious toleration. This
conclusion is echoed by some leaders of established religious groups who view Moon's organization in particular as
"spiritual fascists" bent on depriving members of the abil-
tiy to make free, individual decisions in religious matters.
It is also supported by reports of ex-cult members that
they were denied freedom of thought and choice while within
the cult, and were made to adhere to every detail of the
official theology on pain of spiritual -- and sometimes
physical -- punishment.

DRAWING THE LINE

Inherent in the balancing of interest analysis is the
practical problem of distinguishing between those techniques of persuasion which are necessarily tolerated by society and those which are so harmful as to be unacceptable.
The argument that meaningful distinctions cannot be drawn
between the coercive persuasion practiced by some religious
cults and the practices of other, societally accepted, institutions proceeds by observing that each element or practice utilized in cult-related resocialization is also found
elsewhere. Conventional religious orders often impose a
high degree of isolation by cloistering. Some military
recruiters, Madison Avenue copywriters, and campaigning
politicians use exaggeration, concealment, and "puffing" to
make their product appear more attractive. Revivalists may
at times use guilt manipulation. Officer training schools,
Outward Bound, and executive training institutes sometimes
cause psychological and physical casualties. Thus, the
thought-control processes engaged in by religious cults, it
could be argued, are indistinguishable from those of these
other groups.

There are two responses to this argument. The first
is that some religious cults may expose their indoctrinees
to a greater variety of classic mind control techniques than
do other groups, as well as apply these techniques with
greater intensity. Jesuit and other religious training institutions may isolate the seminarian from the rest of the
world at various stages of the training period, but the
training does not usually involve physiological depletion,
nor does the order deceive the candidate concerning the
duties required of members. Most religious orders are careful to set out the obligations and vows of priesthood in

advance, closely examining the convictions of the candidate
to determine whether the priesthood is best for him and for
the church. Nor do the major denominations concentrate, as
do some religious cults, on the weak, the depressed, or the
psychologically vulnerable. A number of orders, in fact,
utilize psychiatric screening to eliminate those whose interest is an expression of psychiatric or emotional problems.
Others require a waiting or "cooling off" period. Executive
training programs, Outward Bound, and military officer
training all use peer pressure to induce the individual to
adopt new patterns of thinking and behavior, but they rarely, if ever, seek to facilitate this process by physiological depletion. Nor do they deliberately stir up feelings of
dread, doom, guilt, and sinfulness to make the trainee more
receptive to a new view of the world, as some cults do.
Private military schools enroll youths at an early age when
it might be expected that the students are more vulnerable
to forceful indoctrination and less able to resist pressure
to change. Even here, however, the set of means employed is
not so extensive and pervasive as that utilized by some
cults. The students are normally sent home for holidays and
vacations. State requirements ensure that diet, hours of
sleep, and living conditions are adequate to maintain health.
Although peer pressure may be exploited to promote conformity to the school's goals, such pressure is generally applied on a simple reward-punishment basis, rather than by
means of sophisticated psychological techniques aimed at
tapping subconscious fears, anxieties, and guilt feelings,
as is allegedly the case in some cults. Thus, the practices
of few, if any, other societal institutions approach either
the intensity, sophistication, or completeness of the conditioning process found in some cults. A decision to intervene to prevent abuses in this area thus does not by its
own logic require intervention in other areas where the
abuses are milder and more easily resisted.

The second answer considers the end-state, or result,
of religious-thought reform. If it should appear that the
harm brought about to individuals and societal institutions
is more extreme and less consensual in nature than changes
produced by everyday communications such as advertising,
then the case for intervention remains intact even though
there might be some incidental overlap in the means utilized. Television commercials may induce ennui and torpor,
but they rarely cause mental breakdowns; Jesuit training
rarely results in broken bones, scabies, or suicide. Even
military training, with its emphasis on replacing civilian
values and thought processes with those of the military,
does not begin to approximate the far-reaching changes often
reported to result from lengthy stays in a Unification

Church or Hare Krishna training environment. Thus, the coercive persuasion of some religious cults may be differentiable from that of other groups and institutions in two key respects -- the means used and the results obtained. Accordingly, courts may order remedial action without fear that such intervention has no principled stopping point.

If, as the foregoing review suggests, religiously motivated thought reform affecting substantial numbers of young persons and their families and resulting in medical, psychological, and societal harm is being practiced by certain cults, then the state has a constitutionally adequate interest in intervening. Although recruitment and indoctrination are carried out under colorably religious auspices, the right to constitutional protection may be diminished because of insincerity and deception, and because thought reform techniques are not essential to the continuing survival of the religious groups involved. If harms are found to be inflicted on unconsenting individuals, the state may interfere without violating the principle that consensual, self-regarding action should be free from state regulation. It seems possible to differentiate the harmful thought control reportedly practiced by such cults as the Unification Church, Hare Krishna, and the Children of God from other, milder forms of influence traditionally tolerated within our society. A variety of remedial measures are available, ranging from simple preventive requirements to procedures aimed at returning a person to his former condition.

There appear to be no insuperable constitutional, moral, or public policy obstacles in the way of state or federal action designed to curb the abuses of religious groups that utilize high-pressure, harmful, and deceptive tactics in recruiting and indoctrinating young members. So long as remedies comport with the least restrictive alternative requirements (i.e., that the remedy utilized be that which is least harmful in its impact on individuals in the religious group) and provide adequate due process procedures and judicial oversight, measures aimed at regulating the private use of mind control by religious or pseudoreligious groups appear to be fully permissible.

NOTES

* Originally published in <u>Society</u> 17 (March/April 1980):25-32.

*DEPROGRAMMING MEMBERS OF RELIGIOUS SECTS

John E. LeMoult
Karpatkin, Pollet and LeMoult
Law Firm, Atlanta, GA

The conflict between established cultures and new religions is an ancient one. It is parallel to and part of the conflict of the generations, the parent-child struggle, youth's quest for identity through conversion, and age's need to preserve meaning and purpose through established values. It is also part of the ongoing friction between established socio-political institutions and the new ideas that transform those institutions.

In times past, society's intolerance of new religions was easily implemented. Early Christians were crucified. Later, members of Christian sects perceived as heretical were burned at the stake, or tortured into submission. Puritans were harried out of England. Quakers, Mormons, Jehovah's Witnesses, Black Muslims, and many others have suffered different forms of religious persecution in America. It is nothing new.

What is new is the way some members of modern society have chosen -- in a supposedly enlightened age of first amendment religious freedom -- to fight new religious ideas. It is called "deprogramming." It consists of taking adherents of religious groups against their wills, confining them, and subjecting them to intense mental, emotional, and sometimes physical pressures until they renounce their religious affiliation. Deprogramming raises profound questions about religious liberty, privacy, and freedom from parental control. The courts and legislatures are just beginning to deal with these questions. This article will attempt to discuss some of the background factors involved, as well as recent developments in the law.

In order to understand the legal issues surrounding deprogramming, it is necessary to take a look at new religious movements and sects, as well as at "deprogrammers" and the methods they employ. This article will consider: (1) the current "high demand" religious groups, and their process of conversion; (2) the deprogrammers and their techniques of behavior modification; (3) the constitutional rights of members of religious sects; (4) the constitutional rights of minors; (5) the legality of abduction and restraint for the purpose of deprogramming; (6) the use of conservatorship proceedings for the purpose of accomplishing deprogramming; and (7) civil suits, a counterattack by targets of deprogramming.

BACKGROUND

New Religious Sects

The emergence of new religious sects in America attracting thousands of young adherents every year would lead one to believe we are undergoing a religious revival. But this is probably not true. There have always been new religious sects, and the diversity in beliefs of the new groups makes the concept of a unified "revival" unlikely. What is probably happening is that middle class young people are beginning to move away from established churches to unorthodox high demand, often authoritarian, sects springing up all over the country.

Fundamentalist, evangelical, pentecostal, or charismatic sects which for decades have practiced "born again" Christianity in Southern Baptist churches, among "Holy Rollers," in black rural churches, and in the faith healing hills of Bible Belt America are now attracting the college educated children of suburban Catholics, Protestants, and Jews. Likewise, the practices of Zen Buddhism, Yoga, Hindu chanting, Transcendental Meditation, Sufi dancing, and Sikh vegetarianism which formerly attracted only a few western urban intellectuals, are now attracting the sons and daughters of Scarsdale, Oak Park, Shaker Heights, and Grosse Point.

The reasons for this shift of middle class youth away from established churches to these new sects are too complex to discuss thoroughly here. Certainly there is a need for an inner-directed, more authoritarian, and less social-conscious Christianity. But the move of many young people away from Christianity and Judaism toward such groups as the International Society for Krishna Consciousness, the Divine Light Mission of Maharaj Ji, and many other eastern religions of a communal type suggests that they are looking for companionship, a sense of participation, a direct experience, a return to nature, and authority that they have not found in their established religions. Now that the political and social battles of the civil rights and antiwar movements have died down, young people searching for abso-

lute answers are investing their energy and commitment in
religions.

Deprogrammers and some parents are convinced that all
of these new sects are part of a mass conspiracy (sometimes
said to be Communist) to brainwash young people and turn
them into "zombies." The deprogrammers lump all different
kinds of groups together, making no effort to differentiate
the beliefs or practices of the many disparate groups. The
charge is made that the new groups have psychologically kidnaped their new devotees, depriving them of their free will,
so that only the most drastic measures can "rescue" them
from this bondage.

The measures employed by deprogrammers include kidnaping, physical restraint, and enforced behavior modification
or "brainwashing" of the very kind they accuse religious
sects of practicing. Deprogrammers justify these methods on
the theory that the young people are "programmed" by the
"cults," and that all the deprogrammers are doing is bringing them back to reality.

Parents are disturbed not only by the new theological
beliefs of their offspring,but also, and perhaps more so,
by the changes in their attitudes and appearances. Pot-
smoking, motorcycle-riding kids become serene quoters of
Scripture or oriental tracts. Young people doff sweaters,
sneakers, and blue jeans for ties, jackets, long skirts, or
flowing saffron robes. Parents assume their once normal
offspring have lost their minds, been "brainwashed." But
what has clearly happened is that the young people have undergone a thing called conversion.

To most Christian groups, conversion is a sudden infu-
sion of grace into the soul, a new birth, accepting Jesus as
one's personal Savior. To eastern religions, it is a slower
opening to the awareness of God within oneself, or the universal Self or Soul or Consciousness underlying all Being.
It is achieved through chanting, yoga, or some form of meditation, and through the abandonment of the lower self (the
ego with its base desires). By means of detachment, one
attains a higher state of enlightenment and oneness with the
essence of the world around him.

The conversion experience has been well described by
William James (1958) in The Varieites of Religious Experience. He considers it a crystallizing of unconscious aims
and wishes, previously "incubated" in "cold" centers of the
mind, and suddenly becoming "hot" -- brought to the surface
by some crisis or experience and occupying the center of

one's thoughts and activities. James says this happens particularly to people in their teens, and that certain psychological and emotional changes are characteristic of all conversions. The fact that a dramatic change takes place in a
converted youth is neither new nor sinister. It may simply
be a case of arriving at a new identity, perhaps a "negative
identity" with respect to the role offered as proper and desirable in one's family.

No one has proved that any religious sect which has
been the target of deprogramming engages in physical restraint, abduction, or any other such practice. What is
probably true of most such groups is that they offer warmth,
friendship, authority, and a prescribed course of conduct
laced with plenty of dogma. No doubt there are serious efforts to influence the thinking of the new adherent, but
these are clearly not "brainwashing," since the adherent is
free to depart if he chooses.

Deprogrammers and Deprogramming

The new, and I believe dangerous, element in this conflict between parents and children is "deprogramming." Deprogrammers are people who, at the request of a parent or
other close relative, will have a member of a religious sect
seized, then hold him against his will and subject him to
mental, emotional, and even physical pressures until he re-
nounces his religious beliefs. Deprogrammers usually work
for a fee, which may easily run as high as $25,000.

The deprogramming process begins with abduction. Often
strong men muscle the subject into a car and take him to a
place where he is cut off from everyone but his captors. He
may be held against his will for upwards of three weeks.
Frequently, however, the initial deprogramming only lasts a
few days. The subject's sleep is limited, and he is told
that he will not be released until his beliefs meet his captors' approval. Members of the deprogramming group, as well
as members of the family, come into the room where the victim is being held and barrage him with questions and denunciations until he has recanted his newly found religious beliefs.

Such deprogramming is described by deprogrammer Ted
Patrick (1976) in his book, Let Our Children Go! He told
one victim, "I can stay here three, four months. Even longer. Nobody's going anywhere." He admits using "Mace" on
people who try to interfere with an abduction, limiting the
sleep of the victim, hiring thugs to help him with his kidnapings, and using real violence on a member of the Hare

Krishna sect.

One would ask where deprogrammers get the authority to make these cosmic judgments about religious sects. What qualifications do they have to adjudge persons "brainwashed" or to apply dangerous methods of enforced behavior modification? Is this a group of psychiatrists, theologians, and social scientists? No. Ted Patrick, for example, says he is a high school dropout. His only training appears to be a working knowledge of the Christian Bible. There is no evidence that he knows anything about religions. Nor are there indications that other deprogrammers are qualified to make judgments about the mind, the soul, God, or the Unborn, Unoriginated, Unformed One.

Since Ted Patrick began deprogramming people in San Diego in 1971, the deprogramming movement has grown tremendously. Patrick claims that he does not deprogram for a profit, but has his expenses paid by the parents who enlist his aid. Deprogramming has, however, become a somewhat costly proposition. People around the country have organized "underground deprogramming networks" with pro-deprogramming chapters in various cities. One lawyer in Tucson, Arizona, has formed a tax-exempt foundation with the purpose of making Tucson the "deprogramming center of the country." All too often, deprogrammers are able to kidnap members of religious organizations without interference by police and local officials -- or even with their cooperation -- and smoothly transport them to places where they can be confined for rapid brainwashing. Free-lance deprogrammers are operating around the country and cashing in on the profit making potential of deprogramming.

Deprogrammers are able to produce many young people who have been deprogrammed and who will testify to the benefits of deprogramming. They will claim that their minds were enslaved and that they have been brought back to reason. I think that this phenomenon is explained by two factors. First, the deprogramming usually reunites the young people with their parents and brings about the kind of reconciliation and attention that many of these young people have been seeking all of their lives. The prodigal's return to the family fold is usually more than enough to compensate for the loss of a new-found religious belief which may have been, in part, a rebellion against the parents in the first place.

Second, the method of deprogramming is really a form of counter-conversion, a system of behavior modification intended to change the victim's beliefs and make him conform

to religious beliefs and practices acceptable to his parents.
It is far more like "brainwashing" than the conversion process by which members join various sects. The restraint,
deprivation of sleep, constant talk, denunciation, alternation of tough and easy talk, emotional appeals, and incessant questioning finally cause a break in the will, giving
the deprogrammers a certain power over the victim. The
"break" described in Patrick's book is not unlike the break
described by Dr. Joost A.M. Meerloo, in his book (Rape of
the Mind, 1961) on brainwashing, as having been suffered by
victims of Nazi interrogation. The result of deprogramming
may well be the kind of "[s]ubmission to and [p]ositive
[i]dentification with the [e]nemy" described by Dr. Meerloo
of POW subjects of brainwashing.

THE LEGAL RIGHTS OF DEPROGRAMMERS' TARGETS

The Rights of Sects and Their Members

The constitutional right of people to practice their
own religion, no matter how unorthodox, or how unacceptable
to parents, relatives, and friends, has recently been the
subject of several cases involving conflict between deprogrammers and religious groups.

The constitutional issue arises because deprogramming
does not take place in a vacuum outside the realm of legal
encounter. Abduction, unlawful restraint, physical assault,
deprivation of sleep, and enforced behavior modification do
not in themselves involve state action when carried out by
private individuals. But when the state condones or assists
such action, constitutional rights are being violated.

Deprogrammers have often received the tacit, if not
open, support of local police, the FBI, and the courts. In
his book, Ted Patrick calls for legal action to stop "the
cults." Such action has been considered in at least six
state legislatures. There have also been McCarthy-like "investigations" of religious "cults" which have resulted in no
prosecutions, but involved plenty of character assassination.

Recently, in New York City, a Queens County grand jury
handed down an indictment against Hare Krishna leaders on
the theory that they had unlawfully imprisoned their members
through "mind control." In California, a judge granted conservatorships over adult members of a religious sect, allowing deprogrammers to do their work. In a New York prosecution of Ted Patrick for unlawful imprisonment several years
ago, the trial judge allowed the defendant, as part of an

effort to prove the defense of justification, to probe and
ridicule the most deeply held beliefs of a religious group.

At issue is the question of whether the courts are ever
allowed to consider the truth or falsity of any religious
belief. Furthermore, there is the question of whether the
courts are allowed to determine that an individual's religious conversion was not voluntary, but resulted from an alleged exercise of mind control. At the heart of the constitutional issue is the nexus between the free exercise clause
of the first amendment and several other basic constitutional rights, particularly that of free speech.

Deprogramming, as a type of outlaw vigilante action,
arose because of parents' inability to charge religious
sects with violation of any known laws. Though deprogrammers charge new religious groups with fraud, they have not
legally proved this. A church or religious group's practice
of accepting voluntary contributions from adult members can
hardly be defined as fraud. Among the thousands of sects
condemned by deprogrammers, there may be some which are in
it only for the money, but generally these groups are dedicated and sincere -- whether or not one accepts their
creeds.

Parents' real concern is not with any allegedly illegal
action on the part of various sects, but with the process by
which new members are proselytized and then confirmed in
their beliefs by leaders of the groups. That process is
speech. Preaching, praying, chanting, teaching, and meditating all constitute practices heavily protected by the Constitution.

The first amendment "embraces two concepts, -- freedom
to believe and freedom to act. The first is absolute but,
in the nature of things, the second cannot be." The freedom
to act may be restricted, but we must distinguish between
those acts which constitute "speech," those acts protected
by other sections of the Constitution, and those acts falling outside of constitutional protection. Any state invasion of a member of a disfavored sect's right to believe not
only interferes with his free exercise of religion as guaranteed by the first amendment, but also is an unconstitu-
tional establishment of religion. When the state applies
differential treatment to various religious beliefs, there
is an establishment of religion. Interference with disfavored religious beliefs by judicial inquiry as to the
truth or falsity of those beliefs or by suppression of members' religious speech is, therefore, a violation of both
aspects of the first amendment.

The Supreme Court has on several occasions indicated
that the first amendment forbids the courts to consider the
truth or falsity of a religion.   In the United States v.
Ballard former Justice Douglas wrote:

> The law knows no heresy, and is committed to the
> support of no dogma, the establishment of no sect.
> ...Men may believe what they cannot prove. They
> may not be put to the proof of their religious
> doctrines or beliefs. Religious experiences which
> are as real as life to some may be incomprehensible
> to others. Yet the fact that they may be beyond
> the ken of mortals does not mean that they can be
> made suspect before the law.

In the United States v. Seeger, the Supreme Court recognized that when Congress required belief in a "Supreme
Being" to qualify a person for conscientious objector status, it did not allow local draft boards to inquire into the
truth of anyone's belief.   "The validity of what he believes
cannot be questioned," said former Justice Clark.   The Court
asked only whether "the claimed belief occupies the same
place in the life of the objector as an orthodox belief in
God holds in the life of one clearly qualified for exemption." This could include "deeply held moral, ethical, or
religious beliefs."

Courts may in certain situations consider the sincerity
with which religious precepts are held, but such an inquiry
must be cautious so as not to encroach on the protected area
of truth or falsity.

In the realm of action, the state may interfere with
those practices of religious groups which pose a threat to
the rights of others or the good order of society. While
one may question the value judgments by which the courts
have arrived at their sometimes conflicting rulings, one
recognizes the validity of the underlying judicial premise
by which the courts have upheld various kinds of legislative
restrictions on religious groups. Thus, the Supreme Court
has upheld the application of laws against polygamy, Sunday
closing laws, compulsory vaccination laws, and child labor
laws, despite a claim that the free exercise of religion was
thereby violated. Other courts have allowed criminal prosecution for drug-related offenses, despite a claim that the
drugs were part of a religion. A free exercise of religion
argument was rejected in cases involving fraudulent securi-
ties activities and the handling of poisonous snakes in violation of statutory prohibitions. Courts have split on requiring submission to blood transfusions.

In the cases where courts have interfered with the activities of religious groups, the interference has usually
involved traditional standards for public health, safety,
and education. Even in these areas, however, the courts
have leaned towards tolerance where it could not be shown
that the act or omission caused real injury.

The area in which courts, particularly the Supreme
Court, have granted the widest latitude of religious sects
is that of expression. Indeed, early Supreme Court decisions upholding the rights of religious groups rested on the
free speech guarantees of the first amendment rather than on
the free exercise clause. In Lovell v. City of Griffin and
Schneider v. New Jersey, the Court allowed Jehovah's Witnesses to distribute religious tracts on the basis of the
free speech clause. In West Virginia State Board of Education v. Barnette, the Court upheld the right of a child to
refuse, on religious grounds, to salute the flag, but again
based its decision on free speech grounds.

Finally, in Cantwell v. Connecticut, the Court brought
the free speech and free exercise clauses together to protect the right of Jehovah's Witnesses to go door-to-door
proselytizing, playing records, distributing literature, and
performing those very types of actions that today's deprogrammers condemn. Like the so-called "cults" which are attacked by deprogrammers, the Jehovah's Witnesses were not
engaged in any action violating traditional standards of
health, safety, or education. The complaint against Cantwell
was essentially no different from the deprogrammers' complaint against the "cults," i.e., that he used speech to indoctrinate others into a false religion, and to wean them
away from the established, respectable religions of the day.

The act of speech by which religious groups attract,
induct, and indoctrinate members must, of necessity, be protected under the Cantwell doctrine. If any such groups
teach their adherents to separate from family, abandon wordly
goods, forfeit a college education, despise political and
social institutions, or denounce other religions, that
teaching is protected free expression. The teachers may not
be prosecuted for teaching; legal sanctions which would ordinarily protect their followers from deprogramming cannot
be lifted because the adherents listen; and the state may
not condone or assist deprogrammers of those who choose to
accept the teaching.

If the state were allowed to determine that proselytizing resulting in conversion were really "brainwashing," it
would be questioning the validity of a religious experience

and thus, as a result, the underlying validity of the religion. It would also be invading the highly protected area of free speech. Such a determination would violate the free exercise, establishment, and free speech clauses of the first amendment.

This matter is squarely presented in the novel New York case of People v. Murphy. The Murphy case grew out of an effort by a Hare Krishna woman to bring charges against her mother and a private detective who had aided in seizing her. She was held for four days of deprogramming. In her testimony before the grand jury, the woman's mother said her daughter was a victim of "mental kidnapping" by the International Society for Krishna Consciousness (Iskcon, Inc.), and that she was only "rescuing her." The grand jury declined to indict the private detective or the parent, then heard testimony on Iskcon, Inc. Subsequently, the grand jury handed down an indictment charging two Krishna leaders and Iskcon, Inc., with restraining the Krishna woman and another member who was unsuccessfully deprogrammed "under circumstances that exposed them to a risk of serious physical injury." The language was based upon the wording of section 135.10 of the New York Penal Law which deals with first degree unlawful imprisonment. Justice John J. Leahy identified the issue as follows:

> The entire crux of the argument propounded by the People is that through "mind control," "brainwashing," and/or "manipulation of mental processes" the defendants destroyed the free will of the alleged victims, obtaining over them mind control to the point of absolute domination and thereby coming within the purview of the issue of unlawful imprisonment.

Justice Leahy then analyzed the law of unlawful imprisonment and pointed out that there was no evidence that the Hare Krishna members had been subject to either physical restraint or deception. Like other converts to the new religious sects, they had freely and voluntarily chosen this radically different way of life.

The court rejected the prosecution's argument that the daily ritual chanting and other activities of the Krishna movement constituted a form of intimidation and restraint over the members. Justice Leahy noted that cases allowing prosecution for unlawful imprisonment involving "psychologically induced confessions, mental disease or defect, hypnosis to destroy a free will, intoxication, and coverture" were not applicable to the charges brought against the Hare

Krishnas. He found that in every case, the defendants were seeking to compel their victims to perform an illegal act by illegal means, such as false representation.

Justice Leahy indicated that he understood the hurt felt by loved ones whose children had given up their worldly possessions, social contacts, and former way of life for a new religion, but came down on the side of allowing individuals to choose their own path to salvation.

Religious proseltyizing and the recruitment of and maintenance of belief through a strict regimen, meditation, chanting, self-denial and the communication of other religious teachings cannot under our laws -- as presently enacted -- be construed as criminal in nature and serve as a basis for a criminal indictment.

The same issue, i.e., whether religious sects use "mind control" to restrain their members, was later presented in the California case of Katz v. Superior Court. That case involved the use of temporary conservatorship proceedings to gain custody of adult members of the Unification Church of the Reverend Sun Myung Moon. They were then to be deprogrammed. One of the issues that arose in the case was whether the orders granted by the lower court, which initially allowed the members of the Moon Church to be turned over to deprogrammers, constituted a violation of their first amendment right to religious freedom. The parents contended that religious freedom was not involved, but that "the sole issue was whether or not the conservatees had been deprived of their reasoning powers by artful and designing persons." The court indicated that an inquiry into such a matter could in itself constitute a violation of first amendment freedoms.

The court noted that there may be "a compelling state interest in preventing fraud under the guise of religious belief," but said that the first amendment applied to the religious acts as well as beliefs of unorthodox sects. For the practices of a religious group to be regulated, they must pose "some substantial threat to public safety, peace or order." The court found no such grounds for governmental regulation in the case of the voluntary religious conversion of the followers of the Reverend Moon. The court said:

We conclude that in the absence of such actions as render the adult believer himself gravely disabled as defined in the law of this state, the processes of this state cannot be used to

deprive the believer of his freedom of action and
to subject him to involuntary treatment.

The American Civil Liberties Union has condemned deprogramming as a violation of first amendment rights. The Annual Convention of the New England Psychological Association,
the National Council of Churches, the World Fellowship of
Religions, and professionals in theology and psychology have
also condemned deprogramming for the same reason.

The issue is not likely to die with these cases, the
first of their kind. The deprogrammers still have the sympathy of police, the courts, and, probably, the general pop-
ulace. There have been serious efforts to obtain legislation which would make it easy for an individual to be forcibly removed from a religious group which deprogrammers consider to practice brainwashing. The next step, of course,
would be to outlaw various practices of the religious groups
themselves. Consider the possibility of a law which would
outlaw brainwashing. How would such a law be applied?
Would the court be entitled to prohibit the Hare Krishna
movement from engaging in ritual chanting? Could pentecostal religious sects be prohibited from speaking in tongues,
fundamentalists from memorizing Bible verses? Could prac-
titioners of Transcendental Meditation, or other types of
meditation, be prohibited from reciting mantras, counting
their breaths, or practicing yoga?

If there were to be laws against brainwashing, such
laws would have to be particularly and carefully drawn.
They would have to prohibit abduction, physical restraint,
involuntary subjugation to indoctrination, deprivation of
sleep, and lengthy and consistent efforts to break the will
of the subject. It is doubtful that any religious group
could ever be prosecuted under such a law, and the effect of
this law would most likely be to impale the deprogrammers on
their own sword. For it is they, and not the religious
groups, who engage in such practices.

THE LEGALITY OF ABDUCTION

Criminal Cases

The book Let Our Children Go! by deprogrammer Ted
Patrick with Tom Dulack states:

[D]eprogramming is the term, and it may be said
to involve kidnapping at the very least, quite
often assault and battery, almost invariably

conspiracy to commit a crime, and illegal restraint. Patrick disputes the charge that saving children from a cult entails illegal behavior;
in any event, he contends that no alternative
exists.

A principle reason police have often refused to take
any action against deprogrammers is that a family member is
always involved. To the police, this can make the affair a
"family matter" which should either be referred to the family courts or dealt with in civil courts. The FBI has, at
times, expressed similar views.

The federal kidnaping statute applies to "[w]hoever unlawfully seizes, confines, inveigles, decoys, kidnaps, abducts, or carries away and holds for ransom or reward or
otherwise any person, except in the case of a minor by the
parent thereof, when: (1) the person is willfully transport-
ed in interstate or foreign commerce...." The phrase "or
otherwise" means that federal law recognizes kinds of kidnapings other than kidnaping for ransom. In most deprogramming cases, the people being kidnaped are not minors, and
therefore the defense available to a parent does not come
into play. Moreover, even if the parent has the defense,
it should not apply to nonfamily deprogrammers. Nevertheless, there has been only one known federal prosecution
under the kidnaping statute for an abduction for purposes of
deprogramming.

The obvious reason for this failure to prosecute is
that the "purpose" of the deprogramming-kidnaping is not one
of the traditional purposes, i.e., ransom, use as a hostage,
white slavery, or sexual abuse. Federal officials apparently have decided to pass over acts which may not fall into
the usual category of socially reprehensible conduct.

However, the Supreme Court has held that kidnaping
within the meaning of the federal statute need not be for
pecuniary benefit or any other illegal purpose. Circuit
courts have held that the kidnaping need not be for ransom
or reward, or some other illegal purpose, and that a specific purpose need not be charged or proved in a kidnaping
case. There is no requirement that the victim of a kidnaping be harmed. Under federal law, it is possible for a parent to be convicted of kidnaping his or her own child where
that child has a legal right to freedom.

In Miller v. United States, the mother and the step-
father of a married seventeen-year-old girl abducted her for
the purpose of forcing her to live with them and work for

them. Prior to her marriage, the girl had lived with her
grandfather. The court upheld the conviction of the step-
father against the claim that he was simply aiding his wife
in assuming control of her daughter.

It is not a defense that the motive of the kidnaper is
pure, or that well-meaning persons have abducted a child for
its own benefit. In United States v. Atchinson the defendant had abducted a five-year-old child in the belief that
the child was being mistreated by its parents. There was no
evidence that the child was harmed by the defendant, and, on
the contrary, there was evidence that the defendant was motivated by concern for the child's well-being. The court
upheld a federal conviction for kidnaping, and a sentence of
six years' imprisonment.

The degree to which abduction for the purpose of deprogramming can be prosecuted under state law varies from
state to state. Generally, the common law crime of kidnaping has been expanded to include the crime of false imprisonment. The elements of the crime depend upon the particular wording of the statute.

As a general rule, one can be prosecuted for kidnaping,
or unlawful imprisonment, without any proof that the act was
performed for financial gain or for some other illegal purpose. The purpose of the kidnaping is usually immaterial.
The purpose of the abduction may serve as a factor of aggra-
vation, or may be used in determining the punishment. An
evil intent may be specifically required for prosecution on
account of kidnaping. As to first degree kidnaping, New
York would appear to be such a state.

New York combines kidnaping and unlawful imprisonment
under the same article of the Penal Law. The key terms are
"restrain" and "abduct." One is guilty of kidnaping if he
"abducts" a person. One is guilty of unlawful imprisonment
if he "restrains" another person. In New York there is a
crucial distinction between "kidnaping" and "unlawful imprisonment." It is the distinction between "genuine kidnaping" and those many other types of abduction or restraint
which include lesser offenses against the rights of the unwilling victim.

It seems doubtful that the acts of deprogrammers would
fulfill the specific intent requirement of New York's first
degree kidnaping statute. First degree kidnaping requires
either death; or intent to injure, sexually abuse, or ter-
rorize a person, or to collect ransom, advance a felony, or
interfere with a governmental function. Second degree kid-

naping, however, simply requires that the victim be abducted.
Although second degree kidnaping requires a criminal intent,
it appears that intent to abduct is sufficient, without regard to the motive. Thus, a second degree kidnaping prosecution in New York of those who abducted a person for deprogramming would appear to be in order.

In any New York prosecution for kidnaping, it is an affirmative defense that "(a) the defendant was a relative of
the person abducted, and (b) his sole purpose was to assume
control of such person." Hence, a New York kidnaping charge
could not be successfully brought against a person who abducted a relative for deprogramming. The statutory defense
does not extend, however, to unrelated abductors. In most
states a parent cannot be charged with kidnaping his own
child. But where a parent does not have legal custody, he
can be guilty of kidnaping.

In New York, the less serious offense of unlawful imprisonment also appears to be applicable to abduction for
the purpose of deprogramming. For unlawful imprisonment to
constitute a first degree offense, the restraint must expose
the victim to a "risk of serious physical injury." This
might apply if an abduction for deprogramming were particularly violent. Second degree unlawful imprisonment occurs
when the defendant "restrains" another person.

Ted Patrick has escaped conviction in New York for second degree unlawful imprisonment of a person aged twenty.
In a case involving his attempt to abduct Daniel Voll for
deprogramming, Patrick claimed he was only helping the parents of the young man save him from an injury greater than
the seizure of Voll. He asserted the justification defenses
in sections 35.05(2) and 35.10(1) of the New York Penal Law.

The first of these defenses, that in section 35.05(2),
requires an "emergency situation" in which public or private
injury is "imminent." Even if one accepts the dubious proposition that membership in a particular religious group
caused "injury," could such injury be deemed "imminent" requiring emergency measures. The other justification defense,
in section 35.10(1), allows a parent or someone else assigned to care for a person under twenty-one to use physical
force, but not deadly physical force, as he reasonable believes it necessary for the discipline or welfare of the
young person. Both of these justification defenses are general defenses which must be disproved beyond a reasonable
doubt by the prosecution.

At the time of this prosecution of Patrick, the age of
majority in New York was twenty-one, and section 35.10(1)

John E. LeMoult

applied to the parent of a "minor." Since the attempt to
abduct Voll occurred two weeks prior to his twenty-first
birthday, he would have been considered a minor unless emancipated. The prosecuting attorney, Juan U. Ortiz, argued
that Voll, who had been living on his own, was emancipated.

The trial judge allowed the jury to get deeply involved
in value judgments about the rightness or wrongness of
Voll's religion. The result was a trial of Voll's religion
rather than of Ted Patrick. The defense was permitted to
introduce wide-ranging evidence in an attempt to ridicule
the devoutly held beliefs of Voll's evangelical Protestant
fellowship. No evidence was offered to show that this
group was engaged in anything unlawful or even mildly improper. Instead, it was the fundamental theological beliefs
and practices of the group that came under the court's scrutiny.

The defense argued that Patrick, hired by Voll's parents, was their agent, and should have the benefit of the
general defenses under section 35, if available to the parents, who were not on trial. The prosecution argued that
these were personal defenses and should not apply to hired
abductors -- just as the defense of one conspirator does not
shield a co-conspirator. The judge, however, instructed the
jury that Patrick could claim those general defenses available to the parents. Since these defenses must be disproved
by the prosecution beyond a reasonable doubt, extraordinary
latitude is given to hired assailants if the agency theory
is accepted. Patrick was acquitted.

The application of the defense of justification under
section 35.05(2) of the New York Penal Law, requiring an
emergency situation, to the attempted abduction of Voll is a
perversion of the intent of the New York Legislature in en-
acting this section. The Temporary Commission on the Re-
vision of the New York Penal Law indicated that the section
should be narrowly construed so as to apply to areas of
"technically criminal behavior which virtually no one would
consider improper." Illustrative is the burning of real
property to prevent a forest fire, or confining a person to
halt an epidemic. It does not justify such things as mercy
killings committed out of disagreement with "the morality or
advisability of the law." By logical extension, it does not
apply to abductions committed out of disagreement with the
"morality" or advisability of the protection of the first
amendment provides to religious practices carried out by an
individual. Traditionally, the defense of "justification"
or "necessity" applied only where the defendant was forced
to act by reason of physical forces of nature rather than

acts of other human beings.

In the subsequent case of United States v. Patrick, a
federal district judge in the State of Washington, on a motion by the defendant, dismissed kidnaping charges against
Ted Patrick on a mixed theory of "justification" and lack of
criminal intent. The court seemed to ignore the fact that
under the federal kidnaping statute "motive" or "purpose" is
not a defense, and that in any event the defenses available
to a parent should not be available to the parent's agent.

More recently, courts have begun to disallow the defense of justification in prosecutions for false imprisonment of a target of deprogramming. In Orange County, California, a court sentenced Ted Patrick to a year in prison,
with all but sixty days suspended, on account of his false
imprisonment of a member of the Hare Krishna sect. The
court held, as a matter of law, that the defense of justification could not be introduced at trial.

In Denver, Colorado, where Patrick was charged with
false imprisonment of two young women who were not then members of any religious sect, the appeals court affirmed the
conviction despite Patrick's argument that there were sufficient facts presented at trial to prove justification. The
appeals court noted that the proper procedure for proving
such a defense is to make an offer of proof, out of the
presence of the jury, and let the court rule whether such a
defense is available. On the central question, the court
ruled:

> First, for the "choice of evils" defense to be
> available there must be an imminent public or
> private injury about to occur which requires
> emergency action. See   18-1-702(1), C.R.S.
> 1973. Here, there was no evidence of such a
> situation...."

The defense of justification, or "choice of evils," is
obviously improper in such prosecutions for a violent crime
against the person like kidnaping, false imprisonment, assault, or one of the other possible crimes which might arise
out of deprogramming. Aside from the question of "emergency" or "imminence," there is the more central question of
"injury." As United States v. Ballard, Katz v. Superior
Court, and People v. Murphy make clear, it is beyond the
competence of the courts (including juries) to determine the
truth or falsity of any religious belief or practice. To
argue that a particular religious practice causes mental
"injury" to the young adherent is to challenge the first

amendment. Only where it can be shown (in camera) that some other real injury such as fraud, assault, restraint, or abduction has occurred should such a defense be allowed.

Conservatorship Proceedings: Kidnaping by Court Order

In an effort to avoid the civil and criminal pitfalls of their profession, deprogrammers have turned to conservatorship proceedings as a means of legally gaining control over their victims. Conservatorship proceedings are designed to preserve the property "of persons who are unable to manage their own affairs...because of debilitating factors which create a condition falling short of incompetency...."

Under the laws of most states, it would be impossible to have a young person, enthralled by his new path to salvation, declared incompetent or mentally ill. One would search in vain to find "brainwashed zombies" listed in any of the standard texts on mental disorders. Indeed, the things parents complain of most -- renunciation of worldly things, total dedication to the group or group leader, change in personality, flat affect, serenity, and apparent rejection of family and former friends -- do not fit within any of the categories of mental disease.

Generally, the requirements for appointment of a guardian or committee and a judicial declaration of incompetence are a privation of reasoning faculties, or an inability to act with discretion in the ordinary affairs of life. In some states, it is necessary that a person be declared legally insane before a guardianship can be imposed. Generally, however, an inability to protect oneself or to manage one's property will suffice. Irrespective of the legal standard, however, "incompetency" is a strong term carrying strong implications.

Not so with conservatorship. There the implication of mental illness is substantially eliminated, and the onus of "incompetency" avoided. A conservator can be appointed simply because the conservatee is unable to manage his property by reason of some disabling factor, which need not amount to incompetence or justify the imposition of a committeeship.

Deprogrammers have seized upon this device to obtain court orders giving them control over the target. There is now in circulation a "Legal Deprogramming Kit" with forms entitled "Petition for Appointment of Temporary Guardian," "Order Appointing Temporary Guardian for Junior Doe, Order Setting Hearing To Show Cause and Injunction," and sample medical and other attachments. One psychologist teamed up

with two lawyers who specialize in such "legal" deprogrammings to provide them with appropriate testimony. Once the
court order has been obtained, the target may be seized by a
sheriff and police, then turned over the deprogrammers.

The psychiatric testimony offered in such proceedings
can be of somewhat dubious quality, drawing on the faith of
the true believer in deprogramming. While the case of People
v. Murphy was pending in the Supreme Court for Queens
County, New York, the father of one of the persons involved
in the case attempted to have his adult Hare Krishna son declared incompetent. This was not a conservatorship proceeding, but was similar in purpose. The psychiatrist who testified on the father's behalf had observed the son, and
stated that the son's lack of signs of mental disorder was
the firmest indication that he was a victim of mind control.

New York's conservatorship statute is taken from the
Uniform Probate Code. Like most conservatorship statutes,
it deals only with the question of conserving the property
of someone under a disability. The civil rights of the person over whom the proceeding is brought are specifically
protected. Indeed, the very purpose of such a proceeding is
to avoid the interference with civil rights which might be
encompassed in a declaration of incompetency or civil commitment. In its legislative memorandum accompanying New
York's conservatorship statute, the legislature stated:

> The conservatorship procedure provides a flexi-
> ble means for protecting the property of per-
> sons with serious debility and gives the court
> the power to set limits upon the authority of
> the conservator and to insure that the conser-
> vatee has an adequate allowance for his person-
> al needs. The civil rights of the conservatee
> are not affected. The title to the conservatee's
> property remains in him and the conservatee has
> the power to dispose of his property by will if
> he possesses the requisite testament capacity.
> Adequate procedures are incorporated to protect
> the constitutional rights of the person who is
> the subject of the proceeding.

Parents and deprogrammers have obtained a number of orders of temporary guardianship, or conservatorship, and have
used the temporary control gained over sect members as an
opportunity to deprogram them. There has, however, been
very little judicial discussion of the legality of using
conservatorship proceedings to strip a person of the legal
rights which would ordinarily protect him from deprogramming.

The leading case on such use of conservatorship proceedings -- the first, and so far the only significant judicial analysis of this practice -- is Katz v. Superior Court.
There, the California appellate court had to rule upon the
validity of temporary orders of conservatorship granted by
the lower court over several members of the Unification
Church, all over twenty-one years of age. The California
conservatorship statute in effect at the time the orders
were granted provided that a conservator could be appointed
over a person "likely to be deceived or imposed upon by artful or designing persons." Lawyers for the parents used
this language to justify orders allowing them temporary control over the unwilling "Moonies." The case was unusual in
that the proposed conservatees were given notice of the proceedings and allowed to present testimony in a hearing which
lasted eleven days. Generally, when an order of temporary
conservatorship is sought for purposes of deprogramming, the
target is not notified, to prevent him from mounting a successful defense or escaping.

The conservatorship statute in California permits the
appointment of a conservator "with or without notice as the
court or judge may require, upon a verified petition establishing good cause." Ex parte conservatorship proceedings
allowed under California law are similar to those in certain
other states. In ex parte proceedings, the parents and deprogrammers can come into court with affidavits by cooperating psychiatrists or psychologists, and obtain temporary
power over the sect member without any opportunity for the
member to respond with his or her own psychiatric evidence
and personal testimony. Having secured the temporary order,
the deprogrammers will often achieve victory, since it may
take no more than a few days to deprogram someone. In the
Katz case, deprogramming began very soon after the temporary
conservatorship orders were granted by the lower court.
Though the appellate court quickly moved to ban deprogramming, two of the five young people renounced the Unification
Church one day after the appellate court's order was issued.

The appellate court in Katz noted, "The lower court's
orders following the hearing...contain no findings of fact
which would disclose the ground or grounds on which the orders were based." The court below had issued orders appointing conservators without finding that the conservatees were
insane, incompetent, or unable to manage their own property.
Apparently, it was enough for the lower court that the young
people had joined an unorthodox religious sect, and that the
parents were concerned about their welfare. The judge
stated:

It's not a simple case. As I said, we're talking about the very essence of life here, mother,
father and children....This is the essence of
civilization. The family unit is a micro-civil-
ization. That's what it is. A great civilization is made of many, many great families, and
that's what's before this Court.

One of the reasons that I made this Decision, I
could see the love here of a parent for his
child, and I don't even have to go beyond that.

One clinical psychologist who had examined the members
of the Unification Church on behalf of their parents testified, in the words of the court, that what she observed in
them "did not fit into any class under headings offered in a
standard psychiatric and psychological diagnostic and statistical manual." She expressed her opinion that members of
the Unification Church were objects of coercive persuasion
by the Church. A psychiatrist hired by the parents expressed a similar view as to coercive persuasion, and seemed concerned about the young people's change in "affects," their
"limited ability towards abstractions," and the influence
apparently exerted on them by "an outside authority." A
clinical psychologist who testified on behalf of the proposed conservatees stated that all were normal based on the
tests he had conducted. These tests, he said, would reveal
symptoms found in prisoners of war, but did not show such
symptoms in this case. He specifically repudiated certain
symptoms relied upon by the parents' experts.

The court found that the orders of conservatorship
should not have been granted on the evidence, even if given
the interpretation most favorable to the parents. It did
not need to rest its determination on this ground, however,
because it held that the "likely to be deceived...by artful
and designing persons" language of the statute was too vague
to be used to remove an adult's freedom. The court emphasized that statutes, whether civil or criminal, which interfere with fundamental constitutional rights must be certain
in their application.

The court held that the granting of such conservatorship orders violated the church members' constitutional
right to religious freedom. It noted that courts have no
special competence to judge the validity or invalidity of
one's chosen religion, or the process by which one arrives
at this belief. The statute at issue was totally inappro-
priate when applied to matters of faith and belief:

Although the words "likely to be deceived or imposed upon by artful or designing persons" may
have some meaning when applied to the loss of
property which can be measured, they are too
vague to be applied in the world of ideas. In
an age of subliminal advertising, television
exposure, and psychological salesmanships,
everyone is exposed to artful and designing
persons at every turn. It is impossible to
measure the degree of likelihood that some will
succumb. In the field of beliefs, and particularly religious tenets, it is difficult, if not
impossible, to establish a universal truth
against which deceit and imposition can be
measured.

The Katz case made plain the truly illegal nature of
"legal deprogramming" through conservatorship proceedings.
Nevertheless, deprogrammers will surely continue in their
attempts to use legally sanctioned means to accomplish
their goal.

A Response: Civil Suits by Deprogrammers' Targets

For many victims who seek redress after abduction by
deprogrammers, criminal prosecution is too harsh a remedy.
While they may wish to prosecute deprogrammers, they may be
unwilling to charge their parents with criminal acts. Moreover, how do they get around the indifference of police and
prosecutors? In addition, those seized by court order cannot press criminal charges. The solution may be bringing a
civil tort action, and seeking protective and injunctive
orders.

At just about every stage of the deprogramming process
there are acts committed by the relatives, deprogrammers,
and other participants which could lead to civil liability.
A number of actions have been commenced against such persons,
and judgments have been recovered. Several actions are
still in progress and awaiting trial. While parents may
have a defense to criminal charges of kidnaping and false
imprisonment, there is generally no immunity to tort actions
by their offspring.

The act by which a victim of deprogramming is originally seized would generally constitute an assault and battery
-- sometimes a serious one. There may also be assault and
battery at other times during the ordeal. The physical restraint imposed upon the unwilling victim would certainly
constitute unlawful imprisonment. The intense psychological

pressure placed upon the victim would constitute intentional
infliction of emotional distress, particularly because it is
accompanied by false imprisonment and invasion of privacy.
Some complaints charge a separate tort of invasion of privacy. Suits have also been brought charging abuse of process and medical malpractice on account of parents', deprogrammers', or medical personnels' participation in conservatorship or civil commitment proceedings.

The use by deprogrammers of conservatorship proceedings
or other civil actions such as a declaration of incompetency,
appointment of a guardian or committee, or habeas corpus,
gives rise to the possibility that the victim can bring an
action under the federal civil rights statutes. This theory
has been pleaded in a number of complaints against deprogrammers. The concept revolves around the use of the courts
and court officers, including sheriffs, to accomplish a denial of the plaintiff's basic rights to freedom of religion,
association, privacy, and speech.

Under section 1983, private parties may not be sued for
acts which are not performed "under color of law." But
where the private act is performed pursuant to authority
granted by state law or in collaboration with state officials, a suit may be brought. Private detectives can be
sued under section 1983. Of course, police and sheriffs can
be sued under section 1983, but not for executing court orders regular on their face or carrying out private pursuits
outside the scope of official duties.

Section 1985 permits actions against private persons
for conspiracies which involve no state action. Under this
theory, private conspirators were subject to an action where
they broke up a religious service, thereby interfering with
the congregation's freedom of religion. Thus, the right of
action under section 1985(2) and (3) may be more accessible
to plaintiffs than that under section 1983.

The New York Family Court Act confers jurisdiction on
the family court over actions constituting disorderly conduct, harassment, menancing [sic], reckless endangerment,
[and] an assault or an attempted assault between spouses or
between parent and child or between members of the same family or household. The court has the power to issue an order
of protection, and violation of such an order is contempt of
court. A number of other states have family or domestic
relations courts with similar powers.

CONCLUSION

Deprogrammers have received much favorable publicity in the media, and from all appearances have a thriving business. They do not oppose the principle of religious liberty, they say, but merely want to make sure that everyone has the opportunity to espouse beliefs which they consider acceptable -- even if that means holding persons against their wills and forcing them to listen. Many people have persuaded themselves that to accept or condone deprogramming is not inconsistent with upholding religious liberty, or liberty in general. Sensibilities which would be quickly aroused if "religious freaks" were not involved have been lulled into complacency by the strong accusations leveled against targeted groups -- even though these accusations remain substantially or totally unproven.

Abandoning legal protections for a particular segment of society whose beliefs are disapproved is a dangerous experiment. Deprogramming has been used to change not only religious beliefs, but also political and social attitudes. A powerful weapon is being formed which can render anyone with a relative who opposes his lifestyle vulnerable to a judicial determination as to whether he can continue it -- even though he is a peaceable citizen who has broken no laws. Can we afford to say nothing when we see young people being stuffed into cars, locked up in motel rooms accused, and manhandled because they will not espouse the goals of society at large?

The responsibility for answering this question has largely fallen to the courts. Some courts have said yes, violence may be used to break a religious affiliation perceived as mentally injurious. Others have condemned illegal means used by deprogrammers. Fortunately, the most recent judicial decisions have rejected the claims of justification asserted by the deprogrammers, and have vindicated the constitutional right to practice the religion of one's choice -- however unorthodox it may seem to others.

NOTES

* Originally published in Fordham Law Review 46 (1978):599-634.

CONSTITUTIONAL LAW AND MARGINAL RELIGIONS

University of Montana

Decisions of courts at all levels throughout the seventies were negative about claims of deprogrammed plaintiffs against parents and deprogrammers. Parents were not punished for kidnapping, and deprogrammers generally were let off with token payment of either compensatory or punitive damages (deprogrammers also fared well in criminal proceedings by reliance on the defense of necessity or justification). The problem for those who have suffered pain and injury at the hands of deprogrammers is to fashion a cause of action that courts will recognize as a constitutional ground on which to justify punishment of deprogramming-style vigilante justice. And, recently, they have been able to do so successfully. Recently, in cases from 1978 to 1981, a broad, new advance in defense of religious freedom has been forged.

Causes of action in favor of deprogrammed plaintiffs have been successfully based on Title 42 of the United States Code. Section 1985 (3) (number amended in 1976 to 1985 (c). This part of the Civil Rights Act was passed in 1981 and popularly dubbed the Ku Klux Klan Act. It was part of a package of Reconstruction legislation aimed at protecting the rights of emancipated blacks; it was one congressional implementation of the Fourteenth Amendment (1868), particularly its Section 1 language to the effect that no laws can abridge privileges or immunities of citizens, and that no State can deprive any person of life, liberty or property without due process of law, and that equal protection of the law is afforded all without exception.

Section 1985 (c) is aimed at rooting out racial conspiracies of whites against blacks. It states that two or more people cannot act on an agreement to deprive any person or class of persons the equal protection of the laws, or of equal privileges and immunities under the laws; nor can they injure another in person or property, or deprive him of having and exercising any right or privilege of a citizen. Should such injury occur, the Act concludes, "the party so injured or deprived may have an action for the recovery of damages occasioned by such injury or deprivation, against

any one or more of the conspirators." An earlier section,
1983, uses similar language but covers instances in which
color of state law is involved.

The Klan Act (1985 (c) lay dormant for many years.
Briefly, a 1971 Supreme Court case, Griffin v. Breckenridge
(403 U.S. 88) resurrected the section and broadened its applicability and its availability as a constitutional recourse for causes of civil action. What Griffin makes viable is an argument that the state need not be involved in
any way so long as private, invidiously class-based discrimination is injuriously inflicted by persons in conspiracy
against a member or members of a discrete, identifiable
group (e.g., blacks, women, Moonies). Griffin provides the
way for an injured member of a despised group to find redress in the courts. Such plaintiffs are required to show:
(1) a conspiracy, (2) whose purpose is to deprive anyone of
equal protection, or equal privileges and immunities, (3)
an act in furtherance of the conspiracy, and (4) an injury
to another or deprivation of any citizen's rights or privileges. And: "The language requiring intent to deprive of
equal protection, or equal privileges and immunities, means
that there must be some racial, or perhaps otherwise class-
based, invidiously discriminatory animus behind the conspirators' action, "so plaintiffs must also show that they
are members of a group or class so abhorred by the conspirators that such animus motivates the conspiracy"
(Griffin v. Breckenridge, 102). In racial cases, Griffin
easily finds a source of congressional authority in Section 2 of the Thirteenth Amendment, empowering enforcement
of the prohibition of slavery. In addition, and this is
the crucial point for new religious movement cases,
Griffin explicitly finds a source of power in any denial of
the right to travel interstate; equally explicitly, it
states that other constitutional ways to reach private conspiracies may be possible, and leaves open whether Section
5 of the Fourteenth Amendment, empowering enforcement of
the due process and equal protection clauses, is one such
source of power. Later courts have split on this last issue.

I said that a broad new advance in defense of religious freedom has been forged in the wake of Griffin. Let
me simply refer briefly to a few examples of the case law
embodying this judicial remedy. These cases are affirmations of Section 1985 (c) which agree that, specifically,
a deprogrammed plaintiff has fashioned a remedy, stated a
cause of action properly, and reached a constitutional
source of authority on the basis of which the court can
act to redress injuries, again specifically, to punish con-

spiring parents and deprogrammers.

(1) <u>Rankin v. Howard</u>, 457 F. Supp. 70, appeal 633 F. 2d 844 (1980). This Arizona case involves an adult member of the Unification Church whose father obtained a conservatorship order in Kansas, perhaps fraudulently, because Rankin was not a resident of the Kansas county where the order was granted. Under the order, Marcus Rankin was flown to Kansas, then to Phoenix, and deprogramming was attempted under the auspices of the Freedom of Thought Foundation. On defendants' motion to dismiss Rankin's many-pronged suit, Judge Muecke ruled: (a) that the Kansas judge was covered by judicial immunity, so Rankin's 1983, color of state law, complaint was dismissed; (b) that Rankin had successfully stated a cause of action under 1985 (c) (conspiracy to deprive, overt act, and deprivation of rights); (c) that a religious group may indeed be counted as a class for 1985 (c) purposes; and (d) that Rankin's having been deprived of his constitutional right to free interstate travel brings into play a legitimate ground for congressional power to reach the conspiracy. Rankin appealed what was already a substantial victory, and in the 9th Circuit, Judge Wright gave him a further triumph by ruling that the Kansas judge may not in fact be immune if he knew that he lacked jurisdiction over a non-resident, and that as a result Rankin's 1983 cause of action may be equally allowable along with his 1985 (c) success in the lower court. Cases in which conservatorships are involved usually try 1983 as a cause of action along with 1985 (c), because a judge's action triggers the color of state law element, as, sometimes does police action aiding kidnapping parents and their agents. Without a conservatorship or some other state official angle, 1985 (c), standing by itself, is the choice. Pursuing both (Richard Ben-Veniste was Rankin's attorney), he was granted a 1985 (c) cause of action, then also 1983 on appeal because judicial immunity was not granted outright by the 9th Circuit appeal court.

(2) <u>Ward v. Connor</u>, 595 F. Supp. 434, appeal 657 F. 2d 45. In a Norfolk, Virginia, United States District Court, a deprogrammed Unification Church plaintiff lost a 1985 (c) cause of action against his kidnapping deprogrammers because the judge found that his church membership did not qualify as a class, that the defendants' benevolent concern negated the necessary discriminatory animus, and that alleged deprivation of his right to travel failed to reach a congressional source of power which would allow the court to act. The 4th Circuit Court of Appeals reversed on all these points, finding the necessary discriminatory motivation, a source of authority in deprivation of Ward's right to travel, and his religious ties sufficient

to bring in a 1985 (c) cause of action against his abductors. The court refused to consider the Section 5 of the
Fourteenth Amendment source-of-power issue, but here is
another clear victory for a deprogrammed plaintiff seeking
redress in the courts for what he has experienced as a pro-
foundly insulting injury to his right to equality and the
equal concern of the law, in short, to his dignity as a
citizen and his right to define his own belief.

Coercive deprogramming cases afford extraordinarily
dramatic instances of the link between unjustified specula-
tion about emergency and untutored prejudice. Since the
role popular media play in the establishment of opinion
about new religious movements is so great, a broad avenue
devoted to purveying a skewed view of "the cults" has become extremely well-trafficked. Media reportage about minority religious groups is heavily couched in prejudicial
lingo. "That which we would destroy, we first label pejor-
atively: A religion becomes a cult; proselytizing becomes
brainwashing; persuasion becomes propaganda; missionaries
become subversive agents; retreats, monasteries, and con-
vents become prisons; holy ritual becomes bizarre conduct;
religious observances become aberrant behavior; devotion
and meditation become psychopathic trances" (Gutman, 1977:
210). Terms like these have dominated newspaper, magazine,
and television accounts of Moonies and Hare Krishnas for
over a decade, and of course the overwhelming tragedy of
Jonestown exacerbated already irresistible tendencies
among journalists to trade on such inflammatory language.
A vastly powerful influence over public opinion is being
exercised on a daily basis when we add to that the media's
tendency to trot out "atrocity stories" and anecdotal evidence drawn particularly fron successfully deprogrammed
apostates.

> Coercive deprogrammings had a number of effects
> on the fortunes of the new religions. Foremost
> was their immediate discrediting through the
> media by the production of apostates of the new
> religions. A number of coercively deprogrammed
> ex-"cult" members engaged in face-saving at-
> tempts to account for their period of member-
> ship in these deviant groups, and, prompted by
> deprogrammers (who had an interest in portray-
> ing themselves as valid "liberators" of a per-
> nicious captivity) as well as parents (who also
> sought an extraordinary explanation of their
> offspring's questing in unconventional groups,
> yet wanted to avoid marking them with any per-
> manent stigma), they recounted a fairly standard

litany of horrors ranging from claims that they
were manipulatively recruited and brainwashed
into "cults" to various tales of deliberate
family estrangement, deceptive fund-raising,
and political conspiracy or illegal lobbying.
By telling such stories, apostates absolved
their families as well as themselves of any
responsibility for their errant behavior and
paid the price of contrition, thereby reentering
the previously rejected community. Thus, the
stories not only resolved the families' problem
of explaining offspring's deviance, but through
their "smoking gun" quality as eye-witness evidence they seriously discredited many new religions.... Overall, the single most important
effect of deprogramming was the creation of the
apostate role and accompanying atrocity stories
(Shupe and Bromley, 1980:166).

An emergency situation called the victimization of our
children by totalistic minority religious groups is here
being constructed by the media; and that can only feed
flames of prejudice which were, unsurprisingly, rekindled
by Jonestown.

Dworkin defines prejudice in a precise and helpful
way. Prejudices are postures of jugement which rely on
considerations which ought to be excluded by our conven-
tions (1977:219). Trials, for example, are structured by
careful circumscription of reliable evidence; prejudicial
hearsay may not be admitted. More generally, "Our conven-
tions stipulate some ground rules or moral judgment which
obtain even apart from such special contexts, the most important of which is that a man must not be held morally
inferior on the basis of some physical, racial or other
characteristic he cannot help having" (Dworkin, 1977:249-
50). Varied and complex factors of background, reading,
and contemporary influence combine to produce stances of
prejudice in an individual, denying equal concern and respect for another of a different race or ethnic group, or
of a different sexual or religious persuasion. Good reasons or justifications for holding such views are, nearly
by definition, lacking. Sheer emotional knee-jerk reaction
(phobia or obsession); rationalizations based on erroneous
factual understanding, say, about racial inferiority; or
"parroting" (arguments of the "everyone knows that" sort):
these, alone or in combination, rather than good (and dis-
cussable) reasons are the sinews of prejudice (Dworkin,
1977:230). They cancel a claim to hold a moral position.
We can generalize about majority opinion in society. But

that is not necessarily to strike a point about a genuine
moral position, for prejudice rather than reason may under-
lie opinions even of a democratic majority. Its fear and
abhorrence of some novel religious phenomena may rest on
rationalization, unsupported assumptions of fact, and on
vague perceptions of threat to the family, established religions, and the shared religious assumptions of the
Republic (Shepherd, 1978, passim). "The principles of democracy we follow do not call for the enforcement of the
consensus, for the belief that prejudices, personal aver-
sions and rationalizations do not justify restricting another's freedom itself occupies a critical and fundamental
position in our popular morality" (Dworkin, 1977:254).
Moral positions grounded in reason, not prejudices grounded
in feeling, are enforceable by law, and so, when small religious groups are commonly despised, policies about them
must be based on our reasoned principles of individual
rights and not on the community's emotional aversion, even
when it is very widely shared.

Fundamental rights, like the right to equality, may
not be abridged in the name of general welfare or general
utility if arguments about putative social gains from discriminatory policies are erected either upon prejudice or
on an exaggerated account of an imminent emergency (not a
clear, present, and momentous danger), or both. The moral
right to equality was made a legal right in religious matters by the First and Fourteenth Amendments, and also by
the Civil Rights Acts. These rights are not about those of
democratic majorities, rather they are specifically rights
which individuals hold even when the majority of people
might think that society is worse off for allowing, say,
groups like the Alamo Foundation or Love Israel or The New
Testament Missionary Fellowship to operate in our midst,
and this kind of right holds as well when we find our children joining up with movements widely perceived as grotes-
que and harmful outfits. Arguments justifying drastic in-
terventions such as coercive deprogramming find warrant in
the claim that an emergency situation exists when our children choose to worship these strange gods and to live on
low protein diets and to chant and to solicit in airports.
Society may well be worse off for allowing these things to
happen, and grief and distress among families broken up because of them are hard things to blink. Yet whatever we
may speculate about social and familial well-being, kidnapping and forcible deconversion are certain and profound
insults both to individual dignity and to the fundamental
rights of treatment as an equal. In strong form: people
in our society have the constitutional right to be intolerant and dogmatic, and to believe in and peddle mental and
spiritual poison so long as they do so within the law.

In less strong form: what the Constitution protects
against is the persecution of minorities. Embedded in constitutional language securing rights are principles about
equality and independence. These principles and rights
protect minorities against the will of the majority, which
may be based not so much on balancing moral principles as
it is on prejudice combined with an unconvincing diagnosis
of social emergency. If we allow prejudice to prevail
over individual rights as a consequence, then we are con-
straining liberty and negating equality because we despise
the way of life preferred by another.

> Laws that recognize and protect common inter-
> ests, like laws against violence and monopoly,
> offer no insult to any class or individual;
> but laws that constrain one man, on the sole
> ground that he is incompetent to decide what
> is right for himself, are profoundly insulting
> to him. They make him intellectually and
> morally subservient to the conformists who
> form the majority, and deny him the indepen-
> dence to which he is entitled (Dworkin, 263).

The state may never assess one sort of group membership,
especially a religious one, inherently inferior to others
regardless of majoritarian preferences. Religious minorities cannot be persecuted by government because of official policies committing the state to tolerance and, more
important, because of essential or underlying principles
committing the state to treatment of all citizens as
equals.

The argument that it is hard to find real conflicts
between general welfare and treatment of everyone as an
equal (Miller, 1981:387-91) will not wash in the face of
cases which have arisen from anti-cult hostility unleashed
upon adult members of minority new religious movements.
When state officials are directly involved in depriving
freedom and the right to unfettered religious exercise, as
for example, when police openly aid deprogrammers in kidnapping and restraining a new religious group member, then
the stricture that the state may not treat groups differ-
entially comes into play. Discrimination among groups,
reflecting parental preferences and subjecting members of
only some groups to tacitly sanctioned illegal acts, is
precisely what the Constitution protects against. There
can be no establishment of religion and all are guaranteed
the pursuit of religious truth according to their own
lights. The antecedent or "natural" right to treatment as
an equal is hence secured in theory, although endlessly

difficult to be assured about in practice. Constitutionally, though, these present the easier cases. What happens
if, wholly apart from state action or state sanction, parents and their hired agents band together in conspiracy to
rob cultic adherents of their rightful religious liberties,
and to treat them in an invidiously discriminatory way because their new views and allegiances are despised?

Throughout the sixties and early seventies, judicial
decisions laid the groundwork for the law to reach and
punish private conspiracies which had the effect of denying the treatment as an equal not only to racial minorities but to members of other despised groups as well.
All the details of interpretation of these decisions are
arguable and far from solidly set. But although the lower
courts are divided, precedents are clearly available now
to secure the rights of individuals implied by Fourteenth
Amendment restrictions on state authority over citizens.
Judicial activism has more and more insisted on duties of
the states correlative with these restrictions, and the
duties are affirmative -- states must act to ensure that
rights are not abrogated in the private sphere just as
they must maintain vigilance to avoid abridgement of rights
engineered by state officials. An expansion of federal
authority to secure rights in practice parallels similar
developments at the federal level aimed at reducing in-
equalities of material welfare. Many sorts of cases have
elicited this extension of national power, and those involving people discriminated against and harmed because of
their religious persuasions are only one. But constitutionally they are vital because violations of both the
First and Fourteenth Amendments, as well as disputed implied rights such as privacy and travel, are directly implicated in nearly all of them.

If the state has affirmative duties to prevent in-
equalities and harms stemming from invidious discrimina-
tions, the source of failure to afford treatment as an
equal to all is irrelevant: private actions as well as
state involvements (or failure to get involved) must be
regulable and punishable. And this is the direction in
which recent constitutional adjudication has moved. The
Fourteenth Amendment rights at stake have received more and
more specificity, so deprogrammed plaintiffs, for example,
have only recently been afforded constitutional ability to
state a cause of action that will hold up in very particular circumstances. The rights in question are not vague
rights against all the world. They are rather rights a-
gainst particular persons or groups engaged in activities
having the practical effect of denying fundamental rights.

States through their judicial authorities are therefore
finally being required to carry out in practice the duties
demanded by Fourteenth Amendment Section 1 language. "The
Fourteenth Amendment says nothing of rights; it speaks
only of duties and it lays duties only upon the State. The
exactly correlative rights are to have the State perform
its duties" (Cox, 1968:65).

Freedom to choose and define one's own religious belief is clearly guaranteed by the Constitution in the
First Amendment and, less directly, in other binding pas-
sages as well. Constitutional guarantees of the most significant kind have never been automatically applicable
however. They must be won over and over as new challenges
to them arise in new specific circumstances. The deprogramming cases are important not only because they have
brought forth a new way to secure old rights in practice,
but also because they have built on recent precedent to
expand and extend our whole idea of constitutional rights
and the affirmative duties of the states with regard to
them. This advance is unintelligible apart from its historical rootage in the struggle for racial equality in
this country. This story is the dramatic illustration of
Cox's now famous dictum that the idea of equality, once
loosed, "is not easily cabined" (1966:91).

As Cox has stated more recently (Newsweek, 28 September 1981, p. 18) and the reason why 1985 deprogramming
cases afford such vital legal protection to minorities:

> Our country was founded upon the principle that
> there are fundamental human rights that should
> be beyond the reach of any government...includ-
> ing even a majority of the representative Congress
> or state legislature.
>   The ultimate bulwark of those rights is the
> Bill of Rights and the Fourteenth Amendment, in-
> terpreted and applied by an independent judiciary
> ... A right is only as good as the remedy.
>   A constitutional right is at the mercy of
> legislative majorities unless supported by a
> judicial remedy.

CONSERVATORSHIPS AND DEPROGRAMMING: LEGAL AND POLITICAL PROSPECTS

David G. Bromley
Virginia Commonwealth University

The contemporary controversy over new religious movements has spawned a whole series of legal issues ranging from
tax exemption and public solicitation to health and child-
rearing practices. However, it has been the allegation that
new religions employ manipulative, coercive thought control
techniques to recruit and retain members which has been at
the center of the new religions controversy. The numerous
other charges made against new religions (ranging from sexual
deviations to financial irregularities to political subversion) have largely been intended to arouse public indignation
and thereby win broad based support for the campaign against
"cults."

It has been a belief on the part of parents that something mysterious and injurious has been done to their children which has precipitated the outcry against "cults." Allegations by former members of these groups that they were
brainwashed and helped to brainwash others has only served
to confirm family members' worst fears. Family members have
banded together to seek legislative and judicial redress,
and many have engaged deprogrammers to "rescue" and "deprogram" sons and daughters in new religious movements. For
their part, new religions have vehemently protested against
repression and denial of basic civil liberties. They have
contested anti-cult legislative initiatives and have supported civil and criminal actions against deprogrammers.

Since the new religions controversy has now spanned a
decade, the arguments and strategies of both sides have had
sufficient opportunity to develop. This paper reviews the
major legal positions which have emerged out of this controversy. In addition, the problems and prospects for deprogramming are considered since extra-legal actions may continue irrespective of any developing legal consensus.

THE ANTI-CULT POSITION

Opponents of new religious movements have contended that many if not most of these groups are manipulative, destructive "cults." In its baldest form the anti-cultists have formulated a conspiracy theory: unscrupulous gurus have used coercive mind control techniques to reduce unwitting, idealistic youth to virtual automatons in a quest for power and wealth. Gurus are the causal agents; wealth and power are the motives; brainwashing is the means by which youth can become implicated in these fraudulent, pseudo-religious enterprises. The elements of this theory can be found in lists of the essential characteristics of cults compiled by anti-cultists. Shapiro (1977:83), for example, listed eight such characteristics:

1. Demands complete obedience to and subservience to one individual, who purports to be God, the Messiah or some form of, or a messenger of, the deity.
2. Requires separation from society. Association with nonmembers is discouraged, except to gain money or to proseltyize.
3. Discourages any form of self-development. Education is scorned and the self image is totally destroyed.
4. Teaches hatred of parents, organized religion and, sometimes, the U.S. government.
5. Does not have concern for the material body; feels only the soul is important.
6. Takes all material possessions (past, present and future) for its own use. Members are not permitted to own anything in their own names.
7. Makes it almost impossible for a member to leave, either through physical restraints or psychologic fears.
8. Maintains the member in a "brainwashed" state through destructive behavior modification techniques.

Marcia Rudin (1979/1980:24-30) has compiled a longer but similar list:

1. Members swear total allegiance to an all-powerful leader whom they may believe to be a Messiah.
2. Rational through is discouraged or forbidden.
3. Cult recruitment techniques are often deceptive.

4. The cult psychologically weakens the follower
   and makes him believe his problems can be
   solved only by the group.
5. The new cults expertly manipulate guilt.
6. Cult members are isolated from the outside
   world, cut off from their pasts, from school,
   job, family and friends as well as from information from newspapers, radio, and television.
7. The cult or its leader makes every career or
   life decision for the follower.
8. To attract idealistic members, some cults
   promise to raise money to improve society
   and help the poor.
9. Cult followers often work full-time for the
   group.
10. The cults are anti-woman, anti-child, and
    anti-family.
11. Some cult members believe that they are
    elite members of an "elect" survival group
    in a world that is coming to an end.
12. Many of these groups share a philosophy which
    allows the ends to justify the means.
13. The cults often are shrouded in an aura of
    secrecy and mystery.
14. An atmosphere of violence of potential vio-
    lence frequently surrounds the cults.

Based upon these characteristics of "cults" and the implicitly or explicitly implied dangerous, destructive practices
that emanate from them, anti-cult spokespersons have advocated a variety of legal, and sometimes extra-legal remedies.

Richard Delgado has been the primary proponent of legal controls over new religious movements. In his extensive
analyses of legal issues associated with the new religions
controversy (1982; 1980; 1979-1980; 1977) Delgado has spec-
ified conditions under which legal regulation of religious
practice might be possible and then has attempted to demonstrate that cult practices meet those conditions. His legal arguments are buttressed with evidence supplied primarily by psychologists and psychiatrists sympathetic to the
anti-cult position (Clark, 1979a, 1979b, 1978a, 1978b;
Singer, 1979a, 1979b, 1978; Galper, 1976).

Delgado's principal argument has been that the thought
reform practices of "cults" result in physical/psychologi-
cal injury. Major focus has been on harm to individuals
since the primary remedies and controls have centered on

removing individuals from new religions. Delgado has asserted that cult membership tends to produce neurotic or psychotic symptoms that potentially are irreversible. Such symptoms are caused by systematic food and sleep deprivation, lack of opportunity for reality testing, and a sensory barrage which narrows the individual's focus of attention and increases suggestibility. Individuals subjected to this physical and psychological onslaught are further compelled to break off relationships with non-members (including family), give up educational and career plans and adopt a rigid stereotypical world view. The result, Delgado has contended, is an individual who is caught up in a group which stresses dependency, emotional commitment and black and white thinking over autonomy, rationality and complex, critical analysis. Individuals have been plagued with feelings of guilt, worthlessness, apathy and depression. Individuals may be adversely affected in other ways as well since groups' beliefs may lead to inadequate diet and medical care, forfeiture of money and possessions, and abusive child-rearing practices.

It is Delgado's position that intervention by the courts is both within the scope of judicial powers and consistent with case law precedent. The essence of Delgado's argument is that "cult" recruitment and socialization tactics have the effect of diminishing individual free will. There is, he has stated, deliberate manipulation of knowledge and capacity such that an individual never possesses sufficient amounts of each simultaneously to act autonomously. As he has put it (1980:28):

> The process by which an individual becomes a
> member of certain cults appears arranged in
> such a way that knowledge and capacity, the
> classic ingredients of an informed consent,
> are maintained in an inverse relationship:
> when capacity is high, the recruits' know-
> ledge of its practices is low; when know-
> ledge is high, capacity is reduced.

From Delgado's perspective substantial personal and social injury gives the state a right to legal intervention. He has insisted that because the tactics resulting in such harm have been carried out under "colorly religious auspices" state intervention should not be precluded. First Amendment protections have been limited in cases where behavior is socially harmful, not essential to the group's system of belief, or motivated by political/economic rather than religious concerns. Since voluntariness has been substantially reduced such harms could not be regarded as con-

sensual and hence protected by constitutional strictures.
As he summed it up (1980:33):

> There appear to be no insuperable constitutional,
> moral or public policy obstacles in the way of
> state or federal action designed to curb the
> abuses of religious groups that utilize high-
> pressure, harmful and deceptive tactics in re-
> cruiting and indoctrinating young members. So
> long as remedies comport with the least restric-
> tive alternative requirements...and provide ade-
> quate due process procedures and judicial over-
> sight, measures aimed at regulating the private
> use of mind control by religious or pseudoreli-
> gious groups appear to be fully permissible.

Delgado's own concern about the implications of state intervention for religious liberty has been reduced since he has
concluded that "cults" constitute a special category of
groups which "may expose their indoctrinees to a greater
variety of classic mind control techniques as well as apply
these techniques with greater intensity" (1980:32). Further, he has argued that prohibiting such techniques would
not prevent these groups from existing or even from recruiting and continuing to practice their religious beliefs.
Finally, he has concluded that other legitimate groups would
not be endangered since intervention against the stronger
techniques of cults would not make imperative action against
less serious abuses and meaningful distinctions between
cults and other groups could be obtained if means used and
results obtained were considered (1980:33).

Cults have been accused of social as well as individual harms. Threats to social institutions include harm to
family relationships and potential for violence. Among the
alleged violations of family relationships have been acceptance of minors into cult membership, deliberate creation
of hostility toward parents by sons and daughters, hiding
converts to avoid parental contact or "rescue," treatment
of women as inferiors, marriage or remarriage without following proper legal procedures or even informing family
members, and lack of minimal parental or medical care.
Evidence for potential violence has included the stockpil-
ing of weapons by certain groups, creation of enemies lists,
authoritarian control over followers by leaders, and a
tendency by members to become converts to other totalistic
groups. Naturally, the specter of Jonestown has loomed behind allegations of potential violence. These and other
allegations of social injury, while secondary to the main
thrust of Delgado's argument, have been used to buttress

his contention that legal intervention against new religious movements is warranted.

    In a recent and tangential argument he has asserted
that cult practices also violate thirteenth amendment prohibitions against slavery. On the one hand, he has contended (1979-1980:52) that "rigidly hierarchical, authoritarian and isolated living arrangements established by certain religious cults, with the aid of intensive thought
manipulation techniques, contravene the thirteenth amendment." On the other hand, he has derived a second argument
that such arrangements "violate a number of values protected
by the thirteenth amendment, giving rise to a compelling
interest in their abatement" even if they do not constitute
slavery. This line of argument was proferred for several
reasons: (1) the issue of initial voluntariness was avoided
and the objective state of affairs evaluated instead, (2)
slavery is prohibited absolutely, (3) medical and psychiatric testimony became unnecessary, and (4) the individual
member's apparent compliance became irrelevant. He concluded this argument by asserting that "Remedies under the
thirteenth amendment can and should be implemented to limit
the unique but harmful brand of slavery that cults impose
on their members (1979-1980:67).

    Based upon such claims of individual and social injury,
Delgado has enumerated a variety of remedies for abuses by
cults. Recommended remedies have varied with the stage (of
the "cult brainwashing experience") at which they are directed and have conformed to the principle of "least harmful available option." Preventive remedies include self
identification by recruiters, a mandatory cooling off period in which recruits would be required to separate themselves from the group, public education programs which would
focus on risks associated with groups employing thought reform techniques, prohibition of proseltyization, licensing
of individuals permitted to engage in "psychologically in-
trusive practices," and legal status for statements by individuals that they desired rescue in the event they should
become trapped in a cult. Post-induction remedies, all of
which were premised upon the assumption that few cult members could exit these groups voluntarily, include mutual
reassessment, conservatorship powers, and deprogramming (using "carefully defined guidelines"). Other assorted remedies involve tort actions for damages sustained while in a
cult (e.g., false imprisonment, intentional infliction of
emotional distress), civil actions to recover money and
possessions donated to cults, and various criminal actions
(e.g., unlawful imprisonment, kidnapping, slavery).

LEGAL ASSESSMENTS OF
INTERVENTION PROPOSALS

The response by legal scholars to the type of intervention proposed by Delgado and others must be understood in
the context of generic constitutional guarantees of religious liberty and precedent setting cases which have become
guidelines for resolution of contemporary disputes. The
broad parameters of religious freedom in the United States
were defined by the first amendment prohibitions on Congress
from making any law with respect to an establishment of
religion or preventing the free exercise of religion. The
establishment clause of the first amendment has constituted
a kind of prior restraint on legislatures, prohibiting either advancement or inhibition of religion, while the free
exercise clause has constituted a post factum redress for
infringement on individual exercise.

Like other constitutionally protected freedoms, the
free exercise of religion is subject to legal restraint under some conditions. A distinction has developed between
freedom of belief, which is absolutely guaranteed, and freedom of action, which could be constrained. Actions, whether or not they were premised on religious beliefs, have
been restrained when they threatened the established social
order or the rights of other individuals. So, for example,
the Mormon practice of polygamy was not accorded free exercise protection on the basis that it constituted a threat
to established marriage and family practices and snake handling was deemed a threat to public safety. It has frequently been observed that this distinction between belief and
action is arbitrary since it is implausible that deeply
held beliefs would not be manifested in some type of action.
Restraint on action, therefore, would almost inevitably involve some degree of restraint on belief. Fortunately perhaps, the courts have not systematically pursued this be-
lief-action dichotomy in rendering decisions; rather the
courts have chosen to limit the right of free exercise only
when a clash between free exercise and state interests
emerged <u>and</u> a compelling state interest in restraint could
be demonstrated.

Prior to the decade of the 1960's the courts were relatively liberal in identifying and ruling in favor of such
state interests. Two landmark cases reversed this priority
and shifted the burden of proof to the state to demonstrate
a compelling state interest. The 1963 <u>Sherbert v. Werner</u>
case involved a member of the Seventh Day Adventist Church
who was fired for refusing to work on Saturday. She was
refused unemployment compensation benefits by the South

Carolina courts because she had failed to accept work involving Saturday employment. Upon determining that Mrs.
Sherbert was sincere in her belief and that the state was
interfering with the practice of her religion (by forcing
her to choose between religious precepts and unemployment
benefits) the Court concluded that no compelling state interest had been shown nor had it been demonstrated that alternative remedies were lacking which would avoid infringement on first amendment rights. The 1972 Wisconsin v.
Yoder case involved prosecution of Old Order Amish and Conservative Amish Mennonites under school attendance laws for
refusal to enroll their children in the post-elementary public education system. The justices ruled that Amish objec-
tions to formal education beyond the eighth grade were
rooted in religious precept, that the state's enforcement
of compulsory education would undermine the practice of
Amish religious beliefs, and that the state did not have a
sufficiently compelling interest to override free exercise
protections.

Out of these two cases have come the elements of what
has come to be known as the Sherbert-Yoder balancing test.
According to Shepherd (1981:12), the five elements of the
balancing test are as follows:

    1. Are the religious beliefs in question sincerely
        held?
    2. Are the religious practices under review ger-
        mane to the religious belief system?
    3. Would carrying out the state's wishes con-
        stitute a substantial infringement on the
        religious practice?
    4. Is the interest of the state compelling? Does
        the religious practice perpetrate some grave
        abuse of a statutory prohibition or obligation?
    5. Are there alternative means of regulation by
        which the state's interest is served but the
        free exercise of religion is less burdened?

It is in terms of these recent precedent setting cases that
current intervention proposals must be evaluated.

Conservatorships/Guardianships

    The most significant legal issue raised in the contem-
porary cult controversy has been the issuing of conservatorships to parents of members of new religious groups. The
conservatorship issue has become the center of legal conflict for several reasons. First, the primary goal of parents has been extrication of offspring from "cults," and

conservatorships would permit this. Existing conservatorship laws have already been used on numerous occasions for
this purpose, and broadening conservatorship provisions
would constitute a major victory for the anti-cultists.
Second, expanding conservatorship powers has been the major
legislative thrust of the anti-cultists. Bills passed both
houses of the legislature in New York during two consecutive
legislative sessions; passage was overturned in both instances by gubernatorial veto. Virtually identical legislation has been introduced in a number of other states although no other comparable success has been achieved.
Third, if successful, conservatorship bills would place the
state in the position of physically intervening to remove
adult individuals from certain religious groups and evaluating their mental health status by virtue of their having
joined these groups. Numerous more conventional religious
organizations have been drawn into the conservatorship issue as a result of the broad implications of such legislation for religious liberty.

Many states have enacted guardian and/or conservator
provisions. Typically such statutes apply to minors, elder-
ly, and/or mentally incompetent individuals who have been
deemed incompetent in conducting their own affairs. The
most common conservatorship powers are financial and are
implemented when individuals appear to be in danger of seriously mismanaging their finances or being victimized by
"artful and designing persons." More extensive powers are
often available if incapacities are more severe. In recent
years, parents of converts to new religions have sought to
gain legal custody of their offspring through the use of
temporary conservatorships (i.e., a few weeks to a few
months, depending on the state) for the purpose at least of
separating the individual from the group for this period
and often for the purpose of deprogramming the son or daughter in their custody. At the same time, the anti-cultists
have sought to broaden the scope of conservatorship statutes to explicitly cover affiliation with controversial new
religions and to ease the process of obtaining conservatorships in such cases.

Beginning in 1975 conservatorships were used to place
members of new religious groups in the custody of family
members. A number of ex parte conservatorships were issued
in California, for example. As Spendlove (1976:1110) has
noted, these conservatorships were not very difficult to
obtain:

Temporary conservatorships have been issued upon
petitions which have done nothing but recite the
technical requirements of the statutes -- that
the cultist was unable to properly care for his
person or property and is likely to be deceived
by artful and designing persons -- and making
conclusionary allegations that the cultist
showed abrupt personality changes, had transmitted assets to the leaders of the religious
group, and appeared to be the victim of mind
control through hypnosis, mesmerism, or brainwashing.

Simply granting conservatorship power to family members
without adversarial hearings and without substantiating evidence, however, raised the possibility of a variety of a-
buses. Greene (1977:1052) warned that "Guardianship statutes are subject to abuse if courts routinely assume that
parents invariably have the best interests of their children at heart, or that membership in particular religious
cults indicates mental incapacity." Other observers were
even more pointed in their concerns; the New York University Law Review (Note, 1978:1289) concluded:

The imposition of conservatorships on members
of unconventional religious groups is uncom-
fortably close to the suppression of citizens'
rights to pursue, join and practice the religion of their choice. Once it is conceded that
the religious beliefs and practices of one
group are the proper business of another, the
opportunities for mischief are limitless...
If conservatorships are upheld as a legitimate
weapon with which to combat unconventional
religious beliefs and practices, the courts
will be setting off a series of unjustifiable
investigations, accusations and prosecutions
that will go on without forseeable end, jeop-
ardizing the atmosphere of free discussion of,
adherence to, and dissent from religious views
that the free exercise clause was designed to
protect.

Interestingly, the current campaign to broaden conservatorship powers has come at a time when states already
have begun a move to restrict them. Recent statutory
changes have limited granting of conservatorships only to
situations where extreme self-endangerment was clearly evident. These developments have confronted the anti-cultists
with a more formidable challenge, for a lifestyle (however

bizarre by conventional standards) would not constitute
grounds for legal intervention unless there were an immediate and extreme danger to the individual. As Greene (1977:
1054) pointedly observed in a discussion of Hare Krishna:

> ...the advent of the Hare Krishna religious as-
> sociation, with its emphasis upon chanting, its
> pristine values, and the uncommon appearance of
> its members, epitomizes a situation in which an
> unconventional lifestyle frequently evokes a pe-
> jorative psychiatric labeling of the individual
> devotee. Embittered or disappointed parents may
> obtain the support of a psychiatrist who could
> apply his own norms in determining the presence
> of mental illness... These proceedings, there-
> fore, allow a select group of individuals to re-
> strict the permissible range of religious wor-
> ship, contrary to the fundamental American tra-
> dition of religious freedom.

From an anti-cult perspective the future may be even more
bleak since judicial precedents in some states have gone
further in the direction of restricting conservatorships
than even the revised statutes. Spendlove (1976:1118) concluded that, "In light of recent developments in due process as applied to emergency commitment to mental hospitals,
the Arizona temporary guardian statute and the California
temporary conservator statute appear to violate due process." With respect to the California statute, she asserted (Spendlove, 1976:1121-1122) it is:

> ...unconstitutional on its face (and) would cer-
> tainly be unconstitutional as used to appoint ex
> parte temporary conservators for cultists...
> Cultists who are put under temporary conserva-
> torships for the purpose of being subjected to
> deprogramming are condemned to suffer grievous
> loss out of proportion to any governmental in-
> terest in making sure they do not harm them-
> selves or others.

Whatever the degree of restrictiveness involved in the
granting of conservatorships, legal analysts concur that
there are numerous legal/constitutional problems with using
conservatorship powers as a means of extricating individuals from new religions. This would particularly be the
case where conservatorships were granted so that deprogramming could take place.

One major problem facing the anti-cultists has been
that virtually all of the target "cults" possess legal
standing as religions. Under these conditions the possibilities for legal intervention are dramatically narrowed. It
would be virtually impossible to grant conservatorships or
permit deprogrammings without intruding upon the forbidden
territory of individual religious beliefs. Such intrusion
occurs when "a court requires a sect member not only to
testify to his sincerity but to prove to the court's satisfaction that he is not mentally incompetent by virtue of
holding his faith" (Note, 1978:1269). Since it has been
the lifestyles and practices within such groups, which are
direct outgrowths of beliefs, that have been the sources of
complaints from parents, violation of constitutional boundaries would be most difficult to avoid. Shapiro (1978:795)
details the implications of linking mental competence to
religious beliefs:

> As it focuses on the specific issue of incom-
> petence, a court must not put an individual to
> the proof of his beliefs. Nor can an indivi-
> dual be required to show that his religious
> beliefs are conventional or socially acceptable;
> or that he chose his beliefs by a rational pro-
> cess or according to an internally consistent
> logical system. In particular, adherents who
> "subject this reason to the demands of faith,"
> and demonstrate the depth of their commitment
> by insisting upon their beliefs as ultimate con-
> cerns, should not find the intensity of their
> faith being used as proof of their incompetence.
> Otherwise, the fact of adherence to a particular
> faith could itself become evidence of mind con-
> trol, and the only way to show control over
> one's mind would be to renounce one's religion.

The case would be even clearer in the case of deprogramming.
Spendlove (1976:1135-1136) made the point quite clearly:

> ...deprogramming is a technique the specific
> aim of which is not merely to change a cultist's
> behavior, but to alter his religious beliefs...
> A court which allowed a parent custody of his
> child in order to have him deprogrammed would
> be violating the child's first amendment rights.

A second problem concerns demonstrating that coercive
mind control practices have been utilized to recruit and
retain "cult" members, which has always been the center-
piece of anti-cult ideology. Indeed, the whole concept of

brainwashing remains at issue. As Shapiro (1978:786) put
it:

> The literature on brainwashing agrees that is
> generally involves isolation of the subject,
> stress, a feeling that the brainwasher controls
> the subject's environment completely, dehuman-
> ization, a loss of identity, and a resultant
> conformance to the brainwasher's wishes. But
> no one agrees on the relative importance of the
> various elements, the "quantum" of each required
> to brainwash, the structural or theoretical re-
> lationship among the elements, or even the pro-
> per label of the end result.

Even if individuals exhibit behavior consistent with a
brainwashing model, it is far from certain that the behavior in question is the product of brainwashing. For example, anti-cult proponents have used absolute obedience to
a "cult" leader as evidence of thought control. However,
since courts must focus only on sincerity (rather than content) of belief, this argument could easily be turned on
its head. As the New York University Law Review (Note,
1978:1271) put it, "The zealous commitment and unyielding
devotion displayed by most sect members would make it difficult to argue their beliefs are not sincerely held."
Further, as Homer (1974:640) has observed, extreme compliance would be expected if a devotee believed in a religious
leader:

> He may act in accordance with the leader's
> orders unfailingly and unquestioningly from a
> belief that, for example, the leader speaks
> the will of God. In such a case that belief
> is inextricably bound up in the will and
> thought processes of the member. Interfering
> in such a situation would require a prior
> finding that the member's belief that God
> speaks through the cult leader is false and
> that, therefore, the cause of the members'
> dependence is "thought control."

In general, anti-cultists have not been very successful in substantiating claims of mental coercion that would
meet legal standards for granting conservatorships. As the
New York University Law Review concluded, "Despite the public ballyhoo over and concern about brainwashing activities,
no court that has conducted an evidentiary hearing has
found that any religious organization has subjected its adherents to mind control, coercive persuasion or brainwash-

ing" (Note, 1978:1281). The burden of proof with respect
to brainwashing is very heavy. Shapiro (1978:785) has observed:

> The bare assertion that an individual has been
> "brainwashed" should not prove that he is in-
> competent to control his own mind and to adopt
> religious beliefs. In deciding the issue of
> religious competency, courts should examine
> both the specific coercive methods applied to
> the individual and the degree to which the in-
> dividual has retained the capacity to make valid
> choices in spite of the coercion involved. Only
> where a court concludes that both factors coin-
> cide -- that the individual has been subjected
> to a process of coercive persuasion and that as
> a result of the coercion he now lacks capacity
> to adopt a genuine belief -- should it author-
> ize treatment of the individual for his reli-
> gious incapacity. Such a finding of mind con-
> trol would reflect the far-reaching conclusion
> that the individual lacks a basic characteristic
> of being a "person." Where treatment is auth-
> orized, it should be limited to restoring the
> person's mental capacity to form independent
> beliefs.

Of course, the case could be made in a much easier and compelling fashion if physical restraint could be demonstrated.
However, satisfactory evidence on this point has also been
lacking. As the author observed (Note, 1978:1280):

> Parents requesting conservatorships have been
> conspicuously unable to furnish proof that their
> children have been physically restrained. In
> Katz, for example, there was no evidence that
> the members were denied the freedom to come and
> go as they pleased either during the period of
> their introduction to the (Unification) Church
> and inculcation to its values or thereafter.

Even if anti-cult protagonists could demonstrate some
degree of thought control, such evidence might well be insufficient given the necessity of demonstrating an overriding state interest in intervention and the serious intrusion inherent in granting conservatorships. Shapiro (1978:
769) asserted that, "According to the balancing test set
forth in Sherbert v. Werner, even an incidental burden on
the free exercise of religion is constitutionally justified
only by a 'compelling state interest'." However, as the

New York University Law Review (Note, 1978:1272) has pointed out, conservatorships are not an inconsequential remedy:

>Unquestionably, the conservatorship procedure
works a substantial interference. The extreme
powers of temporary conservators...not only
interfere with but negate the members' free exercise rights.... (There is) a total and direct
denial of the members' ability to practice their
religion and a serious threat to the freedom of
their co-religionists.

The problem of demonstrating compelling state interests is
evidenced by numerous court cases in which, for example,
individuals have been permitted to forego medical treatment
on the basis of religious beliefs even in life-threatening
situations. Such cases indicate that courts are unlikely
to find self injury or harm to physical and mental health
sufficiently compelling to support the granting of conservatorships. As the author (Note, 1978:1279) concluded:

>...the sect members do not engage in conduct
that injures or threatens harm to the legitimate
interests of others. The absence of any such
injury distinguishes this case from virtually
every decision in which the courts have found
a compelling governmental interest sufficient
to outweigh a religious claim. The state's
interest in preventing self-endangerment should
not, in and of itself, justify the granting of
conservatorships.

This last conclusion anticipates another line of argument put forward by anti-cultists. Proponents have attempted to justify conservatorships on the basis that
"cults" are fraudulent (i.e., not religious groups at all)
and do substantial social as well as personal injury. However, in comparing the characteristics of contemporary new
religions against the standards set in Seeger, Ballard and
subsequent cases the New York University Law Review concluded (Note, 1978:1267):

>The Unification Church and other sects like it
clearly satisfy (such) definitions. In fact
an organization such as the Unification Church
would present an easy case even under a more
narrow definition than those recently offered
by the judiciary.

Spendlove has concurred (1976:1133):

It seems clear that the beliefs of most cultists
would be protected by the free exercise clause.
The Hare Krishna sect has recently been held to
be a religion within the meaning of the first
amendment and the Unification Church would probably also be held protected, since it completely
meets the criteria set out in Fellowship of
Humanity.

Moore (1980:655), despite a much more openly critical stance
toward new religions, conceded that the same was true for
Scientology, citing the Founding Church of Scientology v.
United States case:

> Despite an attempt by the United States Attorney
> to condemn the therapeutic process, the publica-
> tions and the marketing thereof, as false and
> misleading, the court of appeals found that the
> Scientologists had made out an unrebutted prima
> facie case that they were in fact a religion and
> were not guilty of violating any federal laws.

The further argument that "fraudulent cults" do substantial social injury, particularly to the family, also
fails with respect to the proposed remedy. Legal scholars
have pointed out that demonstrating fraud or illicit political activity, for example, would not specifically help in
gaining conservatorships. While a variety of other legal
remedies, both civil and criminal, might be sought for such
alleged violations, the sincerity of devotees' religious
beliefs would not be contingent upon the integrity of sincerity of leaders' beliefs and actions. As the New York
University Law Review (Note, 1978:1286-1287) stated:

> None of these possible societal harms, however,
> need to be combatted by the imposition of tempo-
> rary conservatorships. Such putative harms
> should have no bearing whatsoever on the right
> of the devotees to practice their religion.

Assessments of intervention based upon ruptured family relationships have yielded similar conclusions. The New York
University Law Review (Note, 1978:1285) asserted:

> Although the state has an interest in protect-
> ing the family relationship from disintegration,
> this interest is overcome by an adult's right
> to free exercise of religion... Here the sect
> members involved are emancipated adults, free
> from parental authority and free to adopt their
> own religions and world views.

Homer (1974:623) reached a similar conclusion:

> While practices such as these may seem extreme
> and inexcusable to some, there would appear to
> be no satisfactory rationale for state inter-
> vention here...(Adherents) have joined the par-
> ticular sect voluntarily, have chosen to accept
> its teachings and strictures and when given the
> choice of repudiating parents or family or leav-
> ing the sect, have opted to remain in the sect.
> To justify infringement here, the state would
> seemingly need to establish either that a mem-
> ber was being unlawfully imprisoned by the sect
> or that there was no meaningful consent by a
> member of the sects attitudes and actions
> against his parents.

He went on to make the even broader assertion (1974:637)
that "no cases have been reported in which a court has held
that the interest in affirming parental authority over an
emancipated child outweighed an individual's interest in the
preservation of his religious freedom.

Deprogramming

Conservatorships/guardianships and deprogramming frequently have gone hand-in-hand since the former usually have
been obtained to facilitate the latter. Nevertheless, deprogramming must be treated separately for analytic purposes
since conservatorships have not inevitably been accompanied
by deprogramming and deprogramming frequently has been carried out without benefit of legal custody. It should be emphasized that what the anti-cultists term deprogramming in
actuality ranges from voluntary dialogues in which converts
to new religions agree to separate themselves from the group
temporarily and "hear the other side" to forcible abductions.
We shall be dealing here only with cases where members have
not consented to participate in the deprogramming process.

Virtually all legal analysts have concurred that forcible deprogramming almost always violates the law. Even
those relatively supportive of controls over "cults" have
rejected deprogramming. For example, Rosenzweig (1979-1980:
156) stated:

> As a self-help remedy, deprogramming has been
> utilized by parents with the assistance of pro-
> fessional deprogrammers to expunge the altered
> world perspective of indoctrinees. The process
> usually involves abduction and physical res-

traint, and is not only potentially illegal
but also directly violative of the absolute
right to religious belief. It entails assaults upon the sect members physical and
mental integrity.

LeMoult (1978:606) has gone even further in condemning deprogramming, asserting that, "It is far more like brainwashing than the conversion process by which members join various sects."

Precisely what offenses might be involved in any particular deprogramming varies, depending upon jurisdictional
statutes and the course of events. Greene (1977:1047) has
asserted that both "the forced removal of the worshipper
from the group and his subsequent physical detention may
constitute false imprisonment or kidnapping." LeMoult (1978:
623-625), however, has noted that state kidnapping statutes
vary and hence deprogramming may not constitute first degree
kidnapping although abduction/deprogramming would be prose-
cutable as either second degree kidnapping or false imprisonment in most states.

The most systematic strategy that deprogrammers have
employed to avoid conviction on criminal charges has been
the "necessity defense." Traditionally, defendants have escaped conviction when they have been able to demonstrate
that they had "violated a law to avoid a greater evil than
the law was designed to prevent" (Pierson, 1981:273). The
defense in deprogramming cases usually has rested on two
sets of arguments -- that parents undertook deprogramming
because they had reasonable cause to believe their children
were in physical and/or psychological danger and that deprogrammers were necessary agents who rendered vital assistance
to parents. Historically, however, the necessity defense
has been used where "forces of nature" compelled action
(LeMoult, 1978; Greene, 1977), and legal scholars have expressed considerable skepticism about its extension to cases
involving pressure by other individuals. LeMoult (1978:629),
for example, asserted that "The defense of justification, or
'choice of evils,' is obviously improper in such prosecutions for a violent crime against person-like kidnapping,
false imprisonment, or one of the other possible crimes
which might arise out of deprogramming." Greene (1977:1047-
1048) was even more critical:

...the act of necessity which exonerates a defendant from criminal liability must be a lesser
harm than that which may have befallen the victim had no action been taken. The forced removal

and prolonged detention and depravity of a
cultist is at best an equivocal act of parental
good faith. At worst, the experience is a terrifying, violent event tinged with gangsterism.
Thus, the harm inflicted by "deprogramming" may
in fact be greater than the harm it avoids.
Finally, even if the "necessity defense" may be
appropriately asserted by parents, extension to
the deprogrammer cannot be founded upon theories
of agency law.

By far the most sophisticated analysis of the applicability of the necessity defense to deprogramming cases has
been conducted by Pierson (1981). He has argued that the
legitimacy of a necessity defense rests on three sets of
factors: (1) the harms created by deprogramming, (2) the
harms avoided by deprogramming and (3) the reasonableness of
parents' beliefs that the second set of harms outweighed the
first. It is Pierson's position that substantial harms ac-
crue as a result of deprogramming both because of the criminal actions accompanying abduction/restraint and because of
the threats to freedom of religion. As he put it (1981:297):

> Most of the characteristics of cult membership
> on which deprogrammers rely to justify their
> activities -- isolation from the rest of society,
> devotion to the cult as a surrogate family, and
> adherence to peculiar beliefs and practices di-
> rectly affects deprogrammed individuals, and
> also harms the cults. In addition to depriving
> cults of members' services and support, depro-
> gramming may generate a chilling effect that
> hampers their recruiting efforts.

With respect to harms avoided, Pierson has contended
that most anti-cult allegations against new religions would
constitute balancing harms only if an individual could not
voluntarily consent to such conditions. He stipulated that
the recruitment and socialization activities of new religions, which have been termed brainwashing, in fact constitute advocacy of religious beliefs. He concluded (1981:302)
that:

> The brainwashing argument may assume that there
> are "normal" religious beliefs and "constructive"
> religious practices from which cults deviate and
> that deprogramming allows individuals to appre-
> ciate. It also assumes that some individuals are
> capable of influencing others in a manner so
> clearly contrary to their best interests that it

is permissible to restrict the influence. It
overlooks, however, the Supreme Court's consistent rejection of both the former and latter
assumptions.

Except in cases of imminent, serious physical injury/damage,
therefore, intervention by deprogrammers would not be protected. And, given the force associated with deprogramming,
inadequate diet or lack of sufficient sleep would not constitute adequate grounds. Psychological problems would be
excluded entirely unless an individual were demonstrably unable to exercise independent judgement.

Finally, Pierson considered the conditions under which
defendants might be legally exonerated on the basis of a
reasonable belief that the balance of harms justified deprogramming. He asserted that, at a minimum, specific evidence
(e.g., correspondence out of character with previous communication, personal contact suggesting incapacity to render
independent judgements, blockage of contact with offspring
by a "cult") was necessary to legitimate "rescue." Of
course, such subjective evidence would be subject to later
scrutiny for reasonableness and specificity. In addition,
other viable legal alternatives, such as conservatorships,
must have been duly considered prior to the undertaking of
extra-legal action. He concluded (1981:306) that:

> The choice of evils defense will thus rarely ex-
> onerate parents of adult cult members, and will
> virtually neve exonerate professional deprogram-
> mers. Deprogramming constitutes a lesser evil
> only if the cult member appears incapable of ex-
> ercising independent judgement or risks severe
> injury. Even in these situations, courts should
> reject the defense if viable legal alternatives
> were available.

Thus, the necessity defense appears to hold little security
for deprogrammers in the long run despite a number of successful applications in recent years. As the full legal implications and precedent cases are more widely disseminated,
it seems likely that courts will be increasingly less receptive to such arguments.

Based on the preceding analysis the long term legal
prospects facing the anti-cultists appear discouraging. In
addition to a general lack of support for such legal proposals, however, deprogrammers also run the risk of civil
suits (Siegel, 1978:826-828). Civil suits offer a number
of advantages such as avoiding the necessity of implicating

parents in legal action and offsetting the failure of law
enforcement agencies to prosecute deprogrammers. LeMoult
(1978:636-637) has identified a number of offenses including assault and battery, unlawful imprisonment, invasion of
privacy and medical malpractice which might be pursued in
civil proceedings.

Shepherd (this volume) has suggested that suits under
the 1985 (c) section of the Civil Rights Act constitute a
basis for civil suits against deprogrammers. He summarizes
the intent of this act as follows:

> Section 1985 (c) is aimed at rooting out racial
> conspiracies of whites against blacks. It
> states that two or more people cannot act on an
> agreement to deprive any person or class of
> persons the equal protection of the laws, or of
> equal privileges and immunities under the laws;
> nor can they injure another in person or prop-
> erty, or deprive him of having and exercising
> any right or privilege of a citizen.

In order to bring suit under the provisions of this act a
plaintiff must show a conspiracy which has as its intent
deprivation of equal protection, an act which furthers the
conspiracy and injury or deprivation of rights and privileges. Shepherd sees in recent court cases "affirmations
of Section 1985 (c) which agree that, specifically, a deprogrammed plaintiff has fashioned a remedy, stated a cause of
action properly, and reached a constitution source of authority on the basis of which the court can act to redress
injuries, again specifically, to punish conspiring parents
and deprogrammers." Taken together, Shepherd argues, these
cases constitute a broadening state mandate to affirmative-
ly move to prevent injury resulting from discrimination.

> The Fourteenth Amendment rights at stake have
> received more and more specificity, so depro-
> grammed plaintiffs, for example, have only
> recently been afforded constitutional ability
> to state a cause of action that will hold up
> in very particular circumstances. The rights
> in question are not vague rights against all
> the world. They are rather rights against
> particular persons or groups engaged in acti-
> vities having the practical effect of denying
> fundamental rights.

Babbit (1979:254) reached a similar conclusion. She stated
that, "If the plaintiff can thus state a cause of action,

trial upon the merits will likely result in vindication of
his constitutional right to join the religious group he
pleases regardless of public or private feelings against
that religious group." If these analyses are correct, then
a pattern of findings against deprogrammers should begin to
emerge.

THE FUTURE OF THE NEW RELIGIONS CONFLICT

Legal scholars have given opponents of the new religions little cause for optimism about the use of conservatorship provisions to extricate individuals from "cults."
However, this bleak assessment has not blunted the anti-
cultists drive for such legislation in a number of states
(Shupe and Bromley, 1980, forthcoming). Expanded conservatorship powers were approved by both houses of the legislature in New York in each of the last two legislative sessions although vetoed by the Governor. Of course, even if
such legislation became law in New York or elsewhere, it
would immediately be subjected to judicial challenge and
appeal all the way to the Supreme Court should that prove
necessary. If conservatorship legislation initiatives fail,
what form will the new religions controversy assume?

The intensity of the conflict may moderate somewhat
over the next decade. A number of new religions are moving
toward more stable, conventional organizational forms as (1)
the first cohorts of recruits reach ages at which domestic
and occupational futives can no longer be ignored, (2) the
cost of long term opposition from anti-cult groups and major
institutions continues to mount, (3) new religions form more
complex, quasi-bureaucratic structures which are inherently
more conservative, and (4) links formed with various conventional groups as part of a defense/cooptation strategy exert
a moderating influence. In addition, a variety of services
are developing to deal with issues raised by the conversion
and deconversion processes. Several "mediation" services
have been proposed or established which have as their objective reduction of fear, misunderstanding and communication
barriers among family members where one family member has
joined a new religion. Counseling groups have been created
to assist leavetakers who face various personal problems as
they seek to re-assume conventional identities and careers
(Shupe and Bromley, forthcoming). While such initiatives
will hardly resolve the conflict, they may reduce the number
of individuals who feel that extreme action is necessary.

At the same time, the conflict is likely to become more
institutionalized. Over the last decade anti-cult groups

have created more sophisticated and stable organizations
and experimented with various strategies for combatting new
religions. These groups may not continue to receive the
same publicity, but they probably will continue their efforts as have groups opposed to earlier new religions such
as Christian Science, Mormonism and Jehovah's Witness (Shupe
and Bromley, forthcoming). Efforts by anti-cult organizations to increase the number of groups designated as "cults,"
to gain political and financial support for the study of
"destructive cultism" and to find alternative legal strategies to conservatorships suggest a long-term organizational
posture.

Among the alternatives to conservatorships which have
received some attention are disclosure legislation and civil
suits against leaders of new religions. Support for disclosure requirements has come from those who see such legislation as a form of consumer protection. Siegel (1978:820-
821), for example, stated:

> Surely the marketplace of ideas and religious
> philosophies is as needful of an informed pub-
> lic as is the commercial area. It would thus
> seem reasonable to require that religious as-
> sociations, in making representations, conform
> to a standard of disclosure similar to that
> required in the marketing of products. No
> freedom of activity would be sacrificed.

The primary appeal of such legislation is that supporters
see no intrusion on constitutionally protected individual
beliefs. Rosenzweig (1979-1980:158) asserted:

> Unlike legalized deprogramming, disclosure leg-
> islation does not directly impinge upon the
> constitutional rights of religious sects or
> their members. In addition, it does not un-
> reasonably burden a sect's free exercise of
> religious worship.

The viability of disclosure legislation remains largely un-
tested since, with the exception of provisions governing
public solicitation, bills have yet to be introduced in
state legislatures or subjected to judicial review.

A variety of possible civil actions against religious
groups, leaders or members are possible under existing
statutes for false imprisonment, fraud or intentional infliction of emotional distress. In the case of false imprisonment physical restraint must be demonstrated, and par-

ents of converts to new religions have not been successful
in presenting evidence of such restraint. Successful suit
for fraud would essentially involve demonstrating that a
"cult" was not religious, and the pattern of court decisions
on the religious status of new religious movements is not
encouraging of this position. Finally, outrageous, purpose-
ful acts designed to create mental anguish could constitute
the basis for civil suit (Greene, 1977:1041). There is
judicial precedent for such suits although none involve current new religions. Greene (1977:1043) does cite one instance of a successful civil suit for malicious prosecution
involving the Church of Scientology. In Allard v. Church of
Scientology of California the plaintiff was awarded damages
after the court found that "the church had a policy of
tricking, harassing, and destroying its enemies, thus indicating that the association had probably not instigated the
criminal action in order to obtain justice. The problem
with all such civil suits is that they involve individually
constructed cases and time consuming, expensive litigation.
The few extreme cases which might produce courtroom vic-
tories would not address the concerns of most parents, and
anti-cult groups lack the financial capacity to sustain a
concerted campaign of civil suits.

    Extra-legal deprogramming seems destined to continue
over the next few years. Even if new religious groups do
moderate somewhat, parental concern is likely to remain
great and legal remedies remain elusive. As case precedents
build up, the likelihood of conservatorships being granted
will decrease (although sympathetic local magistrates still
may be found who will side with distraught parents). Thus
some parents probably will continue to assume the risks of
extra-legal action. Several factors combine to support the
perpetuation of extra-legal deprogramming despite the theoretical availability of legal sanctions.

    First, law enforcement agencies and courts often have
been reluctant to intervene in deprogrammings, regarding
such incidents as family disputes. Homer (1974:640), for
example, cites reports that "Police in several jurisdictions
have refused to register complaints made by emancipated
children against parents who had abducted them on grounds it
involved only a family squabble." LeMount (1978:1253) made
a similar observation, noting the role of grand juries and
juries as well:

        The usual pattern was for a sect member's parents,
        accompanied by a professional deprogrammer and his
        assistants, to forcibly abduct the member from the
        commune or a public place and transport him to a
        home or motel room for a deprogramming session.

The element of state action in self-help situations was passive: police declined to intervene,
viewing the kidnapings as "family matters" best
resolved outside the courts; grand juries refused to indict and petit juries to convict the
abudctors.

Thus, even though the necessity defense does not appear to
be applicable to deprogramming cases, it has been used successfully. Juries have been swayed by the testimony of distraught parents and deprogrammers have been seen as their
agents.

Second, deprogrammers have been increasingly more careful to implicate parents or other family members in abductions and deprogrammings in order to avoid civil or criminal
prosecution. Ted Patrick has been quite explicit on this
point (Patrick and Dulack, 1976:270):

From my research into the subject I was reason-
ably well assured that a parent would not be
prosecuted for kidnaping his own child, especially if the child was a minor. With that in
mind, I began to formulate the basis of my approach to seizing the children and deprogramming
them. The first rule was always to have at
least one of the parents present when we went to
snatch somebody. The parents would have to make
the first physical contact; then, no matter who
assisted them afterwards, it would be parents
who were responsible. And if a parent was not
committing a crime by seizing his or her child,
no one else could be considered an accessory to
a crime.

Third, deprogrammers have been able to exploit a variety of legal loopholes to conduct deprogrammings. For example, in some cases parents have been able to gain writs
of habeus corpus on the grounds that their children were
being held against their wills; in other cases parents have
been granted temporary conservatorships which were immediately challenged in court. However, if parents were able
to gain even brief custody of their children as a result of
such actions, deprogramming might be complete before counter
legal action could be undertaken. Spendlove (1976:1106)
reports:

...lawyers have succeeded in getting hearings
granted on the validity of conservatorships,
but this legal maneuver has not been of practical value. Usually deprogrammers remove cultists

on a Friday afternoon. Even if the cultist has
signed a retainer agreement with an attorney, to
take effect if he mysteriously disappears, his
attorney cannot file a petition for termination
of conservatorship until Monday morning. Since
the court frequently seals the files in cult
conservatorship cases, the cultist's attorney
may be delayed in determining which court issued
the conservatorship order. After a petition is
filed in the correct court, there may be 2 or 3
days further delay before a hearing is held and
service of process on the deprogrammers made.
Deprogramming usually takes 3 days or less, and
so is finished by the time a hearing on petition
to terminate the conservatorship is granted.

Finally, legal proceedings normally will be initiated
only if deprogramming "fails." While the "success" rate of
deprogrammers is unknown, there have been a substantial number of cases in which members of new religions have left
their groups following deprogramming and thereupon had no
interest in prosecution of deprogrammers. When the "success" rate is added to cases in which parents are implicated
and police and courts refuse involvement, deprogrammers
stand a reasonable chance of avoiding serious legal penalty.
Of course, with few exceptions deprogramming is not a full
time occupation, and there is considerable turnover in the
ranks of deprogrammers. This turnover means that it is unlikely that most deprogrammers will be prosecuted on multiple occasions, and hence even if penalties are imposed,
they are typically minimal.

CONCLUSIONS

The central legal issue in the new religions controversy has been brainwashing/deprogramming since opponents of
these groups have sought legal custody of their adult children and forcible abductions have occurred when judicial
remedies were unavailable. The reactions to intervention
strategies proposed by opponents of new religion have not
been encouraging. The application of the balancing test
principles to proposed conservatorship laws or state intervention on the basis of mental incapacity has consistently
indicated a serious infringement upon first amendment liberties. Other legal options, such as civil suits or disclosure legislation, might be pursued, but these options to not
offer the simple, uniform remedy anti-cultists seek. Despite these discouraging legal prospects opponents of new
religions may continue to engage in extra-legal deprogram-

ming. Sympathetic hearings from law enforcement and judicial officials, "successful" deprogrammings, and legal loopholes may keep alive vigilante style tactics given the intensity of family conflicts and the lucrativeness of the deprogramming enterprise.

V

CONCLUSIONS AND IMPLICATIONS

In the four preceding sections of this book we have presented an array of data on and analyses of the brainwashing/
deprogramming controversy. This evidence suggests several
conclusions: (1) subversion theories have recurred throughout American religious history whenever the status quo was
threatened, and the major elements of those theories have
been remarkably predictable and repetitive, (2) both affiliation with and exit from new religious movements conform to
broader social science understandings of recruitment, socialization and defection processes and do not require the
application of more controversial and extreme theories such
as brainwashing, and (3) there are a range of social and
psychological consequences of affiliation with new religious
movements (as there are for all groups and movements) but
certainly no consistent pattern of injurious consequences as
implied in the brainwashing and deprogramming metaphors.
These conclusions raise a number of other issues. If individuals are not programmed (i.e., brainwashed), then what is
deprogramming? Why have these reciprocal processes been so
vigorously proffered and defended? What are the social consequences of interpreting new religious movements in terms
of such metaphors. It is to such issues and to a broader
consideration of the meaning and significance of brainwash--
ing and deprogramming that the papers in this section are
addressed.

Hargrove's thoughtful historically and sociologically
informed paper interprets brainwashing as a contemporary
"evil eye" theory. Conversion always involves a transformation of a convert's organizing framework of meaning.
Given such a transformation it is not surprising that negative feelings develop between insiders (who rely on new
sources of authority, writings and lines of reasoning) and
outsiders (who regard such innovations as bizarre). The
question remains, however, why American society, which
stresses personal autonomy, has fallen back on brainwashing
as an explanation. Hargrove argues that we have lost our
ability to take seriously the place of religion in social
life. Indeed, religion has become largely a leisure-time,
privatized phenomenon. Since we do not take religious seriously, we do not incorporate the making of religious
choices into the socialization process in any significant
way. Furthermore we have tended to overlook the very real

human needs which are satisfied through religious commitments. As a result, we are shocked when others do take religion seriously and the religious impulse intrudes on our
rationalistic, individualistic social order as forcefully as
it has.

Kelley attacks deprogramming from a civil libertarian
perspective. He is particularly dismayed over state intervention in the new religions controversy through the enact-
ment or extension of conservatorship provisions. He argues
that new religious movements, which do take religion seriously, are precisely the groups which need first amendment
protections and for which such protections were designed.
As Kelly sees it, if religious liberty is to have meaning,
then individuals must have the right to subject their reason
to the demands of faith and follow out the self-imposed demands of this faith. Referring to deprogramming as "spiritual gang rape," he contends that separating individuals from
other believers and attacking their religious tenets strikes
at the very heart of religious liberty, the ability to freely hold religious convictions and commitments.

Robbins, Anthony and McCarthy analyze the utility of
"brainwashing" as a social weapon with which to attack new
religions. They point out that this metaphor allows authorities to insist that it is not doctrines but coercive techniques that are at issue even though it is the beliefs and
associated practices which trigger the allegations of mind
control. Brainwashing is an ideal conceptual weapon given
the virtual impossibility of demonstrating that it has not
taken place. Free will is, after all, a cultural presumption rather than an empirical fact. In addition, portraying
religious devotees as passive objects rather than as active
participants in the conversion process legitimates repressive reversal techniques which can be defined as remedial
and therapeutic. Thus the authors see brainwashing as a
thinly disguised tactic for legitimating social repression.

In the final paper, Barker in one sense turns the brain-
washing/deprogramming controversy on its head by emunerating
the positive functions deprogramming may have for new religious movements. The deprogrammer becomes a bogey man;
group solidarity is strengthened by his lurking presence.
Deprogrammers and deprogramming confirm new religious' doctrines about the corruption of the outside world. The fact
that deprogrammers are not resoundingly renounced by the
public at large and by public officials provides convincing
evidence that conventional society is hopelessly corrupt
and apathetic. Confronting such an array of forces only
serves to harden resolve. These feelings are exacerbated

by deprogramming situations in which the most viable means
of escape for victims is to violate the moral precepts of
their groups and adopt the "corrupt" attitudes and practices
of their captors. Barker also observes that deprogramming
heightens family tensions. Fear of deprogramming reduces
candor and communication with parents and contributes to a
process of spiraling mistrust. While not denying the heavy
costs a fortress lifestyle and mentality imposes on new religions, Barker concludes that anti-cult groups contribute
in a significant way to the state of affairs they ostensibly
oppose.

*SOCIAL SOURCES AND CONSEQUENCES
OF THE BRAINWASHING CONTROVERSY

Barbara Hargrove
Iliff School of Theology, Denver, CO

One of the most potentially explosive issues in American society today is the controversy over "brainwashing" and
its proposed remedy, "deprogramming." Whatever the initial
facts of the case, the charges and countercharges, the mobilization of legal and ecclesiastical machinery on one
side or the other, the genuine distress of many of the parties involved, all indicate a level of social disruption
that is highly uncomfortable, if not downright dangerous to
the society at large. If one assumes, then, that what is
going on should be defined as a social malady, there is
clearly a need to seek a cure. Since our definition of the
source of an illness suggests where we search for its cure,
an initial task is to seek out the origins of the charges of
brainwashing. There are at least two types of origins to
consider: the kind of activity which brings on such charges,
and the cultural or experiential bases for applying the term
"brainwashing" to them.

There are charges that young people who are recruited
to such groups as Sun Myung Moon's Unification Church, Hare
Krishna, or the Children of God have undergone a "total
change of personality." They have rejected their families
and their families' values, cut off ties with former friends,
given up cherished career patterns and hobbies. They are
said to show evidence of psychosis, of schizophrenia, a loss
of creativity. They are described as exhibiting robot-like
behavior, or having a typical glassy-eyed "thousand-mile
stare." They no longer engage in a rational discussion,
it is said, but keep using the jargon and advancing the
ideology of the group. They have totally surrounded themselves with group members -- or have been surrounded by them
-- so that they never hear anything that might shake their
newfound way of looking at the world.

It is assumed that this behavior is the product of a
deliberate, sinister, and highly sophisticated plot to take
over the minds and souls of young people and turn them into
"robots." This is done, supposedly, through forced isola-

tion, deprivation of food, sleep, and most essentials, psychological persuasion of the most coercive kind, and other forcible measures which sometimes assume mythological proportions in the conversation of parents and former members who have gone through deprogramming, which is the reversal of that process. All evidence points to the fact that organized deprogramming has become at least as much a social movement as the groups it seeks to oppose.

Given the evidence that deprogramming, based as it is on a definition of brainwashing which requires reversal, contains the possibility of an equal level of psychological manipulation, former members who have undergone this process may scarcely be expected to be reliable witnesses. It then becomes important to see if other explanations of members' behavior are also possible, perhaps even more accurate, yielding insights which might lead to other suggested responses more effective and less socially disruptive than the techniques used in the deprogramming movement.

One obvious question to ask is whether these young converts are simply that, converts to a religious group which is labeled deviant by the society, or at least by that portion of the society from which they have come. There is little doubt that most of the groups originally accused of brainwashing fall into the deviant category, though there is also evidence that the charges are spreading to less deviant ones. For example, a number of conservative Christian groups have been so challenged, and similar charges were raised last spring by parents of several students of the University of Kansas who converted to Roman Catholicism and entered a monastic order in France after a humanities course about such orders in medieval society. In the long run, no religious group is likely to be considered normative if it demands total commitment in the form of withdrawal from ordinary career patterns of familiar social networks.

This is not only true now, but can be found throughout history. A glance through church history will turn up large numbers of people, many of them young, who caused their families great anguish by taking seriously the Biblical injunction from Matthew 10: "He who loves father or mother more than me is not worthy of me, and he who does not take up his cross and follow me is not worthy of me." Further, Christian missionaries in many areas of the world have been accused of stealing the children of the local people and bewitching them with their foreign religion. And there is a long and rather recent folklore of kidnapping as the source of converts to Mormonism, however ridic-

Barbara Hargrove

ulous that may seem today. Were those conversions essentially the same as those now being experienced by recruits
to the Unification Church of Sun Myung Moon, Hare Krishna,
the Children of God, or some other such group? How do
classical descriptions cf conversion compare with what can
be observed in such cases?

The classic psychological description of conversion
remains that of William James, and is a valuable point of
reference. Speaking of the areas of a person's consciousness which are the centers of greatest activity and concentration, James (1963:136) said:

> Now there may be great oscillation in the emo-
> tional interest, and the hot places may shift
> before one almost as rapidly as the sparks that
> run through burnt-up paper. Then we have the
> wavering or divided self....Or the focus of
> excitement and heat, the point of view from
> which the sin is taken, may come to lie perma-
> nently within a certain system; and then, if
> the change be a religious one, we call it a
> conversion, especially if it be by crisis, or
> sudden. Let us hereafter, in speaking of the
> hotplace in a man's consciousness, the group
> of ideas to which he devotes himself, and from
> which he works, call it the habitual centre of
> his personal energy. It makes a great differ-
> ence to a man whether one set of his ideas, or
> another, be the centre of his energy; and it
> makes a great difference, as regards any set of
> ideas which he may possess, whether they become
> central or remain peripheral in him. To say
> that a man is "converted" means, in these terms,
> that religious ideas, previously peripheral in
> his consciousness, now take a central place,
> and that religious aims from the habitual cen-
> tre of his energy.

Sociclogists have added the dimension of social reinforcement to this kind of understanding of conversion.
Our attention focuses as it does, they say, because it is
a common human practice to organize the many experiences
and sense impressions of daily life into some kind of meaningful categories, so that we can make generalizations that
allow us to learn from experience, find one another's behavior predictable, and otherwise understand our lives as
meaningful. Those generalizations gain reality for us as
we share them with other people, and in fact are caught up
in our language, our behavior patterns, and our sense of
identity as persons.

The convert is a person who shifts this overall organizing framework of meaning from one pattern to another which is significantly different. It is a little like comparing a relief map of the country to a political map, where seeing the area organized into mountain ranges, river valleys, and the like, typically calls forth a considerably different response from that to a map showing states, counties, and cities. The territory is the same, but its meaning seems altered.

Usually people learn the basic features of their reality "map" in the family, and find it reinforced, if expanded, in the later socialization of such institutions as school and church. Definitions that are significantly different from those widely shared in the society may result in difficulty in the economic and political realm as well as in these more formative institutions. So a person who turns to a different "map" for his or her authority as a guide to meaning can be seen as an indication of failure of parents or school or church -- a badge of shame to them.

At the same time, there are reasons for negative feelings toward family and old friends on the part of the convert. As Berger (1967:51) has put it:

> ...the individual who wishes to convert, and
> (more importantly) to "stay converted" must
> engineer his social life in accordance with
> this purpose. Thus he must dissociate himself
> from those individuals or groups that consti-
> tuted the plausibility structure of his past
> religious reality, and associate himself all
> the more intensively and (if possible) exclu-
> sively with those who serve to maintain his
> new one. Put succinctly, migration between
> religious worlds implies migration between
> their respective plausibility structures.
> This fact is as relevant for those who wish
> to foster such migrations as for those wish-
> ing to prevent them. In other words, the same
> social-psychological problem is involved in
> evangelism and in the "care of souls."

The convert's new frame of reference (or as Berger puts it, the new plausibility structure) relies not only on the direct response of other members of the group he or she has joined, but also on certain authorities they share -- sacred writings, leaders of the movement, and the like. Part of the changed behavior seen in a convert may be found in this choice of new bases of authority and legitimation, from which new lines of reasoning will arise. It is much more comfortable to be among people for whom such approaches seem rational and right, to be with people who share the same categories and authorities. Often, even if the new way of looking at the world does not necessarily call for changed behavior or appearance, people may adopt certain characteristic styles of action or address in order to identify one another as fellow-believers, to know who it is one may expect to share common assumptions, to talk with without defensiveness, and to give mutual aid in what has been defined as a common struggle.

To others who do not share their frame of reference, (and of course this includes the families and friends with whom the former worldview was shared) such a change in accepted categories of meaning and sources of authority seems a clear loss of rationality. The convert will no longer "listen to reason." His or her attention is fixed elsewhere, so that they may <u>seem</u> a thousand miles away, regardless of whether their eyes actually have a "thousand-mile stare." New styles of response and new priorities concerning ideal personality types may well lead to the appearance of an abrupt change in personality patterns. In fact, if one assumes any accuracy in the concept of the "looking-glass self," one may expect a personality change as the convert sees an entirely different reflection of himself or herself in the response of members of a group whose understanding of the nature and the place of the person is different from what has previously been experienced. And this new self, which may seem far more satisfactory than the old self that was left behind, may not be enhanced by the same patterns or goals as the old one. All this, of course, is completely unfathomable to those who assume that the old self still exists in the familiar body of their child or friend.

Harvey Cox has suggested that in all societies where new religious movements have attracted young people, their parents and others in the "establishment" will develop some "evil eye" theory, insisting that their children have been bewitched. (One is reminded of the tale of the Pied Piper of Hamelin.) "Brainwashing," in that case, may be seen as the "evil eye" theory appropriate to a modern scientific culture. Psychological technology is something we understand a little about, and that we understand to be amenable to counteraction by improved technology. This kind of definition of conversion also fits our common tendency to define any deviance as illness. Conversion in this instance is simply a case of induced mental illness. With its etiology so defined, the cure then is apparent: call in the doctor -- in this case the psychiatrist -- to administer the cure he is professionally trained to provide.

There are, however, certain weaknesses to this way of
dealing with religious conversion. At the first and most
shallow level, one may note that many of the deprogrammers
are not professional psychiatrists, but rather make use of
"package treatments" based on psychological principles --
a sort of patent medicine approach to this kind of deviance
which carries its own dangers of misuse. More serious, however is the relegation of the individual in such cases to
the passive role of the patient, the object of psychological manipulation not only in the first instance of willful
persuasion, but also in the process of returning the convert to a "normal" worldview. There is no place in this
model for "do-it-yourself" activities, no expectation of
any exercise of the human will, no notion of a person making voluntary choices. In fact, if it is a problem that
many of the deprogrammers are not properly certified professionals, it is likely to be seen as even more dangerous
for the individual to attempt to assume conscious control
of his or her own life and strive to make some kind of
personal choice between the views which have been presented.
There is, then, in this "evil eye" theory no more place for
rational decision-making or personal freedom of choice than
could be found in the old theories of witchcraft, sorcery,
and possession.

In a society which aspires toward values of individual
autonomy, why should we find such a theory so widely applied to situations of recruitment to religions which are
considered deviant? Perhaps we have forgotten other explanations which might have carried with them more satisfactory methods of dealing with the situation.

One of the things we have lost is the ability to take
seriously the place and language of religion as a valid
part of human life. In this case, it was assumed that
there were true religions and false religions, and that it
was an important function of family and society to teach
people as they were growing up to distinguish the one from
the other. Clearly this led to many abuses, the Inquisition being only the most notorious, but it provided several
useful ideas as well. First, there was an assumption that
there was a connection between religious identification and
a system of values one lived by, that was part of the normal pattern of involvement in human life. Such an assumption then allows individuals to test various religious approaches for inconsistency, hypocrisy, irrelevance, or
wrong direction. It allows the exercise of a discrimina-
ting view toward religious systems while still taking them
seriously, and thus tends to lead to the development of
ways of training people to ask significant questions of

religious groups concerning their doctrines, practices, and goals. In a secular society, where religion is not taken seriously, neither is serious attention given to the development of skills in making religious choices. Without such training, young people are indeed subjects of undue manipulation by the purveyors of religious schemes.

A failure to recognize the importance of religion in the society leads to overlooking those human needs which are most often served by religious involvement. In particular, a secular society which prides itself on being objectively rational in the scientific mode may offer little challenge or hope to the young person who longs to be fully involved in activity which is of value, even at personal risk or danger. Objective rationality has a hard time satisfying those who would be heroes, who spurn the pragmatic tests of self-interest. And many of the groups in question have the particular appeal of calling converts to become saviors of the world, however they define the salvation they would offer.

A second general way in which we may have become incapable of seeing factors operating in the current situation comes from what has been called the privatization of religion. In modern secular society religion is tolerated as a leisure time activity of the private sphere of one's life, possibly aesthetically enriching or capable of satisfying the need for voluntary association, but nothing more. In this frame of reference there is no basis for considering any public consequences of religion other than its pacifying effect as an "opiate of the masses" or its contribution to social mobility through providing the informal contacts and group skills available in any voluntary association.

Consequently, when a religious group sets out to save the world, no one takes the claim seriously enough to ask what the public consequences of that doctrine might be. Several of the groups which hope to save the world soon exhibit a kind of authoritarian mentality which, should their movement prove successful, could lead to a highly repressive kind of society with a sacred legitimation which is particularly hard to context. But since religion is defined as a private affair, no one has suggested to potential converts that they carefully weigh the possible public consequences of the groups they might join.

Time and time again, converts give as their reason for joining a group the fact that here they had found people who cared about one another, and who cared for them as persons. The other questions, those of doctrine or public

consequence, were never even considered until group reinforcement had already made the doctrine seem reasonable
and the consequences right. At this point, the assumption
that people can be brainwashed has essentially become a
self-fulfilling prophecy. Without any basis on which to
ask questions of the group, they join it out of felt needs,
out of hungers which have not been satisfied in their lives
outside the group, and then submit themselves willingly to
its influence.

An "evil eye" definition of conversion has both its
source and its consequences in the willingness by members
of the dominant society to avoid dealing with those weakness of the society that create needs which are met by new
religious groups. Bewitchment or brainwashing must be the
fault of the deceiver, not of those whose children are
deceived nor of the society from which they come. No critical examination of other possible causes is thought necessary. And so no remedial action is required other than
the exorcism of the evil influence.

That way of dealing with the situation is always open
to the kind of criticism carried in the parable of the man
who, freed from an evil spirit, swept out the house of his
soul so thoroughly that the spirit returned with seven even
more evil companions. To assume that the sole source of
religious conversion is the evil influence of the converter
is to refuse to deal with sources of the conversion which
should be faced by those most concerned.

Why are young people so impressed by a group of people
who show genuine love and concern? Have they never met
such responses elsewhere? Why is it so attractive to be
recruited to save the world? In what ways have recruits
come to understand that it is so in need of saving? What
are the interstices of our culture through which important
human needs are falling unmet, and how may these be filled?
These are the kinds of questions which conversions elicit,
and which definitions like brainwashing allow us to ignore.

Solutions like deprogramming reinforce a view of
humankind as incapable of decision-making or any exercise
of the will. They reflect a kind of scientific determinism
that is frequently identified as a source of youthful dis-
content, and in fact as a source of conversions to new
lifestyles and meaning systems. If one assumes that individual lives are entirely the product of impersonal social
forces, and that all human responses are the result of some
kind of conditioning, then it becomes very difficult for a
person to see any particular meaning in his or her life.

Yet there are expectations in our society that the particular task of youth is to choose a career pattern and life
plan that will be meaningful. It seems logical that,
placed in this position, young people should be attracted
to groups which offer such meaning, and that they might
consider it a sinister act if they are pursued by people
bent on conditioning them to a different response.

Much of the ideology behind the deprogramming movement
has involved a critique of the religious groups for sub-
stituting a communal will for the autonomy of the individual. But the basic view of humanity which underlies the
method of deprogramming is less one of autonomy and more
that of a stimulus-response psychology which is indeed
"beyond freedom and dignity." The young people involved
appear to be given the choice between being directed by
an authoritarian community or used as subjects of an abstract technology. Thus while some of the religious movements appear to be authoritarian and potentially if not
actually repressive, so also do the methods by which they
are opposed. It is not much of a choice to pick domination
by psychological manipulators over that by religious dema-
gogues. In fact, the latter at least seen to offer more of
the warmth of human community than do the deprogrammers.

It is true that there is much illusion in a philosophy
that says, "I am the master of my fate, the captain of my
soul." Yet the very number and variety of influences and
institutions by which any person is shaped may create the
conditions of genuine decision-making. The responsibilities of freedom are heavy in a modern, pluralistic society
where the range of choice may seem almost beyond the ability of the individual's powers of discrimination.

Since the situation of much of today's youth lies in
that area of freedom and choice, there are two directions
in which members of the society may move to support them in
that highly ambiguous situation. They may reduce the area
of choice, either through deliberate manipulation or coercion, or through providing membership in some authoritarian
group. Or they may provide definite training in the making
of choices, along with the inculcation of a sense of autonomy, a belief that one is truly capable of choosing values,
goals, and commitments, and that those choices are significant and the commitments meaningful.

This second course may well require rethinking the importance of a religious approach to existence, both for the
individual and in the public sphere. At least in the past,
religion has been a source of meaning and a focus of commitment for a great number of people. There is a need to

question the hasty assumption often found in a secular society as well as a number of religious groups, that all
religious choices must be either authoritarian or thoroughly privatized, lest that assumption become a self-fulfilling prophecy that pushes people into unnecessary
choices of religious systems that are not functional in a
democratic society.

A definition of conversion which takes seriously the
ability of human beings to make decisions of their own,
the legitimacy of a religious worldview, and the public
potential of religious action is one which would allow for
the development of skills to make these things possible.
It also opens the possibility that some of the choices, and
the commitments they engender, could be made within the
mainstream of the society, and be devoted to making it an
environment less conducive to deviant choices which might
prove, in the long run, simply wrong.

* Originally published in Society 17 (March-April 1980):
  20-24.

*DEPROGRAMMING AND RELIGIOUS LIBERTY

Dean M. Kelley
National Council of Churches

Ever since the term "deprogramming" entered our national
vocabulary several years go, civil libertarians have been
hard pressed to map the battlefront of this emotional controversy. Arrayed on one side are a plethora of new, high-
demand "cult" religions which, dismayed observers allege, en-
share and exploit impressionable young people through "mind
control" and "brainwashing." On the other side are the parents of the new converts who increasingly are resorting to
deprogramming -- which admittedly involves kidnapping and
physical restraint -- to restore their children, at great
expense, to what the parents perceive as "normal." Lost in
the shuffle somewhere is the First Amendment to the Constitution whose protection of religious freedom the new religions
and their adherents claim as their own. What is going on
here? Are civil liberties being infringed, and, if so, by
whom?

Recently, the legal parameters of the issue were defined
by two diametrically opposed court decisions -- one in New
York, and the other in California. The first case, in
Queens County, New York, involved two members of the Hare
Krishna movement, Ed Shapiro and Merylee Kreshour. When both
Shapiro and Kreshour were forceably detained by their parents
and subjected to deprogramming by a private detective named
Galen Kelly, they filed a complaint with the local district
attorney. As a result of a subsequent grand jury investigation, however, the complaint against the parents and the deprogrammer was thrown out, and instead the leaders of the local Krishna Temple were themselves indicted for kidnapping
and unlawful detention through "mind control."

Obscured by the hue and cry of distraught parents who
see their children being duped by "bogus" religions is an examination of what the process of deprogramming actually entails. It is really nothing more than a euphemism for behavior modification. The practice originated in San Diego,
California, under the leadership of a man named Ted Patrick,
a former (volunteer) community relations aide to Governor
Ronald Reagan. The object of the deprogrammers is to restore
new converts of unorthodox religious groups to society by

309

dissuading them from their new-found beliefs. Kidnapping is
the method used for these "rescues."

Deprogrammers -- displaying a certain amount of uni-
formity -- always grab the victim at a time when he is least
expecting it. There are usually three or four people who
stuff the victim into a car and drive him off to some hotel,
motel, or private home. He can be locked up in a room for
up to three weeks, though usually the deprogramming takes
only a few days. The victim is deprived of sleep and food
and told that he will be held until he capitulates. One
such scene, related with all the drama and pathos of a B
grade war movie, was described by Ted Patrick himself in his
recent book, Let Our Children Go:

> We hurried downstairs to the examining room where
> Dr. Shapiro conducted his practice, and there was
> Ed, a tall thin boy, his head shaven, still wear-
> ing his robes and his beads, chanting and scream-
> ing. "Get me a pair of scissors," I said. "Scis-
> sors? What for?" "First thing we're going to do
> is cut that knot of hair off his head."
>
> Ed came to attention. "What? Who are you? What
> right do you have to go cutting my hair? I have
> a right to wear this. It's part of my religion.
> I'm a legal adult. I'm twenty years old." "Shut
> up and sit down." I told him. "Just shut your
> mouth and listen."
>
> "I won't listen. I don't have to listen. I want
> to leave!" "Well, you're not going to leave.
> Where's those scissors?" Four of his relatives
> held him down and I cut off the tuft of hair they
> all wear on the back of their heads and I removed
> the beads from around his neck. As soon as we
> let him up, he started chanting again at the top
> of his voice, "Hare Krishna, Hare Krishna, Hare
> Hare..."
>
> In the game room Dr. Shapiro had a lot of lovely
> and expensive art objects and souvenirs he col-
> lected over the years and Ed began smashing them,
> one by one, just ripping the place apart, chant-
> ing all the while...I took him by the arms and
> flung him into a corner up against the wall, and
> I said, "All right, you hatchet-head son of a
> bitch, you move out of there and I'll knock your
> goddamned head off."

I picked Ed up by the front of his shirt and
marched him backwards across the room, slamming
him bodily against the wall. "You listen to me!
You so much as wiggle your toes again, I'm gonna put my fist down your throat!" His eyes got
bigger and bigger with fear. He sat down abruptly.
I had a picture of Prabhupada and I tore it up in
front of him and said, "There's the no-good son of
a bitch you worship. And you call him God!" The
usual line of approach.

This "usual line of approach" has become a burgeoning
business. Some programming entrepreneurs are charged $10,000
to $14,000, plus expenses, for deprogrammings, even if ulti-
mately unsuccessful. A tax-exempt foundation has been set up
in Tucson, Arizona, with Alexander, a protege of Patrick, and
his wife as full-time resident deprogrammers, assisted as
needed by two lawyers and a psychologist. There are networks
of enthusiasts for deprogramming who circulate periodic newsletters telling how the battle goes in various parts of the
country, generating letters to encourage cooperative prosecutors or to discount critics of deprogramming.

On the surface, it may seem that controversy over deprogramming is purely a personal matter, involving as it does
the interaction between parent and child. But, while the origins of the issue may have been private, familial disputes,
the intrusion of state agencies -- the courts, local police,
state legislatures -- raises the problem to a much more serious level. One of the necessary elements of civil liberties
issues is the violation of individual rights by the state.
At first the element of state action in deprogramming was
passive or covert at most: police refusing to intervene in
deprogramming because it was a "family matter" or -- as
Patrick relates in his book -- quietly cooperating with the
family; prosecutors declining to prosecute admitted abductions and kidnappings; grand juries refusing to indict; or
petit juries refusing to convict.

But now state action in support of deprogramming has es-
calated. It is no longer passive but active, no longer covert but overt. Legislatures in several states are being
asked to enact or to expand laws permitting conservatorships
or guardianships to be granted by court order in cases of
persons -- of whatever age -- who are not able to manage
their own affairs or to protect them from "artful and designing persons," as a bill recommended by a special committee of
the Vermont Legislature puts it.

Thus a parent, relative or friend could go into court
and obtain an order assigning custody of an adult whose reli-

gious convictions or behavior were suspect for the purpose
of forceably returning that person to "normal." Membership
in an esoteric cult would be prima facie evidence of the
need for such a court order, and even that might not be necessary. Deprogramming has already been attempted, though
not under court order, on persons belonging to long-estab-
lished religious bodies such as a female member of a Roman
Catholic Community in Canada and a male member of the Epis-
copal Church of the Redeemer in Houston; people belonging to
a political group like the Socialist Labor Party; and even
on persons not belonging to any group as in the case of two
girls in Denver whom Patrick was hired to bring back to the
strict tutelage of their Greek Orthodox families.

So who is safe? If someone doesn't like the way you
talk or act or the people with whom you associate, they can
hire a deprogrammer to go after you, grab you by force, take
you off to a secluded place, and work you over until you consent to act in a manner acceptable to them.

The admittedly illegal abductions of deprogramming are
justified by the claim that they are necessary to prevent a
worse evil, the capture of innocent, idealistic young people
by the pernicious cults. Visions are conjured up of adolescents enslaved to an alien Moloch, bound to an endless round
of mindless and abject servitude, obliterating from their
lives the bright promise of upwardly-mobile business and professional careers. Such a picture was the defense used by
Ted Patrick when he was brought to trial for kidnapping a
young adherent to the New Testament Missionary Fellowship,
and it worked. The argument had the remarkable effect of
putting the religious group on trial, obliging it to try to
justify its religious beliefs and practices. What is going
on here?

Most, if not all, of the behavior associated with the
so-called cult religious movements will seem bizarre and
mystifying only to those largely innocent of any knowledge of
church history or, in deed, of human history. What we are
seeing in these groups today is not something new, but something old; a phenomenon sometimes labeled <u>conversion</u>. Thirty or 40 years ago, similar anxieties were stirred by the
Jehovah's Witnesses and their aggressive proselytizing. The
Mormons were widely feared and despised in the nineteenth
century, driven by state militias from one haven after another. The early Quakers were detested and persecuted for
their persistent efforts to persuade others to their beliefs.

Intense and zealous movements are very frightening to
the adherents of more casual and conventional faiths. They
divide communities and tear families apart, creating tension,

friction and turmoil. Such movements are aggressive, not
heeding any consideration but the propagation of the True
Faith. The idea that families are -- or should be -- spared
this kind of dissension finds little basis in history. Consider this statement from the New Testament.

> Do not think that I have come to bring peace on
> earth; I have come not to bring peace, but a
> sword. For I have come to set a man against
> his father, and a daughter against her mother,
> and a daughter-in-law against her mother-in-law;
> and a man's foes will be those of his own house-
> hold. He who loves father or mother more than
> me is not worthy of me; and he who loves son or
> daughter more than me is not worthy of me; and
> he who does not take up his cross and follow me
> is not worthy of me (Matthew 10:34-38).

These words, attributed to Jesus, do not fall graciously upon
the ear. People seem to have difficulty remembering them.
Yet, there is no truer description of the perils of conversion, of being caught up in a new faith.

Giovanni Bernadone lived in the twelfth century, son of
a successful businessman. When he sold some cloth from his
father's warehouse to rebuild a ruined church, the elder
Bernadone took him to the local bishop to disinherit him. At
that moment, he removed all of his clothes, returned them to
his father and went on his way in a monk's cloak to pursue
his religious convictions. History now remembers him as St.
Francis of Assisi -- instead of the prosperous textile mer-
chant he could have become. St. Clare's family is said to
have restrained her bodily from joining the band of followers
of St. Francis of Assisi. Legend has it that St. Thomas of
Aquinas' family confined him in a room with a prostitute to
demonstrate the pleasures of secular existence as opposed to
the regimen of the Dominican order he wanted to join.

Undeniably, the conversion of their children to an alien
faith is a devastating experience to parents, who see it as a
repudiation of all they stand for. This anguish is only
heightened when the cults are portrayed as rackets, monstrous
hoaxes, or alien political cabals. But these hysterical pro-
jections do not necessarily help us to understand what is going on here. To offer an economic or political explanation
for an ostensibly religious phenomenon is to miss the direct
and elemental dynamic of religious motivation, which has often proved more powerful than economic or political motivations.

Human beings have an unquenchable need to make sense of
their life experience in the largest conceptual framework
they can conceive. This need is especially acute in adoles-
cence when the emerging adult must find his or her own explanation that makes sense. The received family faith does-
n't always accomplish that -- at least not without some exploring, testing and comparing -- to which we owe the expansion and modification of religious traditions. Without some
effective anchorage in a system of ultimate meaning, human
beings are susceptible to despair, rage, bitterness and anxiety. They become prone to the maladies of meaninglessness
that are increasingly prevalent in our society. The need to
fill this void of meaninglessness has been an important force
in human history.

All of our great systems of ultimate meaning -- religions -- began as intense, high-demand movements that claimed
all the time, energy and thoughts of the believers. Characteristically, these movements have believed that they had the
Truth, all the Truth, and that other religions were essentially false. They have required rigid discipline and un-
questioning obedience from the faithful while attempting to
shield them from the insidious temptations of the world,
particularly those most likely to draw the new convert back
into old, depraved ways -- family and former friends.

People who expect new religious movements to be bland
effusions of vague, diffuse amiability and good intentions
are naturally not going to recognize what is going on in the
groups we are witnessing today. It is precisely because
such groups believe that religion is serious business, that
it matters for one's eternal salvation what one believes and
does in this life, that they transmit to the less fervent
public an elemental quality that is both disconcerting and
frightening. But these are the very groups which most benefit the people whose need for religion is acute and who are
not reached by the more placid faiths. They are the very
groups which most need, deserve, and test the protections
of religious liberty guaranteed by the First Amendment.

To call these groups "cults" is to use a perjorative
term to denigrate them without recognizing the constructive
function they may be serving for present and future adherents. Many people don't realize that there is a high degree
of normal turnover in the membership of these groups without
the intervention of deprogrammers; in fact, probably to a
higher degree when uncertain adherents don't feel threatened
into greater solidarity with the group by deprogramming activity. Neither the groups nor the deprogrammers like to
admit this natural flux of disaffection, since it suggests
doubts about both the vitality of the group and the need for

deprogrammers.

Part of the religious dynamic at work in these situations is the most powerful reagent in human affairs: concentrated personal attention. Adolescents who have been rather
ignored by their families and peers find themselves suddenly
the center of attention by attractive young people who spend
hours working and talking with them to bring them into the
loving circle of the group. It's interesting that the parental antidote for this so-called captivity by the religious
movements is an equal and opposite dose of concentrated,
protracted personal attention -- deprogramming.

Young people whose parents try to dissuade them from
their new religious commitments face a difficult emotional
dilemma. Not wanting to argue with or hurt their parents,
nor to compromise their own beliefs, the children often clam
up, waiting for the storm of criticism to subside -- they
then are described by the parents as acting like "zombies."
This type of behavior is often the catalyst which causes parents to seek the help of deprogrammers to counteract what
they perceive as "brainwashing" and "mind control." But that
perception -- clouded as it is by strong emotion -- is really
a highly suppositious and elaborate explanation for behavior
which seems much easier to explain without it.

Is it possible that this is a new set of terms used to
discredit behavior which society does not approve; to make
its perpetrators persons whose rights and intentions can be
considered invalid? Is there such a thing as "brainwashing"
at all, or is it a term we use to justify events and behavior
we do not want to explain in more rational ways? Parents want
to believe that some mystical or magic force must be to blame
to keep them from having to think the unthinkable: that a
free choice has been made for some other faith, another way
of life.

Deprogrammers claim to want only to restore the free use
of a young person's reason so that he or she can exercise
"freedom of choice," that is, to choose freely any course except the religious commitment that led to the deprogramming.
Reason and free choice are great goods won at high cost in
human history. However, they are neither the only nor the
highest goods in human experience, and indeed, have led to --
or at least not prevented -- much conflict and suffering.

The meaning of true liberty, especially religious liberty, is that persons must be free to subject their reason to
the demands of faith if they want to do so, however bizarre
and unreasonable that faith may seem to others. People must
be free to live out other understandings of the good life

than those accepted by conventional society if they want to
do so, as long as they do not harm others or impair their
rights.

Consider the many cases where deprogramming has been
"successful." The result is often a person who is "de-
pleted" -- apathetic, drifting, brittle -- unable to take up
new interests. This condition has lasted for a year or more
in some cases, unless the victim of deprogramming finds a
purpose in life, as some have done, deprogramming others.
Post-deprogramming denunciations of the religious group as a
"hoax" should be suspect to some degree. After a person has
doubly defected -- once from parental values and then from
the religious group -- strong pressures for self-justification and the expiation of guilt are set in motion. These
often take the form of insisting, "I was fooled, I was taken
in, I was victimized," statements that mainly reflect the
difference between being in and being out.

Of course the great criticism leveled against the new,
high-demand religious movements is that they use force or
coercion to gain and retain converts. If that is true, it
is as illegal and repugnant as deprogramming, and should be
punished in a court of law where evidence is required to
prove criminal conduct. Until proof is adduced, however,
these charges remain mere allegations. In fact, the weight
of evidence runs the other way, against those who admit using force in the physical abduction of cult members. The religious groups themselves should want to bend over backward
to avoid even the appearance of taking unfair advantage of
young people, but it is not the responsibility of government
to compel religious groups to behave in a manner that outsiders will consider suitably decorous.

A part of religious liberty is the right of all of us to
make what seem to others to be foolish choices, to be hoodwinked or to be exploited, for the sake of what seems to us
to be the Truth. This is no justification for illegal activities by such groups, however, and this article is not intended as a defense or apologia for them. If they are fronts
for foreign governments, then let that be investigated and
proven. If they are using their tax exemption for illegal or
non-religious purposes, then let that be demonstrated and the
exemption revoked. But mere disputes about religious truth,
about differences of religious practice such as diet, prayer,
study or almsgathering are not matters in which government is
empowered to interfere.

This is not to ignore the anguish of parents who feel
that their children have been taken from them. But anguish
is not the only possible response to such a situation, and it

has certainly been exploited and exacerbated to hysterical
levels by deprogrammers who, in turn, feed off it like pre-
dators.

Let us not forget that the anguish of parents is not
the only anguish involved here. Let us give equal consideration to the feelings -- and rights -- of young people who
go about in daily dread of being physically seized and subjected to protracted spiritual gang-rape until they yield
their most cherished religious commitments. That is what's
going on here. That is the element that makes deprogramming
the most serious violation of our religious liberty in this
generation, and why it must clearly be seen as criminal. It
should be prosecuted, not just as any other kidnapping, undertaken for mercenary motives would be, but even more vigorously, since it strikes at the most precious and vulnerable
portion of the victim's life, religious convictions and commitments.

Our nation was founded on the principle of religious
freedom. After 200 years of trial and error with state-es-
tablished churches in the various colonies, it really could
not have been otherwise. The religious ferment in colonial
America, especially during the Great Awakening of the mid-
eighteenth century, familiarized the authors of our Constitution with a wide variety of zealous and evangelical sects.
And it was encroachment upon this sort of fervor that the
founders sought to prevent.

"Because we hold it for a fundamental and undeniable
truth that religion...can be directed only by reason and conviction, not by force of violence," James Madison told the
Virginia Assembly in 1785, "the religion of every man must be
left to the conviction and conscience of every man; and it is
the right of every man to exercise it as they may dictate.
That right is, in its nature, an unalienable right." Is the
right freely to exercise religious beliefs as one sees fit
any less imperative today than in Madison's time?

One may argue, of course, that Madison had no knowledge
of the alien nature of the Eastern sects emerging in our
country today or of the potential to destroy one's free will
through behavior modification. However, faiths as alien to
Madison as the Krishna Consciousness Movement is to a contemporary Virginia Episcopalian certainly existed in eighteenth
century America. And thus far, only deprogrammers themselves
have been proven to use the mind-numbing techniques of behavior modification.

Deprogramming is a basic and fundamental violation of
the constitutional guarantees to freedom of speech and asso-

ciation. But it is the encroachment upon the individual's
religious freedom, the very right to think and to believe,
that is most repugnant. Unlike many constitutional principles which have either been subject to the ebb and flow of
judicial interpretation or have grown slowly from the well-
spring of precedent, the right freely to exercise religious
beliefs has remained close to a judicial absolute. The
First Amendment is very clear.

In the legal battle over deprogramming Justice Douglas
probably expressed it best writing for the majority in the
1944 Court decision in U.S. v. Ballard: "The Fathers of the
Constitution were not unaware of the varied and extreme
views of religious sects... They fashioned a charter of
government which envisaged the widest possible toleration
of conflicting views. Man's relation to his God was made
no concern of the state. He was granted the right to worship as he pleased and to answer to no man for the verity of
his religious views."

NOTES

* Originally published in Civil Liberties Review (July/
August 1977):23-33.

*LEGITIMATING REPRESSION

Thomas Robbins
Central Michigan University
Dick Anthony
Graduate Theological Union
James McCarthy
Sanctuary Institute

Allegations are frequently made to the effect that devotees of today's "cults" have been subjected to "mind control," "brainwashing" or "mental coercion" which has destroyed their free will and created a pattern of involuntary
servitude. In effect, such arguments implicitly affirm the
functional equivalence of peer pressure with physical constraint.

A continuum of psychiatric attitudes can be identified
regarding the viability of the brainwashing notion and its
application to contemporary religious movements such as Hare
Krishna or the Unification Church. At one pole is the absolutist perspective of the noted "anti-psychiatrist" Dr.
Thomas Szasz, who asks, "What is brainwashing? Are there,
as the term implies, two kinds of brains: washed and unwash-
ed?" According to Dr. Szasz (1976), "brainwashing is a metaphor. A person can no more wash another's brain with coercion or conversation than he can make him bleed with a cutting remark....However, we do not call all types of personal
or psychological influences brainwashing. We reserve this
term for influences of which we disapprove."

A less absolutist position has been articulated by Dr.
Walter Reich (1976) who has argued that the revival of
fifties' mystiques of brainwashing threatens the credibility
of forensic psychiatry, "so painfully won," and undermines
the foundations of criminal law, which "is based on the assumption of personal responsibility for one's own behavior."
While the concept of schizophrenia also undermines voluntaristic notions of personal autonomy and responsibility, evo-
cations of schizophrenia are based on "a core of widely
shared scientific and clinical experience," which is not the
case with alleged "brainwashing." Accordingly, "Psychiatry
endangers itself -- debases its coinage -- by entering areas
in which it lacks adequate expertise."

Farther along the continuum are the views of a number
of scholars who believe that there does exist a devastating
brainwashing process, which, however, is a very rare occurrence in the West and entails a traumatic sequence of brutal
physical abuse and threats of physical extinction. Psychologists Alan Scheflin and Edward Opton comment in The Mind
Manipulators (1978:23): "Substantial facts do support the
brainwashing concept as a description of an extreme form of
persuasion in a context of torture." The authors acknowledge that elements of classical brainwashing syndromes are
indeed present in cultist indoctrination processes but they
are substantially attenuated. "Isolation is the factor that
most closely ties so-called brainwashing to religious cults;
it is a central facet of each. But when one looks closely,
any apparent similarity dissolves.... In religious cults the
degree of isolation varies from group to group, but usually
it is of necessity only partial.... Sometimes the supposed
isolation vanishes completely when one questions it" (1978:
61). Moonies witnessing on city streets or operating busi-
nesses are subject to numerous influences the Unification
Church cannot really control. Sometimes a putatively robot-
ized candidate for deprogramming is actually living and/or
working outside of a stigmatized group to which he nevertheless feels committed. Groups such as Hare Krishna and the
Unification Church, while regimented and totalistic in several respects, are ultimately not true "total institutions"
which totally control access to and egress from their premises, i.e., many persons emerge from these movements to voluntarily without abduction and/or seizure by police,[1] and
many who are proselytized and who even participate in initial indoctrination workshops do not return for further sessions (Barker, forthcoming; Galanter et. al., 1980).

Finally, we come to the formulations of a number of
psychiatrists and psychologists who affirm not only that
mind control, brainwashing, and psychological kidnapping are
meaningful and viable scientific concepts, but that such notions may easily be generalized from contexts involving
tangible and overt intimidation (e.g., POW camps) to formally voluntary religious contexts. Dr. Kevin Gilmartin, who
has been associated with the Freedom of Thought Foundation
in Tucson, speaks in an interview in Human Behavior (Sage,
1976) of "socially induced ego regression" in which an en-
capsulated convert relinquishes 'reality testing' and 'ego
functioning' (i.e., thinking for oneself) and acquiesces
completely to the "expectancies and demands of the social
unit." In such situations the term psychological kidnapping
is appropriate. Victims of psychological kidnapping qua socially induced ego regression are really being "held against
their will because the cognitive and volitional state known

as will is removed from the individual" (Sage, 1976:47).
Such persons may have the illusion of free thought but they
are in fact incapable of freely exercising their will and
are enslaved by the cult.

Pro-deprogramming psychiatrists and psychologists thus
tend to typify cult converts as manifesting pathological
states (e.g., ego regression). Given the existence of a
definite group indoctrination process, a key inference is
made that the putatively dysfunctional mental state is totally and exclusively socially induced. The essential latent premise is that no one could ever voluntarily relinquish (even temporarily) intellectual freedom and advanced
ego functioning.[2] This seems to be a rather dubious premise.
For centuries individuals have joined totalistic movements
and willingly surrendered elements of intellectual freedom
and flexibility in exchange for psychological rewards associated with a sense of normative structure, a sense of purpose and meaning in one's biography, or relief from anxiety
and anomie. In Pagan and Christian in an Age of Anxiety
(1963), E.R. Dodds argues that Christianity appealed to persons in the later Roman empire in part because "it lifted
the burden of freedom from the shoulders of the individual:
one choice, one irrevocable choice, and the road to salvation was clear...in an age of anxiety any 'totalist' creed
exerts a powerful attraction" (Dodds, 1963:133-134). Similarly, Mark Rasmussen, who observed a Unification Church
workshop, writes (1977:14), "The desire to abandon reason
for emotion had to be present before the person came to the
workshop...and the new identity that emerged from the workshop experience was an assertion of self that came from submission.... It was a willful submission."

Can it really ever be empirically determined whether
someone's alleged ego regression has been exclusively socially induced? Dr. Gilmartin acknowledges that cult devotees are often alienated persons who wander from group to
group, checking out different alternate life-styles and
meaning systems. But might not such "seekers" be seeking a
totalistic commitment at least temporarily as a sort of experimental identity-game? An oppressive bureaucratic society may systematically rob the individual of a sense of
authenticity and personal responsibility such that only a
decisive surrender to an overpowering totalistic demiurge
can provide some persons with a sense of helplessness. Dr.
Gilmartin has acknowledged that persons may freely enter
authoritarian movements, "but once the social process begins, the individual is not freely capable of exercising
free will to leave" (Sage, 1976:47). Yet movements such as
Hare Krishna or the Unification Church seem to have substantial turnover; numerous participants have apparently found

it possible to leave these groups without abduction, court
custody orders, or deprogramming.

RELIGIOUS PERSECUTION

The metaphor of brainwashing is best understood as a
social weapon which provides a "libertarian" rationale for
the suppression of unpopular social movements and belief
systems. The notion of brainwashing is an ideal social weapon because: (1) it implies that authorities are not trying
to suppress opinion, as they are not concerned with the content of a belief but rather with the way in which it has
been induced; (2) its applicability can never really be disproved (how is the presence of free will established?); and
(3) it implies that religious devotees are passive recipients of social conditioning rather than seekers of meaning
and commitment exercising constitutional freedoms.

The utility of the brainwashing concept as social weapon derives in part from its implication that concern is being directed not at the content of a belief or opinion but
at the manner in which this belief has been developed (i.e.,
via brainwashing). Allegedly it is not what one believes
but how one believes and how one has come to believe which
is being scrutinized. Utilizing this rationale, one can apply pressure to religious and political movements and even
subject their adherents to forcible confinement and counter-
indoctrination without conceding any intention of suppress-
ing a point of view.

Deprogrammers and anti-cult activists assert that the
relevant issue is not freedom of religion but freedom of
thought; that is, freedom from the insidious mind control to
which cults are accused of subjecting their members. But
candidates for deprogramming are generally assumed to be
brainwashed simply by virtue of their affiliation with a
certain religious sect. When deprogrammers, outraged parents, and anti-cult activists have their way, adult cult
converts are subject to deprogramming without prior hearings
in which they may contest allegations of their incompetence
and without prior psychiatric examinations. More importantly, a deprogrammee's mind is considered to be liberated from
conditioning only when he actually recants his beliefs.
There does not seem to be an expectation that successful deprogramming might transform a rigid Moonist into a thinking
Moonist. It appears that cult devotees are viewed as brainwashed more or less by definition; i.e., formal affiliation
with a group and adherence to a belief system is made the
essential criterion for determining whether one is mentally
competent.

The claim by deprogrammers and anti-cult activists not to be persecuting opinions cannot be seriously maintained. Dave Gressler, a successfully deprogrammed former Moon convert, recalls that deprogrammers "tried to prove that Moon's theology was wrong and a ripoff" (Sage, 1976:46). Bible study is used in some modes of deprogramming (Kim, 1977). The basic aim of deprogramming, which one supporter refers to as "deindoctrination" (Levine, 1980), is to produce a re-cantation, and the devotee who does not recant is not considered to have been successfully deprogrammed. Whether or not extreme brutality is used, the conclusion appears warrented that deprogramming is essentially coercive suppression of deviant beliefs. The protest against brainwashing is in part a protest against the adherence of persons to certain beliefs: Moonist, Communist, etc.

The essential subjectivity of brainwashing and mind control notions lends itself to exploitation as a weapon of repression. It is always possible to argue that this or that monastery or commune intertwines rituals and doctrines in such a way as to lock converts into rigid thought patterns. Somehow it is only foreign communists and domestic religious minorities who use mind control techniques. This selectivity ought to make one suspicious of brainwashing allegations as essentially ideological. Indeed, Marxists and radical social critics maintain that we are all "one dimensional men" brainwashed via capitalist "ideological hegemony" over the media.

The subjectivity of brainwashing notions renders them invulnerable to falsification. "Free will" is hardly a very tangible or empirical concept. In the absence of tangible physical coercion, what shall be the criteria for inferring a washed brain or an imprisoned will? It is impossible to disprove allegations of mind control. If, for example, one reminds a deprogrammer, as one of the authors has, that many potential Moon converts do not return after sampling a weekend workshop, or that many converts find it possible to drop out of the movement without benefit of deprogramming, one merely elicits the reply that Moon's mind control technique, which depends on exploiting the victim's hidden guilt complexes, only works on certain personality types, but it is not therefore any less of a coercive technique of psychological kidnapping. But this sounds suspiciously like a free choice situation: an advertiser, politician, or guru presents a stimulus and some fish bite and others do not, depending upon personality and social background factors.

While one can never decisively disprove or falsify allegations of brainwashing, it is easy to present "facts" which appear to sustain such allegations. One can cite the fact that sectarian communes are frequently in relatively inaccessible places and are thus allegedly difficult to leave. One can present valid evidence of dissimulation and manipulation by cults, especially the Unification Church. Finally, one can report heavy-handed and systematic indoctrination processes and the application of intense peer group pressures to potential converts. But is the presence or absence of free will a "fact" epistemologically equivalent to whether or not Guru X has a Swiss bank account? Impervious to strict criteria of falsifiability but easy to "prove" by assembling facts in an epistemological void, mind control and brainwashing are ideal conceptual tools for legitimating repression.

Psychologists and psychiatrists who approve of deprogramming generally tend to typify sectarians as manifesting various psychopathological states such as ego regression, blunted affect, or lack of creativity, and then assume that such effects can be viewed as entirely socially induced. Thus, at a celebrated 1977 custody hearing in San Francisco, Dr. Margaret Singer (who had previously been an expert witness in Patty Hearst's defense) and Dr. Samuel Benson testified that Moonies they had examined exhibited blunted affect, defective memories, limited vocabulary, deficiencies in their knowledge of current events, and "artificial happiness." Dr. Singer conceded that this pattern did not fall into any standard classification of mental illness, but called it a syndrome associated with coercive persuasion, a term which was used interchangeably with brainwashing (Collier, 1977).

Dr. Singer and Dr. Benson's testimony was contradicted by the testimony of Dr. Allan Gershon, who interviewed and administered multiple tests to the same Moonist subjects and reported that their scores were within the normal range. A valid objection might also have been made to a notion such as "artificial happiness," as if "happiness" were an objective state rather than an intrinsically subjective feeling (thus, if one feels happy, one is happy, although conceivably one ought not to be happy spreading the authoritarian message of Reverend Moon).

If, however, we take the Singer-Benson "findings" at face value, what can we really infer about brainwashing? Data relating to the psychological state of a subject says nothing in and of itself about how the subject developed this state. Under certain conditions it may be reasonable to attribute responsibility for developmental states to cap-

tors or experimenters, but such responsibility cannot simply
be assumed without a context of either a controlled experiment or raw physical coercion without any formal choice element. But even if we were to assume that responsibility for
developmental pathological states can definitely be attributed to the subject's involvement with a cult, this still
hardly warrants an inference of involuntary coercive persuasion. It is conceivable that conversion to a rigid and dogmatic ideology may have the consequence of reducing intellectual flexibility and creativity. Cognitive rigidity may
indeed by the consequence of voluntary conversion to certain
movements and meaning systems, and need not imply that converts have been "coerced."[3]

TOWARD THE THERAPEUTIC STATE

The dubious notions of brainwashing and mind control
express moral disapproval of the way in which someone has
been influenced by someone else. The terms lend a spurious
scientific rationale to such disapprobation. The brainwashing metaphor evokes the medical model of deviant behavior as
symptomatic of pathology. The brainwashee's thought processes are viewed as involuntary symptoms; i.e., he can no more
control his thoughts than someone with measles can control
his skin rash. He must therefore be restrained and controlled for his own good so that he may be cured (Robbins and
Anthony, 1982).

The medical model appeals to a society in moral crisis
because it has an aura of scientific objectivity, and the
implicit moral judgments involved in the exercise of social
control are downplayed. In a period of shifting values,
authorities are disinclined to acknowledge punitive or repressive intent. Thus the state increases its reliance upon
psychiatrists who can provide it with benevolent therapeutic
rationales to control dissidents. Brainwashing thus becomes
a conceptual tool of the "therapeutic state" which, as
Richard Stivers notes, has created its clientele "by developing categories of deviance which reflected an assumption
of illness. Psychopath, alcoholic, and drug addict are categories applied to those whose sexual, drinking, and drug
behavior is thought to be beyond their control" (Stivers,
1975:384). A special category may now be emerging for persons whose religious behavior is thought to be beyond their
control. Some psychiatrists now claim the right to decide
which religions are legitimate and which are not.[4]

The brainwashing concept implies that cult converts are
essentially passive victims and conditioned zombie-robots.

As such they cannot claim the same rights as pertain to
rational and responsible individuals in full possession of
their faculties. They can therefore be forcibly confined
without the usual due process. The application of such
terms as brainwashing or mind control to the activities of
religious movements lays a conceptual groundwork for detach-
ing numerous devotees from their civil liberties and subjecting them to what might otherwise be deemed arbitrary
procedures.

Are converts to regimented and totalistic sects mere
passive victims of conditioning? There are alternative con-
ceptualizations with different implications. One of them is
Robert Lifton's (1970) "protean man" concept. Contemporary
protean man is not really a passive and static product of
conditioning, rather he is one who continually recreates his
self-concept and exchanges and negotiates new identity games
-- hence the rapid turnover of groups such as Hare Krishna
or the Unification Church, and the tendency for many converts to "new religions" to have what James Richardson (1980)
has termed "conversion careers" entailing sequences of ex-
perimentation with various groups and lifestyles.

It is also possible to conceptualize sectarian conversions as exchanges in which the "burden of freedom" is re-
linquished in exchange for normative structure, anxiety relief, and cognitive closure. Mark Rasmussen (1977), a participant-observer personally hostile to Moonism, makes the
following comment on the converts he interacted with as a
participant-observer:

> I had to accept that a good number of them chose
> that identity, not falling into it because they
> lacked the strength to make it on their own, but
> taking it up because there were things that Moon
> offered them that they valued. I think the
> Moonies gave up a lot in their regimented devo-
> tion -- they gave up the chance to think, to
> read, to confront -- and the struggle for me was
> to recognize and respect the fact that they found
> in Moon something that was more important to them
> than certain things I value.

Of course, the valued "things that Moon offered them"
may lose their attractiveness along with their novelty over
time. Rather than acknowledge that they were temporarily
quite willing to surrender freedom of thought, some excon-
verts may prefer to externalize responsibility for prior
commitments and affirm that they were brainwashed. This
disavowal of responsibility is encouraged by deprogrammers

and many therapists who work in "rehabilitating" ex-converts.

It is conceivable that the context of an oppressive
bureaucratic society erodes the sense of personal autonomy
and authenticity that is encouraged by traditionally domi-
nate normative orientations. Social movements may provide
contexts for operationalizing social identities autonomous
from bureaucratic instrumental roles and depersonalized
"mass society" settings. The fragmentation of daily life
into limited segments involves individuals in impersonal
bureaucratic institutions of work and study enhances the appeal of commitment to an all-embracing system which will in-
tegrate one's life and give meaning to one's existence.
Given the structurally volatile and marginal status of over-
educated postadolescents in a society with high levels of
unemployment and underemployment, an upsurge of youth movements is not a surprising development; nor is it really
shocking that a number of these groups regiment converts and
segregate them from mainstream structures and processes
which are not capable of meeting the expressive needs of
many young persons or even of providing them with satisfactory employment. Such movements, however, tend to have a
rapid turnover and frequently evolve over time in a more
adaptive and accommodative direction.

In a culture pervaded by anomie, one cannot really infer coercive manipulation or brainwashing from seemingly
irrational patterns of self-renunciation and asceticism.
The philosopher William Barrett has made this point elo-
quently:

> The frenzies of asceticism, which may seem mere
> aberration and abnormality to our secular minds,
> are in fact the inevitable means to which the
> human animal is driven to give meaning to his
> existence. Rather than be meaningless, we shall
> find ourselves seeking out devices of our own
> that are equally extreme. We create by denying
> ourselves. So long as we drive ourselves in the
> toils of some discipline we cannot believe that
> our life is meaningless. In the tensions of the
> will -- the simultaneous striving and surrender
> -- the ghost of nihilism departs.

NOTES

1. This has very recently been acknowledged by some fervent critics of the Unification Church. Cf. "Moon Organization Changing," The Advisor, Sept./Oct., 1982. This article summarizes a report by Ex-Moon, an organization of former devotees who are strongly antipathetic to the Unification Church. The report concludes that the organization has an "incredible turnover rate." Many persons leave in part because "after initial indoctrination members have increasing contact with the outside world ....There are many opportunities for being influenced by the outside world." A number of studies by sociologists have also concluded that there is a large voluntary defection rate in "cults." For references to numerous relevant studies see Robbins and Anthony (1982) and Anthony, Robbins and Needleman (forthcoming).

2. Thus the fact, reported by several studies, that only a third or less of cult converts are significantly disturbed prior to conversion is often treated as evidence that converts are victimized by mind control techniques which override free will. But this is only logical if it is assumed that converts must be either disturbed misfits or unmotivated victims, i.e., no healthy person could willingly join a cult. See Singer (1979).

3. In a provocative law review article, Robert Shapiro (1978) contends that allegations of mental pathology and brainwashing against cults are based on arbitrary transvaluations of the intensity of faith, i.e., indications of dogmatism, fervor and fanaticism are interpreted as signs of psychological damage or mind control.

4. Sometimes the criteria employed are rather subjective and moralistic, e.g., one psychiatrist, noted as a crusader against cults, was quoted by a newspaper to the effect that disconnectedness from conventional institutions such as the family or churches differentiated "destructive" cults from acceptable cults. This criterion would pinpoint almost all millenarian messianic and apocalyptic sects, including early Christianity, as "destructive." Cf. Glen Collins, "The Reasons 'Normal' Kids Fall for Cults," San Francisco Chronicle, 23 March 1982.

* Originally published in Society 17 (March-April 1980): 39-42.

WITH ENEMIES LIKE THAT:
SOME FUNCTIONS OF DEPROGRAMMING AS AN AID
TO SECTARIAN MEMBERSHIP

Eileen Barker
London School of Economics and
Political Science

This paper is not concerned with the rights or wrongs of deprogramming, nor is it even concerned with the objective facts of what occurs during the deprogramming process. Rather it describes some of the consequences of the existence of the institution of deprogramming in so far as it serves a positive function for the very organizations which the deprogrammers wish to attack and from which they wish to remove members. In other words it seeks to show how, while deprogramming may rescue or, according to one's perspective, recapture some individuals from a sectarian allegiance, it can also serve to reinforce the hold of the sect over its membership. Not only can one find the most fervent, even fanatical, members of a movement among those who had been subjected to deprogramming but it is also as a result of the very existence of the practice that many of those who have had not such personal experience will have their allegiance strengthened.

The deprogrammer has offered himself as a bogey man par excellence and like most bogey men he can be invoked quite explicitly as a spur to action in the face of apathy. On one occasion I heard the members at a Unification Church centre being harangued for their lack of spirit and organizing power because they had not mended a gate post although it had been knocked down several weeks before. "That is the sort of negligence that lets in deprogrammers" they were told by their leader. I was not clear whether it was spiritual or physical entry to which he was referring. I am not sure that the abashed members knew either. Perhaps it was both. It did not matter. Before the day was out the gate post was mended.

The practice of deprogramming does however have considerably more far reaching consequences for the movement and its relations with the outside world than this rather trivial example might suggest. One important element in the

process whereby these consequences come into being, and one
upon which this paper will concentrate, is the testimony.
It is the practice of most evangelical groups that members
will publicly testify or witness to their conversion. They
will tell other members and potential converts the story of
their rebirth -- how, through seeing the light, they have
been born again into a true faith. The more wickedly depraved they were before, the more wonderful and miraculous
the conversion.

Those who have studied such movements quickly come to
recognize these testimonies and learn methodologically to
bracket them off into a category of carefully constructed
reality which is best separated from other, less oft repeated, information. It is not that those who witness in
this manner are deliberately fabricating their stories, but
rather that through the constant tellings there is a process
of natural selection going on. The bits that "work" are re-
tained and elaborated while those bits that do not have such
an effect on the listener are dropped. The style of the
testimony becomes polished and can be very moving. A speak-
er, with tears in his eyes, might confess that God is inspiring him as well as others as he tells his story. The
giving of a testimony functions to reinforce the belief of
both teller and listener in the rightness of the life that
the convert has chosen and the error of any other way of
life.

In recent years it has become possible to recognize a
second type of testimony -- that of the returned deprogramee. Perhaps it is not altogether surprising that, unlike the members of a religious community who have just returned from a routine visit to their parents, those who have
just escaped from the clutches of the famous -- or infamous
-- "Black Lightning" (the name commonly given to the most
well known of all the deprogrammers, Ted Patrick) will have
plenty of opportunity to repeat their accounts of the experience to a spell bound audience. They will have overcome
evil in order to return to the fold; and the testimonies,
like those of conversion, will, with each telling, become
ever more efficient in their presentation of the good inside, bad outside image. And, in like fashion, one can see
the solidarity of the community being reaffirmed and reinforced.

A similar process producing a mirror image of this
dualistic perspective can be seen just as effectively at
work among those who oppose the new religious movements.
Parents wanting to find out about the strange group their
daughter has just joined are likely to be regaled with bizarre and frightening stories by a Parent and Concerned

Persons' Organization which, again not altogether surprisingly, selects in the telling of its own testimonies the
kind of information which most clearly "works" to prove that
there is a very real cause for concern and action by the
parents.

Inside the Unification Church the story of the girl
whose mother had told her during a deprogramming session "I
would rather you were dead than a Moonie" testifies to the
sort of hurtful cruelty to which a mother in the outside
world can submit her daughter. Outside the Unification
Church this unmaternal statement has its counterpart in the
well rehearsed reports of a Moonie telling his mother she
was an agent of Satan and he never wanted to set eyes of
her again. Such eminently quotable stories of filial rejection testify that all Moonies are obviously out of their
minds and in desperate need of deprogramming. Both sides
are reassured in their negative definition of the other side
by what can at times only be described as wallowing in sensational proofs that it is we who are the goodies and they
are the baddies. Neither side is going to waste much fuel
as it fans the flames of its opponents' wickedness when
this implies its own self righteousness. And deprogramming
provides plenty of fuel for the Unification Church.

The typical deprogramming testimony tells how deprogrammers in particular and the outside world in general define all that the Church members believe to be good and
true as false and wicked, and how all that is false and
wicked they applaud as good and true. The testimony tells
how the Church members are kidnapped and held against their
will. They may beg, plead, scream and fight, but they will
be forcibly detained until they manage to escape or their
captors are convinced their mission has been successfully
accomplished. The reports dramatically testify to a series
of indignities which follow the kidnapping. The deprogrammer may pin his victims to the floor, tie them to a bed,
take away their clothes -- there are whispers of sexual attacks having taken place in some cases. The personal insults which are continuously hurled at the Church members
take such forms as telling them that they are pimps who
have been prostituting themselves for Moon (e.g., Patrick,
1976) whose photograph is likely to be spat upon and torn
up in front of his helpless followers. All the members
have learned to hold most sacred and dear is defamed and
blasphemed against by the relentless deprogrammers.

But while the deprogrammer might claim that he is better acquainted than the average members with the Unification theology as set out in the Divine Principle, the returning member will testify to how very little outsiders

really understand about the true purpose of the Church, its
doctrines and its actions. One such testifier who had escaped through a window after three days of captivity denied
feeling anything but anger and contempt for his captors.
"Everything they said persuaded me that Principle was right
and they were wrong," he said. "They were so full of hate
and negativity. They never once mentioned love."

     According to the Divine Principle, the present period
is one of immense importance. All the signs indicate that
it is the time of the Second Coming, and it is essential
that each member plays his part in fighting the Satanic forces of evil if the Kingdom of God is to be realized on
earth. While at its most simple deprogramming is a violation of the right of individuals to believe and to lead the
sort of lives that they have chosen to lead; at another
level it is seen as a way of trying to prevent a Church member from playing his role in restoring the world to the
state that God had planned when He first created Adam and
Eve in the Garden of Eden. For believers it is clear that
this is a time in which Satan is going to be pulling out all
the stops to prevent God's victory, and it is not difficult
for them to recognize deprogramming as one such stop. That
parents, and indeed whole sections of society, should be
drawn into either performing or condoning wicked (and often
illegal) action can be seen as clear evidence that the
Divine Principle is a true and predictively correct doctrine.

     Outside agencies and individual bystanders emerge as
either corrupt or hopelessly apathetic. Members of the
great American public "just do not want to be involved."
When appealed to in the street by a deranged looking youth
who may have escaped from his captors without any shoes on
his feet, they look embarrassed and pass by on the other
side as the respectable looking parents bundle their pro-
testing offspring into a waiting car. Police turn a blind
eye or, not infrequently, they will even help with the illegal kidnapping (Patrick, 1976:109). Medical staff at
hospitals to which the member is taken will at best remain
neutral, but they may set themselves up as 'experts' ready
to pronounce on the mental incompetence of the 'patient'
(usually charging a grossly exaggerated fee for asking ridiculous questions and drawing even more outrageously ridiculous conclusions from the silence or angry scorn they receive in answer).

     As the battles over deprogramming have moved to the
courts, the Unification Church members have felt increasingly victimized and frustrated in their attempts to enjoy
the rights that they believe the First Amendment confers
upon them. "To provoke the righteous indignation of those

who have reached their twenties after an individualistical-
ly oriented education in the United States, little needs to
be added to the pronouncement of a judge (Horowitz, 1978:
206) who, in granting a conservatorship order to some
parents and allowing them to turn the children over to deprogrammers, declared that 'a child is a child even though
the parent may be ninety and the child sixty'... The parents are still in charge..."

The hypocrisy of the outside world is held up to ridicule and utter scorn. How, the members will demand, can
people in the outside world dare to justify such brute
force by saying that they are de-programming? It is they,
not the Unification Church members whom they accuse, who
are the brainwashers. So far as the use of physical coercion is concerned the Moonies can testify to an unassail-
able moral headstart over the deprogrammers -- a headstart
that seems so blatantly obvious to people who are convinced
they joined the movement of their own free will that any
comparison between the two processes must be nothing short
of insulting idiocy. A world that seems to condone deprogramming on the grounds that it is performing a necessary
antidote to conversion, is a world either gone mad with
twisted values employed in demonic rationalizations or
lulled into an apathetic abrogation of any responsibility
to uphold basic human rights and values.

Such beliefs are further reinforced as the testimonies
continue. Although the intense pressure of the initial deprogramming seldom lasts for more than a few days, the
Moonie has no way of knowing this will be so in his case.
He will report that his captors told him "We've got all the
time in the world and we're going to keep you here till you
come to your senses." While he may have felt anger and
frustration at the aggression, he will testify that the
most unbearable thing he had to endure was the uncertainty
and the feelings of complete impotence during his enforced
separation from anyone who understood. "I felt so alone --
there was no one I could turn to -- I saw no hope of escape
-- I believed that I was completely alone in the world --
apart from God."

The testimonies seldom admit to any real doubts that
the victim might have felt during deprogramming. He will
say he eventually realized that the only strategy open to
him was to pretend to fall in with the deprogrammers in the
hope that he might pave the way for an opportunity to escape. He might testify that he was keeping a secret diary
that could prove to the police (and of course himself) that
he had never really denounced his faith. If he signed a

declaration that he no longer believed in the teachings of
the Unification Church and that he would never return, he
might add that the lawyers had told him that this would not
stand up in a court of law as he had had to sign under dur-
ess. The most important consequence to which he will
testify is that by pretending to give in, he was relieved
of the terrible pressure and utter exhaustion to which he
had been continually subjected: "At last I was able to fall
asleep with God."

But even if his captors are convinced that they have
been successful in their task, they will know that after
the critical "recanting" there follows a period during
which the erstwhile member is sometimes described as
"floating." And it will be suspected that he could still
return to the movement unless he is very carefully watched.
The deprogrammers will say that he has to be gradually
"readjusted" to the "normal" world through mixing with
carefully selected people of his own age. The Church member will testify that, in order to persuade his parents or
custodians that he was genuinely "back to normal," he had
to say and do all sorts of things that are anathema to followers of the Divine Principle. "I had to keep remembering
to swear that I had to drink and talk about women 'pieces
of skirt,' and things, just so that they would trust me
enough to give me the chance to escape... I knew then that
the hypocrisy of the world was such that it was only by doing the very things God teaches us are wrong, that they
would think I was alright."

While it might be suspected that, despite protesta-
tions to the contrary, several of those who were deprogrammed did entertain very real doubts about the Unification
Church during the course of the experience, it can also be
surmised that some of those who had doubts were helped to
overcome these when they were thrust back into an "Unprin-
cipled" world which seemed to have forsaken practically all
moral, spiritual or idealistic standards. Even making al-
lowances for the exaggerated memories of individuals' conversion testimonies, it is certainly the case that many of
those who join the Unification Church were as much pushed
by what they disliked in the society they lived in, as
pulled by the lure of the Unification Church or its members. An enforced reversion to the kind of life style
that they may have rejected before joining the Church, and
which they had certainly learned to reject after joining
it, can merely serve to prove to the individual that the
Church was right all along.

Despite the bravado to be found in the testimonies, most of those who have been subjected to deprogramming were very, very frightened and the member may well testify to having experienced moments of sheer terror. This can be combined with a certain degree of self recrimination for not having been strong or good enough in some way, although of course he eventually wins as one does in all good testimonies that survive the telling. Odd touches of humour may pepper the stories too. These allow for both the heightening and relief of tension. One girl, for example, produced such an effect while describing a session with Ted Patrick:

> He put his hands round my throat and pushed me
> back so that the chair was right back. I
> thought I was going to die. I was sure he
> was killing me. I thought, "this is what they
> do to martyrs; this way I'll get to be a
> martyr." Then I thought, "Martyrs are always
> good people. Would they find out I wasn't
> really all that good?

The laughter thus evoked gives rise to feelings of warmth and security in being with those who, while strong in their resolve, do nonetheless share one's own human frailty. It functions as a reassuring affirmation of membership of the persecuted community of believers. But however comforting the laughter, the fear too is easily transmitted; and the listener begins to wonder what he will do if he ever finds himself in such a situation. Will he be able to keep praying hard enough not to hear the lies that will be shouted at him? Will he be brace enough to cut his wrists like the sister who saw this as the only way of getting to the neutral territory of a hospital so that she could demand her rights and let her Unification Church Family know where she was being held?

It is perhaps in the relationship that members have with their parents that some of the most poignant and tragic consequences of deprogramming are to be observed. One of the charges most often levelled at the Unification Church is that it separates children from their parents and certainly many young people, having joined the Church, see far less of their parents than they might otherwise have done. It is also the case however that among the considerable repercussions of the institution of deprogramming (one very direct consequence) has been the provision for the Unification Church of a reason for being unwilling to let members visit their parents. Stories circulate of how trusting children have gone home and found themselves confronted with a team of deprogrammers. As such incidents increased in number, mistrust of parents grew among the

Church leaders and members and visits home became less frequent. Parents became more desperate and would beg their
son or daughter to come home for a special occasion such
as a family wedding. They sent messages saying they were
ill or perhaps even dying. The member might then have gone
home and found himself being bundled into a car and swept
off to some remote motel. Any plea that has been employed
to lure a Moonie into a situation where he or she could be
kidnapped has become a source of deep suspicion whenever it
is used, however legitimately, by other parents. Those who
escape and return nearly always testify to the element of
incredulity they experienced. They had somehow always
trusted their parents; they had not believed their parents
could do this to them. Their parents had even said that
although they disagreed with the Unification Church, they
respected their child's right to do what he wanted and
they would not interfere with his decision however much
they thought he was in error. The incredulity and sur-
prised hurt testified to by the returned member infects
his listeners with unease and suspicion. That is what
their parents have said -- is it possible that they too
could be planning such a thing?

     The spiral of mistrust builds up as parents who might
initially have been prepared to respect their child's decision while disagreeing with it, feel surprise and hurt
that their son should be suspicious of them. "How could he
mistrust us?" they want to know. "After all these years,
after all we have done for him -- all we've given him --
how could he think we would do anything like that?" Reports they read in the media play upon these worst fears.
The parents start to testify that on realizing what was
going through their child's mind they just felt it was like
being with a complete stranger ("Something awful must have
happened to him to make him think of us like that -- he
could not be himself"). They feel that they have to do
something. The spiral can then reach a stage where the
parents become so upset that they do in fact contact the
deprogrammers. And the members of the Unification Church
are reinforced in their suspicions and furnished with further proof that parents whom one might have trusted did in
fact turn out to be kidnappers.

     It must, of course, be stressed that the above de-
scription is greatly oversimplified; many more factors are
involved. But the point to be made is that deprogramming
contributes to an accelerating drift between the parents
and children. There develops between them what might almost be called an institutionalized distrust. This gets
no better when the son or daughter tries to re-establish a
relationship and finds that the parents seem to be incap-

able of understanding just what an indignity it was to
which they subjected their son or daughter. "Now -- we'll
see each other sometimes" one testimony concludes, "but I
still don't dare go home alone. We're polite enough, but
they have never ever apologized for what happened. Not
once have they said they were sorry. They just don't seem
to realize what it did to me and how it hurt me."

Accompanying the spirals of mistrust and hurt which
are undoubtedly felt very deeply by both parties, one can
see a further exacerbation of the situation in the explanations given by the protagonists for each other's actions.
Each side, in trying to understand the apparently incomprehensible behavior of the other, employs a rhetoric of determinism that inevitably leads to a sense of hopelessness
that either of them could possibly be able to communicate
with the other. This is evidenced in the "more in sorrow
than in anger" temper of the testimonies. The Unification
Church member, far from heaping wrath and blame upon his
parents, testifies that deep down underneath they are really good, loving parents who were just weak and/or unfortunate enough to be persuaded against their better judgement.
The real blame lies with the sensational media, jealous
clergy, scheming communists, spiteful friends, avaricious
deprogrammers or, more simply, with Satan. "I know they
could never have agreed to it unless they were forced into
it" the member insists. The parents might well agree that
they were forced into it but according to them it is the
Unification Church that left them with no other option.
Furthermore, their rhetoric of determinism asserts that
only brainwashing could explain their child's being a member of the movement. Any element of free choice would be
literally unimaginable.

Both sides find themselves in positions where it is
only those on the same side as themselves who can share
any realistic understanding of what is going on. Those
most involved, the parents and their children, have,
through their respective explanations of the others' behavior, taken the capacity to reason for him or herself
away from the very person with whom they might most have
wanted to communicate. Each sees the other as under the
evil influence of agents who must be attacked and destroyed. It is despite and even possibly because of the testimonial avowals of filial understanding and forgiveness
(which most parents would probably find insufferably pa-
tronizing) that the members are pushed further away from
their families into a more complete identification with
the Unification Church. The whole process has, in effect,
clarified the position for the member. It is he who has
chosen to remain free and successfully fought for his

choice; the experience has reinforced his commitment, and
through his escape and denial of the outside world he has
proved to himself and to others exactly where he stands.
One member testified quite explicitly, "The deprogramming
helped alot. Others are suffering from an identity crisis
-- I have been through it all at one time. God can trust
me."

But while the Church member who has survived deprogramming may be assured of the trust that exists between
God, himself and his fellow believers, it is also obvious
that there will be little trust left between him and the
outside world. It is at this juncture that another consequence of deprogramming can be noted. The process has not
only created a situation in which the Unification Church
member finds that his parents have betrayed his trust in
them, it has also led to a situation in which he finds that
he must deceive them. He has, he will testify, been forced
into a position in which he has had to declare that he has
denounced his religion in order to be able to return to his
chosen way of life. He has secretly had to plan how to
convince his parents that he can be left alone long enough
to get the car keys, to make the essential telephone call,
to do whatever is necessary to arrange his escape. In
other words, deprogramming has produced a situation in
which not only can the Unification Church member testify
that he has been the recipient of deception, but that the
deception of others has forced him too to be deceitful.
There have been times during interviews or casual conversation when members have admitted to feeling unease about
some of the methods that are employed within the Unification Church. The concept of "Heavenly Deception" has
given rise to many a niggling doubt and anxiety, but not
once have I heard a single doubt expressed over any deception employed to secure escape from deprogrammers, which
is accepted as a clear and unchallengeable case of necessity. The outside world would seem to demand to be deceived -- no honest person could do otherwise if he is to
be true to his beliefs and to serve God as his conscience
demands.

In order to attempt an illustration of the extent to
which the testimony can be used to create a particular set
of attitudes, this paper will end with a brief look at a
publication which purportedly advocated deprogramming, but,
through the selection and presentation of the material, did
in fact manage to "work" in persuading its readers in quite
the opposite direction. An organization calling itself
POWER (People's Organized Workshop on Ersatz Religion) appeared on the London scene towards the end of 1976. POWER
proclaimed itself intent on introducing deprogramming into

England on a scale comparable to that in the United States. It sent out newsletters and circulated a nine page document entitled Deprogramming: The Constructive Destruction of Belief. A Manual of Technique. The Manual advocated techniques like "Shame-inducement through nudity," "Food Termination," "Destruction of Holy Works," "Sleep Withdrawal" and "Aggressive Sex" (which, it explained, the subject often quite wrongly confuses with rape).

When I saw the Manual I took it to be an example of sick humour -- at best a satrical joke in rather bad taste. I was astonished to learn that it was being taken perfectly seriously. The media issued statements of shocked horror and reported that the Home Office was looking into the matter. Academics discussed it in hushed, voyeuristic seminars. Eminent psychiatrists declared that such methods really should not be advocated and they hoped most sincerely that they would not be allowed to spread in this country. There was also considerable concern generated on the part of those on whose side POWER claimed to stand. An officer of one evangelical group which has devoted considerable time, energy and money to exposing the cults told me of the terrible embarrassment POWER was causing them. "People think we go along with everything they say," she complained. "I wish they'd shut up -- they're really not helping us at all." It did not seem to have crossed her mind that this could be exactly why the Manual might have been put out in the first place. What she was worried about was the way her group was being lumped together with POWER in the public eye. These were just not the friends that she would have chosen.

Had those who read the Manual with such horror looked at it a bit more carefully they might have noticed that although the techniques and many of the attitudes overtly advocated were certainly similar to those used by genuine deprogrammers, the selection, the focusing and the effects (in fact the whole psychology of the publication) belonged to a sectarian testimony, not to that of a deprogrammer. Let me try to give a couple of examples to illustrate this claim. Taking first the paragraph under the heading "Philosophical and Moral Questions" one reads (POWER, n.d.:9):

> These are no concern of the (deprogramming)
> Technician and are best left to philosophers
> and moralists to worry about. The mission
> of the technician is simply to serve the
> interests of his client with all his profes-
> sional skill in return for a well-earned fee.
> His only other duty is to ensure that the
> subject is brought to the required state.

This reflects a sectarian testimony that deprogrammers (a)
see themselves as having a mission and (b) do not accept
any moral responsibility whatsoever as (c) they are only in
it for the money which (d) may need to be defended for its
exorbitance (Ted Patrick's charging $25,000 for a case is
quoted earlier in the Manual). Furthermore, (e) the object
of the exercise is stated as that of bringing the subject
to a "desired state" which (f) is defined purely in terms
of the interests of the client.

    In the reading of a genuine deprogrammer's testimony
-- and Let Our Children Go is possibly the best available
-- one certainly can get the impression that the deprogrammer sees himself as having a mission -- that is proclaimed
with messianic zeal. He will also insist on the profes-
sionalism of the skills involved in deprogramming. (We
are in fact warned that those who leave a cult without the
benefit of the profession will remain "programmed" and
suffer the unfortunate consequences.) Patrick however also
testifies that he is definitely not in it for the money (he
has indeed suffered enormous financial disadvantages); he
has been continually villified and attacked for his actions
which he only carries out to try to help those whom no one
else will help. He is responsible for what he does; indeed, he not only accepts responsibility, he testifies to
it and is martyred for it. Furthermore, the object of the
whole exercise is, in the deprogrammer's testimony, to release the subject from a programmed state and after that it
is up to the subject to make up his or her own (now free)
mind about what he or she chooses to do. The clients (the
parents) too have only their child's interests at heart,
not their own. They are willing for their child to follow
the religion of his choice, but they have got to be sure it
is a religion and it is his choice.

    The second example is to be found among a list of se-
lected cases which are quoted in the Manual, (POWER, n.d.:
8):

    Debby Dugeon, now aged 22, had been a member of
    the United Church since her childhood. In late
    1974, having been a convert to Roman Catholicism
    for over a year, Debby's parents hired Ted Patrick
    to deprogramme their daughter. Ted flew her from
    Canada to his home in the U.S.A. where he and
    four assistants started to work on her. Unfortun-
    ately this could not be completed because Debby
    had managed to tell the Canadian Police that she
    would be gone for only two weeks. Ted and his
    team were therefore forced to release the girl

and she has, regrettably, returned to Roman
Catholicism (Toronto Star, March 11, 1975).

Apart from the uses of language (and age) which would
seem to indicate sectarian testimony, it is extremely unlikely that any deprogrammer would select the statement
"she has, regrettably, returned to Roman Catholicism."
This is not to suggest that certain parents might not be
extremely upset were they to find their son or daughter
espousing the Church of Rome. Nor is it to suggest that
this particular deprogramming attempt did not take place.
It is not without significance however that it is not one
of those Patrick himself featured in Let Our Children Go.
In that book, all the subjects selected are from movements
that are not only comparatively new and unknown but which
also can be and indeed were (with a certain degree of social safety) denounced for their wicked practices at considerable length. It would not require much sensitivity to
one's audience to know that selecting reports of deprogramming converts to Roman Catholicism could well be counter-
productive. On the other hand, it is exactly the sort of
story upon which the sectarian would focus if he wanted to
raise doubts about the practice. As Catholics, we find
ourselves pushed into asking, really "programmed" in the
same way as members of the new cults are? If so, might
this mean that the cult members are not actually quite as
"brainwashed" as was being suggested? Or does it perhaps
suggest that all those who do not belong to -- what was it?
-- the United Church -- might be deprogrammed to the "desired state?" It is only a few years to 1984. If converts
to Roman Catholicism are to be deprogrammed, where will it
stop? Quis custodiet ipsos custodes?

What POWER and the Manual illustrate is that, by selecting the evidence from one point of view while apparently putting the opposite point of view -- by testifying to
the ammunition of the opposition in a way that is actually
informed by the perspective of the victims of deprogramming
-- the very practices that from the "genuine" deprogramming
perspective might seem necessary and desirable can come to
be viewed with disgust and considerable disquiet. The
authors of the Manual had realized at least some of the
potential of deprogramming as a weapon which could effectively be turned against itself.

SUMMARY AND CONCLUSIONS

Since the time of Simmel (at least), sociologists have
been aware of the extent to which groups exhibit an in-

creased internal cohesion or group solidarity as they face
the enemy without. The Jewish ghetto or the nation at war
are familiar examples. Practically every student knows
the title if not the content of Coser's Functions of Conflict (1976). This paper has argued that in the case of
the Unification Church deprogramming has provided one such
shared, external focus. It illuminates practices of deception, cruelty, coercion and persecution which provide proof
that the teachings of the Church are true, that these are
indeed the Last Days and there is a very real urgency to
fight the battle against Satan with every fibre of one's
being at every moment of each day. Deprogramming rein-
forces what Mary Douglas would call a "strong group position." It can result in binding the members together as
partners in crime as they find themselves with a justification (perhaps a duty) to take on the devil on this own
terms and employ his tools of secrecy and scheming in their
task of restoring a world over which he seems to have do-
minion. "Heavenly deception" is vindicated by the sins of
the world. When all is painted in black and white the
equation of two blacks making a white becomes a plausible
calculation.

    And deprogramming certainly contributes to an emphasis
of the black and white dualistic perspective of the good
inside and the bad outside. The boundary between "them"
and "us" is strengthened as mutual mistrust and suspicion
grow in an ever accelerating spiral, each side reacting to
the other's reactions by reinforcing their worst suspicions
of the other. Through constant rehearsal, the testimonies
of the protagonists (see Wallis, 1976) select and celebrate
these aspects of their respective experiences which best
legitimate their own position while damming that of the
other side. Reconciliation and communication between those
most directly involved, the parents and their children, becomes increasingly unlikely as both employ a rhetoric of
determinism in their attempts to find an explanation of the
others' incomprehensible behavior. Having defined the
other as helpless under the influence of evil forces, they
can only turn to those on the same side of the polarised
divide as themselves for comfort and support when faced
with the fear and suspicion engendered by the diverse testimonies. It is not to his family of origin but the Family
of God to which the Unification Church member feels he has
to turn for truth and security. The existence and the process of deprogramming bear witness that outside the Unification Church is a world in which all that the members have
ever taught to believe was true and good is considered evil
and wrong, and that all they have been taught to believe
was shallow, false and evil is seen as good and desirable

(or at least considered "normal"). Those who believe in love and truth have a duty and responsibility to unite together under the leadership of God in the only place that seems to have a remnant of Godly sanity left in it.

When sociologists write papers on a particular aspect of a subject it is sometimes assumed that they are denying or are ignorant of other aspects of that subject. This occasionally means that writers are pushed into a position where they end up producing nothing but a collection of qualifications, describing everything in general and, consequently, nothing in particular. In the hope that no such assumptions will be made for a single contribution to a book devoted entirely to deprogramming I have risked sticking rigorously to very restricted terms of reference and have tried only to spell out some of the ways in which deprogramming serves to reinforce rather than diminish the hold a sect has over its members.

Of course deprogramming has consequences which are negative for the groups whose members it claims. The loss of numbers is, in itself, certainly not an insignificant cost. Furthermore, the publicity that has been generated (with the attendant testimonies of parents and others) will obviously frighten off many a potential convert as well as putting many more on the alert so that any sect member putting a foot wrong and doing or saying something which might otherwise go unnoticed will be immediately pounced upon and help up as an example.

Less obviously, but possibly more crucially for the future of the Unification Church, if the movement is to grow beyond a certain critical size it is likely that some sort of accommodation to and with the rest of society will become increasingly necessary. (This can be argued on a number of counts -- the economic and the recruiting ones being only the most obvious.) It may well be that there is some threshold point at which the spirals of polarization which function to give internal support to a group with sectarian status will need to switch to spirals of accommodation if they are to support a group of denominational status. But although there are definite signs that the leadership of the Unification Church is making an all out effort to improve public relations and to cull support from a wider audience, it is not at all clear that such a critical point in the movement's history has yet arrived -- if indeed it ever will.

And of course there are hundreds of other variables influencing the state of the Unification Church and other movements affected by deprogramming, both in their internal

structures and in their relations with the rest of the
society. Some of these I have described elsewhere (Barker,
1978a; 1978b; 1979). In this essay, however, I have attempted no more than to draw out a single thread from a
very complicated tapestry in order to look at some of the
ways in which it would not be altogether empty bravado (although extremely unlikely) for members of a small religious
sect to say of deprogrammers "With enemies like that.....".

BIBLIOGRAPHY

Adams, Robert L. and Robert J. Fox. "Mainlining Jesus: The New Trip." Society 9 (February 1972):50-56.

Adorno, Theodore W. Negative Dialectics. New York: Seabury, 1973.

Ahlstrom, Sydney E. A Religious History of the American People. New Haven: Yale University Press, 1972.

Andrews, Edward D. The People Called Shakers: A Search for the Perfect Society. New York: Dover Publications, 1963.

Anthony, Dick, Madeline Doucas and Thomas G. Curtis. "Patients and Pilgrims: Changing Attitudes Toward Psychotherapy of Converts to Eastern Mysticism." American Behavioral Scientist 20 (July/August):861-886.

Anthony, Dick, Thomas Robbins and Jacob Needleman, eds. Conversion, Coercion and Commitment in New Religious Movements. New York: Crossroads Books, forthcoming.

Asch, Solomon E. Social Psychology. New York: Prentice-Hall, 1952.

_____. "Effects of Group Pressure Upon the Modification and Distortion of Judgements." Groups, Leadership and Men. Edited by H. Gvetzkow. Pittsburg, Carnegie Press, 1951.

Babbie, E. and D. Stone. "What Have You Gotten After You 'Get It'?: An Evaluation of Awareness Training Participants." Presented at the 129th Annual Meeting of the American Psychiatric Association, Miami Beach, Florida, May 1976.

Babbitt, Ellen M. "The Deprogramming of Religious Sect Members: A Private Right of Action Under Section 1985 (3)." Northwestern University Law Review 74 (1979): 229-254.

Balch, Robert W. "Looking Behind the Scenes in a Religious
    Cult: Implications for the Study of Conversion." Socio-
    logical Analysis 41 (Summer 1980):137-143.

Balch, Robert W. and David Taylor. "Seekers and Saucers:
    The Role of the Cultic Milieu in Joining a UFO Cult."
    Conversion Careers. Edited by James T. Richardson.
    Beverly Hills, CA: Sage, 1978.

_____. "Walking Out of the Door of Your Life: Becoming
    a Member of a Contemporary UFO Cult." Paper presented
    at the annual meeting of the Pacific Sociological Asso-
    ciation, San Diego, CA, 1976.

Barker, Eileen. "Resistible Coercion: The Significance of
    Failure Rates in Conversion and Commitment in the Uni-
    fication Church." Conversion, Coercion and Commitment
    in New Religious Movements. Edited by Dick Anthony,
    Thomas Robbins and Jacob Needleman. New York: Cross-
    roads Books, forthcoming.

_____. "Who'd Be a Moonie? A Comparative Study of
    Those Who Join the Unification Church in Britain." The
    Social Impact of New Religious Movements. Edited by
    Bryan Wilson. New York: Rose of Sharon Press, 1981:pp.
    59-96.

_____. "Whose Service is Perfect Freedom: The Concept
    of Spiritual Well-Being in Relation to Rev. Sun Myung
    Moon's Unification Church in Britain." Spiritual
    Well-Being. Edited by David O. Moberg. Washington,
    DC: University Press of America, 1979.

_____. "Confessions of a Methodological Schizophrenic:
    Problems Encountered in the Study of Rev. Sun Myung
    Moon's Unification Church." Institute for the Study of
    Worship and Religious Architecture Research Bulletin,
    University of Birmingham, 1978a.

_____. "Living the Divine Principle: Inside the Rev-
    erend Sun Myung Moon's Unification Church in Britain."
    Archives de Sciences Sociales des Religions 45 (1978b):
    71-83.

Barrett, William. "On Returning to Religion." Commentary
    62 (November):38.

Bauer, Raymond A. "Brainwashing: Psychology or Demonology."
    Journal of Social Issues 13 (1957):41-47.

Baum, Gregory. "Does the World Remain Disenchanged?" Social Research 37 (Summer 1970):153-202.

Beckford, James A. "Accounting for Conversion." British Journal of Sociology 29 (1978a):249-262.

_____. "Through the Looking-Glass and Out the Other Side: Withdrawal from Rev. Moon's Unification Church." Les Archives De Sciences Sociales Des Religions 45 (1978b):95-116.

Bellah, Robert N. "New Religious Consciousness and the Crisis in Modernity." The New Religious Consciousness. Edited by Charles Y. Glock and Robert N. Bellah. Berkeley: University of California Press, 1976, pp. 333-352.

Berg, Moses David. The Basic Mo Letters. Geneva: The Children of God, 1976.

Berger, Peter. The Sacred Canopy. Garden City, NY: Doubleday, 1967.

_____. An Invitation to Sociology. Garden City: Doubleday, 1963.

Berger, Peter L. and Thomas Luckmann. The Social Construction of Reality. Garden City, NY: Anchor Books, 1966.

Biderman, Albert D. "The Image of 'Brainwashing'." Public Opinion References Quarterly 26 (1962):547-563.

_____. "Communist Attempts to Elicit False Confessions from Air Force Prisoners of War." Bulletin of the New York Academy of Medicine 33 (September 1957): 616-625.

Bogart, Robert W. "A Critique of Existential Sociology." Social Research 44 (Fall 1977):502-528.

Bromley, David and Anson Shupe Jr. "Moonies" in America: Cult, Church and Crusade. Beverly Hills, CA: Sage Publications, 1979.

_____. "Financing the New Religions: A Resource Mobilization Approach." Journal for the Scientific Study of Religion 19 (September 1980a):227-239.

_____. "Just a Few Years Seem Like a Lifetime: A Role
Theory Approach to Participation in Religious Movements."
Research in Social Movements, Conflict and Change.
Edited by Louis Kriesberg. Greenwich, CT: JAI Press,
1979b, pp. 159-186.

_____. "The Tnevnoc Cult." Sociological Analysis 40
(1979c):361-366.

Bromley, David G., Anson D. Shupe, Jr. and Joseph C.
Ventimiglia. "Atrocity Tales, the Unification Church
and the Social Construction of Evil." Journal of Communication 29 (1979):42-53.

Brown, R.H. A Poetic for Sociology. New York: Cambridge
University Press, 1977.

Clark, John. "Cults." Journal of the American Medical
Association 242 (1979a):279-281.

_____. "Sudden Personal Change and the Maintenance of
Critical Governmental Institutions." Paper presented
at the annual meeting of the International Society for
Political Psychology, Washington, DC, 1979b.

_____. "Problems in Referral of Cult Members."
Journal of the National Association of Private Psychiatric Hospitals 9 (1978a):27-29.

_____. "We are all Cultists at Heart." Newsday,
November 30, 1978b.

Clark, John, Michael D. Langone, Robert E. Schacter and
Roger C.G. Daly. Destructive Cult Conversion: Theory,
Research and Treatment. Weston, MA: American Family
Foundation, 1981.

Coleman, Lee. Psychiatry the Faithbreaker: How Psychiatry
is Promoting Bigotry in America. Sacramento, CA:
Printing Dynamics, 1982.

Coleman, Lee and Trudy Solomon. "Parens Patrie 'Treatment':
Legal Punishment in Disguise." Hastings Constitutional
Law Quarterly 3 (1976):345-362.

Collier, Peter. "Bringing Home the Moonies." New Times,
June, 1977.

Conway, Flo and Jim Siegelman. Snapping. New York: J.B.
Lippincott, 1978.

_____. "Information Disease: How Cults Created a New Mental Illness." Science Digest (January 1982):87-92.

Coser, Lewis. The Functions of Social Conflict. New York: Free Press, 1956.

Cox, Archibald. The Warren Court: Constitutional Decision as an Instrument of Reform. Cambridge: Harvard University Press, 1968.

_____. "Don't Overrule the Court." Newsweek, 28 September 1981, p. 18.

_____. "The Supreme Court 1965 Term. Foreword: Constitutional Adjudication and the Promotion of Human Rights." Harvard Law Review 80 (1966):91.

Cox, Harvey. "Myths Sanctioning Religious Persecution." A Time for Consideration. Edited by M. Darrol Bryant and Herbert Richardson. New York: Edwin Mellen Press, 1978, pp. 3-10.

Dahrendorf, Ralph. Class and Class Conflict in Industrial Society. Stanford, CA: Stanford University Press, 1959.

Damrell, Joseph. Seeking Spiritual Meaning: The World of Vedanta. Beverly Hills, CA: Sage, 1977.

Daner, Francine. The American Children of KRSNA. Chicago: Holt, Rinehart and Winston, 1976.

_____. "The American Children of Krsna: A Study of the Hare Krsna Movement." Ph.D. dissertation, University of Illinois, Urbana, 1973.

Davis, David B. "Themes of Countersubversion." The Missouri Valley Historical Review 47 (September 1960): 205-224.

Davis, Rex and James T. Richardson. "The Organization and Functioning of the Children of God." Sociological Analysis 37 (1975):321-340.

Delgado, Richard. "Awaiting the Verdict on Recruitment." The Center Magazine 15 (March/April 1982):18-24.

_____. "Limits to Proselytizing." Society 17 (March/April 1980):25-32.

_____. "Religious Totalism as Slavery." New York University Review of Law and Social Change 9 (1979-1980):51-68.

_____. "Ascription of Criminal States of Mind: Toward a Defense Theory for the Coercively Persuaded ("Brainwashed") Defendant." Minnesota Law Review 63 (November 1978):1-34.

_____. "Organically Induced Behavioral Change in Correctional Institutions: Release Decisions and the 'New Man' Phenomenon." Southern California Law Review 50 (1977a):215-270.

_____. "Religious Totalism: Gentle and Ungentle Persuasion Under the First Amendment." Southern California Law Review 51 (1977b):1-100.

Deutsch, Alexander. "Observations on a Sidewalk Ashram." Archives of General Psychiatry 32 (February 1975):166-175.

Dodds, E.R. Pagan and Christian in an Age of Anxiety. New York: Norton, 1963.

Doress, Irvin and Jack N. Porter. "Kids in Cults." In Gods We Trust: New Patterns of Religious Pluralism in America. Edited by Thomas Robbins and Dick Anthony. New Brunswick, NJ: Transaction, 1981.

Douglas, Jack and John Johnson, eds. Existential Sociology. Cambridge: Cambridge University Press, 1977.

Downton, James V. Jr. Sacred Journies: The Conversion of Young Americans to Divine Light Mission. New York: Columbia University Press, 1979.

Dupuy, Homer. "The Psychological Section of the Current Health and Nutrition Examination Survey." Proceedings of the Public Health Conference on Records and Statistics (1972). DHEW Publication HRA 74-1214. Rockville, MD: National Center for Health Statistics, 1973.

Durkheim, Emile. The Rules of Sociological Method. New York: MacMillan, 1938.

Dworkin, Ronald. Taking Rights Seriously. Cambridge: Harvard University Press, 1977.

Edwards, Christopher. Crazy for God. Englewood Clifss, NJ: Prentice-Hall, 1979.

Ellwood, Robert. Religious and Spiritual Groups in Modern America. Englewood Cliffs, NJ: Prentice-Hall, 1973.

Enroth, Ronald M. The Lure of the Cults. Chappaqua, NY: Christian Herald Books, 1979.

_____. Youth, Brainwashing and the Extremist Cults. Grand Rapids, MI: Zondervan, 1977.

Erikson, Erik. Ghandi's Truth: On the Origins of Militant Non-Violence. New York: W.W. Norton, 1969.

_____. Young Man Luther: A Study in Psychoanalysis and History. New York: W.W. Norton, 1958.

Erikson, Kai. Wayward Puritans: A Study in the Sociology of Deviance. New York: Wiley, 1966.

Farber, I.E., Harry F. Harlow and Louis J. West. "Brainwashing, Conditioning and DDD." Sociometry 20 (December 1957):271-285.

Festinger, Leon. A Theory of Cognitive Dissonance. Evanston, IL: Row, Peterson, 1957.

Festinger, Leon, Henry W. Riecken and Stanley Schacter. When Prophecy Fails: A Social and Psychological Study of a Modern Group that Predicted the Destruction of the World. New York: Harper Torchbooks, 1964.

Flacks, Richard. "The Liberated Generation: An Exploration of the Roots of Student Protest." Conformity, Resistance and Self-Determination: The Individual and Authority. Edited by Richard Flacks. Boston: Little, Brown, 1973.

Flinn, Frank K. Law v. Religion: "Cults," "Brainwashing," "Deprogramming," Conservatorship." n.d.

Forbes, I.F., H.F. Harlow and L.J. West. "Brainwashing, Conditioning and DDD." Sociometry 20 (1951):271-285.

Foster, Sir J. Enquiry into the Practice and Effects of Scientology. London: H.M.S.O., 1971.

Frank, Jerome. Persuasion and Healing. New York: Schocken Books, 1963.

Galanter, Marc. "Psychological Induction into the Large-
    Group: Findings from a Modern Religious Sect." American
    Journal of Psychiatry 137 (1980):1574-1579.

_____. "The 'Relief Effect': A Sociobiologic Model for
    Neurotic Distress and Large-Group Therapy." American
    Journal of Psychiatry 135 (May 1978):588-591.

Galanter, Marc and Peter Buckley. "Evangelical Religion and
    Meditation: Psychotherapeutic Effects." Journal of Ner-
    vous and Mental Disease 166 (October 1978):685-691.

Galanter, Marc, Richard Rabkin, Judith Rabkin and Alexander
    Deutsch. "The 'Moonies': A Psychological Study of Con-
    version and Membership in a Contemporary Religious Sect."
    American Journal of Psychiatry 136 (February 1979):165-
    170.

Galanter, Marc, Richard Stillman, Richard J. Wyatt, Tom B.
    Vaughan, Herbert Weingartner and Fran L. Nurnberg.
    "Marihuana and Social Behavior: A Controlled Study."
    Archives of General Psychiatry 30 (April 1974):518-521.

Galper, Marvin F. "The Cult Indoctrinee: A New Clinical
    Syndrome." Paper presented to the Tampa-St. Petersburg
    Psychiatric Society, Tampa-St. Petersburg, FL, 1976.

Garkinkel, Harold. "Conditions of Successful Degredation
    Ceremonies." American Journal of Sociology 61 (March
    1956):420-424.

Gay, Anne C. and George R. Gay. "Haight-Ashbury: Evolution
    of a Drug Culture in a Decade of Mendancity." Journal
    of Psychedelic Drugs 4 (Fall 1971):81-90.

Gellhorn, Ernst and William F. Kiely. "Mystical States of
    Consciousness: Neurophysiological and Clinical Aspects."
    Journal of Nervous and Mental Disease 154 (June 1972):
    399-405.

Gergen, Kenneth J. and M. Jorawski. "Emergence of an Al-
    ternative Metatheory of Social Psychology." The Review
    of Personality and Social Psychology. Edited by L.
    Wheeler. Beverly Hills, CA: Sage, 1980.

Gerlach, Luther P. and Virginia H. Hine. "Five Factors
    Crucial to the Growth and Spread of a Modern Religious
    Movement." Journal for the Scientific Study of Reli-
    gion 7 (Spring 1968):23-40.

Glueck, Bernard and Charles F. Stroebel. "Biofeedback and Meditation in the Treatment of Psychiatric Illnesses." Comprehensive Psychiatry 16 (July/August 1975):303-321.

Goffman, Erving. "Alienation from Interaction." Human Relations 10 (February 1957):47-60.

Gordon, David. "Identity and Social Commitment." Identity and Religion. Edited by H. Mol. London: Sage, 1978.

Greeley, Andrew M. Ecstasy: A Way of Knowing. Englewood Cliffs, NJ: Prentice-Hall, 1974.

_____. "Superstition, Ecstasy and Tribal Consciousness." Social Research (Summer 1970):203-211.

Greene, Robert H. "People v. Religious Cults: Legal Guidelines for Criminal Activities, Tort Liability and Parental Remedies." Suffolk Law Review 11 (1977):1025-1058.

Gutmann, David. "The Premature Gerontocracy: Themes of Aging and Dying in the Youth Culture." Social Research 39 (Autumn 1972):416-448.

Gutman, Jeremiah S. "Constitutional and Legal Dimensions of Deprogramming." Deprogramming the Issue. Edited by Herbert Richardson. Toronto: Institute of Christian Thought, St. Michael's College, University of Toronto, 1977, pp. 208-216.

Habermas, Jurgen. Theory and Practice. Boston: Beacon, 1973.

_____. Knowledge and Human Interests. Boston: Beacon, 1971.

Hall, John R. The Ways Out: Utopian Communal Groups in an Age of Babylon. New York: Routledge and Kegan Paul, 1978.

Hargrove, Barbara. "Evil Eyes and Religious Choices." Society 17 (1980):20-24.

Heys, M. The Anticultist Newsletter. (London, England), 10 August 1976.

Hine, Virginia. "Bridge Burners: Commitment and Participation." Sociological Analysis 31 (Summer 1970):61-66.

Hinkle, Lawrence E. and Harold G. Wolff. "Communist Interrogation and Indoctrination of 'Enemies of the State'."
A.M.A. Archives of Neurological Psychiatry 76 (August
1956):115-174.

Holsti, Ole. Content Analysis for the Social Sciences and
Humanities. Reading, MA: Addison-Wesley, 1969.

Holzer, Burkart. Reality Construction in Society. Cambridge, MA: Schenkman, 1968.

Homer, David. "Abduction, Religious Sects and the Free Exercise Guarantee." Syracuse Law Review 25 (1974):623-
645.

Horowitz, Irving L., ed. Science, Sin and Scholarship: The
Politics of Reverend Moon and the Unification Church.
Cambridge, MA: MIT Press, 1978.

Horton, Paul C. "The Mystical Experience as a Suicide Preventive." American Journal of Psychiatry 130 (March
1973):294-296.

Howard, John R. The Cutting Edge: Social Movements and Social Change in America. Philadelphia: J.B. Lippencott,
1974.

Hunter, Edward. Brainwashing: From Pavlov to Power. New
York: The Bookmailer, 1956.

_____. Brainwashing in Red China. New York: Vanguard,
1951.

James, William. The Varieties of Religious Experience.
Expanded Version. New Hyde Park, NY: University Books,
1963.

Judah, S. Stillson. Hare Krishna and the Counterculture.
New York: Wiley, 1974.

_____. "New Religions and Religious Liberty." Under-
standing the New Religions. Edited by Jacob Needleman
and George Baker. New York: Seabury, 1978, pp. 201-208.

Kandel, Denise. "Adolescent Marihuana Use: Role of Parents
and Peers." Science, 14 September 1973, pp. 1067-1070.

Kanter, Rosabeth M. Commitment and Community: Communes and
Utopias in Sociological Perspective. Cambridge:
Harvard University Press, 1972.

Kelman, Herbert C. "Compliance, Identification and Internalization: Three Processes of Attitude Change."
   Conflict Resolution 2 (1958):51-60.

Kilbourne, Brock. "An Analysis of the Conway and Siegleman
   Data." University of Nevada, Reno, 1982.

Kilbourne, Brock and James T. Richardson. "From Privatization to Communalization of Religious Experience: Evidence for a Countertrend." University of Nevada, Reno,
   1982.

Kim, Byong Suh. "Deprogramming and Subjective Reality."
   Sociological Analysis 40 (Fall 1979):197-207.

Lasswell, Harold D, Daniel Lerner and Ithel de Sola Pool.
   The Comparative Study of Symbols. Stanford, CA: Stanford University Press, 1952.

LeMoult, John. "Deprogramming Members of Religious Sects.
   Fordham Law Review 46 (1978):599-634.

Levin, Theodore M. and Leonard S. Zegano. "Adolescent
   Identity Crisis and Religious Conversion: Implications
   for Psychotherapy." British Journal of Medical Psychology 47 (March 1974):73-82.

Levine, Edward. "Deprogramming Without Tears." Society 17
   (March/April 1980):34-38.

Levine, Edward. "Religious Cults: Their Implications for
   Society and the Democratic Process." Paper presented
   at the annual meeting of the International Society for
   Political Psychology, Washington, 1979.

Levine, Mark. "The Free Exercise Clause as a Defense to
   Involuntary Civil Commitment: Bringing Mental Illness
   into Religion." Albany Law Review 39 (1974):144-156.

Levine, Saul V. and Nancy E. Salter. "Youth and Contemporary Religious Movements: Psychosocial Findings." Cana-
   dian Psychiatric Association Journal 21 (1976):411-420.

Lieberman, Merton A. and Jill R. Gardner. "Institutional
   Alternatives to Psychotherapy: A Study of Growth Center
   Users." Archives of General Psychiatry 36 (February
   1976):157-162.

Lieberman, Morton A., Nancy Salow, Gary R. Bond and Janet
    Riebstein. "The Psychotherapeutic Impact of Women's
    Consciousness-Raising Groups." Archives of General Psy-
    chiatry 36 (February 1979):161-168.

Lifton, Robert. Boundaries. New York: Random House, 1970.

_____. Thought Reform and the Psychology of Totalism.
    New York: W.W. Norton, 1963.

_____. "The Appeal of the Death Trip." New York Times
    Magazine, 7 January 1979, pp. 26-31.

_____. "Thought Reform of Western Civilians in Chinese
    Communist Prisons." Psychiatry 19 (May 1956):173-195.

Lin, N. Foundations of Social Research. New York: McGraw
    Hill, 1976.

Lofland, John. Doomsday Cult. Revised Edition. New York:
    Irvington Press, 1977.

_____. "Becoming a 'World Saver' Revisited." Conver-
    sion Careers. Edited by James T. Richardson. Beverly
    Hills, CA: Sage, 1978, pp. 10-23.

Lofland, John and Rodney Stark. "Becoming a World Saver: A
    Theory of Conversion to a Deviant Perspective." Ameri-
    can Sociological Review 30 (December 1965):862-874.

Luckman, Thomas. The Invisible Religion. New York: Mac-
    millan, 1967.

Lynch, R.R. "Toward a Theory of Conversion and Commitment
    to the Occult." Conversion Careers. Edited by James
    T. Richardson. Beverly Hills, CA: Sage, 1978.

McNemar, Richard. The Other Side of the Question. Cincin-
    nati, OH: Looker, Reynolds and Co., 1819.

Mannheim, Karl. Ideology and Utopia: An Introduction to
    the Sociology of Knowledge. New York: Harcourt, Brace,
    Jovanovich, 1936.

Marcuse, Herbert. One Dimensional Man. Boston: Beacon,
    1964.

Maslow, Abraham H. Religions, Values, and Peak Experiences.
    New York: Viking Press, 1964.

Mead, George H. <u>Mind, Self and Society</u>. Chicago: University of Chicago Press, 1934.

Meerloo, Joost A.M. <u>The Rape of the Mind</u>. New York: Grosset and Dunlap, 1956.

_____. "The Pavlovian Strategy as a Weapon in Menticide." <u>American Journal of Psychiatry</u> 110 (May 1954): 809-813.

_____. "The Crime of Menticide." <u>American Journal of Psychiatry</u> 107 (February 1951):594-598.

Miller, Henry. "On Hanging Loose and Loving: The Dilemma of Present Youth." <u>Journal of Social Issues</u> 27 (1971): 35-46.

Miller, James G. "Brainwashing: Present and Future." <u>Journal of Social Issues</u> 13 (1957):48-55.

Miller, Richard W. "Rights and Reality." <u>The Philosophical Review</u> 90 (1981):383-407.

Mills, C. Wright. "Situated Actions and Vocabularies of Motive." <u>American Sociological Review</u> 6 (1940):904-913.

Mitchell, Dave, Cathy Mitchell and Richard Ofshe. <u>The Light on Synanon</u>. New York: Seaview Books, 1980.

Moloney, James C. "Psychiatric Self-Abandon and Extortion of Confessions." <u>International Journal of Psycho-Analysis</u> 36 (1955):53-60.

Monk, Maria. <u>Awful Disclosures of the Hotel Dieu Nunnery of Montreal</u>. New York, 1836.

Moore, Joey P. "Piercing the Religious Veil of the So-Called Cults." <u>Pepperdine Law Review</u> 7 (Spring 1980): 655-710.

National Commission on Marihuana and Drug Abuse. <u>Drug Use in America: Problem in Perspective</u>. Washington, DC: U.S. Government Printing Office, 1973.

New Hampshire, State of. <u>Report of the Examination of the Shakers of Canterbury and Enfield, Before the New Hampshire Legislature</u>. Concord, 1849.

Nicholi, Armand M. II. "A New Dimension of the Youth Culture." American Journal of Psychiatry 131 (April 1974):
396-401.

Niebuhr, Richard H., The Social Sources of Denominationalism.
New York: Meredian Books, 1957.

Nordquist, Ted. Ananda Cooperative Village. Uppsala,
Sweden, Religionhistoriska Institunionen, 1978.

"Note: Conservatorships and Religious Cults: Divining a
Theory of Free Exercise." New York University Law
Review 53 (1978):1247-1289.

Partridge, William L. The Hippie Ghetto. New York: Holt,
Rinehart and Winston, 1973.

Patrick, Ted and Tom Dulak. Let Our Children Go. New York:
E.P. Dutton and Co., Inc., 1976.

Pattison, E. Mansell, A. Lapins Nikolays and Hans A. Doerr.
"Faith Healing: A Study of Personality and Function."
Journal of Nervous and Mental Disease 157 (December
1973):397-409.

Pavlos, Andrew J. The Cult Experience. Westport, CT:
Greenwood Press, 1982.

People's Organized Workshop on Ersatz Religion. Deprogramming: The Constructive Destruction of Belief. A Manual
of Technique. London, England: n.d.

Peterson, Donald W. and Armand L. Mauss. "The Cross and
the Commune: An Interpretation of the Jesus People."
Pp. 261-279 in Charles Y. Glock, ed. Religion in Sociological Perspective. Belmont, MA: Wadsworth, 1973.

Pierson, Kit. "Cults, Deprogrammers, and the Necessity
Defense." Michigan Law Review 80 (December 1981): 271-
311.

Piette, Maximin. John Wesley in the Evaluation of Protes-
tantism. London: Sheed and Ward, 1937. 569 pp.

Pilarzyk, Thomas. "The Origin, Development and Decline of
a Youth Culture Religion: An Application of Sectariani-
zation Theory." Review of Religious Research 20 (Fall
1978).

Poythress, Norman G. "Behavior Modification, Brainwashing, Religion, and the Law." Journal of Religion and Health 17 (1978):238-243.

Prus, Robert C. "Religious Recruitment and the Management of Dissonance." Sociological Inquiry 46 (1976):127-134.

Psathas, George and Frances Waksler, eds. Phenomenological Sociology. New York: John Wiley, 1973.

Rasmussen, Mark. "Promising People the Moon: A View from the Inside." State and Mind (November/December 1977).

_____. "How Sun Myung Moon Lures America's Children." McCall's, September 1976, p. 102.

Reed, Rebecca T. Six Months in a Convent. Boston: Russell, Odorne and Metcalf, 1835.

Reich, Charles A. "Causes and Consequences of the Jesus Movement in the United States." Bulletin of the International Conference on Sociology of Religion 26-30 (August 1973):395-405.

Reich, Walter. "Brainwashing, Psychiatry and the Law." Psychiatry 39 (November 1976).

Richardson, James T., ed. Conversion Careers: In and Out of New Religions. Beverly Hills, CA: Sage, 1978.

Richardson, James T. "Financing the New Religions: A Broader View." Journal for the Scientific Study of Religion 21 (September 1982):255-268.

_____. "Conversion, Brainwashing and Deprogramming." The Center Magazine 15 (March/April 1982):18-24.

_____. "Conversion Careers." Society 17 (March/ April 1980):47-50.

_____. "A New Paradigm for Conversion Research." Paper presented at the annual meeting of the International Society for Political Psychology, Washington, DC, 1979.

Richardson, James T. and Brock Kilbourne. "Violence and the New Religions." Paper presented at the annual meeting of the Society for the Scientific Study of Religion, Baltimore, 1982.

Richardson, James T., Robert B. Simmonds and Mary W. Harder.
"Thought Reform and the Jesus Movement." Youth and
Society 4 (December 1972):185-200.

Richardson, James T., Mary Stewart and Robert Simmonds.
Organized Miracles: A Study of a Contemporary Youth Com-
munal Fundamentalist Organization. New Brunswick, NJ:
Transaction Books, 1979.

_____. "Researching a Fundamentalist Commune." Under-
standing the New Religions. Edited by Jacob Needleman
and George Baker. New York: Seabury Press, 1978, pp.
235-251.

Richardson, James T. and Mary Stewart. "Conversion Process
Models and the Jesus Movement." Conversion Careers.
Edited by James T. Richardson. Beverly Hills, CA: Sage,
1978.

Richardson, James T., Jan van der Lans and Frans Derks.
"Voluntary Disaffiliation, Expulsion and Deprogramming:
An Analysis of Ways of Leaving Social Groups." Paper
presented at the annual meeting of the Association for
the Sociology of Religion, Toronto, Canada, August,
1981.

Robbins, Thomas L. "Contemporary 'Post-Drug' Cults: A Comparison of Two Movements." Ph.D. dissertation, University of North Carolina, Chapel Hill, 1973.

_____. "Religious Movements, the State and the Law:
Reconceptualizing 'The Cult Problem'." New York University Review of Law and Social Change 9 (1979-1980):
33-49.

_____. "Eastern Mysticism and the Resocialization of
Drug Users." Journal for the Scientific Study of Religion 8 (Fall 1969):308-317.

Robbins, Thomas and Dick Anthony. "Deprogramming, Brainwashing, and the Medicalization of Deviant Religious
Groups." Social Problems 29 (February 1982):283-297.

_____. "Religious Movements, Families and Brainwash-
ing." Society 17 (May/June 1980a):77-83.

_____. "The Limits of Coercive Persuasion as an Ex-
planation for Conversion to Authoritarian Sects." Political Psychology 2 (1980b):27-37.

_____. "New Religions, Families and Brainwashing."
Society 15 (1978):77-83.

_____. "Getting Straight with Meher Baba: A Study of
Mysticism, Drug Rehabilitation and Postadolescent Role
Conflict." Journal for the Scientific Study of Religion
11 (June 1972):122-140.

Robbins, Thomas L., Dick Anthony and Thomas Curtis. "Youth
Culture Religious Movements: Evaluating the Integrative
Hypothesis." Sociological Quarterly 16 (Winter 1975):
48-64.

_____. "The Limits of Symbolic Realism: Problems of
Empathetic Field Observation in a Sectarian Context."
Journal for the Scientific Study of Religion 12 (1973):
259-272.

Rosenzweig, Charles. "High Demand Sects: Disclosure Legislation and the Free Exercise Clause." New England Law
Review 15 (1979-1980):128-159.

Ross, A. Private notes and personal communications, 1975-
1976.

Rozak, Theodore. Where the Wasteland Ends. Garden City:
Doubleday, 1973.

_____. The Making of a Counterculture. Garden City:
Doubleday, 1969.

Ruiz, Pedro and John Langrad. "Psychiatry and Folk Healing:
A Dichotomy." American Journal of Psychiatry 133 (January 1976):95-97.

Sage, Wayne. "The War on Cults." Human Behavior (October
1976).

Salonen, Neil. "Memo from Mr. Salonen to Group Leaders."
Barrytown, NY, Unification Church, 1974.

Santucci, P.S. and G. Winokur. "Brainwashing as a Factor
in Psychiatric Illness. AMA Archives of Neurology and
Psychiatry 74 (1955):11-16.

Sargant, William. Battle for the Mind. New York: Doubleday, 1957.

_____. "The Mechanism of Conversion." British Medical
Journal 2 (1951):311-316.

Scales, H.L. "Lifton Finds Adolescents Vulnerable to Cult
    Recruiting." Journal for the American Family Foundation
    2 (1980):1.

Scheflein, Alan and Edward Opton. The Mind Manipulators.
    New York: Paddington, 1978.

Schein, Edgar F. Interpersonal Communications, Group Soli-
    darity and Social Influence." Sociometry 23 (1960):148-
    161.

_____. "Reactions and Patterns to Severe, Chronic
    Stress in American Army Prisoners of War of the Chinese."
    Journal of Social Issues 13 (1957):321-330.

_____. "The Chinese Indoctrination Program for Pris-
    oners of War." Psychiatry 19 (May 1956):149-172.

Schein, Edgar H., Inge Schneier and Curtis H. Becker.
    Coercive Persuasion. New York: W.W. Norton, 1961.

Schutz, Alfred. On Phenomenology and Social Relations.
    Chicago: University of Chicago Press, 1970.

Shutz, Alfred and Thomas Luckmann. The Structure of the
    Life-World. Evanston, IL: Northwestern University
    Press, 1973.

Schutz, William C. The Interpersonal Underworld. Palo
    Alto, CA: Science and Behavior Books, 1966. 242 pp.

Scott, Marvin B. and Scott Lyman. "'Accounts.'" American
    Sociological Review 33 (1968):46-62.

Shafi, Mohammed, Richard Lovely and Robert Jaffee. "Medi-
    tation and the Prevention of Alcohol Aubse." American
    Journal of Psychiatry 132 (September 1975):942-945.

_____. "Meditation and Marijuana." American Journal
    of Psychiatry 131 (January 1974):60-63.

Shapiro, Arthur K., Elmer Struening, Elaine Shapiro and
    Harvey Barten. "Prognostic Correlates of Psychotherapy
    in Psychiatric Outpatients." American Journal of Psy-
    chiatry 133 (July 1976):802-808.

Shapiro, Eli. "Destructive Cultism." American Family Phy-
    sician 15 (February 1977):80-83.

Shapiro, Robert. "'Mind Control' or Intensity of Faith: The Constitutional Protection of Religious Beliefs." Harvard Civil Rights - Civil Liberties Law Review 13 (1978): 751-797.

Shepherd, William C. "Legal Protection for Freedom of Religion." The Center Magazine 15 (March/April 1982a):30-33.

_____. "The Prosecutors Reach: Legal Issues Stemming from the New Religious Movements." The Journal of the American Academy of Religion 50 (1982b):187-214.

_____. "The New Religions and the Religion of the Republic." Journal of the American Academy of Religion 44 (1978):509-525.

_____. "Religion and the Counter Culture: A New Religiosity." Sociological Inquiry 42 (1972):3-9.

Shimano, Eido Tai and Donald B. Douglas. "On Research in Zen." American Journal of Psychiatry 132 (December 1975):1300-1302.

Shupe, Anson D., Jr. and David G. Bromley. The New Vigilantes: Deprogrammers, Anti-Cultists and the New Religions. Beverly Hills, CA: Sage, 1980.

_____. "The Moonies and the Anti-Cultists: Movement and Countermovement in Conflict." Sociological Analysis 40 (Winter 1979):325-366.

Shupe, Anson D., Jr., Roger Spielmann and Sam Stigall. "Deprogramming: The New Exorcism. American Behavioral Scientist 20 (July/August 1977):941-956.

Siegel, Terri I. "Deprogramming Religious Cultists." Loyola of Los Angeles Law Review 11 (September 1978): 807-828.

Simon, Justin. "Observations on 67 Patients Who Took Erhard Seminars Training." American Journal of Psychiatry 135 (June 1978):686-691.

Singer, Margaret. "Coming Out of the Cults." Psychology Today (January 1979a):72-82.

_____. "Psychological Mechanisms of Cult Affiliation." Paper presented at the annual meeting of the American Psychological Association, New York, 1979b.

_____. "Therapy with Ex-Cult Members." Journal of the National Association of Private Psychiatric Hospitals 9 (1978):15-19.

Skolnick, Jerome. The Politics of Protest. New York: Bantam Books, 1969.

Skonovd, Norman. "Apostasy: The Process of Defection from Religious Totalism." Ph.D. Dissertation, University of California Davis, 1981.

Slater, Philip. The Pursuit of Lonliness: American Culture at the Breaking Point. Boston: Beacon Press, 1970.

Smelser, Neil. The Theory of Collective Behavior. New York: Free Press, 1963.

_____. Some Determinants of Destructive Behavior." Sanctions for Evil. Edited by Nevitt Sanford and Craig Comstock. Boston: Beacon Press, 1971.

Snow, David. "The Disengagement Process: A Neglected Problem in Participant Observation Research." Qualitative Sociology 3 (1980):100-122.

Snow, David, L.A. Aurcher, Jr., and S. Ekland-Olson. "Social Networks and Social Movements: A Microstructural Approach to Differential Recruitment." American Sociological Review 45 (1980):787-801.

Society of Believers. Investigator: or a Defense of the Order, Government and Economy of the United Society Called Shakers, Against Sundry Charges and Legislative Proceedings. Pleasant Hill, KY: Society of Believers, 1828.

Solomon, Trudy. "Integrating the 'Moonie' Experience." In Gods We Trust: New Patterns of Religious Pluralism in America. Edited by Thomas Robbins and Dick Anthony. New Brunswick, NJ: Transaction, 1981, pp. 275-294.

Solomon, Trudy and A. Pines. "Brainwashing and Psychotherapy: The Case of Children in Residential Treatment." Paper presented at the meeting of the Western Psychological Association, Seattle, 1977.

Somit, Albert. "Brainwashing." International Encyclopedia of the Social Sciences, Volume 1. Edited by D.L. Sills. New York: Macmillan and Free Press, 1968.

Sontag, Frederick. Sun Myung Moon and the Unification Church. Nashville: Abingdon, 1977.

Spendlove, Gretta. "Legal Issues in the Use of Guardianship Procedures to Remove Members of Cults." Arizona Law Review 18 (1976):1095-1039.

Stark, Rodney. "Psychopathology and Religious Commitment." Review of Religious Research 12 (1971):165-176.

Stoner, Carrol and Jo Anne Parke. All God's Children. Radnor, PA: Chilton, 1977.

Strauss, Ansalem. Mirrors and Masks. Glencoe, IL: Free Press, 1959.

Straus, Roger. "Religious Conversion as a Personal and Collective Accomplishment." Sociological Analysis 40 (1979):158-165.

_____. "Changing Oneself: Seekers and the Creative Transformation of Life Experience." Doing Social Life. Edited by John Lofland. New York: Wiley, 1976.

Strivers, R. "Social Control in the Technological Society." The Collective Definition of Deviance. Edited by R. Strivers and F. Davis. New York: The Free Press, 1975.

Szasz, Thomas. "Some Call It Brainwashing." New Republic, March 1976.

Taylor, David. "The Social Organization of Recruitment in the Unification Church." M.A. Thesis, University of Montana, 1978.

Thompson, Daniel P. Shaker Lovers, and Other Tales. Burlington: C. Goodrich and S.B. Nichols, 1848.

Tiryakian, Edward A. "Toward the Sociology of Esoteric Culture." American Journal of Sociology 78 (November 1972):491-502.

_____. "Existential Phenomenology and the Sociological Tradition." American Sociological Review 30 (October 1965):674-688.

Toch, Hans. The Social Psychology of Social Movements. Indianapolis: Bobbs-Merrill, 1965.

Toulmin, S. "Contemporary Scientific Mythology." Meta-physical Beliefs. Edited by A. McIntyre. London: S.C.M. Press, 1957.

Travisano, Richard V. "Alternation and Conversion as Quali-tatively Different Transformations." Life as Theater: A Dramaturgical Sourcebook. Edited by Dennis Brissett and Charles Edgley. Chicago: Aldine, 1975.

_____. "Alternation and Conversion as Qualitatively Different Transformations." Social Psychology Through Symbolic Interaction. Edited by G.P. Stone and M. Garverman. Waltham, MA: Ginn-Blaisdell, 1970.

Trice, Harrison M. "The Affiliation Motive and Readings to Join Alcoholics Anonymous." Quarterly Journal of Studies on Alcoholism 20 (1959):313-320.

Troeltsch, Ernst. The Social Teaching of the Christian Church. London: George Allen and Unwin, 1931.

Truzzi, Marcello. "The Occult Revival and Popular Culture: Some Random Observations on the Old and Nouveaux Witch." Sociological Quarterly 13 (Winter 1972):16-36.

Underwood, Betty and Barbara Underwood. Hostage to Heaven. New York: Potter, 1979.

Ungerleider, J. Thomas and David K. Wellisch. "Coercive Persuasion (Brainwashing), Religious Cults, and Depro-gramming." American Journal of Psychiatry 136 (March 1979a):279-282.

_____. "Psychiatrists' Involvement in Cultism, Thought Control and Deprogramming." Psychiatric Opin-ion 16 (January 1979b):10-15.

Verdier, Paul. Brainwashing and the Cults. Redondo Beach, CA: Institute of Behavioral Conditioning, 1977.

Wallis, Roy. The Road to Total Freedom: A Sociological Analysis of Scientology. London: Heineman Education Books, 1976.

_____. "Ideology, Authority, and the Development of Cultic Movements." Social Reserach 41 (Summer 1974): 299-327.

Weber, Max. The Sociology of Religion. Boston: Beacon, 1963.

Weider, D. Lawrence and Don H. Zimmerman. "Becoming a Freak: Pathways into the Counter-Culture." Youth and Society 7 (March 1976):311-344.

West, Louis J. "Psychiatry, Brainwashing and the American Character." American Journal of Psychiatry 120 (March 1964):842-850.

White, R.K. Value-Analysis: The Nature and Use of the Method. Glen Gardiner, NJ: Libertarian Press, 1951.

Wilson, John. Introduction to Social Movements. New York: Basic Books, 1973.

Wilson, W.P. "Mental Health Benefits of Religious Salvation." Diseases of the Nervous System 33 (1972):382-386.

Winokur, George. "Brainwashing: A Social Phenomenon of Our Time." Human Organization 13 (Winter 1955):16-18.

Wood, Alan T. with Jack Vitek. Moonstruck. New York: William Morrow, 1979.

World Christian Liberation Front. An account of a W.C.L.F. member's observations of the Unification Church in Berkeley, California, 1975.

Zablocki, Benjamin. The Joyful Community. Baltimore: Penguin, 1971.

_____. "Problems of Anarchism in Hippie Communes." Pp. 167-177 in Rosabeth M. Kanter, ed. Communes: Creating and Managing the Collective Life. New York: Harper and Row, 1973.

Zald, Mayer and Roberta Ash. "Social Movement Organizations: Growth, Decay and Change." Social Forces 44 (1966):327-341.

Zimbardo, Philip and Cynthia Hartley. "The Nature and Extent of Recruiting Contact Between Cults and High School in the Bay Area of San Francisco." Paper presented at conference on "Conversion, Coercion and Commitment in New Religious Movements" sponsored by the Graduate Theological Union, Center for the Study of New Religious Movements, Berkeley, 1981.

Zygmunt, Joseph. "Movements and Motives: Some Unresolved Issues in the Psychology and Social Movements." Human Relations 25 (November 1972):449-487.

For price information or a complete book list write:

The Edwin Mellen Press
P.O. Box 450
Lewiston, New York 14092